# Toward a Feminist Theory
## of the State

D0761574

# TOWARD
# A FEMINIST THEORY
# OF THE STATE

*Catharine A. MacKinnon*

*Harvard University Press*
*Cambridge, Massachusetts*
*London, England*

First Harvard University Press paperback edition, 1991

*Library of Congress Cataloging-in-Publication Data*
MacKinnon, Catharine A.
    Toward a feminist theory of the state / Catharine
A. MacKinnon.
        p. cm.
    Bibliography: p.
    Includes index.
    ISBN 0-674-89645-9 (alk. paper) (cloth)
    ISBN 0-674-89646-7 (paper)
    1. Women—Legal status, laws, etc.   2. Women
and socialism.
    I. Title.
    K644.M33   1989
    346.01'34—dc20
    [342.6134]     89-7540
                    CIP

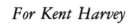

*For Kent Harvey*

# Contents

# *Preface*

Writing a book over an eighteen-year period becomes, eventually, much like coauthoring it with one's previous selves. The results in this case are at once a collaborative intellectual odyssey and a sustained theoretical argument.

This book analyzes how social power shapes the way we know and how the way we know shapes social power in terms of the social inequality between women and men. In broadest terms, it explores the significance gender hierarchy has for the relation between knowledge and politics. In other words, it engages sexual politics on the level of epistemology.

The argument begins with the respective claims of marxism and feminism to analyze inequality as such, moves to reconstruct feminism on the epistemic level through a critique of sexuality as central to women's status, and concludes by exploring the institutional power of the state on the more particularized terrain of women's social construction and treatment by law.

Marxism is its point of departure because marxism is the contemporary theoretical tradition that— whatever its limitations—confronts organized social dominance, analyzes it in dynamic rather than static terms, identifies social forces that systematically shape social imperatives, and seeks to explain human freedom both within and against history. It confronts class, which is real. It offers both a critique of the inevitability and inner coherence of social injustice and a theory of the necessity and possibilities of change.

My original intention was to explore the connections, contradictions, and conflicts between the marxist and feminist theories of consciousness, as they grounded each theory's approach to social order and social change. Through comparing each theory's notion of the relation between the mental and physical forms in which dominance was enforced, I wanted to compare feminism's explanation for the subjection of women, understood to be the condition Adrienne Rich described in 1972 as "shared, unnecessary, and political," with marxism's explanation for the exploitation of the working class. I thought the women's movement had an understanding of consciousness that could contribute to understanding and confronting social hegemony.

I began trying to disentangle the economic from the sexual roots of women's inequality: Is it sexism or capitalism? Is it a box or a bag? In this form, the question was intractable because it referred to realities that appeared fused in the world. The inquiry devolved into a question about the factor to be isolated: Is it sex or class? Is it a particle or a wave? Chapters 2, 3, and 4 were written in the mid-1970s to explore each theory's answer to the other's questions on these levels. The exercise in mutual critique cleared ground, focused problems, and exposed inadequacies, but it did not solve the world/mind problem each theory posed the other. However essential they are to the theory that emerged, these chapters may for this reason seem groping and comparatively primitive.

My initial strategy assumed that feminism had a theory of male dominance: an account of its key concrete sites and laws of motion, an analysis of why and how it happened and why (perhaps even how) it could be ended. I assumed, in short, that feminism had a theory of gender as marxism had a theory of class. As it became clear that this was not the case in the way I had thought, the project shifted from locating and explicating such a theory to creating one by distilling feminist practice, from attempting to connect feminism and marxism on equal terms to attempting to create a feminist theory that could stand on its own.

Sheldon Wolin had described "epic theory" as a response not to "crises in techniques of inquiry" but to "crises in the world" in the sense that "problems-in-the-world" take precedence over and determine "problems-in-a-theory." An epic theory identifies basic principles in political life which produce errors and mistakes in social "arrangements, decisions, and beliefs" and which cannot be dismissed as episodic. Scientific theories, Wolin argued, attempt explanation and technique; epic theories, by contrast, provide "a symbolic picture of an ordered whole" that is "systematically deranged." Most theories attempt to change one's view of the world; "only epic theory attempts to change the world itself" ("Political Theory as a Vocation," *American Political Science Review* 63 [1967]: 1079–80). Marx's critique of capitalism and Plato's critique of Athenian democracy were examples.

Seen in these terms, feminism offered a rich description of the variables and locales of sexism and several possible explanations for it. The work of Mary Wollstonecraft, Charlotte Perkins Gilman, and Simone de Beauvoir were examples. It also offered a complex and explosive practice in which a theory seemed immanent. But except for a few major beginnings—such as the work of Kate Millett and Andrea Dworkin—feminism had no account of male power as an ordered yet deranged whole. Feminism began to seem an epic indictment in search of a theory, an epic theory in need of writing.

The project thus became a meta-inquiry into theory itself—Is it feminism or marxism? Is it relativity or quantum mechanics?— requiring the exploration of method presented in Part II. Unpacking the feminist approach to consciousness revealed a relation between one means through which sex inequality is produced in the world and the world it produces: the relation between objectification, the hierarchy between self as being and other as thing, and objectivity, the hierarchy between the knowing subject and the known object. Epistemology and politics emerged as two mutually enforcing sides of the same unequal coin. A theory of the state which was at once social and discrete, conceptual and applied, became possible as the state was seen to participate in the sexual politics of male dominance by enforcing its epistemology through law. In a very real sense, the project went from marxism to feminism through method to analyze congealed power in its legal form, and state power emerged as male power.

As the work progressed, publication of earlier versions of parts of this book (listed on page 321) gave me the benefit of the misunderstandings, distortions, and misreadings of a wide readership. This experience suggests that it must be said that this book does not try to explain everything. It attempts an analysis of gender which can explain the pervasive and crucial place sex occupies as a dimension that is socially pervasive and, in its own sense, structural. It seeks to understand gender as a form of power and power in its gendered forms. To look for the place of gender in everything is not to reduce everything to gender.

For example, it is not possible to discuss sex without taking account of Black women's experience of gender. To the considerable degree to which this experience is inseparable from the experience of racism, many features of sex cannot be discussed without racial particularity. I attempt to avoid the fetishized abstractions of race and class (and sex) which so commonly appear under the rubric "difference" and to analyze experiences and demarcating forces that occupy society concretely and particularly—for example, "Black women" instead of "racial differences." All women possess ethnic (and other definitive) particularities that mark their femaleness; at the same time their femaleness marks their particularities and constitutes one. Such a recognition, far from undermining the feminist project, comprises, defines, and sets standards for it. It also does not reduce race to sex. Rather, it suggests that comprehension and change in racial inequality are essential to comprehension and change in sex inequality, with implications that link comprehending and changing sexism to comprehending and changing racism. In this light, to proliferate "feminisms" (a white racist feminism?) in the face of women's diversity is the latest attempt of liberal pluralism to evade the challenge women's reality poses to theory, simply because the theoretical forms those realities demand have yet to be created. At the same time, this book does not pretend to present an even incipiently adequate analysis of race and sex, far less of race, sex, and class. That further work— building on writings by authors of color such as those cited in this volume, stunning efforts in fiction and literary criticism, developments in the social world and advances in political practice and analysis, and recent contributions in the legal arena by women such as Kimberle Crenshaw, Mari Matsuda, Cathy Scarborough, and Patricia Williams—will take at least another eighteen years.

This book is also not a moral tract. It is not about right and wrong or what I think is good and bad to think or do. It is about what *is,* the meaning of what is, and the way what is, is enforced. It is a theoretical argument in critical form which moves in a new direction; it does not advance an ideal (sex equality is taken, at least nominally, as an agreed-upon social ideal) or a blueprint for the future.

Some key terms and concepts used in this volume seem to require prophylactic clarification beyond their use. I use the verb *deconstruct* in its ordinary sense, having used it before the deconstruction school made the term mean what it now means. (Deconstruction notwithstanding, reading this preface is not a substitute for reading this book.) I do not defend "subjectivity" over "objectivity" or elevate "differences" over "sameness" but criticize the method that produces these symbiotic antinomies. To say that feminism is "post-marxist" does not mean that feminism leaves class behind. It means that feminism worthy of the name absorbs and moves beyond marxist methodology, leaving theories that do not in the liberal dustbin.

Much has been made of a supposed distinction between sex and gender. Sex is thought to be the more biological, gender the more social; the relation of each to sexuality varies. I see sexuality as fundamental to gender and as fundamentally social. Biology becomes the social meaning of biology within the system of sex inequality much as race becomes ethnicity within a system of racial inequality. Both are social and political in a system that does not rest independently on biological differences in any respect. In this light, the sex/gender distinction looks like a nature/culture distinction in the sense criticized by Sherry Ortner in "Is Female to Male as Nature Is to Culture?" *Feminist Studies* 8 (Fall 1982). I use sex and gender relatively interchangeably.

The term *sexual* refers to sexuality; it is not the adjectival form of *sex* in the sense of gender. Sexuality is not confined to that which is done as pleasure in bed or as an ostensible reproductive act; it does not refer exclusively to genital contact or arousal or sensation, or narrowly to sex-desire or libido or eros. Sexuality is conceived as a far broader social phenomenon, as nothing less than the dynamic of sex as social hierarchy, its pleasure the experience of power in its gendered form. Assessment of the potential of this concept for analysis of social hierarchy should be based on this understanding (developed in Chapter 9). Connections between courtly love and nuclear war, sexual stereotyping and women's poverty, sadomasochistic pornography and lynching, sex discrimination and prohibitions on homosexual marriage and miscegenation seem remote if sexuality is cabined, less so if it roams social hierarchy unconfined.

This book is not an idealist argument that law can solve the problems of the world or that if legal arguments are better made, courts will see the error of their ways. It recognizes the power of the state and the consciousness- and legitimacy-conferring power of law as political realities that women ignore at their peril. It recognizes the legal forum as a particularly but not singularly powerful one. It does not advance a critique of "rights" per se but of their form and content as male, hence exclusionary and limited and limiting. It is one thing for upper-class white men to repudiate rights as intrinsically liberal and individualistic and useless and alienating; they have them in fact even as they purport to relinquish them in theory. It is another to reformulate the relation between life and law on the basis of the experience of the subordinated, the disadvantaged, the dispossessed, the silenced—in other words, to create a jurisprudence of change. In this as in all other respects, the title term *toward* is a considered one.

For readers who may be interested, this work has been previously published in fragments and in almost reverse order of its writing. At the same time, much of my other work on specific areas of law presents practical proposals for solving some of the theoretical shortcomings first diagnosed here. The analysis that became Chapter 1—an attempt to conceive the relation between marxism and feminism—was written in 1971–72, revised in 1975, and published in *Signs* in 1982. The ideas for Chapter 12 on sex equality were largely conceptualized in 1973–74. It presents a critique of the "same treatment" versus "different treatment" fixation of sex discrimination law, a resolution to which became the theory of sexual harassment published in *Sexual Harassment of Working Women* (New Haven: Yale University Press, 1979) and adopted by the courts. Chapter 9, written largely in 1981 and published in *Signs* in 1983, criticized the law of rape in a way that has contributed to some rape law reform. Chapter 10 scrutinizes existing concepts and law of abortion in light of the analysis of sexuality and the private as a realm of sex inequality. The argument that legal abortion is a sex equality right awaits affirmative development. Chapter 11 criticizes obscenity law in a way that, together with the work of Andrea Dworkin, provided a basis for the theory underlying the civil rights ordinances against pornography designed first in late 1983. An earlier collection, *Feminism Unmodified: Discourses on Life and Law* (Harvard University Press, 1987), presented spoken versions of some of these arguments at earlier stages. As Lindsay Waters, editor of that volume and this one, characterized the relation between them: "You've seen the movie, now read the book."

This volume presents my argument in its original unity, shape, and order. Hopefully, it exposes the coherence underlying the approach taken in earlier publications. It may also help counter the tendency to reduce a theory's implications for political understanding to what has been made of it in legal practice.

This book does not aspire to locate itself within academic literatures or trends or discourses. It aspires to create, on its own terms, a feminist theory of the state; to this end, it uses works that are useful. Most of the groundbreaking contributions to feminist theory were made by the women's movement in the 1970s through practice; some of its insights were published in journals, obscure newsletters, and some books. Major intellectual contributions were made by women based mostly outside universities, women such as Andrea Dworkin, Audre Lorde, Kate Millett, and Adrienne Rich. Other crucial work outside the academy has been done by writers such as Susan Griffin, Robin Morgan, Gloria Steinem, and John Stoltenberg. Some academic work has been essential to this project. Without Diana E. H. Russell's extraordinary research on sexual abuse, the theory of sexuality as advanced in Chapter 9 would not have been possible. Other feminists whose scholarly writings have been especially helpful or stimulating include Kathleen Barry, Pauline Bart, Phyllis Chesler, Nancy Cott, Mary Daly, Teresa de Lauretis, Marilyn Frye, Carol Gilligan, Heidi Hartmann, Alison Jaggar, Gerda Lerner, Kristin Luker, Carole Pateman, Barbara Smith, and Elizabeth Spelman. Most of these women have been active in the women's movement as well as in scholarship, and it shows. Some scholars have attempted to respond to some of the challenges leveled in this book, without yet, in my view, making the criticisms obsolete. The fact remains that, even when exceptions like these are recognized, academic reformulation of feminist insights has too often added little of substance. This has been most true in legal academia. I accordingly reference the original (movement-based) expressions of the ideas I use wherever possible.

Some readers have wondered: If perspective participates in situation and if situation is divided by power, how will we talk to each other? The fact that some people do not like an argument or observation, or feel threatened or uncomfortable or find it difficult, does not make it wrong or impossible or untrue. Many readers (in the Kantian tradition) say that if a discourse is not generalized, universal, and agreed-upon, it is exclusionary. The problem, however, is that the generalized, universal, or agreed-upon never did solve the disagreements, resolve the differences, cohere the specifics, and generalize the particularities. Rather, it assimilated them to a false universal that imposed agreement, submerged specificity, and silenced particularity. The anxiety about engaged theory is particularly marked among those whose particularities formed the prior universal. What they face from this critique is not losing a dialogue but beginning one, a more equal and larger and inclusionary one. They do face losing the advance exclusivity of their point of view's claim to truth—that is, their power. And we continue to talk about it.

Other earlier readers have had a related problem. Adhering to science as a standard for theory, they have suggested that the theorist must be stripped of commitments, community, experience, and feelings to know the truth about society. If knowledge is located instead in a critical embrace of those same commitments, a recognition of community context, a skeptical grasp of the roots and consequences of experience as well as its limitations, and an attempt at awareness of the social determinations of emotions, these factors are made accessible to theory. Such a theory does not deny that the theorist is determined by the very factors the theory documents for everyone else. Theory becomes a social endeavor inseparable from collective situation. Situated theory is concrete and changing rather than abstract and totalizing, working from the viewpoint of powerlessness to political understanding toward social transformation. This posture places the theorist inside the world and the work, not above or outside them—which, to be frank, is where the theorist has been all along.

It is said that thus speaking from the inside runs the risk of not being compelling to those who are not already convinced. This may be because much prior theory has adopted the position of dominance and needed to disguise that fact to support the illusion that it was speaking for everyone. Whatever its disabilities, speaking from the position of subordination does not have this one. In any event, I accept the risk of the engaged theorist without really believing that many readers are thereby excluded. The alternative has too often been compelling to no one.

My sense that method has something to do with women probably first crystallized with a passing witticism by Leo Weinstein of Smith College that " 'really' is the feminine expletive." He also taught political theory and constitutional law at the same time and took my writing seriously. Robert A. Dahl, one of the world's few practicing pluralists and ten nicest men, engaged this project patiently, supportively, and intelligently for a very long time. Paul Brest was the first to think it deserved an audience in the legal academy; Shelly Rosaldo was the first to decide it deserved to be published. Faculty, students, librarians, and staff at Yale, Harvard, Stanford, Minnesota, UCLA, Chicago, and Osgoode Hall (York University) law schools have contributed to its development. Over my objections to theory books, Lindsay Waters convinced me to publish this one. Ann Hawthorne was the most helpful and least intrusive manuscript editor ever.

The intrepid Karen E. Davis, my research assistant through thick and thin, has been resourceful, dedicated, and persistent beyond belief; her contributions, always crucial, have become increasingly substantive over time. Alison Walsh helped greatly checking citations at a difficult moment. Suzanne Levitt tracked down vast numbers of final fugitive footnotes with intelligence, energy, and astonishing good humor. Anne E. Simon delivered pungently her always valuable insights. The work could not have been completed without the help of Pat Butler, Twiss Butler, Phyllis Langer, and David Satz. My Canadian colleagues—especially Mary Eberts, Christie Jefferson, and Elizabeth Lennon—provided an intellectually rewarding, humanly sensible, receptive, and insightful community in which to explore the implications of these ideas. My parents, to whom this work was dedicated in its earlier incarnation as a doctoral thesis, have been supportive throughout.

Kent Harvey and Andrea Dworkin have been my colleagues and friends. They contributed to this work on every level. My thanks to them, finally, cannot be expressed but can only be lived.

*New Haven, Connecticut*
*May 1989*

Surely it was time someone invented a new plot, or that the author came out from the bushes.

—Virginia Woolf, *Between the Acts*

I imagined myself sitting on the end of a beam of light and imagined what I would see.

—Albert Einstein

# I. FEMINISM AND MARXISM

# 1 | *The Problem of Marxism and Feminism*

Marxism and feminism are one and that one is Marxism.
—Heidi Hartmann and Amy
  Bridges, "The Unhappy Marriage
  of Marxism and Feminism"

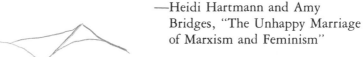

$S$exuality is to feminism what work is to marxism: that which is most one's own, yet most taken away. Marxist theory argues that society is fundamentally constructed of the relations people form as they do and make things needed to survive humanly. Work is the social process of shaping and transforming the material and social worlds, creating people as social beings as they create value. It is that activity by which people become who they are. Class is its structure, production its consequence, capital a congealed form, and control its issue.

Implicit in feminist theory is a parallel argument: the molding, direction, and expression of sexuality organizes society into two sexes: women and men. This division underlies the totality of social relations. Sexuality is the social process through which social relations of gender are created, organized, expressed, and directed, creating the social beings we know as women and men, as their relations create society. As work is to marxism, sexuality to feminism is socially constructed yet constructing, universal as activity yet historically specific, jointly comprised of matter and mind. As the organized expropriation of the work of some for the benefit of others defines a class, workers, the organized expropriation of the sexuality of some for the use of others defines the sex, woman. Heterosexuality is its social structure, desire its internal dynamic, gender and family its congealed forms, sex roles its qualities generalized to social persona, reproduction a consequence, and control its issue.

Marxism and feminism provide accounts of the way social arrangements of patterned and cumulative disparity can be internally rational and systematic yet unjust. Both are theories of power, its social derivations and its maldistribution. Both are theories of social inequality. In unequal societies, gender and with it sexual desire and kinship structures, like value and with it acquisitiveness and the forms of property ownership, are considered presocial, part of the natural world, primordial or magical or aboriginal. As marxism exposes value as a social creation, feminism exposes desire as socially relational, internally necessary to unequal social orders but historically contingent.[1]

The specificity of marxism and feminism is not incidental. To be deprived of control over work relations in marxism, over sexual relations in feminism, defines each theory's conception of lack of power per se. They do not mean to exist side by side, pluralistically, to ensure that two separate spheres of social life are not overlooked, the interests of two discrete groups are not obscured, or the contributions of two sets of variables are not ignored. They exist to argue, respectively, that the relations in which many work and few gain, in which some dominate and others are subordinated, in which some fuck and others get fucked and everybody knows what those words mean,[2] are the prime moment of politics.

What if the claims of each theory are taken equally seriously, each on its own terms? Can two social processes be basic at once? Can two groups be subordinated in conflicting ways, or do they merely crosscut? Can two theories, each of which purports to account for the same thing—power as such—be reconciled? Confronted on equal terms, these theories at minimum pose fundamental questions for each other. Is male dominance a creation of capitalism, or is capitalism one expression of male dominance? What does it mean for class analysis if a social group is defined and exploited through means that seem largely independent of the organization of production, if in forms appropriate to it? What does it mean for a sex-based analysis if capitalism might not be materially altered if it were fully sex integrated or even controlled by women? Supposing that the structure and interests served by the socialist state and the capitalist state differ in class terms, are they equally predicated upon sex inequality? To the extent their forms and behaviors resemble one another, could gender be their commonality? Is there a relationship between the wealth of wealthy men and the poverty of poor women? Is there a relationship between the power of some classes over others and the power of all men over all women? Is there a relationship between the fact that the few have ruled the many and the fact that those few have been men?

Instead of confronting these questions, marxists and feminists have usually either dismissed or, in the more active form of the same thing, subsumed each other. Marxists have criticized feminism as bourgeois in theory and in practice, meaning that feminism works in the interest of the ruling class. They argue that to analyze society in terms of sex ignores the primacy of class and glosses over class divisions among women, dividing the proletariat. Feminist demands, it is claimed, could be fully satisfied within capitalism, so their pursuit undermines and deflects the effort for basic change. Efforts to eliminate barriers to women's personhood—arguments for access to life chances without regard to sex—are seen as liberal and individualistic. Whatever women have in common is considered to be based in nature, not in society. When cross-cultural analyses of women's social conditions do not seem to support this analysis, women's conditions are seen as not common or shared, and analyses that claim they are, are called totalizing and ahistorical. When cross-cultural analyses of women's social conditions do support this analysis, women's status is seen as a universal, or analyses based on it are considered to lack cultural specificity. The women's movement's focus upon attitudes, beliefs, and emotions as powerful components of social reality is criticized as formally idealist; the composition of the women's movement, purportedly of middle-class educated women, is advanced as an explanation for its opportunism.

Feminists charge that marxism is male defined in theory and in practice, meaning that it moves within the worldview and in the interest of men. Feminists argue that analyzing society exclusively in class terms ignores the distinctive social experiences of the sexes, obscuring women's unity. Marxist demands, it is claimed, could be (and in part have been) satisfied without altering women's inequality to men. Feminists have often found that working-class movements and the left undervalue women's work and concerns, neglect the role of feelings and beliefs in a focus on institutional and material change, denigrate women in practice and in everyday life, and in general fail to distinguish themselves from any other ideology or group dominated by male interests, where justice for women is concerned. Marxists and feminists each accuse the other of seeking what in each one's terms is reform—alterations that appease and assuage and improve in accommodation to structures of inequality—where, again in each one's terms, a fundamental transformation is required. At its most extreme, the mutual perception is not only that the other's analysis is wrong, but that its success would be a defeat.

Neither set of allegations is groundless. In the feminist view, sex, in analysis and in reality, does divide classes, a fact marxists have been more inclined to deny or ignore than to explain or change. Marxists, similarly, have seen parts of the women's movement function as a special interest group to advance the class-privileged: educated and professional women. At the same time, to consider this group coextensive with "the women's movement" precludes questioning the social processes that give disproportionate visibility to the movement's least broadly based segment. Accepting a middle-class definition of the women's movement has distorted perception of its actual composition and made invisible the diverse ways in which many women—notably Black women and working-class women—have long moved against gendered determinants. But advocates of women's interests have not always been class conscious; some have exploited class-based arguments for advantage, even when the interests of women, working-class women, were thereby obscured.

In 1866, for example, in an act often thought to inaugurate the first wave of feminism, John Stuart Mill petitioned the English Parliament for women's suffrage with the following partial justification: "Under whatever conditions, and within whatever limits, men are admitted to suffrage, there is not a shadow of justification for not admitting women under the same. The majority of women of any class are not likely to differ in political opinion from the majority of men in the same class."[3] Perhaps Mill meant that, to the extent class determines opinion, sex is irrelevant. In this sense, the argument narrowly fits the purpose of eliminating gender as a restriction on the vote. Mill personally supported universal suffrage. And, as it happened, working-class men got the vote before women of any class. But this argument can also justify limiting the extension of the franchise to women who "belong to" men of the same class that already exercises it—in which light it is both demeaning to all women and works to the detriment of the excluded underclass, "their" women included.

This kind of reasoning has been confined neither to the issue of the vote nor to the nineteenth century. Mill's logic is embedded in the theoretical structure of liberalism that underlies much contemporary feminist theory and justifies much of the marxist critique. His view that women should be allowed to engage in politics was an expression of Mill's concern that the state not restrict individuals' self-government, their freedom to develop talents for their own growth, and their ability to contribute to society for the good of humanity. As an empirical rationalist, he resisted attributing to biology what could be explained as social conditioning. As a kind of utilitarian, he found most sex-based inequalities inaccurate or dubious, inefficient, and therefore unjust. That women should have the liberty, as individuals, to achieve the limits of self-development without arbitrary interference extended to women Mill's meritocratic goal of the self-made man, condemning (what has since come to be termed) sexism as an irrational interference with personal initiative and laissez-faire.

The hospitality of such an analysis to marxist concerns is problematic. Mill's argument could be extended to cover class as one more arbitrary, socially conditioned factor that produces inefficient development of talent and unjust distribution of resources among individuals. But although this extrapolation might be in a sense materialist, it would not be a class analysis. Mill himself does not even allow for income leveling. Unequal distribution of wealth is exactly what laissez-faire and unregulated personal initiative produce. The individual concept of rights which this theory requires on a juridical level (especially but not only in the economic sphere), a concept that produces the tension in liberalism between liberty for each and equality among all, pervades liberal feminism, substantiating the criticism that feminism is for the privileged few.

The marxist criticism that feminism focuses upon feelings and attitudes is also based on something real: the importance to feminism of women's own perceptions of their situation. The practice of consciousness raising, not only or even primarily as a concrete event but more as a collective approach to critique and change, has been a technique of analysis, structure of organization, method of practice, and theory of social change of the women's movement.[4] In consciousness-raising groups, which were common in the United States in the 1970s, the impact of male dominance was concretely uncovered and analyzed through the collective speaking of women's experience from the perspective of that experience. Because marxists tend to conceive of powerlessness, first and last, as concrete and externally imposed, they believe that it must be concretely and externally undone to be changed. Through consciousness raising taken more broadly, women's powerlessness was found to be both externally imposed and deeply internalized. For example, femininity is women's identity to women as well as women's desirability to men—indeed, it becomes identity to women because it is imposed through men's standards for desirability in women. From this practical analytic, a distinctly feminist concept of consciousness and its place in social order and change has emerged. It does not substitute one set of professed ideas for another and declare change, in the mode of liberal idealism. Nevertheless, what marxism conceives as change in consciousness is not, within marxism, a form of social change in itself. For feminism, it can be, but this is because women's oppression is not just in the head, so feminist consciousness is not just in the head either. But to the materially deprived, the pain, isolation, and thingification of women who have been pampered and pacified into nonpersonhood is difficult to swallow as a form of oppression. As a result, changing it is difficult to see as a form of liberation in any but the most reduced sense. This model is particularly difficult to swallow for women who will never carry a briefcase and whom no man has ever put on a pedestal.

Marxism, similarly, has not been just misunderstood. Marxist theory has traditionally attempted to comprehend all meaningful social variance in class terms. In this respect, sex parallels race and nation as an undigested but persistently salient challenge to the exclusivity or even the primacy of class as social explanation. Marxists typically extend class to cover women, a division and submersion that, to feminism, is inadequate to women's divergent, diverse, and common experience. For example, in 1912 Rosa Luxemburg addressed a group of women on the issue of suffrage:

> Most of these bourgeois women who act like lionesses in the struggle against "male prerogatives" would trot like docile lambs in the camp of conservative and clerical reaction if they had the suffrage. Indeed, they would certainly be a good deal more reactionary than the male part

of their class. Aside from the few who have taken jobs or professions, the bourgeoisie do not take part in social production. They are nothing but co-consumers of the surplus product their men extort from the proletariat. They are parasites of the parasites of the social body.[5]

Luxemburg's sympathies lay with "proletarian women," who derive their right to vote from being "productive for society like the men."[6] Her blind spot to gender occupied the same place in her perspective that Mill's blind spot to class did in his. Mill defended women's suffrage on gender grounds with a logic that excluded working-class women; Luxemburg defended women's suffrage on class grounds, although the vote would have benefited women without regard to class.

Women as women, women unmodified by class distinctions and apart from nature, were simply unthinkable to Mill, as to most liberals, and to Luxemburg, as to most marxists. Feminist theory asks marxism: what *is* class for women? Luxemburg, again like Mill within her own frame of reference, subliminally recognized that women derive their class position from their personal alliances with men. This may help explain why women do not unite against male dominance, but it does not explain that dominance, which cuts across class lines even as it takes some forms peculiar to classes. What distinguishes the bourgeois woman from her domestic servant is that the latter is paid (if barely), while the former is kept (if contingently). Is this a difference in social productivity or only in its measures, measures that themselves may be products of women's undervalued status? The tasks the women perform and their availability for sexual access and reproductive use are strikingly similar. Luxemburg saw the bourgeois woman of her time as a "parasite of a parasite" but failed to consider her possible commonality with the proletarian woman who is the slave of a slave. In the case of bourgeois women, to limit the analysis of women's status to their relationship to capitalism and to limit this analysis to their relations to capitalism through men is to see only its vicarious aspect. To fail to do this in the case of proletarian women is to miss its vicarious aspect. In both cases, to define women's status solely in class terms is entirely to miss their status as women defined through relations with men, which is a defining relational status they share even though the men through whom they acquire it differ.

Feminist observations of women's situation in socialist countries, though not conclusive on the contribution of marxist theory to understanding women's situation, have supported the feminist theoretical critique.[7] In the feminist view, socialist countries have solved many social problems—women's subordination not included. The criticism is not that socialism has not automatically liberated women in the process of transforming production (assuming that this transformation is occurring). Nor is it to diminish the significance of such changes for women: "There is a difference between a society in which sexism is expressed in the form of female infanticide and a society in which sexism takes the form of unequal representation on the Central Committee. And the difference is worth dying for."[8] Some feminists, however, have more difficulty separating the two: "It seems to me that a country that wiped out the tsetse fly can by fiat put an equal number of women on the Central Committee."[9] The basic feminist criticism is that these countries do not make a priority of working to change women's status relative to men that distinguishes them from nonsocialist societies in the way that their pursuit of other goals distinguishes them. Capitalist countries value women in terms of their "merit" by male standards; in socialist countries women seem invisible except in their capacity as "workers." This term seldom includes the work that remains women's distinctive service to men, regardless of the politics of those men: housework, prostitution and other sexual servicing, childbearing, childrearing. Sexual violence is typically barely mentioned. The concern of socialist and socialist revolutionary leadership for ending women's confinement to traditional roles too often seems limited to making their labor available to the regime, leading feminists to wonder whose interests are served by this version of liberation. Women become as free as men to work outside the home while men remain free from work within it. The same pattern occurs under capitalism. When woman's labor or militancy suits the needs of emergency, she is suddenly man's equal, only to regress when the urgency recedes.[10] Feminists do not argue that it means the same to women to be on the bottom in a feudal regime, a capitalist regime, and a socialist regime. The commonality is that, despite real changes, bottom is bottom.

Where such attitudes and practices come to be criticized, as in Cuba or China, changes appear gradual and precarious, as they do in capitalist countries, even where the effort looks major. If seizures of

state and productive power overturn work relations, they do not
overturn sex relations at the same time or in the same way, as a class
analysis of sex would, and in some cases did, predict and promise.[11]
Sexual violence, for example, is unchanged. Neither technology nor
socialism, both of which purport to alter women's role at the point of
production, has ever yet equalized women's status relative to men,
even in the workforce. Nothing has. Sex equality appears to require a
separate effort—an effort with necessary economic dimensions, potentially supported by a revolutionary regime and shaped by transformed
relations to production—but a separate effort nonetheless. In light of
these experiences, women's struggles, whether under capitalist or
socialist regimes, appear to feminists to have more in common with
each other than with marxist struggles anywhere.[12]

Attempts to create a synthesis between marxism and feminism,
termed socialist-feminism, have recognized neither the separate integrity of each theory nor the depth of the antagonism between them.
Many attempts at a unified theory began as an effort to justify women's
struggles in marxist terms, as if only that could make them legitimate.
Although feminism has largely redirected its efforts from justifying
itself within any other perspective to developing a perspective of its
own, this anxiety lurks under many synthetic attempts. The juxtapo-
sitions that result emerge as unconfronted as they started: feminist or
marxist, usually the latter. Socialist-feminist practice often divides
along the same lines, consisting largely in organizational cross-
memberships and mutual support on specific issues, with more
support by women of issues of the left than by the left of women's
issues.[13] Women with feminist sympathies urge attention to women's
issues by left or labor groups; marxist women pursue issues of class
within feminist groups; explicitly socialist-feminist groups come
together and divide, often at the hyphen.

Most attempts at synthesis try to integrate or explain the appeal of
feminism by incorporating issues feminism identifies as central—the
family, housework, sexuality, reproduction, socialization, personal
life—within an essentially unchanged marxian analysis.[14] According
to what type of marxist the theorist is, women become a caste, a
stratum, a cultural group, a division in civil society, a secondary
contradiction, or a nonantagonistic contradiction. Women's liberation
becomes a precondition, a measure of society's general emancipation,
part of the superstructure, or an important aspect of the class struggle.

No matter how perceptive about the contribution of feminism or how sympathetic to women's interests, these attempts cast feminism, ultimately, as a movement within marxism.[15] Most commonly, women are reduced to some other category, such as "women workers," which is then treated as coextensive with all women.[16] Or, in what has become near reflex, women become "the family," as if this single form of women's definition and confinement, which is then divided on class lines, can be presumed to be the crucible of women's determination.[17] A common approach to treating women's situation as coterminous with the family is to make women's circumstances the occasion for reconciling Marx with Freud. Such work is typically more Freudian than marxist, leaving feminism as the jumping-off point.[18]

Or, the marxist meaning of reproduction, the iteration of productive relations, is punned into an analysis of biological reproduction, as if women's bodily differences from men must account for their subordination to men; and as if this social analogue to the biological makes women's definition material, therefore based on a division of "labor" after all, therefore real, therefore potentially unequal. Sometimes reproduction refers to biological reproduction, sometimes to the reproduction of daily life, as in housework, sometimes to both.[19] Family-based theories of women's status analyze biological reproduction as part of the family, while work-based theories see it as work. Sexuality, if noticed at all, is, like "everyday life,"[20] analyzed in gender-neutral terms, as if its social meaning can be presumed to be the same, or coequal, or complementary, for women and men.[21] Although a unified theory of social inequality is prefigured in these strategies of subordination, staged progression, and assimilation of women's concerns to left concerns, at most an uneven combination is accomplished. Some works push these limits.[22] But socialist-feminism basically stands before the task of synthesis as if nothing essential to either theory fundamentally opposes their wedding—often as if the union had already occurred and need only be celebrated. However sympathetically, "the woman question" is always reduced to some other question, instead of being seen as *the* question, calling for analysis on its own terms.

# 2 | A Feminist Critique of Marx and Engels

We often romanticize what we have first despised.
—Wendell Berry, *The Gift of Good Land*

To Marx, women were defined by nature, not by society. To him, sex was within that "material substratum" that was not subject to social analysis, making his explicit references to women or to sex largely peripheral or parenthetical.[1] With issues of sex, unlike with class, Marx did not see that the line between the social and the pre-social is a line society draws. Marx ridiculed treating value and class as if they were natural givens. He bitingly criticized theories that treated class as if it arose spontaneously and operated mechanistically yet harmoniously in accord with natural laws. He identified such theories as justifications for an unjust status quo. Yet this is exactly the way he treated gender. Even when women produced commodities as waged labor, Marx wrote about them primarily as mothers, housekeepers, and members of the weaker sex. His work shares with liberal theory the view that women naturally belong where they are socially placed.

Engels, by contrast, considered women's status a social phenomenon that needed explanation. He just failed to explain it. Expanding upon Marx's few suggestive comments, Engels tried to explain women's subordination within a theory of the historical development of the family in the context of class relations. Beneath Engels' veneer of dialectical dynamism lies a static, positivistic materialism that reifies woman socially to such an extent that her status might as well have been considered naturally determined. Marx and Engels each take for granted crucial features of relations between the sexes: Marx because woman is nature and nature is given, and Engels because woman is the family and he is largely uncritical of woman's work and sexual role within it.

Marx's theories of the division of labor and the social relations of production under capitalism were at the core of his theory of social life, as his views of women were not. In this context, Marx offered the analysis that differences "in the sexual act" were the original division of labor. "With [the increase of needs, productivity, population] there develops the division of labor, which was originally nothing but the division of labor in the sexual act, then that division of labor which develops spontaneously or 'naturally' by virtue of natural predisposition (e.g., physical strength), needs, accidents, etc. etc."[2] The reproductive difference of function between women and men apparently constitutes a division of labor. It is unclear whether this "original" division then extends itself to become other divisions, or whether this "original" division is a primary or cardinal example that other divisions then replicate or parallel or pattern themselves after. Marx accounts for neither the view that the gender difference of function in reproduction is more "original" than other differences of function that do not fall along gender lines; nor the view that reproduction is a species of labor; nor the appropriateness or necessity of the extension or duplication of this division throughout society. But then the gender division is not his subject; it is merely the "origin" of his real subject, the class division.

Still one wonders why other differences of function do not constitute or underlie a division of labor, but sex does. When discussing the division of labor under capitalism, Marx sees the question of which individual gets which task, or becomes a member of which class, as originally an accident that then becomes historically fixed: an "accidental repartition gets repeated, develops advantages of its own, and gradually ossifies into a systematic division of labor."[3] Not so gender. Which sex gets which task is first a matter of biology and remains so throughout economic changes. Discussing woman's work in the home, Marx states: "The distribution of the work within the family, and the regulation of the labor-time of the several members, depend as well upon the differences of age and sex as upon natural conditions . . . Within a family . . . there springs up naturally a division of labour, caused by differences of sex and age, a division that is consequently based on a purely physical foundation." Women are assigned housework by nature. Marx then abandons sex to discuss relations between tribes, for which "the physiological division of labor [sex and age] is the starting-point."[4]

Because women's role was naturally defined, Marx's view of the relationship of nature to labor is instructive. Nature's produce is "spontaneous." Society produces through the human activity of work: "material wealth that is not the spontaneous product of Nature, must invariably owe [its] existence to a special productive activity, exercised with a definite aim, an activity that appropriates particular nature-given materials to particular human wants."[5] Appropriating materials of nature, with intent to modify them to satisfy human wants, is a creative and purposive, as well as adaptive, activity. Nature produces of itself; work transforms the world.

Nature's forms change naturally or not at all. Labor's organization is social and is therefore subject to human intervention. "If we take away the useful labor expended upon them, a material substratum is always left, which is furnished by Nature without the help of man. The latter can work only as Nature does, that is by changing the form of matter. Nay more, in this work of changing the form he [man] is constantly helped by natural forces. We see, then, that labour is not the only source of material wealth, of use-values produced by labour. As William Petty puts it, labour is its father and the earth is its mother."[6] Mother/woman is, is nature; father/man works, is social. The creative, active, transformative process of work is identified with the male, while the female is identified with the matter to be worked upon and transformed. Neither human reproduction nor housework features the intentionality and control of appropriating and modifying naturally given materials which characterize the labor process in socialist thought. Actually, factory work under capitalism possesses few of these characteristics, yet it is considered for that reason alienated rather than spontaneous and natural.

To the extent that man's relation to nature is given by nature, relations between the sexes will also be defined by nature. To the extent that man's relation to nature has, for Marx, a social aspect—and it does—his relation to woman will have a social aspect. This may be the meaning of Marx's statement "The production of life, both of one's own labor and of fresh life in procreation, now appears as a double relationship: on the one hand as a natural, on the other as a social relationship."[7] From a feminist perspective, women have no more special relation to nature "naturally" than men do; their relation to nature, like men's, is a social product. Man's relation to nature is probably equally profound and determinative of his being, but he is not socially limited to it. Men's supposed superior strength does not confine them to being beasts of burden. Men also reproduce; women also labor. If one applied Marx's approach to class to the problem of sex, one might try to understand the connection between a physical fact—say, male physical strength or female maternity—and the social relations that give that fact a limiting and lived meaning. One might try to identify the material interest of those who gain by such an arrangement, rather than abandoning the task of social explanation on the level of physiological observation, as Marx does with sex.

Marx thought that capitalism distorted the family by bringing women into social production under capitalist conditions. This development was both detrimental and historically progressive, much like the impact of capitalism on other aspects of social relations. The destructive impact of capitalism upon the family was deplored largely in terms of its impact on woman's performance of her sex role. The introduction of machinery permitted the enrollment of "every member of the workman's family, without distinction of age or sex," so the working man who had previously sold his own labor power "now sells his wife and child" in addition. They do not even sell themselves; he sells them. To Marx, this arrangement resulted in the "physical deterioration . . . of the woman" and usurped "the place not only of the children's play but also of free labour at home within moderate limits for support of the family."[8] Perhaps dinner was not ready on time. This theorist, so sensitive to the contribution of labor to the creation of value and to its expropriation for the benefit of others, could see the work women do in the home only as free labor, when the only sense in which it is free is that it is unpaid.

When the cotton crisis turned women out of factory jobs, Marx found partial consolation in the fact that "women now had sufficient leisure to give their infants the breast . . . They had time to learn to cook. Unfortunately, the acquisition of this art occurred at a time when they had nothing to cook. But from this we see how capital . . . has usurped the labor necessary in the home of the family. This crisis was also utilized to teach sewing . . ." Even women who do the same work men do are understood in terms of the cooking and sewing they should be doing at home—and, but for the excesses of capitalism, they would be doing. Marx further attributes the high death rate of children, "apart from local causes, principally . . . to the employment of the mothers away from their homes . . . [There] arises an unnatural estrangement between mother and child . . . the mothers become to a grievous extent denaturalized toward their offspring."[9] The harm capitalism does to male workers is not measured by its distortion of their family relationships or the denaturing of men to their children, but women's employment itself means working women's children are neglected. Apparently, under the standard against which Marx compares capitalist distortions, the wife stays home, cooking and sewing and nursing children, while the husband goes off to work. When men work, they become workers, Marx's human beings. When women work, they remain wives and mothers, inadequate ones.[10]

Although he usually abjures moral critique as a bourgeois fetish, Marx displays moral sensitivities on women's work. Abhorring the "moral degradation caused by capitalistic exploitation of women and children," Marx observes: "Before the labour of women and children under 10 years of age was forbidden in mines, capitalists considered employment of naked women and girls, often in company with men, so far sanctioned by their moral code, and especially by their ledgers, that it was only after the passing of the Act that they had recourse to machinery."[11] It is unclear how nudity is profitable. When men are exploited, it is a problem of exploitation; when women are exploited, it is a problem of morality.[12]

Marx did not see the buying and selling of women for sexual use as natural, as liberal theorists tend to do, nor did he reject it as immoral, like the conservatives. In his early work, Marx criticized the man of money, for whom even "the species-relationship itself, the relationship of man to woman, etc., becomes an object of commerce! Woman is bartered."[13] He does not inquire why it is woman who is bartered, nor mention by or to whom. He criticizes "crude and thoughtless communism" for merely transforming private possession of women into collective possession of women; "in which a woman becomes a piece of communal and common property."[14] The woman thus "passes from marriage to general prostitution." He terms the exploitation of women in prostitution as "only a specific expression of the general prostitution of the labourer." The capitalist is analogous to the pimp. Although the analysis is fragmentary and largely metaphorical, prostitution *is* social exploitation, not merely morally condemned. Marx does not inquire why it is overwhelmingly women who are prostitutes, given that men also marry and are exploited as workers. In his later work with Engels, Marx observed that the bourgeoisie are hypocritical in deploring prostitution because "bourgeois marriage is in reality a system of wives in common." He is clear that the abolition of the present system of production "must bring with it the abolition of the community of women springing from that system, i.e., of prostitution both public and private."[15] He does not say why prostitution, which has adapted to every changed economic structure, must necessarily end with the abolition of capitalism.

One of Marx's most widely assimilated views of women has been that the working woman is a liability to the working class because women are more exploitable. To Marx, women's employment contributes to undermining the power of the working man to resist the hegemony of capitalism. "By the excessive addition of women and children to the ranks of the workers, machinery at last breaks down the resistance which the male operatives of the manufacturing period continued to oppose to the despotism of capital." Mechanization and consequent attempts to prolong the working day are resisted by that "repellant yet elastic natural barrier, man." This resistance is undermined by "the more pliant and docile character of the women and children employed on [machine work]."[16] Women are more exploitable than men, not just more exploited, their character a cause rather than a result of their material condition. Women are exceptions to every rule of social analysis Marx developed for the analysis of human beings in society. They are defined in terms of their biology, with children as incompletely adult, in need of special protection, not real workers even when they work.[17] The woman who works outside the home is a class enemy by nature. The possibility that working-class women are specially exploited by capital—and with proper support and organization might be able to hold out for higher wages, better conditions, and fight mechanization—is absent. Men who work for lower wages are a special kind of organizing problem. Woman's exploitability makes her a liability to the working class unless she stays home.

Marx did find progressive potential in women working outside the home, as he did in much of capitalism. "However terrible and disgusting the dissolution, under the capitalist system, of the old family ties may appear, nevertheless, modern industry, by assigning as it does an important part in the process of production, outside the domestic sphere, to women, to young persons, and to children of both sexes, creates a new economic foundation for a higher form of the family and of the relations between the sexes." He also found it obvious that "the fact of the collective working group being composed of individuals of both sexes and all ages must necessarily, under suitable conditions, become a source of human development . . . [although in its capitalist form] that fact is a pestiferous source of corruption and slavery."[18] Sex in marriage was another thing, however: "the sanctification of the sexual instinct through exclusivity, the checking of instinct by laws, the moral beauty which makes nature's commandment idea in the form of an emotional bond—[this is] the spiritual essence of marriage."[19] Yet Marx perceived that under capitalism relations within the family "remain unattacked, in theory, because they are the practical basis on which the bourgeoisie has erected its domination, and because in their bourgeois form they are the conditions which make the bourgeois a bourgeois."[20] In spite of his brief insights into women's condition, he did not systematically see that he shared what he considered natural, and his considering it *as* natural, with the bourgeois society he otherwise criticized.

Whatever one can say about Marx's treatment of women, his first failing and best defense are that the problems of women concerned him only in passing. Friedrich Engels can be neither so accused or excused. His *Origin of the Family, Private Property, and the State* is the seminal marxist attempt to understand and explain women's subordination. The work has been widely criticized, mostly for its data, but its approach has been influential. Often through Lenin, who adopted many of its essentials, the approach and direction of Engels' reasoning, if not all of its specifics, have become orthodox marxism on "the woman question."

To Engels, women are oppressed as a group through the specific form of the family in class society. In pre-class sexually egalitarian social orders, labor was divided by sex. Not until the rise of private property, and with it class society, did that division become hierarchical. Anthropological evidence is used to demonstrate this argument. Under capitalism, women divide into "the bourgeois family" and "the proletarian family," as "personal life" reflections of capitalism's productive relations. Women's economic dependence is a critical nexus between exploitative class relations and the nuclear family structure. Women are not socially subordinate because of biological dependence, but because of the place to which class society relegates their reproductive capacity. Engels applies this analysis to housework and childcare, women's traditional work, and to monogamy and prostitution, issues of women's sexuality. Socialism would end women's oppression by integrating them into the workforce, transforming their isolated "private" work in the home into "public" social production. By eliminating the public/private split incident to the divisions between classes under capitalism, socialism provides the essential condition for women's emancipation.[21]

Engels thus grants that women are specially oppressed, that they are second-class citizens compared with men, that this occurs structurally in the family, antedates the current economic order, and needs to be changed. Engels attempts to set women's subjection within a totality of necessary but changeable social relations—as necessary and changeable as class society. His work holds out the promise that women's situation has been grasped within a theory of social transformation that would also revolutionize class relations. He suggests, at least, that women's equality, including their entry into the wage labor force on an equal basis with men, would do more to change capitalist society than simply advance women as a group within it.

Engels' work has had a continuing impact on contemporary theorists.[22] Adaptations and extensions of his themes are often qualified by ritual disclaimers of his data while appropriating his "insights"[23] or "socio-historical approach,"[24] or claiming to reach his "conclusions . . . by a different route."[25] Engels' views are often most accurately reflected when he is not quoted.[26] Zaretsky, for example, begins his analysis of the relation between socialism and feminism with: "To talk about ending male supremacy takes us right back to the dawn of history—to the creation of the family and class society." He argues that the personal is "a realm cut off from society" under capitalism, developed in response to the socialization of commodity production, where woman is oppressed because she is isolated.[27] Socialism is the solution. Many contemporary marxists also share a tendency, in which Engels and liberal theory are indistinguishable, to interpret the division between work and life under capitalism in terms of coincident divisions between market and home, public and private, male and female spheres. While Engels' account is not universally accepted by marxists, despite, or perhaps because of, the fact that he is widely misinterpreted—a fate his account deserves—his general approach to women's situation is sufficiently accepted among marxists and socialist-feminists as not even to be mentioned by name or footnoted.[28] Or, one often suspects, read.

Engels legitimates women's interests within class analysis by subordinating those interests to his version of class analysis. His attempt to explain women's situation fails less because of his sexism than because of the nature of his materialism; rather, the positivism— more specifically the objectivism—of his materialism requires his sexism. He not only does, but must, assume male dominance at the very points at which it is to be explained. His account works only if essential features of male ascendancy are given; it moves from one epoch to another only if sex-divided control of tasks, and the qualities of male and female sexuality under male dominance, are presupposed. His positivism makes the inaccuracy of his data fatal. He describes what he thinks, attributes it to what he sees, and then ascribes coherence and necessary dynamism to it. In his theory, if something exists, it is necessary that it exist; this does not explain *why* one thing exists instead of something else. What becomes of such a theory if the facts turn out not to exist, or as with sex equality—never to have existed? Perhaps this is why Engels must believe that women were once supreme, despite data and suggestions to the contrary, for eventual equality of the sexes to be historically imaginable. He is dependent for explanation on a teleology of what is; he must explain what is in terms of what is, not in terms of what is not. Sex equality, unfortunately, is not.

According to Engels, women's status is produced through social forces that give rise to "the origin of the family, private property, and the state." He assumes that answering the question "How did it happen that women were first subordinated to men?" is the same as addressing the question "Why are women oppressed and how can we change it?" He equates the temporally first with the persistently fundamental. For Engels, capitalism presents the most highly evolved form both of woman's subjection and of economic class antagonism; that subjection must therefore be understood in its capitalist form if it is to be changed. But woman's oppression, he also finds, predates capitalism; it arises with the first class society. Engels does not situate history within the present so as to tell whether or not fighting capitalism is fighting all of woman's subordination.

In his double sense, women "originally" became "degraded, enthralled, the slave of man's lust, a mere instrument for breeding children" when and because female monogamy was required to guarantee paternity for the inheritance of private property. The same exclusive appropriation of surplus product in the form of private property divided society into antagonistic classes, first into pre-capitalist forms (slave, feudal, mercantile) and later into the capitalist form, as commodity production became generalized. These developments increasingly required a state to contain the social conflict between classes for the advantage of the ruling classes. Thus the rise of private property, class divisions, women's oppression, and the state "coincided with" and required each other, linking the exploitation of man by man in production and social control through the instrument of the state with the subordination of woman to man in monogamy and household drudgery.[29]

Before these four "coincident" developments inaugurated "civilization," Engels argued, labor was divided by sex within the clan, often with women in domestic roles, but woman's social power was equal to or greater than man's. In pairing marriage, the family form which preceded monogamy, woman was supreme in the household, and lineage was reckoned according to "mother right." With the rise of private property, the unity of the clan dissolved into antagonistic classes and isolated family units. As production shifted out of the household, leaving women behind in it, and more private wealth accumulated in men's hands, lineage came to be traced by "father right," marking what Engels called "the world historical defeat of the female sex."[30] The socialization of housework and the full entry of women into production is necessary to end women's isolation in the family and her subordination to men within it. Woman's liberation will therefore come with the end of the private property ownership and class relations that caused her oppression.

Engels summarizes his view in an often quoted and as often misread paragraph:

Monogamous marriage comes on the scene as the subjugation of one sex by the other; it announces a struggle between the sexes unknown throughout the whole previous pre-historic period. The first division of labor is that between man and woman for the propagation of children . . . the first class opposition that appears in history coincides with that of the female sex by the male. Monogamous marriage was a great historical step forward; nevertheless, together with slavery and private wealth it opens the period that has lasted until today in which every step forward is also relatively a step backward, in which prosperity and development for some is won through the misery and frustration of others. It is the cellular form of civilized society in which the nature of the oppositions and contradictions fully active in that society can be already studied.[31]

Of this analysis, Wilhelm Reich wrote that "Engels . . . correctly surmised the nature of the relationships . . . the origin of class divisions was to be found in the antithesis between man and woman."[32] Kate Millett concludes that Engels views "sexual dominance [as] the keystone to the total structure of human injustice."[33] Both interpretations share a one-sided social causality with Engels, yet both read Engels' causality precisely backward. Engels does not think that a division of labor, on the basis of sex or anything else, is inherently exploitative. The first division of labor, he says, was by sex for the propagation of children. The first class opposition, on the other hand, was presumably between slaves and slave owners. The *antagonism* between women and men—not the division of labor between women and men—arose with economic classes. In Engels' view, classes and sexual antagonism "coincided" in that they developed at the same time, but they did not coincide in the sense of falling along the same lines.

Women were not a class for Engels. He cannot be taken to mean, as he often is, that "this first class division among women and men forms the basis for the exploitation of the working class," nor did he think that the oppression of workers "is an extension of" the oppression of women.[34] To Engels, sex divides labor, not relations to the means of production. His widely-quoted spectacular references to woman as man's "slave" ("who only differs from the ordinary courtesan in that she does not let her body on piecework as a wage worker, but sells it once and for all into slavery") and to the man in the family as "the bourgeois [while] the wife represents the proletariat,"[35] though highly suggestive, are essentially metaphors. To argue that women are a class renders capitalism one form of patriarchal society, rather than one form of (economic) class society, in which the patriarchal family is the appropriate family structure. Basing class relations on gender relations would make the fundamental motive force of history a struggle or dialectic between the sexes. This is an argument, but it is not Engels'.[36] In his work, family forms support and respond to changes in economic organization, not to a sex-based historical dialectic. Changes in family forms changing productive structures would be contrary to all that Engels takes historical materialism to be about.[37]

In Engels' history of gender, the transition from group marriage to pairing marriage places woman in the household with one man within a communal setting marked by matrilineal descent. The transition from pairing marriage to monogamy eliminates the communal context and the woman's right to descent, leaving her in the modern nuclear household. Because dialectical materialism claims special competency in explaining social change, the inadequacy of Engels' treatment of these dynamic moments is particularly telling.

Pairing marriage first arose, according to Engels, in the transition from barbarism to savagery, at a time when slavery and private property existed but were not generalized. Class society had not emerged. Although women and men labored in separate spheres, no distinction existed between the public world of men's work and the private world of women's household service. The community was still a large collective household within which both sexes worked to produce goods primarily for use. Pairing marriage was primarily distinguished from the previous communal form in that one man lived with one woman. Men could be polygamous or unfaithful, but infidelity by women was severely punished. Either party could dissolve the marriage bond; children were considered members of the mother's family ("mother right"). Why and how did this form of marital relationship arise to replace group marriage?

> The more the traditional sexual relations lost the naive, primitive character of forest life [sometimes translated "jungle character"] owing to the development of economic conditions with consequent undermining of the old communism and the growing density of population, the more oppressive and humiliating [sometimes translated "degrading"] must the women have felt them to be; and the greater their longing for the right to chastity, of temporary or permanent marriage with one man only, as a way of release [sometimes translated "deliverance"]. This advance could not in any case have originated from the man, if only because it has never occurred to them, even to this day, to renounce the pleasures of actual group marriage.[38]

Engels seems to think that the existence of more people in a smaller space—higher density—of itself generates greater demand for sexual intercourse per woman. The basis for his view that women preferred marriage to one man is unclear. It seems to assume that the present reality that women largely have intercourse at men's will rather than their own was present at the "origin" of this system. Pairing marriage arose because the women, besieged by sexual demands, wanted it. Could not increased population density as well support less intercourse, producing less crowding, or the continuance of extended groups, since people were living so close together anyway? Engels assumes, rather than explains, that a system of restricting women to one man but not restricting men to one woman is an improvement over a system of equal lack of restraint on both. He assumes rather than explains that sexual intercourse with diverse partners is imposed by and desired by men, imposed upon and unwanted by women.[39] Male lust is not explained. Under what conditions would women "long for chastity"? The more marxist approach, methodologically, would be to inquire into the conditions that would create a person who experienced this desire or found such a social rule necessary or advantageous. The fact that men remained able to have many wives or to be unfaithful while women's fidelity was demanded makes one wonder what women gained from the rearrangement. Since "mother right" had supposedly given them supremacy in the clan household, women at this point presumably need not have accepted a situation they did not want.

To assert that frequent and varied sexual intercourse necessarily appeared degrading and oppressive to women fails to explain the "origins" of a society in which it is so. Consequence is presented as cause. The explanation for the social change is: virtuous women wanted husbands. (Unvirtuous women, presumably, were having intercourse with the unfaithful husbands.) Men are ready at all times for "the pleasures of actual group marriage." Here we have the sexed men, the virgins and the whores, characters in the basic pornographic script set before the dawn of history.

Engels goes on: "Just as the wives whom it had formerly been so easy to obtain had now acquired an exchange value and were bought, so also with labor power, particularly since the herds had definitely become family possessions . . . according to the social custom of the time, the man was also the owner of the new source of subsistence, the

cattle, and later of the new instruments of labor, the slaves."[40] Engels
connects things and social meanings, relations between things and
relations between people, with extraordinary offhandedness. How did
wives come to be "obtained," much less sold? Women were sold
because herds were family possessions? What can the power of "mother
right" have been if the wife was purchased by the husband? Labor
power came to be sold "just as" women were sold? How did these
divisions come to be "the social custom of the time"? What made
herds considered wealth in the first place? Why did not women own
or tend herds? Why were not husbands bought and sold? Could it
really be that slavery arose because "The family did not multiply so
rapidly as the cattle. More people were needed to look after them; for
this purpose use could be made of the enemies captured in war, who
could also be bred just as easily as the cattle themselves."[41] Because
cattle reproduce more efficiently than people, slavery arose?

In contrast with this approach to explaining the social status of a
non-class group, Marx asked: "What is a Negro slave? A man of the
black race. The one explanation is as good as the other. A Negro is a
Negro. He only becomes a slave in certain relations. A cotton spinning
jenny is a machine for spinning cotton. It becomes capital only in
certain relations. Torn from these relationships it is no more capital
than gold in itself is money or sugar is the price of sugar."[42] Yet even
Marx was apparently convinced that what makes a domesticated
woman is not social relations, but being a person of the female sex.
Engels proceeds as if one can explain the creation of the social relations
of slavery by pointing to the existence of the need for the work the
slaves performed.

Engels also notes that "the exclusive recognition of the female
parent, owing to the impossibility of recognizing the male parent with
certainty, means that the women—the mothers—are held in high
respect."[43] Out of a context that grants specific social meaning to
descent and maternity, there is no basis to believe that social respect
is a necessary correlate of the only possible system of tracing descent.
Mothers' recognizability need not make them respected. As a prior
matter, it is most unclear why women, a biologically defined group,
are "in the house" at all, or, rather, why the men are not there with
them. Engels says, "According to the division of labor within the
family at that time, it was the man's part to obtain food and the
instruments of labor necessary for the purpose. He therefore also

owned the instruments of labor, and in the event of husband and wife separating, he took them with him, just as she retained her household goods."[44] To Engels, this state of affairs does not require explanation. Woman's place in the household is an extension of the division of labor between the sexes—originally nonexploitative and "for purposes of procreation only." How did it become housework? This question is addressed at most by: "The division of labor between the two sexes is determined by quite other causes than by the position of women in society. Among peoples where the women have to work far harder than we think suitable, there is often much more real respect for women than among our Europeans." Engels does not specify the "quite other causes" that determine this division of labor between the sexes. It does not seem to have occurred to him that the social division of labor might influence the social position of the people who fill the roles, as well as the reverse. He reassures us that the hard-working woman of barbaric times "was regarded among her people as a real lady . . . was also a lady in character."[45] Just in case anyone is worried that socialism, by having women do real work, would make women un ladylike.

No other division of labor in Engels' account divides work along the same lines as another human characteristic in the way sex does. Other than the division between the sexes, divisions of labor separate "men" in production. Each advance in the division of labor fully supersedes the previous historical one.[46] "The division of labor slowly insinuates itself into this process of production. It undermines the collectivity of production and appropriation, elevates appropriation by individuals into the general rule, and thus creates exchange between individuals . . . Gradually commodity production becomes the dominating form."[47] It would seem that when work is divided between women and men (as it continues to be under capitalism without being superseded) Engels feels no need to explain it, but sees it as justified by unspecified "quite other causes." But when work is divided between men and men in production, particularly in class society, it lies at the root of the exploitation of one class by another.[48]

Even when Engels grants that women engage in production—not just socially necessary labor—he cannot manage to conclude that they derive social power from it. To the extent women have power, it comes from their role as mothers and is exercised in the home. Men are workers, even when women engage in production and men are recognizable parents.[49] Men derive neither power nor social position from paternity; they derive these from their role in production. Engels' analysis of pairing marriage precisely tracks liberal theory. A split between home and work is defined in terms of a split between male- and female-dominated spheres, and social power for women is reckoned not by relation to production but by sex.

Engels' purpose is to explain how male dominance occurred. Yet it is present before it is supposed to have happened. The picture of pairing marriage that emerges looks like nothing so much as class society under male supremacy: women are "obtained" or sold as wives, they labor in the house; men own and control the dominant means of subsistence, women are sexually possessed. This arrangement does not describe the exceptions to the general rule later to emerge full-blown in class society, but the general conditions of women's life in this period. Although antagonism between women and men is not supposed to have begun until civilization, the relations described here do not look especially harmonious, unless one thinks of them as somehow suitable. One is left wondering how female monogamy, "father right," and other oppressive features of class society could make women's lives substantively worse and sexual relations newly antagonistic.

With the generalization of private property and class relations, the communal family was replaced by the modern nuclear family. The nuclear family is characterized by monogamy "for women only" for the sole purpose of "mak[ing] the man supreme in the family and to propagate, as the future heirs to his wealth, children indisputably his own." Only the husband can dissolve the marriage bond. Female monogamy is accompanied by male adultery, hetaerism, and prostitution: "the step from pairing marriage to monogamy can be put down to the credit of the men, and historically the essence of this was to make the position of the women worse and the infidelities of the men easier."[50] The initial stimulus for monogamous marriage came when (and because) improved labor productivity increased social wealth. Considerable wealth could concentrate in the hands of one man. To guarantee that the man's children would inherit this wealth, "father right" had to replace "mother right," a change that Marx said "in general . . . seems to be the most natural transition."[51] In Engels' words, "Thus on the one hand, in proportion as wealth increased it made the man's position in the family more important than the woman's and on the other hand created an impulse to exploit this strengthened position in order to overthrow, in favor of his children, the traditional order of inheritance."[52]

Thus female monogamy arose from the concentration of wealth in the hands of one "man" and from the need to bequeath this wealth to his children.[53] Again many connections between material objects and their social meanings are simply presupposed. Engels assumes that an increase in wealth stimulates private appropriation of that wealth; that private wealth is male owned; that an increase in male-owned private wealth creates a need for its inheritance; and that an increase in wealth by husbands has an effect on relations with their wives in the family. He also assumes that the mother's power in the home both can and must be overthrown in order to guarantee that inheritance will pass to his children, even though under pairing marriage paternity was traceable because female fidelity was demanded. And that descent systems automatically correlate with power.

Why would an increase in the produced numbers of any object above immediate need constitute of itself an increase in wealth, in the sense of having the social consequences wealth has for the individual owner?[54] If increased productivity created surplus wealth, why was it not communally owned? The existence of more things does not dictate the form of social relations their organization will take. Must one assume that people inherently desire to have private possessions? If so, the prospect for socialism under any but subsistence conditions seems dim indeed. Why did not women acquire wealth for themselves? Why was the wealth acquired by men not considered owned by the paired unit? Just because man did the labor of tending herds, why did that mean he owned them? Surely a division of labor does not automatically produce a corresponding division of ownership.

Why does having private property imply a belief that it is important that someone, specifically one's "own" children, acquire it on one's death? A discussion of the social meaning of private property is needed to attach property ownership to fathers through marriage and to children as heirs. Possessiveness of objects, parental possessiveness of children ("his children"), possessiveness of spouses for each other, all require grounding in the meaning of social relations. If, for example, private property ownership reflects positively on personality in a given culture, and if death culturally means the end of personality, one might to want to pass on property to someone with whom one identifies. Inheritance becomes a defense against death by perpetuation of self through the mediation of property ownership, to which end monogamous marriage is (at least for men) a means. Whatever the account, one is needed. Engels proceeds as if the need to bequeath (or own) property is a physical quality of the objects themselves.[55]

Why does an increase in social wealth give men power over women in the household? Even presuming that wealth is male owned, why is it relationally significant between the sexes? Under pairing marriage, women worked in the house, where they were supreme as well as socially coequal. Passing property on to children did not require that "mother right" be overthrown; wealth could pass through the mother, whose maternity is seldom in question. What changed under monogamy was the importance for social power of production outside the home. The reason for that shift in social meaning and its effect for gender relations within the home remains unexplained.

When the home was the center of productive activity, the fact that women labored in the home had ensured female supremacy there. When the home was superseded by the marketplace as a productive center, the fact that women labored in the home ensured male supremacy. This may describe the status of women once commodity production takes over social production, and women are excluded from it. But it explains neither that exclusion on the basis of sex nor its consequences for social power. How did the conception of domestic labor change from "productive" to "unproductive" with the rise of classes? At this point, not the rise of commodity production, women were to have lost power. Apparently, the move to clan society, private property, and monogamy devalued housework, that is, women. As women's work was devalued in society, women were deprived of power within the home. Would it have mattered for women's power whether their work produced a surplus to be accumulated as private wealth if the work were seen as essential production? Engels discusses the change as if work in the home were already trivialized as a result of being given the low value of women. The work itself changed little. Yet once the father had gained increased power through increased wealth in the society,

Mother right . . . had to be overthrown, and overthrown it was. This was by no means so difficult as it looks to us today. For this revolution—one of the most decisive ever experienced by mankind—could take place without disturbing one of the living members of a gens. All could remain what they were. The simple decree [sometimes translated "decision"] sufficed that in the future the offspring of the male members should remain within the gens, but that those of the female should be excluded by being transferred to the gens of their father.[56]

Class power produces gender power. Marxists do not usually allow a "simple decision" to overturn historically based power relations. Seemingly men made this decision. Why did the women, who were supposedly supreme in the family at this time, accept it?

The answer appears to be that when the division of labor between men outside the family changed, the domestic relation inside the family changed.[57] The division of labor within the family before the rise of social classes gave man the important property (such as herds). When the division of labor outside the family became a class relation based upon private property ownership, the domestic relation necessarily changed from female to male supremacy. Leaving aside the questions of why and in what sense men could have "owned" property in the family before private property became the dominant mode of ownership, or why the women were all at home, the essence of the argument seems to be that the power of some men to dominate other men in production gave all men power over all women in the home. Engels explains the distribution of power between men and women in the family as a function of the position of the family unit in social production, which in turn expresses men's relations with men.

From the proposition that class power is the source of male dominance, it follows that only those men who possess class power can oppress women in the family. Engels divides his examination of women under capitalism into a exploration of "the bourgeois family" and "the proletarian family," making clear that the class position of the family unit within which the woman is subordinated defines his understanding of her subordination. Since working-class men command no increased wealth, probably own little private property, and are exploited by the few (men) who do, they lack Engels' prerequisite for male supremacy. The proletarian family lacks property, "for the preservation and inheritance of which monogamy and male supremacy were established; hence there is no incentive to make this male supremacy effective." Further, "now that large scale industry has taken the [proletarian] wife out of the home into the labor market and into the factory, and made her often the breadwinner of the family, no basis for any kind of male supremacy is left in the proletarian household, except perhaps for something of the brutality toward women that has spread since the introduction of monogamy."[58]

Proletarian and bourgeois women differ in the structure of their sexual relations with their husbands. Proletarians experience "sex love"; the bourgeoisie has monogamy. Sex love "assumes that the person loved returns the love; to this extent the woman is on an equal footing with the man." Sex love is intense, possessive, and long-lasting. Its morality asks of a relationship: "Did it spring from love and reciprocated love or not?"[59] Individual marriage is the social form that corresponds to sex love, "as sexual love is by its nature exclusive—although at present this exclusiveness is fully realized only in the woman." Sex love is possible only in proletarian relationships. It "becomes and can only become the real rule among the oppressed classes, which means today among the proletariat . . . the eternal attendants of monogamy, hetaerism and adultery, play only an almost vanishing part."[60] In its relationships, the proletariat, the revolutionary class, prefigures the post-revolutionary society.[61]

The proletarian woman is not, then, oppressed as a woman. She is not dominated by a male in the family. She does not live in monogamy. She is neither socially isolated nor economically dependent, because she takes part in social production, as all women will under socialism. She is not jointly or doubly oppressed. Proletarian women are oppressed when, in working outside the home, they come into contact with capital as workers, a condition they share with working-class men.

The differences between proletarian sexual relationships of sex love and bourgeois sexual relationships of monogamy are highly vaunted but obscure. Sex love in its origins, and even upon its abolition, is merged with monogamy. Individual marriage is the social form of both. Removal of the economic basis for monogamy, and consequent equalization of the sexes, will not free women to experience sex love, but will make men "really" monogamous: "If now the economic considerations also disappear which made women put up with the habitual infidelity of their husbands—concern for their own means of existence and still more for their children's future—then, according to all previous experience, the equality of women thereby achieved will tend infinitely to make men really monogamous than to make women polyandrous."[62] The distinction between sex love and monogamy in Engels' analysis serves to distinguish proletarian women's situation from that of bourgeois women in order to idealize the proletariat. Women of both classes are the exclusive possessions of men. Under socialism, the position of all women changes because private house-keeping is removed into social industry. "The supremacy of the man in marriage is the simple consequence of his economic supremacy, and with the abolition of the latter will disappear of itself."[63] At most this explains why women must tolerate male supremacy; it does not explain why men want it. A clearer example of one-sided causality between material relations and social relations would be hard to find.

Putting housekeeping into social industry "removes all the anxiety about 'consequences' which today is the most essential social—moral as well as economic—factor that prevents a girl from giving herself completely to the man she loves." Knowing that communism will enable men more wholly to own women sexually because women will "give [themselves] completely"—the major barrier to this being housework, which one infers is a euphemism for child care—does not make one particularly look forward to Engels' millennium. He asks whether communism will not "suffice to bring about the gradual growth of unconstrained sexual intercourse and with it a more tolerant public opinion in regard to a maiden's honor and a woman's shame?"[64] How unrestrained sexual intercourse went from being the reason women sought deliverance from group marriage under barbarism to that deliverance itself under communism, not to mention the trans-formation of the meaning of intercourse for women from transforma-tion in property relations, is entirely unexplained, but must be what is meant by vulgar materialism.

Sex love occurs only in proletarian relations, so proletarian women are not oppressed as women; monogamy occurs only in the ruling classes, so only bourgeois women are oppressed as women. Can it be that the entire exploration of the origins of women's oppression produces an explanation that excludes the majority of women? Only those women who benefit from class exploitation—that is, women of the ruling classes—are subordinated to men, and only to ruling-class men. It appears to come to this: women who are oppressed by their class position are not oppressed as women by men, but by capital, while only women who benefit from their class position, bourgeois women, are oppressed as women, and only by men of their class. But how would ruling-class men oppress ruling-class women, since class differential is the basis of sex oppression? And since working-class men cannot oppress ruling-class women, bourgeois women cannot be victims of male dominance either. Once working-class men are disqualified from engaging in male dominance, the oppression of women exists, but there is no account of who is oppressed by it, far less of who is doing it.

Engels explains sexism as a kind of inverse of class oppression, which correlates with no known data; it is consistent with one persistent view on the left that feminism is "bourgeois." It also substantiates a feminist view that much marxist theory, in interpreting gender through class, convolutes simple realities to comprehend gender derivatively if at all. A theory that exempts a favored male group from the problem of male dominance necessarily evades confronting male power over women as a distinctive form of power, interrelated with the class structure but neither derivative from nor a side effect of it.[65]

Engels fails to grasp the impact across classes of women's relationship to the class division itself. He does notice that the tension between women's family duties and public production cuts across classes: "if she carries out her duties in the private service to her family, she remains excluded from public production and unable to earn; and if she wants to take part in public production and earn independently, she cannot carry out family duties. And the wife's position in the factory is the position of women in all branches of business, right up to medicine and the law."[66] Engels does not develop his implicit awareness that the relationship of women to class, while often direct and long-lasting, can also be attenuated or crosscut because it is vicarious as well.

From a feminist perspective, a woman's class position, whether or not she works for wages, is as much or more set through her relation first to her father, then to her husband. It changes through changes in these relations, such as marriage, divorce, or aging. It is more open to change, both up and down, than is a man's in similar material circumstances. Through relations with men, women have considerable class mobility, down as well as up. A favorable marriage can rocket a woman into the ruling class, while her own skills, training, work experience, wage scales, and attitudes, were she on her own, would command few requisites for economic independence or mobility. Divorce or aging can devalue a woman economically as her connections or attractiveness to men declines. Women's relation to men's relation to production fixes a woman's class in a way that cuts across the class position of the work she herself does. If she does exclusively housework, her class position is determined by her husband's work outside the home—in spite of the fact that housework is increasingly similar across classes and, when paid, is considered working-class work. This is not to suggest that women's relation to class is less potent than men's because it is vicarious, but to point out that women's relation to class is mediated through their relations with men.

Engels presupposes throughout, as liberal theorists do, that the distinction between the realm inside the family and the realm outside the family is a distinction between public and private.[67] "Private" means "inside the family." "Public" means the rest of the world. That is, the family is considered to be a truly private space, private for everyone in it—and not just because there is an ideological function served by regarding it so. In analyzing women as a group in terms of their role in the family, and men in terms of their role in social production, Engels precludes seeing social relations, inside as well as outside the family, in terms of a sex-based social division. Are women really treated very differently by male employers in the marketplace from the way they are treated by husbands at home? in the work they do? in the personal and sexual services they perform? in the hierarchy between them? To consider the home "private" is to privatize women's oppression and to render women's status a question of domestic relations to be analyzed as a derivative of the public sphere, rather than setting the family within a totality characterized by a sexual division of power which divides both home and marketplace.

Engels' private/public distinction parallels and reinforces Marx's nature/history distinction by defining women's issues in terms of one side of a descriptive dualism in which women's status is the least subject to direct social change. For Marx, woman's natural role is mirrored in her role as worker; for Engels, woman's natural role is mirrored in her role in the family. To identify women's oppression with the private and the natural, on the left no less than in capitalist society itself, works to subordinate the problem of women's status to the male and dominant spheres and to hide that relegation behind the appearance of addressing it.

The key dynamic assumption in Engels' analysis of woman's situation, that without which Engels' history does not move, is (in a word) sexism. The values, division of labor, and power of male supremacy are presumed at each crucial juncture. The account otherwise collapses into a parade of facts. The subject to be explained—the development of male supremacy—is effectively presumed. As an account of the "origins" of that development, the analysis dissolves into a mythic restatement divided into ascending periods of an essentially static state of woman's subordination, within which one can see growing inequalities but cannot figure out how they started or why they keep getting worse. If the intent was to give "the woman question" a place in marxist theory, it did: woman's place.

Engels' method made this inevitable. His approach to social explanation is rigidly causal, unidirectional, and one-sided. Material conditions alone create social relations; consciousness and materiality do not interact. Thought contemplates things. Objects appear and relate to each other out there, back then. The discourse is mythic in quality, passive in voice. "There arose" certain things; then something "came over" something; this "was bound to bring" that. Theory, for Engels, is far from a dialogue between observer and observed. He does not worry about his own historicity. He totally fails to grasp the subject side of the subject/object relation as socially dynamic.[68] And he takes history as a fixed object within a teleology in which what came before necessarily led to what came after. This is to fail to take the *object* side of the subject/object relation as socially dynamic. One must understand that society could be other than it is in order to explain it, far less to change it. Perhaps one must even understand that society could be other than it is in order to understand why it necessarily is as it is. Engels' empiricism can imagine only the reality he finds, and therefore he can find only the reality he imagines.

# 3 | A Marxist Critique of Feminism

It is true, as Marx says, that history does not walk on its head, but it is also true that it does not think with its feet. Or, one should say rather, that it is neither its "head" nor its "feet" that we have to worry about, but its body.
—Maurice Merleau-Ponty

Does history's body have sex? If so, something of the unity between its head and its feet is left out of account by a reference to its body, singular. Nor is the unity of consciousness—thinking—with materiality—walking—adequately captured by an analysis of a totality that is bifurcated unless that split is exposed and explored. If the life situation of consciousness varies by sex, its wholeness may prove as illusory in social reality as it is obfuscating in theoretical figure. How does history walk through women's lives, think women's thoughts? If this question has never been confronted, might something be missing in the conceptualization not only of women but of history and consciousness as well? Feminism worries about this, altering the stance and persona—the "we"—of the theorist, the practice of theory as an activity, the analysis of consciousness, social life, and the relation between them.

A theory is feminist to the extent it is persuaded that women have been unjustly unequal to men because of the social meaning of their bodies. Feminist theory is critical of gender as a determinant of life chances, finding that it is women who differentially suffer from the distinction of sex. Compared with men, women lack control over their social destinies, their contributions and accomplishments restricted and undervalued, their dignity thwarted, and their physical security violated. The reasons for this, although they vary, are believed to be predominantly social and unjust. To see existing relations between the sexes as a social inequality, rather than as based on inherent differences, is to reject the judgment that those relations express whatever might validly or immutably distinguish the sexes. Although varied accounts of the problem exist, animated by different factors and dynamics as determinants, feminism is distinguished by the view that gender *is* a problem: that what exists now is not equality between the sexes.

Feminism sees women as a group and seeks to define and pursue women's interest. Feminists believe that women share a reality, and search for it, even as they criticize the leveling effects of the social enforcement of its commonalities. Women's commonalities include, they do not transcend, individual uniqueness, profound diversity (such as race and class), time, and place. Feminism's search for a ground is a search for the truth of all women's collectivity in the face of the enforced lie that all women are the same.

What, really, is a woman? Most feminists implicitly assume that biological femaleness is a sufficient index and bond because of what society makes of it: a woman is who lives in a female body. Others locate what women have in common within a shared reality of common treatment as a sex: a woman is who has been treated as one. A few define a woman as one who thinks of herself, or identifies, as one. Most consider women's condition to be a descriptive fact of sex inequality: no woman escapes the meaning of being a woman within a social system that defines one according to gender, and most do. Women's diversity is included in this definition, rather than under-cutting it. Once sameness and difference are supplanted by a substan-tive analysis of position and interest, women become defined politically: since no woman is unaffected by whatever creates and destroys women as such, no woman is without stake in women's situation.

In its search for an account of the social pattern of relations between the sexes and a way to change it, contemporary feminism places women's experience, and the perspective from within that experience, at the center of an inquiry into the lived-out reality of gender. This feminism pays close attention to women's everyday lives and gives priority to women's point of view. In theoretical form, these qualities are not unique to feminism. Phenomenology, for example, conceives everyday life as central; marxism gives priority to the point of view of the group whose dispossession it criticizes. Both the fundamental substantive analysis and epistemological approach of feminism, the feminist stance as a formal theoretical departure, are nonetheless embodied in its practice of these principles. What is women's everyday life? Where and how does one look for it? How does one know and verify that one has found it?

In some feminist work, aspects of ordinary life—such as housework or sexuality—become theoretically primary, the locale or ground of women's subordination. In some feminist theories, women's perspective becomes exclusively legitimate, so that only women can validly reflect on their situation, taking separatism to the level of method. But is there such a thing as women's point of view? Who speaks from it? How can it emerge validly self-reflective from an invalid condition? How can it be identified? How distinguished from delusion? How can anything any woman thinks be called false in a theory that purports to validate all women's experience? If every woman's views are true, regardless of content, how is feminism to criticize the content and process of women's determination, much less change it? Regardless of the weight or place accorded daily life or women's insight, feminist theory probes hidden meanings in ordinariness and proceeds as if the truth of women's condition is accessible to women's collective inquiry. The pursuit of the truth of women's reality is the process of consciousness; the life situation of consciousness, its determination articulated in the minutiae of everyday existence, is what feminist consciousness seeks to be conscious of.

A theory is marxist in the broadest sense to the extent it critically analyzes society's dynamic laws of motion in their totality, materiality, and historicity, combining determinacy with agency, thought with situation, complexly based on interest. If this line is drawn across the feminist tradition, two distinct theoretical approaches emerge. One is liberal, more like the theories Marx criticized; one is radical, more like marxism, at least in its formal dimensions. Other than socialist feminism, the tendencies of liberal feminism and radical feminism divide most major feminist theories and forms of practice, confusingly as well as productively entangled in an unresolved tension.[1] One approach or the other usually dominates a project or theory or author; few are exclusively liberal or exclusively radical. Both tendencies respond to sex inequality; they just have different conceptions of what the problem is, diverging in their accounts of its source, dynamics, and place in society:

what sex is, how it is created, shaped, and socially lived. They also diverge in their accounts of what the wrong of sex inequality is, how it is damaging, and what must be done to change it.

For purposes of analysis, these differences can be discussed in terms of two pervasive if usually inexplicit theoretical presumptions. The first concerns the proper unit of social analysis; the second, the dynamic of their interaction. Liberal feminism takes the individual as the proper unit of analysis and measure of the destructiveness of sexism. For radical feminism, although the person is kept in view, the touchstone for analysis and outrage is the collective "group called women."[2] The difference is one of emphasis, but an emphasis that is all. What kind of collectivity is/are women? Liberal feminism aggregates all women out of each woman. Radical feminism sees all women in each one. In liberalism, women are an aggregate, a plural noun. In radicalism, women is a collective whole, a singular noun, its diverse elements part of its commonality. The fact that an individual might be socially constructed is an outrage and an injury in liberalism; liberal feminism applies this critique to women. In radical theory, the fact of social construction of the individual is accepted and even embraced. Its content—what the person is made into or who she is allowed to be or prevented from being—is what is criticized. Toni McNaron's distinction between humanism and feminism also distinguishes liberal from radical feminism: "humanism is essentially individualistic and ahistorical, while feminism is collective and deeply contextual."[3] The relationship between the individual and the social delineates a split between liberal and radical feminism in their view of the personal. In liberal feminism, the personal is distinguished from the collective; in radical feminism, it comprises it.

From these conceptions of the constitution of the social actors proceeds the analysis of the nature of their social interaction. To liberal feminism, the problem of sex inequality is that law and custom divide the sexes into two arbitrary and irrational gender roles that restrict human potentialities. To radical feminism, sex is a systematic division of social power, a social principle inseparable from the gender of individuals, enforced to women's detriment because it serves the interest of the powerful, that is, men. In the radical view, sexism is not just a disparity to be leveled but a system of subordination to be overthrown. Biological females can and do act for and against its interests, just as biological males can and do, but interest in this system diverges by gender.

In radical feminism, the ultimate independence of sexism from the biology of sex, not only at its source but in its lived-out forms, renders the analysis intrinsically socially based. That male power is systematic and cumulative defines what is political about sex to radical feminist theory—a very different conception of politics from that of liberalism. To liberal feminism, gender differentiation defines sexual politics; undercutting, blurring, or trading gender roles seen as imposed differences changes it. To radical feminism, gender hierarchy defines sexual politics. In this view, only a transformation in the equation of gender (hence gender difference) with dominance, a delegitimation of the sexual dynamic of power and powerlessness as such, can alter it. Radical feminism as a theory is a movement of mind which addresses the most basic questions of politics: the constitution of the person in society; social as against natural determinations of relative status; the relationship between morality, justice, and power; the meaning and possibility of willed action; the role of thought and the theorist in politics; the nature of power and its distribution; the nature of community; the definition of the political itself. Packed into two conceptions of the meanings of "the personal" and "the political" are the meaning of their convergence. The interplay among these themes illuminates feminism's major contours and contributions by exposing some of its least resolved inner tensions

John Stuart Mill's *The Subjection of Women*, published in 1869, remains the most compelling, sympathetic, subtle, perceptive, consistent, coherent, complex, and complete statement of the liberal feminist argument for women's equality. The influence of his wife, Harriet Taylor, doubtless made it the most nearly radical of Mill's essays, exhibiting both the deepest weaknesses and greatest strengths of liberalism. In his *Autobiography,* Mill says his essay *On Liberty* aspires to explore "the importance, to man and society, of a large variety in types of character, and [gives] full freedom to human nature to expand itself in innumerable and conflicting directions."[4] *On Liberty* accordingly asks about "the nature and limits of the power which can be legitimately exercised by society over the individual." Mill's solution was to define limits to "the legitimate interference of collective opinion with individual independence."[5] Most broadly, Mill analyzed the ways government and society distorts individuals' ability to follow the logic of their own lives, in order to reduce or eliminate these limitations. His application of this impulse—this humanism—to women defines his feminism.

Mill's *The Subjection of Women* is the original statement of the view, taken up and extended and transformed by feminists since, that the status of the sexes in the family, particularly in the marriage law, accounts for the inequality of the sexes in society as a whole. Society is "patriarchal."[6] The relations between the sexes are distorted through "the legal subordination of one sex to the other," specifically through the legal inequality between husband and wife in marriage. Upbringing for a domestic role, and the requirements of living it as a sole life option, contort each woman's natural character into that of man's dependent and inferior appendage.[7] "Wrong in itself," this system arose "simply from the fact that from the very earliest twilight of human society, every woman (owing to the value attached to her by men, combined with her inferiority in muscular strength) was found in a state of bondage to some man."[8]

Unequal marriage laws, in his account, began by "recognizing the relations they find already existing between individuals."[9] The resulting inequality was maintained by a combination of force with attitude. Force finally resides in the state; hence the central importance of law to Mill's analysis. Attitude is ingrained opinion based upon "a mass of feeling," specifically a male "instinct of selfishness" which overwhelms reason, because of which "the generality of the male sex cannot yet tolerate the idea of living with an equal."[10] Such laws not only keep women in legal bondage ("There remain no legal slaves, except the mistress of every house") but are "now one of the chief hindrances to human improvement" and happiness.[11]

The heart of Mill's argument is that woman should be man's legal equal so that she can be his social equal because she is his natural equal. To support this, he undertakes to undermine the reasonableness of a catalogue of popular attitudes and observations concerning women's behavior, personality, characteristics, and motivations, then as now women's supposed differences from men. Real differences, to Mill, are individual, and the rest are imposed or otherwise unknowable so long as inequality exists. Central to his analytic strategy is the comparison of women with men. For example, a "nervous temperament" or a tendency to govern and be governed by one's "amatory propensities" may describe some women,[12] but it also describes some men; hence it is not a characteristic of sex. Other qualities may disproportionately characterize women, he says, but they are overgeneralized. Not to admit exceptions for exceptional individuals is to close to women options that society opens to men.

To the extent that other characteristics are true of women, as with intuitiveness, morality, or practicality, in that strange moral (always condescending) reversal that characterizes so many defenses of the female sex, women are seen as comparatively superior: "A woman seldom runs wild after an abstraction."[13] Other differences may, Mill argues, have benefits commensurate with detriments. If woman's brain is sooner fatigued, it may sooner recover. Some allegedly female qualities are found to be misattributed, such as those that vary across cultures.[14] All those qualities that are found to be true to any extent, including women's "deficiency of originality" of mind with attendant lack of desire for fame, are explained largely as "the natural result of their circumstances."[15] Rather than seeing women's existing differences from men as reasons for their unfitness for equality, Mill argues that whatever differences naturally distinguish women from men, or would express themselves as socially beneficial, cannot be known and will not reliably emerge until the compulsory artifice of legal inequality is removed.

The essence of Mill's analysis is that sex inequality is irrational, therefore unjust. Inequality on the basis of sex subjects individuals to other individuals who are not their natural superiors. Sex is necessarily an irrational, therefore unjust, basis for differentiation because sex is a group quality, not an individual one. Women's social development is based upon an average or a generality rather than upon unique attributes. The marriage law, like restrictions on women's access to education and professions, admits no exceptions: "Even if [a general rule] be well grounded in a majority of cases, which it is very likely not to be, there will be a minority of exceptional cases in which it does not hold: and in those it is both an injustice to the individuals, and a detriment to society, to place barriers in the way of their using their faculties for their own benefit and for that of others."[16]

The power of men over women, which comes down to physical force sanctioned by the state, is similarly unjust because it is distributed to men on a group basis, rather than by more precise standards, standards that seem to include class:

Whatever gratification of pride there is in the possession of power, and whatever personal interest in its exercise, is in this case not confined to a limited class, but common to the whole male sex. Instead of being, to most of its supporters, a thing desirable chiefly in the abstract, or, like the political ends usually contended for by factions, of little private importance to any but the leaders, it comes home to the person and hearth of every male head of a family, and of every one who looks forward to being so. The clodhopper exercises, or is to exercise, his share of the power equally with the highest nobleman. [17]

Power among men is power according to merit, including class, or contended for and won, or held "in the abstract." The satisfactions or benefits of such power are not allowed women. Given that men's power over women is also unchecked and unilateral, a maldistribution that Mill sees as "an isolated fact in modern social institutions, a solitary breach of what has become their fundamental law," he is relieved to concede that he has described "the wife's legal position, not her actual treatment." [18] Men do not do what they could do. According to Mill, tenderness produced by nearness, mutual attraction to offspring, and other incidents of sharing a household tend to moderate, even if they do not qualify, men's dominant position.

Women's daily life, in Mill's view, is debilitatingly tedious in ways that vary by class yet remain a constant force in women's subjection. "The superintendence of a household, even when not in other respects laborious, is extremely onerous to the thoughts; it requires incessant vigilance, an eye which no detail escapes, and presents questions for consideration and solution, foreseen and unforeseen, at every hour of the day, from which the person responsible for them can hardly ever shake herself free." A woman who can afford domestic help merely refocuses this imperative into "what is called society . . . the dinner parties, concerts, evening parties, morning visits, letter writing, and all that goes with them . . . All this is over and above the engrossing duty which society imposes exclusively upon women, of making themselves charming." [19]

Women's view of their own situation is complexly treated in Mill's work. "In the first place, women do not accept it." [20] Yet men place real limits upon women's ability to reject it even within themselves:

Men do not want solely the obedience of women, they want their sentiments . . . They have therefore put everything into practice to enslave their minds . . . When we put together three things—first, the natural attraction between the opposite sexes; secondly, the wife's entire dependence on the husband . . . and lastly that the principal object of human pursuit, consideration, and all objects of social ambition can in general be sought or obtained by her only through him, it would be a miracle if the object of being attractive to men had not become the polar star of feminine education and formation of character.[21]

In this analysis—which identifies sexuality and economics as bases for women's condition—women's consent to their place is no less coerced for seeming acquiescent. Women have little choice but to become women, their characters debased, their options obscure or futile, so that they seem willingly to choose their chains. Men have no access to any truth other than this about women: "The truth is, that the position of looking up to another is extremely unpropitious to complete sincerity and openness with him." In fact, Mill doubts whether anybody can know the truth about women. The "influence" of men over women's lives and minds means that one cannot tell what women would think, feel, create, choose, or become, of their own accord and for their own use. "Even the greater part of what women write about women is mere sycophancy to men." Only when social institutions permit "the same free development of originality in women which is possible to men," only "when that time comes, and not before, we shall see, and not merely hear, as much as it is necessary to know of the nature of women, and the adaptation of other things to it."[22] What contemporary feminism terms sexism, then, is in Mill's theory a form of unjust authority that restricts the free development of each woman. Distorting her character to fit her subordination, inequality violates her nature, constrains social efficiency, and obstructs human happiness. Mill's feminism commits him to women's freedom—the absence of such pressures—because each woman is a human being like any other.

From Mill to contemporary forms, liberal theory exhibits five interrelated dimensions that contrast with radical feminist theory, clarifying both. These are: individualism, naturalism, voluntarism, idealism, and moralism.[23] Individualism involves one of liberalism's deepest yet also superficially most apparent notions: what it is to be a person is to be a unique individual, which defines itself against, as distinct from, as not reducible to, any group. The person in radical feminist thought is necessarily socially constituted, affirmatively so through an active yet critical embrace of womanhood as identity. Naturalism is at base an epistemological posture growing out of the search for a ground on which to found true reality perception, a location of constancy, a bedrock beneath social shifts, variance, and relativity. Nature is a fixed, certain, and ultimately knowable reality to which there is tangible demonstrable truth, intersubjectively communicable, regardless of perspective. The idea of naturalism, in fact, is that nature is not an idea, but an object reality, meaning that it is thing. Sex as biology, gender as physical body, occupies this place in liberal feminism. In this view, body originates independently of society or mind; then, to varying degrees but invariably and immutably, it undergirds social relations, limiting change. In radical feminism, the condition of the sexes and the relevant definition of women as a group is conceived as social down to the somatic level. Only incidentally, perhaps even consequentially, is it biological.[24]

The idealism of liberalism consists in its tendency to treat thinking as a sphere unto itself and as the prime mover of social life. Reason becomes a transhistorical logic that motivates persuasion independently of surroundings, advocacy, or audience. Attitudes tend to be identified as the sources and solutions for social problems like sexism, rational argument as the engine of change. The radical feminist theory of consciousness, by contrast, sees thoughts as constituent participants in conditions—more than mere reflections but less than unilinear causes of life settings. Intricately related to its idealism is liberalism's account of correct thought: moralism. Rightness means conforming behavior to rules that are abstractly right or wrong in themselves.[25] From women's experience that such precepts have systematically, often with no logical defect, worked in the interest of men, radical feminism is developing a theory of male power, in which powerlessness is a problem but redistribution of power as currently defined is not its ultimate solution, upon which to build a feminist theory of justice.

The voluntarism of liberalism consists in its notion that social life is comprised of autonomous, intentional, and self-willed actions, with exceptional constraints or qualifications by society or the state. This aggregation of freely-acting persons as the descriptive and prescriptive model of social action is replaced, in radical feminism, with a complex political determinism. Women and women's actions are complex responses to conditions they did not make or control; they are contextualized and situated. Yet their responses contextualize and situate the actions of others. As an individual self, one has little power; but as an other in a social milieu, one ultimately has more. Women struggle to transform conditions, but conditions are not resisted without means given or seized, nor simply because they are determining, nor because women are really free beneath their victimization. With forms of power forged from powerlessness, conditions are resisted, in the radical feminist view, because women somehow resent being violated and used, and because existing conditions deny women a whole life, visions of which are meager and partial but accessible within women's present lives and recaptured past. Women also have access to a clear sense that their lives would be better if they were denigrated less and paid more.

Marxists often speak disparagingly of "bourgeois feminism."[26] Exactly what this means, other than to disparage whatever it is, is as often not apparent. Some suggest that feminism is inherently bourgeois; that is, it inherently works in the interest of the bourgeoisie as a class. Pointing to some feminists' middle-class backgrounds, good educations, and bent for law reform is an attempt to reduce feminism to the class position of some feminists.[27] Even if this description were true of the movement (often it is not), would such a relation between consciousness and material conditions necessarily place opposition to women's social condition in the service of the ruling class? This is a question that marxists take seriously when considering the relation between material conditions and consciousness on the left; it has a long history in the debates over the role of the intellectual in the revolution and the nature of the party. To conclude that the women's movement is bourgeois because it includes women from the bourgeoisie is to resolve a question for feminism which is unresolved for marxism.

Sometimes the epithet "bourgeois feminism," which becomes one word, inaugurates an effort to bring feminism into line with socialism by exorcising its bourgeois analytic elements, beginning with "women." At this juncture, it seems less important to criticize feminism for analyzing a social category other than the one Marx found fundamental than to evaluate the one that feminism analyzes in a marxist light, even if that raises real questions for the primacy of the class division. Clearly, "women" as a category is not "class" as a category, although they overlap in the world. What is the class of a nurse who marries a doctor, continuing to work part-time as a nurse? the woman from an academic family with three children who goes on welfare when her psychoanalyst husband mysteriously disappears? the daughter of a professional mother and middle-management father who worked up from office boy? the secretary who marries her executive boss? the "Sears card" middle-class girl abducted into pornography? the steelworker's daughter in law school? the young runaway fleeing rich suburban incest being pimped downtown? These examples do not mean that class does not exist or that true class mobility is all that significant. They do suggest that women's class status is significantly mediated by women's relation to men.

To marxists, an analysis of "women" seems to imply a movement confined to women. It seems clear that if marxists agreed that women experience a fundamental and strategically located oppression, the autonomy of a movement on behalf of women's interests would not be contested because it was separate. August Bebel argued that "women should expect as little help from the men as workingmen do from the capitalist class."[28] The seeds of autonomous organization exist in any politics based on a group analysis—women, children, Blacks, or workers—particularly when the analysis identifies an antagonism. The notion that a separate oppression creates the need for a separate struggle for liberation, though often ambiguous in practice, is accepted in theory in the case of the working class, because the theory of its specifically critical place in the basic structure of social power—production—is accepted. The proletariat has "radical chains."[29] Are women oppressed as women in a way that is strategic for social power? Do women have radical chains?

Feminists who argue that the division between women and men is the primary social division clearly think so. "The primary social and political distinctions are not even those based on wealth or rank but those based on sex. For the most pertinent and fundamental consideration one can bestow upon our culture is to recognize its basis in patriarchy."[30] The family is often regarded as the key structure for perpetuating patriarchy, modeling authoritarian social relations as it teaches sexual differentiation of social functions. This account of the man/woman division is much like the marxian account of the class division: a social structural response by human beings to a material condition that is essential for survival, maintenance of which is in the interests of those who have the dominant role and against the interests of those who are dominated. In this view, woman's position is clearly rooted in a social division, played out through society in roles, systematically and cumulatively benefiting one group to the detriment of the other. If there is no ultimate explanation offered of why women are "women" and men are "men," neither does marxism explain why some particular individuals (with any other single quality in common) become capitalists and others are workers. If women's oppression is the primary oppression, then women's liberation must be the primary liberation. Women's liberation is thus argued to be basic to social transformation, not merely an index of it. Such an analysis supplies a new basic contradiction, tending to supplant or subsume economic class. To avoid the primacy issue by allowing class divisions to coexist with or crosscut sex, other theorists have argued that women are a caste. But when female liberation from caste status is declared "the basis for social revolution,"[31] the picture is reversed, so that each sex caste layer is divided horizontally in half by class, raising the question of primacy all over again.

Marxist theories disagree with the implication that women are a class and argue that such views divide the proletariat. Barbara Ehrenreich and Dierdre English state: "Women are not a 'class'; they are not uniformly oppressed; they do not all experience sexism in the same ways."[32] Do proletarians, including women, all experience class oppression in the same ways? On the level of the work women do, women's lives are strikingly similar across class. Kate Millett has argued that "economic dependency renders [women's] affiliations with any class a tangential, vicarious, and temporary matter."[33] Evelyn Reed has responded: "To oppose women as a class against men as a class can only result in a diversion of the real class struggle."[34] Marxists seem worried that to posit women and men as classes suggests that women must fight men for their freedom. "What is the logical and inescapable extension of the basic feminist position that the fundamental social division is one of sex, that the oppression of women stems from male supremacy, that all women are 'sisters' if not that women should place themselves on the opposite side of the barricades from their oppressors—from men?"[35] Apparently it is a matter of judgment—perhaps an assessment of importance as much as a deduction from theoretical postulates or empirical evidence—which struggle is "the real class struggle." If women were considered oppressed as a class, marxists should be among the last to protest recourse to the barricades.

Beyond the disagreement over categorical primacy, if one accepts sex as a material social category at all and uses Marx's analysis of class to scrutinize feminist analyses of sex, a substantial body of feminist work can be criticized for the very tendencies Marx criticized in bourgeois theory.[36] Marxists have charged feminism with liberalism of two kinds: idealism, or belief in the power of ideas alone to cause social change; and individualism, or reliance on the individual to effect social change.[37] The first criticism is often presented as addressing attitudes rather than the material base of those attitudes,[38] or as relying on moral persuasion.[39] The theory and practice of consciousness raising (see Chapter 6) can lapse into treating social reality as if it were constructed solely by one's idea of it, so that all that is required for social change is to persuade people of the morality and utility of equality for women to achieve equality by force of reason and exemplary practice.[40] This approach attributes the movement of history to the movement of ideas and changes in these ideas to abstract human reason or to eternal ever-unfolding verities of ever-progressing justice. Marx criticized Hegel and Proudhon for idealism in attributing movements in the material world to movements in reason rather than to alterations in material relations. Marx ridiculed Proudhon's notion that "it was the principle that made the history, and not the history that made the principle."[41] History, to Marx, is moved by people in concrete relation to productive forces and within the social relations that arise from their organization of those forces.[42]

As an example of the feminism to which such a criticism of idealism would apply, Mary Daly in *Gyn/Ecology* speaks less of the creation of women's consciousness by the realities of male power, therefore of the depth of women's damage, and more of its lies and distortions, positing mind change as social change. For instance, in the investigation of suttee, a practice in which Indian widows are supposed to throw themselves upon their dead husband's funeral pyres in grief (and to keep pure), Daly focuses upon demystifying its allegedly voluntary aspects. Women are revealed as drugged, pushed, browbeaten, or otherwise coerced.[43] Comparatively neglected—both as to the women involved and as to the implications for the diagnosis of sexism as illusion—are perhaps suttee's deepest victims: women who want to die when their husband dies, who volunteer for self-immolation because they believe their life is over when his is, women whose consciousness conforms to the materially dismal and frightening prospect of widowhood in Indian society. To the extent the analysis turns on whether the women jump or are pushed, it gives ideas both too much and too little power. In the case of male power, too much, in suggesting that the subordination of women is an idea such that to think it differently is to change it. In the case of female powerlessness, too little, in neglecting the consciousness of the most totally victimized in favor of a critique of the victimization of those whose consciousness, at least, has escaped. Similarly, Susan Griffin, in *Pornography and Silence,* reduces the problem of pornography to the problem of "the pornographic mind."[44] Pornography is opposed to eros in a distinction that is fundamentally psychological rather than interested, something to be un-thought and therefore changed, rather than a form of exploitation rooted in social life which both constitutes and expresses its material realities.

A similar failure to situate thought in social reality is central to Carol Gilligan's work on gender differences in moral reasoning.[45] By establishing that women reason differently from men on moral questions, she revalues that which has accurately distinguished women from men by making it seem as though women's moral reasoning is somehow women's, rather than what male supremacy has attributed to women for its own use. When difference means dominance as it does with gender, for women to affirm differences is to affirm the qualities and characteristics of powerlessness. Women may have an approach to moral reasoning, but it is an approach made both of what is and of what is not allowed to be. To the extent materialism means anything at all, it means that what women have been and thought is what they have been permitted to be and think. Whatever this is, it is not women's, possessive. To treat it as if it were is to leap over the social world to analyze women's situation *as if* equality, in spite of everything, already ineluctably existed.

The woman's morality Gilligan discovers cannot be morality "in a different voice." It can only be morality in the feminine voice, in a higher register.[46] Women are said to value care. Perhaps women value care because men have valued women according to the care they give. Women are said to think in relational terms. Perhaps women think in relational terms because women's social existence is defined in relation to men. The liberal idealism of these works is revealed in the ways they do not take social determination and the realities of power seriously enough. As a matter of sociology of knowledge, it is enlightening, though, that affirming the perspective that has been forced on women is rather widely taken as real progress toward taking women seriously.

Some feminists early in the second wave advanced "feelings" as pure reflection of the external world and therefore unmediated access to truth. The San Francisco Redstockings, for example, asserted: "Our politics begin with our feelings: feelings are a direct response to the events and relationships that we experience; that's how we know what's really going on . . . Information derived from our feelings is our only reliable information, and our political analysis can be trusted only so long as it does not contradict our feelings."[47] This intuitionist approach posits feelings, as Proudhon and others posited reason, as outside society, an internalized reference system for measuring social reality that derives its claim to validity from its place beyond social reach. Surely one is more likely to feel bad than justified when confronting difficulties in a situation that social learning supports, such as motherhood. This response may produce the sense that feelings are an independent basis for understanding reality, that thoughts are able to grasp it only derivatively, and that thinking is socially constructed while feelings are not. Yet feminism has uncovered women's social roles in women's actual feelings and society's standards in women's feelings, both in embracing and in rejecting their roles. If a woman feels anger at not being treated as a full person, this surely refers to social definitions of personhood, possibly even liberal ones, to which men routinely experience entitlement without being subjected to class-based critique. Similarly, feelings of loss of control over one's life may reflect a social standard of self-actualization that requires control as a means to it.

Some feminist practice—such as therapy, crisis intervention, and service work—tends to focus on the individual as if social life were constructed of an amalgam of independent and solitary individuals, so that social change is a matter of moving their lives one by one. Opposing the suggestion that there is a sphere of human social activity which belongs exclusively to each individual as a unit, Marx states: "The individual is the social being. The manifestation of his life—even when it does not appear directly in the form of a communal manifestation, accomplished in association with other men—is . . . a manifestation and affirmation of social life."[48]

Marxist epistemology makes the isolated individual a person without consciousness, unthinkable to self as well as for theory, social order, and social change.

The marxist criticism of feminist individualism often turns into a criticism of its focus on private life, on the supposition that private life is intrinsically the realm of the individual. Thus, Engels said women's emancipation and equality were impossible so long as women were "restricted to housework, which is private."[49] Updated, "the sex occurs on privatized, intimate terrain within the family unit."[50] The husband's authority, the children's demands, and the wife's conditioned conception of a good housekeeper may be seen as "simply the personal means through which economic necessity is expressed inside the family," yet addressing housework is called individualistic and characterized as adopting "primarily interpersonal forms of struggle."[51] The woman "rebels as an isolated individual to the immediate detriment of her husband and children and her actions do not contest the relations of capital directly . . . [Her rebellion is] objectively untenable because she is not part of any union."[52] Presumably, a union of organized labor.

It is difficult to avoid the conclusion that such charges of individualism are disagreements with the analysis that the division between women and men is a basic social division of power, including labor. Similarly, the charge of idealism often turns into the view that the social division between women and men can be attacked only as unreasonable or immoral—which is another way of saying that it is not a matter of exploitation and has no material base. Yet social theory via individual biography surely has its limitations. Consider the following quotation, which exemplifies virtually all the strains in feminist thought singled out for marxist criticism—the focus on the individual, the reflective theory of perception, and the asocial "ideas move life" logic:

> We know that true revolution is a glacial process of unknown cell structures that will evolve out of shared bits of profoundly internalized consciousness. This consciousness, which is at first realized through the painful acknowledgment of hierarchical oppression, is transformed by degrees into the birth of the self and the celebration of spontaneous behavior appropriate to the individual and her perception of the constantly changing environment and social conditions.[53]

Oddly, the most prominent liberalism in feminism is not idealism or individualism but naturalism. Marx observed that class relations are taken as natural, hence static and immutable. "When the economists say that present-day relations, the relations of bourgeois production, are natural, they imply that these are the relations in which wealth is created and productive forces developed in conformity with nature. These relations therefore are themselves natural laws, independent of the influence of time. They are eternal laws which must always govern society."[54] Bourgeois social theory, Marx observed, divides society into two kinds of social institutions, the natural and the artificial.[55] A similar distinction characterizes published feminist thought. Implicit in feminism are answers to the question "What is a woman?" that range from the almost purely biological, in which women are defined by female biology, to the almost purely social, in which women are defined by their social treatment. Many prominent feminist theorists advance implicitly or explicitly biological theories, criticizing society for its artificiality or criticizing the natural as well. In much the same way biology underlies women's social position in the social ideology of both left and right, it underlies some feminism.

It is one thing to identify woman's biology as a part of the terrain on which a struggle for dominance is acted out; it is another to identify woman's biology as the source of that subordination. The first approach certainly identifies an intimate alienation; the second predicates woman's status on the facticity of her biology. As Simone de Beauvoir presents it,

> Here we have the key to the whole mystery. On the biological level, a species is maintained only by creating itself anew, but this creation results only in repeating the same Life in more individuals . . . Her misfortune is to have been biologically destined for the repetition of Life, when even in her own view Life does not carry within itself its reasons for being, reasons that are more important than Life itself.[56]

Here, it is not the meaning society has given woman's bodily functions but the functions themselves, existentially, that oppress women. The biological collapses into the social not because society enforces a meaning of woman's biology, but because woman's body determines her social being as a pre-social matter. The fact of woman's oppression is accounted for by the universal existential fact of her physiology: anatomy is destiny. Since woman is defined by nature, it seems inevitable that she will be oppressed in society, even though this oppression is what Beauvoir clearly seeks to criticize. Thus woman's oppression is present at Beauvoir's account of its birth: "Perhaps, however, if productive work had remained within her strength woman would have accomplished with man the conquest of nature . . . but because she did not share his way of working and thinking, because she remained in bondage to life's mysterious processes, the male did not recognize in her a being like himself."[57] Because this assumes that patriarchy is already institutionalized, man's power over woman cannot be explained, since it was never taken as problematic. Why did the tasks on which woman spent her strength not give her supremacy over man or equality with him? Why was her labor not seen as productive? What is the special relevance of man's conquest of nature to his relation with woman? Why was it not determinative that man failed to share woman's way of working and thinking just as she did not share his? Why was woman's relation to life's mysterious processes seen as bondage while his (hunting, for example) was interpreted as conquest of nature? Why wasn't death, which comes to them equally, as mysterious as life? Most importantly for present purposes, why is what the male saw in her the controlling recognition, rather than what she saw in him or what she saw in other women or in herself? Only if male power is presumed ascendant can unequal social relations be, even existentially, based on the body.

The underlying sociobiological text of naturalist explanations for unequal social status is that the characteristic that members of the dominant group share is the inherent cause of and continuing justification for their dominance, and the characteristics shared by the subordinate groups cause and justify their subordination. In this way, social conditions become universal givens. The same problem arises with Beauvoir's analysis of woman as "other" or the "second sex" to man. It is one thing as description, another as explanation. Why isn't man "other" to woman? Social power is not explained, it is only restated, depriving the critique of any basis other than a moral one.

Building on Beauvoir's account, Shulamith Firestone substitutes sex for class within a dialectical and materialist analysis that takes sex as pre-social:

[B]eneath economics, reality is psychosexual . . . Unlike economic class, sex class sprang directly from a biological reality; men and women were created different, and not equally privileged . . . The biological family is an inherently unequal power distribution . . . In every society to date there has been some form of the biological family and thus there has always been oppression of women and children to varying degrees . . . Thus, it was woman's reproductive biology that accounted for her original and continued oppression.[58]

Her solution is consistent: "the freeing of women from the tyranny of their biology by any means available, and the diffusion of the childbearing role to the society as a whole . . . Childbearing could be taken over by technology."[59] Woman's body is the root of her oppression rather than a rationalization or locale for it. How women, who have not been permitted to control their own bodies or existing technology, would control reproductive technology remains a mystery.

A biological theory of rape within a social critique of the centrality of rape to women's subordination is adopted by Susan Brownmiller, who argues:

Men's structural capacity to rape and woman's corresponding structural vulnerability are as basic to the physiology of both our sexes as the primal act of sex itself. Had it not been for this accident of biology, an accommodation requiring the locking together of two separate parts, penis and vagina, there would be neither copulation nor rape as we know it . . . By anatomical fiat—the inescapable construction of their genital organs—the human male was a natural predator and the human female served as his natural prey.[60]

She does not seem to think it necessary to explain why women do not lurk in bushes and forcibly engulf men, an equal biological possibility for "locking together." Criticizing the law for confusing intercourse with rape, she finds them biologically indistinguishable, leaving one wondering whether she, too, must either alter or acquiesce in the biological.[61] This underlying approach, in some tension with her historical critique of rape, elevates social relations to eternal verities, undercutting any basis for challenging them or for recognizing that they are as man-made, historical, and transitory as the ideas that justify them.[62]

Another variant on feminist naturalism is the view that women are biologically defined by heterosexuality seen as a biological given but not an exclusive social inevitability. For example,

Sexual congress between man and woman is an invasion of the woman
. . . she remains the passive receptive hopeful half of a situation that
was unequal from the start. The fate that woman has to resign herself
to is the knowledge of this biological inequity. A fate that was not
originally the occasion for the social inequities elaborated out of the
biological situation. From this knowledge the woman can now alter her
destiny.[63]

In this analysis, woman's social inequality is not an inevitable
attribute of her biology but biologically inherent in the heterosexual
sex act. The current meaning of sexual relations between women and
men is taken as biologically inevitable. The only thing that is not
inevitable is woman's social oppression through them. Woman's
biology oppresses her only when she relates to men. The basis of the
inequality of the sexes here is seen as the inequality inherent in
heterosexual intercourse as a result of sex-specific anatomy. To
transcend or avoid this in personal life by having sexual relations only
with women—lesbianism—eliminates the gender-based underpinnings of sexual inequality in this view. "For if the phrase biology is
destiny has any meaning for a woman right now it has to be the urgent
project of woman reclaiming herself, her own biology in her image,
and this is why the lesbian is the revolutionary feminist and every
other feminist is a woman who wants a better deal from her old
man."[64] Biological problems have biological solutions.

A psychological form of naturalism is argued by Juliet Mitchell,
who rejects the view that women are biologically destined to be
subordinate to men.[65] She posits a psychoanalytic theory that the
universal unconscious taboo against incest (the foundation of the
Oedipus complex) grounds patriarchy by forcing families to look
outside themselves for species perpetuation in marriage, and thus
requires that women become exchange objects. In the laws of kinship
she takes from Freud, sexual unions between siblings, and between
parents and children, first achieve the rule of cultural law over
biological impulses. The act of establishing social consequences to sex
differences is the same act that inaugurates civilization as human. The
essence of humanity is its ability to enforce these permanent psychological structures, these sexual laws, as social laws. What can
feminism mean when, in the content attributed to the sexual laws,
patriarchy is coextensive with civilization? Although Mitchell pro-

fesses to study society as mediated and reflected in mental life from a feminist standpoint, the Freudian psychic universals she adopts are not seen as socially contingent or even equal. And they are as immutable as biology.

Feminist treatments of childbirth and childrearing reveal other examples of biologically based analyses of women's social existence. A biological analysis tends to assume that the meaning of giving birth and rearing a child is fixed. Beauvoir, for instance, accepts the current social meaning of having children as universal and intrinsic to the act itself: "But in any case giving birth and suckling are not activities, they are natural functions; no project is involved; and that is why woman found in them no reason for a lofty affirmation of her existence—she submitted passively to her biologic fate."[66] Arguably, once a woman can choose not to bear children, to do so would constitute a project, suggesting that childbearing is "natural" only so long as it is "fate." This is not to question Beauvoir's implicit awareness that the motherhood myth has functioned to trick and trap women. It is to argue that this effect is a result of the social implications and consequences of motherhood, its impact on how a woman can spend her time, how she is valued socially, the narrowing of her world and options, rather than to anything intrinsic to motherhood. By attributing the lack of potential for self-affirmation to biology rather than to society, Beauvoir accepts the patriarchal notion that motherhood has a universal invariant significance; she only transvalues it. Others, by attributing the potential for self-affirmation to the very potential that for Beauvoir denies it to women, accept the content of the motherhood fetish, rejecting only its effects on women's social position of relative powerlessness. Yet taking women's biology as the basis of women's liberation only negates biological justifications for women's subordination without questioning their basis.

Taking sex as a "difference" even if a social one, instead of as a material division of power, is a consequence of all these facets of liberalism taken together. In Nancy Chodorow's work, for example, sex inequality becomes sexual differentiation, and sexual differentiation is caused by female mothering, which male children resent and female children emulate. The social fact that mother is a woman and powerless as such is given little recognition in the construction of psyche, and sex inequality is reduced to a problem of psychoanalysis.[67] If the issue is less how the sexes come to be differentiated and more why one sex comes to dominate the other, hence to require differentiation, Chodorow's analysis is less useful. Similarly, in the theory of Dorothy Dinnerstein, women and men participate equally in the "arrangements" of sex roles through which sex differences, created by females' primary parenting, produce the "human malaise of gender."[68] Thus do liberal approaches construe evidence of women's subordination as evidence of women's difference, elevating the body of women's oppression to the level of a universal, a category beyond history.[69]

# 4 | *Attempts at Synthesis*

The value of labor. The labor theory of value. Her labor married to his value. *We were told that Zeus swallowed Metis whole* Her labor *that from his belly* disappearing *she gave him advice.* Her labor not counted in his production. His name given to her labor. The wife of the laborer called working class. The wife of the shopkeeper called petit bourgeois. The wife of the factory owner called bourgeois.

—Susan Griffin, *Woman and Nature*

$T$he aspiration to encompass all inequality within a critique of the "totality" of social life has been a central feature of marxist theory from the beginning.[1] Its ambition for inclusiveness has produced attempts to explain in marxist terms all inequalities marxists have perceived as real.[2] Feminism, by contrast, has not typically regarded the existence of class, or any other social division or theory, as needing to be either subsumed or dismissed, or as a challenge to the theoretical viability or practical primacy of focus upon relations between the sexes. That feminism has seen itself as valid while seeming by marxist standards to advance a less embracing or more partial theory may simply mean that feminism holds itself to a different standard of theoretical adequacy—its own.

Marxism is drawn toward feminism by its recognition that the distinctive condition of women may not be adequately explained by marxism. As a movement within marxist thought, feminism can be traced from its complete subsumption through various forms of subordination to decisive equipoise and break, as the understanding of feminism's challenge to the marxist version of the totality intensifies. Underlying marxist attempts to accommodate or respond to feminism, including most socialist-feminist theories, is one of three approaches: equate and collapse, derive and subordinate, and substitute contradictions. The first equates sex with class, feminism with marxism, in order to collapse the former into the latter. The second derives an analysis of sex from an analysis of class, feminism from marxism, in order to subordinate sex to class, feminism to marxism. The third applies marxist method to sex or feminist method to class.

Distinguishing the three approaches is the analysis of the unit or site or dynamic or women's oppression. Feminism points to the ubiquity of male power in sexual relations; marxism points to the productive sphere, defined as work in the marketplace. An apparent point of convergence often seized upon is "the family," such that conceptions of the family illustrate varieties of attempted theoretical accommodation. The traditional socialist approach tends to see the family (at least the working-class family) and the market as opposed principles in capitalist society, pulling in separate directions. As a separate sphere of privacy, warmth, and individuated human relations, the family is considered antithetical to the impersonality of the marketplace, a refuge from and bulwark against its forces. In this view, the family expresses a contradiction within capitalism. Feminist theory sees the family as a unit of male dominance, a locale of male violence and reproductive exploitation, hence a primary locus of the oppression of women. Far from being contradictory forces, capitalism expresses the same authority structure as does the family, through its organization, distribution of wealth, and resource control.

Influenced by feminism to reexamine the traditional socialist view of the family, some contemporary marxists seek a synthesis with feminism but accomplish at best a hybrid. In their view, home and family are a microcosm and breeding ground of capitalist social relations, the internal dynamics of which are determined by the marketplace and reproduce it. Since feminism is implicitly seen as addressing relationships within the family, marxism as implicitly analyzing the relationship of the family to the society, most attempts at synthesis scrutinize either relationships within the family or the relationship between home and market. The family is analyzed either in terms of its internal dynamics, or as a unit in relation to the larger society; rarely are the two explored together. Sexual relations in the marketplace and property relations within the family tend to be ignored, as are interactions between them.

In approaches that equate and collapse, women's problems are given no specificity or cross-class commonality at all. They are totally subsumed under, telescoped within, assimilated to, a class analysis. To the extent women exist at all within the theory, their problems are eclipsed by those of the working class and their remedy is collapsed into socialism. Lenin, who focuses more upon women's contribution to the socialist revolution than upon the socialist revolution's contribution to women, is an example,[3] with Rosa Luxemburg[4] and some contemporary Marxists.[5] Traditional roles of wife and motherhood are not criticized but are seen as abused by capital—rather than women being seen as abused in and by these roles. Marx paved the way for this view by assessing capitalism's impact on women in terms of its damage to their femininity.[6] The "equation and collapse" view is commonly capsulized in some version of the formulation, "The Socialist who is not a Feminist lacks breadth. The Feminist who is not a Socialist is lacking in Strategy."[7] Socialism correctly understood includes anything that feminism offers women, and, as a practical matter, socialists should not confine themselves to organizing only half of the working class; feminists cannot afford to ignore class issues and, as a practical matter, need socialist support. This formulation glosses over the question of the specific contribution of socialism to ending the subordination of women to men, including under socialism.

The vast majority of marxist or marxist-feminist writers who have considered the so-called woman question adopt a "derivation and subordination" strategy. This grants more separate validity to an analysis of women's condition than the first approach did, but it nevertheless reduces women's oppression to a special dimension of the class question. Thus Sheila Rowbotham has explained the situation of women as the result of capitalism.[8] Most theorists in this category follow Engels, explicitly or implicitly; women's subordination to men, when acknowledged, is seen as caused by class dominance, its cure as the overthrow of class relations. So while some validity is granted to feminism, it is seen as correctly subordinate to, while contributing to the development of, an essentially marxist analysis and an essentially marxist movement. No matter how distinct women's subordination is imagined to be, or how separate a women's movement is cognized, gender contradictions are seen as derivative of class contradictions and as ultimately reducible to them.

Within this framework, sex is derived from class but not equated with it. The classical socialists believed first socialism, then women's liberation. Engels and, later, with more flexibility and insight, Bebel adopted this strategy.[9] Fidel Castro's "revolution within a revolution," which has had a broad impact upon national liberation movements, provides another variation.[10] Although Mao Tsu-tung granted more distinctness to women's status, the approach taken during the Chinese revolution prefigured the Cuban strategy.[11] In this view, the oppression of women by men is addressed within the revolutionary struggle for control over the means of production. The effort is serious, yet it is clear which revolution is within which.

What might be called an "intersection" view is yet another variant of the "derivation and subordination" strategy. It is as if feminism and marxism were vectors, pointing in different directions and crossing at one point: "women workers." The problem of women is hybridized with a class analysis in order to be subsumed within it. The value of feminism is that it helps mobilize and unify the working class. Thus, Nancy Hartsock: "I want to suggest that the women's movement can provide the basis for building a new and authentic American socialism."[12] Alexandra Kollontai exemplifies this tendency historically, as do many contemporary groups on the left and socialist-feminist theoreticians.[13] A final form of "derivation" theory is the "separate but equal" strategy. Here, women's situation is recognized to derive from a distinct set of social dynamics. Change, however, is still reduced to socialism, in a litany by this point clearly forced.[14] Socialism may be modified by the recognition of the specificity of sex, but there is still no analysis of male power, separate but equal remaining unequal.

A third approach, "substitute contradictions," presents a deeper accommodation. The category identified by each theory is taken as valid by the other and methods are cross-applied. Shulamith Firestone exemplifies this approach in some respects. Taking sex as the basic social category, she proposes to apply marxist method to analyze it: "We can attempt to develop a materialist view of history based on sex itself."[15] Similarly, many theorists have recently attempted to use reproduction as a foundation for a materialist analysis of women's situation. Some feminists have taken this approach from the feminist side, subjecting class to consciousness raising: "Class is the way you see the rest of the world, and your place in it."[16]

The most imaginative and complex contemporary attempt at synthesis is the "wages for housework" perspective, which takes a clear long step beyond the "substitute contradictions" approach, aspiring to explain both sex and class within a theory marxian in scope yet feminist in basis. The perspective has precursors in the work of Charlotte Perkins Gilman, who in the last century saw housework as basic to women's inferiority but not to capitalism. She observed: "the salient fact in this discussion is that, whatever the economic value of the domestic industry of women is, they do not get it. The women who do the most work get the least money, and the women who have the most money do the least work." She also perceived that "there is no equality in class between those who do their share of the world's work in the largest, newest, and highest ways, and those who do theirs in the smallest, oldest, lowest ways."[17] Margaret Benston early saw the marginality of housework to capitalism as the material basis for the marginality of women to society as a whole.[18] Peggy Morton conceived housework, hence women, in a central yet subordinate social role.[19] In the work of Mariarosa Dalla Costa, Selma James, Sylvia Federici, and Nicole Cox, "wages for housework" becomes a perspective seeking to explain the subordination of women to men under capitalism in terms of the critical role of housework in capitalist production.[20] The housewife role is then generalized to explain the exploitation, hence powerlessness, of unwaged workers, argued to be the foundation of the exploitation of waged workers. Christine Delphy argues that to see housework as both work and unwaged, necessarily a simultaneous awareness, redefines housework as exploitive and in the process redefines the economic itself.[21] In the end, "wages for housework" theory, in its movement toward feminism, breaks with marxism from the inside.

Marxism's ambivalence about taking women seriously can be traced in contemporary socialist-feminist treatments of the argument that women's work in the home is work. Lise Vogel concluded that "women's domestic labor under capitalism is neither productive nor unproductive."[22] Eli Zaretsky stated: "Housewives are and are not part of the working class. They do and do not confront capital directly."[23] Carol Lopate thought that "we may have to decide that housework is neither production nor consumption."[24] Lotte Femminile argued that "housework is . . . slave labor . . . hence women are a proletarian stratum, though not in the orthodox sense."[25] Much of this reflects an attempt by marxists to adapt Marx's categories to changing perceptions or economic realities. In place of slavish adherence to "point of production" models of laboring, for example, some have decided that service work is now properly capitalist production, discovering a "new working class" in many formerly considered unproductive. Others have moved further toward embracing all "socially necessary labor," and thus all socially necessary laborers, as "critical" in the marxist sense.[26] Some who go further to construe the home as a "social factory" conceive that step as a break with marxism.[27]

Much of this modernization changes rather than merely updates marxist categories. For example, "socially necessary labor time" is not a total of all work that needs to be done in society, such that housework must have been included *sub silentio* all along. Rather, it is an average of all social laboring, so that the product of a fixed amount of labor time varies in value depending upon the average labor time socially required to make a particular good.[28] From this standpoint, one cannot address the question of whether housework is or is not included in socially necessary labor time by acting as if it has always been implicit. The prior question is whether it is or is not social laboring in the sense of abstract labor, laboring for capital.

Marxists fetishize categories when the approach that gives the categories meaning is ignored in favor of treating the categorical products as if they were things with an independent existence, into or outside of which all social life must be shoehorned. Confronted with the suspicion that marxist theory has no account of the particular oppression of women, the response has often been either to explain why women as such fall outside what marxist theory identifies as important, or to scramble to locate a conception in preexisting marxist categories that subsume women's subordination, so that feminism was implicit in marxism all along. The debate over wages for housework exhibits these tendencies. It also confronts marxism and feminism more coequally than any other approach has so far done, even if finally it is on marxist ground. Precisely because marxist economics is the core of marxist politics, this attempt exposes the limits of the possibilities of taking women seriously within marxism.

Wages for housework as a perspective attempts to analyze women's situation and society as a whole. It attempts feminism in revaluing the contribution women have always made, in demonstrating the essentiality and value of women's most degraded and most universal functions. In breaking the ideological tie of that work to women's biology, it attempts to base a claim for a fair share of social product for an activity that almost all women perform, and perform largely for men. It attempts marxism in grounding its analysis of women's oppression in the exploitation—the nonvaluing in the political-

economic sense—of women's work, in arguing for the contribution of
this work to capital and its expansion. In this way, it grounds an
analysis of women's power in her productive role, not incidentally
changing the definition of production. In so doing, wages for
housework makes women's liberation a critical moment in class
struggle. At the same time, women's struggle is united with that of
all unwaged workers, a new stratum of the exploited found beneath
waged slavery. Discussions of wages for housework thus open critical
issues of value; labor and its division by sex and sphere; conceptions of
the meaning, structure, and inner dynamics of the social order of sex
and class; and the sources and strategies for mobilizing political power
toward a social transformation that is conceived as total.

Taken in isolation from its underlying analysis, the actual demand
for a wage for housework is easy to dismiss as systemically equivalent
to a wage increase, with a minimally positive redistributive impact in
favor of women in the home, or a negative effect in keeping them there
by increasing their stake in staying. However, taken as a perspective
on the situation of women in the family and on society as a whole, and
used to raise the issues involved in assessing the impact of marxist
economic analysis on a feminist analysis of the relationship of women
to capital, the issues it raises are substantially more profound.

In this broader sense, the argument in favor of wages for housework
can be stated as six propositions.[29] First, women's nonwaged work in
the home is productive labor for capital, in that women produce their
own labor power as well as men's on a daily and generational basis,
which men then sell to capital for a wage. Second, capitalism keeps
women as a reserve labor pool in a dual sense. Women absorb the
fluctuations in the capitalist market, increasing their productivity to
keep capitalism afloat (by the reproduction of labor power) when
capitalism cannot employ them otherwise, while they remain ready to
go to work directly for capital in periods of expansion for lower wages
than men, because they are used to working for nothing. Third,
women serve as a psychological as well as economic safety valve for
capital. Male workers benefit from women's services and support
personally and sexually. They also benefit materially from women's
unpaid labor, much as capitalists benefit from the labor of workers.
Sex roles in the marketplace are monetized forms of sex roles in the
home. Fourth, male workers, through this system of relations, are
forced into the service of capital through their sense of responsibility

and love for their families, with women at home presented as rewards, as booty in the struggle of men against men. Men thus become compliant workers, willing to accept exploitation in the workplace because of the necessity of supporting a family and the compensations of the (for them) private sphere. That is, capitalism makes male dominance rational for men by giving men a stake in it.

Fifth, women's dependence upon men for money, the medium of power under capitalism, is both a means and a mystification of the power of capital over both sexes. The wage system keeps women subordinate to men at home through keeping the working class subordinate to capital in the workplace—and in order to do so. Sexism thus functions within the home to maintain the power of capital outside the home. Finally, the struggle for a wage for housework would be revolutionary. It would demystify this complex of social relations by exposing women's role as social and essential, not natural and socially marginal. It would give women material independence of male supremacy to some extent by giving women some money of their own, altering the balance of power within the home. It would expose the role of love as an ideological mechanism whereby women's work is controlled and suggest that sex is constrained or unfree because women's material options are unequal to men's. Making women's work more expensive to capital than it presently is, it would raise the cost of production and cut into profits—assuming that the mechanism for paying the wage ensured that it came from profits, as most proponents of the theory assume. Wages for housework would empower women within the home by demystifying the naturalness of their work. By giving women the benefit of their work, the wage would set women up to refuse to do it. The demand for wages for housework presents a theory of women's potential power as women that situates women in class struggle on a feminist basis.

From a feminist standpoint, the argument for a wage for housework recommends itself by focusing upon women's invisible contributions, in its determination to recognize and valorize women's role in society, and in its goal of grounding a claim of women's political power in the existing realities of women's situation. By attacking women's economic dependence upon men, it proposes to alter the balance of advantage in the family. Much recommends the theory from a marxist standpoint as well. If women's work produces male labor power, housewives are an undiscovered sector of the working class whose work product is expropriated and sold by the man in the act of selling his own labor power as a commodity in the marketplace for the benefit of capital. The subordination of women is thus based on the exploitation of her as a worker through men by capital. Women are oppressed by capital—not (or only indirectly) by men, as feminists have claimed, to the consternation of marxists. Women also have strategic power to withdraw from critical productive activity. Their struggle for return on, and control over, their production, together with other class members, widens the struggle to change society.

"Wages for housework" analysis synthesizes the feminist insight that relations between women and men in the home are social relations with the marxist analysis that the "social relations of production" underlie all other social relations. A commodity possesses exchange value because part of the labor of society is allocated to its production in a way that is "subordinate to the division of labor within society."[30] This is how value relations between commodities reflect social relations between persons. Feminism sees the sexual division of labor as a social division of (at least) labor; "wages for housework" analysis sees that this social division between the sexes is also a productive relation. Without analyzing the productive role of women in the home, the notion common to the classical political economists and Marx, that relations between persons as mutually interdependent producers of commodities underlie their social relations, would exclude women as such (unless they work outside the home) from this definition of the foundation of social relations. If women's work is to produce the commodity labor power, women do participate in the exchange of products, which is in essence the exchange of quantities of social laboring.

The systematization of relations between women and men—the perspective that sees these not as relations between particular persons or biological beings, as they have been seen in liberal and other theory, but as a structural social relation between social beings—is central to feminist theory. Speaking of the private property relation, Marx said: "The relationship of private property is labor, capital, and the interconnection between the two . . . and the manner in which they come to confront one another as two persons is for the economist an accidental event which therefore can have only an external explanation."[31] What to Marx was accidental is to feminism, in a sense, a centrally determinate social relation. For feminism, how two individual persons come to confront each other in the family is an accidental event. Their relationship, and the fact that one is a woman and one is a man, is internal and determinate.

The difficulties wages for housework poses for marxism and feminism parallel its benefits. Feminism is concerned that, in practical effect, a wage is conservative in that it would tie women even more securely to the home as a means to a livelihood. A wage would legitimate women's role as homemaker, although in theory men who did housework would be paid too. Depending upon the particular scheme, it could further institutionalize the superiority of the husband, now the woman's employer. More deeply, the analysis may suffer from the same shortcomings that other marxist analyses of women do: to the extent it bases itself in women's work, it fails fully to grasp women's role as women. To give an example of limits that are confined to work, bourgeois women's housework, according to the argument, would not technically produce labor power if bourgeois men did not sell their labor as a commodity in the marketplace. So are bourgeois women not oppressed as women because their labor is not expropriated if their husband does not properly "labor"? The woman is still doing housework for the man. This is merely the "wages for housework" version of the problem encountered with every prior attempt to define women's oppression in class terms. To define women in terms of the class status of "their" men is to accept as the grounds for analysis something that needs to be challenged concerning the determinants of women's power and powerlessness. Finally, feminism finds women oppressed as a sex, one expression of which is economic exploitation. It is difficult to believe that a wage for housework would sexually deobjectify women or eliminate violence against them, for example; independently wealthy as well as middle-class women are sexually abused. "Wages for housework" analysis shows how women are oppressed by capital, which at times looks like a suspicious dodge for concluding that they are oppressed by men—perhaps through capital, but by men nonetheless.

Marxist arguments against wages for housework have centered primarily on a defense of those aspects of the family which feminists have criticized. The family is not an economic sphere, marxists say, but a warm personal place in which people are unique individuals, in contrast to the impersonality and anonymity of the marketplace. The family bond is said to be love,[32] as opposed to that of the market, which is gain. Marx seems to have been of two minds on this point. In some passages he extols the ideal virtues of the family; in others, noting what capitalism has made of it, he attacks: "On what foundation is the present family, the bourgeois family, based? On capital, on private gain . . . the bourgeois sees in his wife a mere instrument of production."[33] Most marxists seem reflexively to think of the family "itself" as a locale of close personal and emotional relationships, "a refuge from the alienation and psychic poverty of work life."[34] The idea of paying women money for working in the family, which amounts to an admission that housework is labor and therefore alienated, implies that it is servicing for the one who pays for it—the male—and love is no compensation. This analysis implies that women otherwise give more than they get. To deny this has been the notion of the family ever since liberalism created the private and put the family in it. The marxist family is rooted in bourgeois reality. Indisputably, a wage for housework and the reconceptualization of the family that it implies violate the male experience of the family, which, to paraphrase Marx, no matter how dissolved it has been in theory, cannot be otherwise from a male point of view.[35]

Other marxists object that the function of the wage under capitalism is not to reward or reflect the production of surplus value, in the home or elsewhere. But labor is not waged because it produces. In fact, it is the lack of a one-to-one relationship between the wage paid on the one hand, and labor expended and value created on the other, that allows capital to accumulate, thus to continue to exist. A wage is paid to enable the worker to subsist so that "he" can continue to produce for capital, not as a reward for, reflection of, or recognition of production. To think that a wage compensates for value created is to idealize capitalism. Whatever extrinsic effects a wage might have on the balance of power between the sexes is a matter of indifference to capital. But no marxists are heard to argue that, therefore, workers should not be paid; nor do they retreat from their position that workers' claim of right to own the means of production is that it is their work that produces value.

Marxists further object that since workers are no more paid for their product by the wage than women currently are, paying women a wage for reproduction of male labor power, from the point of view of capital, would only raise the cost of production. Women in the house are, in this view, already supported by capital through the family wage. Making their contribution explicit by monetizing it might have various effects, but one of them would probably not be to redress the structural relationship whereby women's labor is expropriated. In this sense, wages for housework appears to be a reformist demand, one that leaves the system in place, a demand that women be exploited in the home as men have been in the factory. It would not change the status quo but merely make its hegemony visible. From this perspective it is about as revolutionary as a worker's demand for a wage increase. Few marxists are heard to oppose such demands. But the demand for a wage need not be grounded upon actual creation of surplus value. Many people are paid who, in marxist terms, do not produce surplus value but live off of it. Moreover, laborers who do produce surplus value in the classical sense are not waged for that reason. The particular potential and promise of the "wages for housework" perspective lies in its attempt to examine women's work in the home in the context of a marxist theory of the relation between production and power as a means of analyzing, hence altering, women's status in traditional material terms. The definition of materiality is altered to encompass women's work, but the analysis remains in the marxist tradition to the extent that women's status is still seen as determined by their work.

The most telling criticism that might be made of the "wages for housework" perspective (although no one has made it) is that its economics are more in the tradition of classical political economy than of Marx. Wages for housework shares more of its theoretical grounding with Adam Smith than with Marx.[36] The ways in which Marx moved beyond Smith are the least integral to the approach, giving the marxist charge that feminism is "bourgeois" some content. Specifically, the conception of the labor theory of value which "wages for housework" theory applies to women's work in the home derives more clearly from Smith than from Marx's emphasis upon the contribution of capital to the equation. So while wages for housework "values" women's situation in material terms and exposes the applicability of marxist categories to a conceptualization of women's inequality informed by feminism, as a matter of political economy it takes a step back. It may be argued that the household is the sphere of capitalist society which capital has, so far, penetrated least, its nonmonetization being but an expression of that fact. But while women's work in the home may or may not be pre-capitalist, as many marxists have charged, the "wages for housework" analysis of it tends to be.

Is housework "laboring for capital"? In the *Economic and Philosophic Manuscripts of 1844*, Marx speaks of laboring as life activity and "species-characteristic."[37] The later theory of value advanced in the *Grundrisse* and *Capital* argues that the character of labor is specific to, conditioned and determined by, the particular mode of social production under which it is realized. Social laboring under capitalism, then, must be in some sense "laboring for capital." "Wages for housework" theorists, although they argue that housework produces surplus value for capital, never squarely confront the question of whether housework is laboring for capital. At least five characteristics that identify "laboring for capital" seem to be advanced throughout Marx's work. One is that the surplus product of the labor is appropriated by capital. A second is that the laboring produces a commodity that is exchanged against capital, not revenue. A third is that the production process itself is "capitalized" in that it uses capital goods in the process of production. A fourth is that the costs of the work are considered by capital to be costs that must be driven to a minimum. A fifth is that the work participates in the circuit of producing means of production to produce means of production for the expansion of capital. These characteristics interrelate and sometimes conflict.

The questions raised by "wages for housework" theory are posed by considering this from the *Grundrisse:*

> A presupposition of wage labour, and one of the historic preconditions for capital, is free labour and the exchange of this free labour for money, in order to reproduce and to realize money, to consume the use-value of labour not for individual consumption, but as use-value for money. Another presupposition is the separation of free labor from the objective conditions of its realization—from the means of labour and the material for labour.[38]

At first impression, domestic work does not seem to fit any of these preconditions. It certainly is not free—but then, in what sense does Marx mean that a worker is "free" to sell his labor? In *Capital,* Marx stated that waged labor "in essence . . . always remains forced labor—no matter how much it may seem to result from free contractual agreement."[39] Next, a housewife does not exchange her labor for money. At least, she does not do so directly. The product of her labor, her husband's labor power, according to "wages for housework" advocates, is exchanged for money, which then provides the conditions for her subsistence very much as the exchange of his labor for a wage is thought to provide the conditions of his subsistence. The distinction between "use value . . . for individual consumption" and "use value for money" seems to disqualify household labor as labor conclusively, unless one conceives of the distinction in interpenetrated terms. That is, the use values a woman produces are for individual consumption to regenerate labor power, which is sold for money in the circuit of capital. But this reasoning is circular. If she were paid a wage, her production would be "for money." Would that make it labor, where previously it was not? As to being separated from the means of production, the means of production of housework could be said to be owned by someone who is independent of her—her husband. She must exchange her labor in order to be provided with the means and material of her labor—her body, her sexuality, her femaleness.

Does housework produce labor power? In marxist theory, product is valued in terms of the labor required to produce it. Inputs to the process are valued in terms of the labor required to produce the capital, raw materials, and human energy used up during production. In *Capital,* Marx defined labor power: "By labor power or capacity for labor is understood the aggregate of those mental and physical capabilities existing in a human being, which he exercises whenever he produces a use-value of any description. But in order that . . . labour power [be] offered for sale as a commodity, various conditions must first be fulfilled.[40] The value of labor power is determined by the abstract labor time socially necessary to produce the commodities that the worker purchases. But are commodities the only inputs to the production of labor power—and what is a commodity? "Wages for housework" analysis argues that the production of labor power includes the labor time domestically necessary to make purchased commodities consumable, together with all the services that daily reproduce a human being capable of working.

But is the production of labor power the same as the production of other commodities? The cost of the production of labor power has long been a difficulty in marxian economics. There is an analogous problem in classical economics in the debate over "natural" as opposed to "market" price. The marxist analysis has tended to answer that the cost of the production of labor power is measured by the subsistence wage, a figure set by an autonomous process in the family which socially defines needs and accordingly dictates the level of consumption. But can this process be conceived as independent of market determinations and the processes of exchange? What makes the family autonomous of other social relations? For Marx, the subsistence wage is determined independently of the money wage, yet the subsistence level must be fixed in order for the rate of profit to rise relative to the rate of exploitation of labor; hence the cost of labor power must be taken as fixed also, at least fixed relative to its market price. This then raises a version of the problem of transforming value into price, termed the transformation problem in classical economics. A mechanism to conform price with value seems lacking in the case of the commodity labor power, which raises the question of whether it is bought and sold "at its value" as Marx assumes commodities are. ("If you cannot explain profit upon this supposition, you cannot explain it at all.")[41] The relation between price and value begins to appear socially tautologous rather than socially transformed, with value assigned a priori to certain social contributions and not to others. The fact that work in the family is not included is not explained by such an analysis. The value of labor time is thought to be greater than the value of labor power. Women may contribute to the production of labor power in the home, but labor time is the creature of capital. The question is, what is capital?

The "wages for housework" perspective attempts to ground the production of the commodity labor power in the expenditure of more labor power. It offers a possible explanation for the fluctuations in the level of subsistence which is independent both of the wage and of increased profit margins, built upon the assumption that the cost of labor power is fixed. Because women's work varies to absorb differences in wage rates, women accommodating themselves to increases in the cost of subsistence by working harder, the cost of labor power can be considered fixed by capital. The fluctuations in the subsistence level are thus absorbed by the level of her emiseration, making her dependence a necessary condition for his exploitation, and her own survival a contribution to the functioning of the profit system. The marxist analysis that the rate of surplus value varies with the rate of productivity of labor is also true here, once it is seen to include the hidden productivity of housework, which increases as squeezed by necessity. Thus to Marx's observation that labor power has a historically and culturally given value, "wages for housework" theorists add that one of the "fixed" determinants of that constellation is the wife's labor, which has all the appearance of a fixed condition because women have had so few choices about it.

It seems appropriately marxist that the value of the labor power of some should be produced through the labor of others, making value an entirely relational creation. If this is not the case, it is necessary to argue that something is present in the product which was not present in the relations that produced it. Analyses of labor power often proceed as if labor power were produced by and for capital, yet somehow still sprang out of "nature," not out of social relations. Have women, or women's labor in the family, been that nature? In marxist theory, the character of the productive process as much as its concrete realization (here, direct laboring for capital) creates the character of the product. Is it possible that labor power is the only commodity in capitalist reality which becomes a commodity "for capital" only through the market relations that it enters into after it has already been produced—in this case, beyond the threshold? It is axiomatic social materialism that the abstract character of a product congeals the social relations that produced it.

Marxist theory assumes that previous labor is present in its product, including when that product is the capacity for more labor. The problem here is similar to the problem confronted in traditional marxism of the reduction of skilled to unskilled labor. Does labor invested in creating a skill reappear proportionally, or in some measure determinately, in the value of the product? Is what she puts into him reflected in what he is paid? Or does the labor of the housewife reappear proportionately, or in some way determinately, in the value of the labor her husband sells? To answer the question of whether her work creates value in his labor power, as with the question of the creation of value in skill, it is necessary first to address this question independent of price, then to see if there is a determinate relation between value and price.

It would seem that this problem is no more difficult for housework than it is for the issue of skilled and unskilled labor. In fact, the current lack of a wage for housework makes the condition of price independence easier to satisfy. Instead of transferring the value of skill bit by bit to the product over the lifetime of the laborer, like circulating capital, the wife's substance is transferred bit by bit over her lifetime, to be sold as the product, labor power. Looked at this way, this becomes a Ricardian problem of making the productivity of labor visible in (the distribution of) the product.[42] In Ricardian terms, the question could be phrased: How can the husband's labor be reduced to its component parts of which the wife's labor is one, independent of price, yet still contribute to the determination of the price of the commodity? The "wages for housework" answer is that currently the wife's labor is reflected more in profits than in the price of labor, because although her labor is a cost of production, it is a cost borne by her because it is unwaged. Because of her wagelessness, the contribution, the value, of her work need not be reflected in any price. If she were paid, it would be. This argument fits the Ricardian one-way determination of price by value, such that labor time determines value determines price (or, by deduction, profit). In this scheme, productivity of labor is considered to be determined independent of the market, but the value of labor is seen as a fixed condition independent of accumulation. Implicitly, "wages for housework" theory seems to take a similar view. A more complex view might be that these factors are reciprocally determined. This view requires dispensing with the notion that value is fully determined immediately in the act of laboring, locating value itself in a totality of social relations that include exchange and distribution, labor and capital, women and men.

This move toward concrete meaning, substantivity and specificity, is precisely opposite to the traditional marxist approach, which abstracts and generalizes labor, as capitalism is seen to do. That labor is abstract which creates value, as distinct from use value. Abstract labor is productive activity as such, from which all differences between the various kinds of activities and relations and people—all uniqueness or particularity—have been removed.[43] Thus, abstract labor is "truly realized only as a category of the most modern society where individuals pass with ease from one kind of work to another, making it immaterial to them what particular kind of work may fall to their share."[44] This abstraction reduces labor to its common denominator, the expenditure of human labor power in the abstract.[45] To see labor in the abstract is to see it from the point of view of capital. The products of abstract laboring bear the marks of the abstract relations of social production which characterize commodity-producing societies:

"homogeneous human labor, expenditure of one uniform labor power," is the labor that in capitalism "forms the substance of value."[46]

Is housework abstract labor? A precondition for the abstraction of labor is the exchange of its products. Labor power is certainly exchanged. Abstract labor also requires the indifference of capital and labor to the specificity of the product and the producer. Since capital as such is indifferent to every particularity[47] and exists not only as the totality but also as the abstraction from all its particularities, "the labor which confronts it likewise subjectively has the same totality and abstraction in itself . . . the worker himself is absolutely indifferent to the specificity of his labor; it has no interest for him as such, but only in as much as it is in fact labour and, as such, a use-value for capital."[48] If women subjectively care about men, does that make their work not work? If so, why only in the home and not also in the marketplace?

Perhaps the economic character of the housewife lies in the specificity of her labor in her relation to a specific man who is her "master." But it is exactly by seeing the relations between women and men as a system that feminism has grasped the systemic indifference to the specificity of which woman works for and services which man or many men, such that sexual relations are social relations. If a laborer argued that he labored every day for love because he felt he had to provide for his family, the fact he felt that way would do nothing to the systemic logic of the inner determinations of capitalist production. (He would still be paid.) Instead of arguing that this is the motive force in capitalist relations, the marxist would see this as a necessary but false reflection of the system of relations which creates both such necessities and the ideology that makes people able to endure them, indeed often experiencing eagerness and self-fulfillment in the process. But his labor would be none the less abstract.

Too, the condition of exchange of equal values presupposes the independence of exchangers from any personal ties with each other. "The dissolution of all products and activities into exchange values presupposes the dissolution of all fixed personal relations of dependence in production, as well as all the all-sided dependence of the producers on one another . . . The reciprocal and all-sided dependence of individuals who are indifferent to one another forms their social connection. This social bond is expressed in exchange value."[49] The individuals, the subjects between whom this process occurs, are only exchangers. "As far as the formal character is concerned, there is absolutely no distinction between them . . . As subjects of exchange, their relation is therefore that of equality."[50] Does this mean that women are not entitled to a wage for their housework because they are unequal to men?

Any difference or inequality between persons in exchange is "only purely individual superiority of one individual over another. The difference would be one of natural origin, irrelevant to the nature of the relation as such."[51] Here, the inequality of the sexes obstructs arguing for a wage for housework in marxist terms. But the theory precisely intends to expose the hidden assumptions of male dominance in marxist economics, assumptions that at moments like this seem actually to be supporting capitalism, including its theory of value. "Wages for housework" advocates thus argue, in essence, for the commensurability of women's work in the home with other forms of laboring for capital in order to end the inequality it expresses, in order to contribute to ending the "fixed personal relations of dependence" that are posited as a presupposition for the abstraction of labor necessary for it to have a capitalist character, and thus to be entitled to a wage on capitalist terms. The marxian view seems to reduce to an argument that one must be equal before one can assert a right to equality, that capitalism must value one's work before a movement of political economy to end capitalism can value it, that one must already be independent before one can claim one is entitled to independence. At this juncture, one has to wonder why, really, women's work in the home is unpaid and how its lack of a wage can be justified.

Briefly reviving the "status" problem from the history of the "just price" debate helps illuminate the roots of this difficulty. The equality of labor necessary for Adam Smith's "labor commanded" theory of price,[52] for example, presupposed that the social division of labor occurs among social equals. Thus, to the extent women are socially unequal to men, their labor product will not have equal value. According to marxist analysis, the rise of capitalism rendered status differences unimportant, resolving them into the class division between capitalist and wage-laborer. One problem feminism poses is that women as such have no place in either of these classes in terms of many tasks they perform, unless they are employed in the marketplace. Now suppose that to the extent women do housework, they belong to neither class, but instead occupy a "status," a low one as reflected by the unwaged character of their work. The classical economists saw this problem as an issue for price determination. But it seems equally possible that it contributes to value determination in a way that is not reflected in price, because women do not have the social power to demand a return on their labor, much less a proportional one. In this sense, women's labor seems to pose a neglected aspect of the transformation problem in a way marxist theory has not resolved, in that women's labor contributes to value without, so long as it is unwaged, contributing to price, including the price of production.

Finally, is housework productive or unproductive? Capitalism defines productive labor as that labor the object of which is not use value but the renewal and expansion of capital. This process is endemic to the relations the product enters into, not to the activity or object itself. That is, that labor is productive which exchanges against capital, if capital appropriates the surplus. Ultimately, though, it is unclear how one knows if something is appropriated by capital. The superficial answer is that capital pays for it. But would paying for housework render productive labor that had not been so before? If productive labor is work that contributes to renewing the system as a whole and to the expansion of value, housework is productive. But if productive labor is work that realizes itself against money, all unwaged work is unproductive; and since the worker is unpaid, there is no way of knowing if capital gets value it does not pay for. If the kind of labor is expressed in the value form of the product, the object of laboring will make explicit qualities latent in the productive means. In this sense, housework appears to be as much productive for the man, and by women as a whole for men as a whole, as for capital. If housework were not done as it is in the home, men would have to purchase substitute goods and services in the marketplace, and it would be all the same from the standpoint of capital. Thus the question of who should pay raises the question of who benefits, which is another way of asking where the value comes from, to whose profit it redounds, and how it should be measured.

The "wages for housework" perspective is an attempt to synthesize feminism with marxism which uniquely exposes the dual nature of labor under capitalism as a locus at once of oppression and of possible liberation. It is said that under socialism real social relations between laborers will no longer be disguised as social relations between products. Perhaps women's work reveals the family under socialism to be a new "religion of everyday life"[53] which buys off discontent with the illusion that there is a sphere of life in which relations between people are really that, when they are yet more subtly disguised relations between things. Only feminism has seen this because only feminism has grasped that it is women who have become things.

Taking women's conditions seriously revises existing definitions of social exploitation. When one asks, why is what women do not valued like what men do is valued, the marxist answers are tautologies, defenses of the capitalist status quo—as if contradicting the nature of capitalism were not what class struggle is all about. Wages for housework as a perspective approaches the economic system seeking to explain how women's contribution, and women, are at once invisible and essential. As an apex of synthetic attempts, it forces reexamination both of housework from a marxist point of view and of marxist economics from women's point of view, suggesting that not only must women be included in an analysis from which they have been omitted, not only that any analysis that leaves women out is distorted and partial, but also that it is necessary to recast the vision of the totality to be explained.

Even given the limitations of "wages for housework" theory, what emerges is a simultaneous critique of the society that excludes women from its center and a critique of the marxist theory that can see women only at its periphery. Even when women work, women do not count, even in marxist theory. That women's role is marginal emerges as both real and not true. Women's work has been minimized both in the sense of being prevented from being realized and in the sense that its importance has been precluded from realization. And there is a connection: so long as women are excluded from socially powerful activity, whatever activity women do will reinforce their powerlessness, because women are doing it; and so long as women are doing activities considered socially valueless, women will be valued only for the ways they can be used.

# II. METHOD

Still harping on the same subject, you will exclaim—How can I avoid it, when most of the struggle of an eventful life has been occasioned by the oppressed state of my sex: we reason deeply, when we forcibly feel.

—Mary Wollstonecraft (1794)

In sum, there must be as much difference between our world and the world of men as there is between Euclidean geometric space and curved space, or between classical and quantum mechanics.

—Colette Guillaumin (1982)

# 5 | Consciousness Raising

I am a woman committed to
a politics
of transliteration, the methodology

of a mind
stunned at the suddenly
possible shifts of meaning—for which
like amnesiacs

in a ward on fire, we must
find words
or burn.

     —Olga Broumas, "Artemis"

. . . there is something else: the faith of those despised and
endangered that they are not merely the sum of damages
done to them.

     —Adrienne Rich, "Sources"

Feminism is the first theory to emerge from those whose
interest it affirms. Its method recapitulates as theory
the reality it seeks to capture. As marxist method is dialectical
materialism, feminist method is consciousness raising: the collective
critical reconstitution of the meaning of women's social experience, as
women live through it. Marxism and feminism on this level posit a
different relation between thought and thing, both in terms of the
relationship of the analysis itself to the social life it captures and in
terms of the participation of thought in the social life it analyzes. To
the extent that materialism is scientific it posits and refers to a reality
outside thought which it considers to have an objective—that is, a
nonsocially perspectival—content. Consciousness raising, by contrast,
inquires into an intrinsically social situation, into that mixture of
thought and materiality which comprises gender in the broadest sense.
It approaches its world through a process that shares its determination:
women's consciousness, not as individual or subjective ideas, but as

collective social being. This approach stands inside its own determinations in order to uncover them, just as it criticizes them in order to value them on its own terms—indeed, in order to have its own terms at all. Feminism turns theory itself, the pursuit of a true analysis of social life, into the pursuit of consciousness, and turns an analysis of inequality into a critical embrace of its own determinants. The process is transformative as well as perceptive, since thought and thing are inextricable and reciprocally constitutive of women's oppression, just as the state as coercion and the state as legitimating ideology are indistinguishable, and for the same reasons. The pursuit of consciousness becomes a form of political practice.

Consciousness raising is the process through which the contemporary radical feminist analysis of the situation of women has been shaped and shared. As feminist method and practice, consciousness raising is not confined to groups explicitly organized or named for that purpose. In fact, consciousness raising as discussed here was often not practiced in consciousness-raising groups. Such groups were, however, one medium and forum central to its development as a method of analysis, mode of organizing, form of practice, and technique of political intervention. The characteristic structure, ethic, process, and approach to social change which mark such groups as a development in political theory and practice are integral to many of the substantive contributions of feminist theory. The key to feminist theory consists in its *way* of knowing. Consciousness raising is that way. "[An] oppressed group must at once shatter the self-reflecting world which encircles it and, at the same time, project its own image onto history. In order to discover its own identity as distinct from that of the oppressor, it has to become visible to itself. All revolutionary movements create their own way of seeing."[1] One way to analyze feminism as a theory is to describe the process of consciousness raising as it occurred in consciousness-raising groups.

As constituted in the 1960s and 1970s, consciousness-raising groups were many women's first explicit contact with acknowledged feminism. Springing up spontaneously in the context of friendship networks, colleges and universities, women's centers, neighborhoods, churches, and shared work or workplaces, they were truly grassroots. Many aimed for diversity in age, marital status, occupation, education, physical ability, sexuality, race and ethnicity, class, or political views.

Others chose uniformity on the same bases. Some groups proceeded biographically, each woman presenting her life as she wished to tell it. Some moved topically, using subject focuses such as virginity crises, relations among women, mothers, body image, and early sexual experiences to orient discussion. Some read books and shared literature. Some addressed current urgencies as they arose, supporting women through difficult passages or encouraging them to confront situations they had avoided. Many developed a flexible combination of formats. Few could or wanted to stick to a topic if a member was falling apart, yet crises were seldom so clarifying or continuous as entirely to obviate the need for other focus.

Participants typically agreed on an ethic of openness, honesty, and self-awareness. If a member felt she could not discuss an intimate problem or felt coerced to do so, this was typically taken as a group failure. Other usual norms included a commitment to attend meetings and to keep information confidential. Although leadership patterns often emerged, and verbal and emotional skills recognizably varied, equality within the group was a goal that reflected a value of nonhierarchical organization and a commitment to confronting sources of inequality on the basis of which members felt subordinated or excluded.

What brought women to these groups is difficult to distinguish from what happened once they were there. As with any complex social interaction, from laboratory experiment to revolution, it is often difficult to separate the assumptions from the discoveries, the ripeness of conditions from the precipitating spark. Where does consciousness come from? The effectiveness of consciousness raising is difficult to apportion between the process itself and the women who choose to engage in it. The initial recruiting impulse seems to be a response to an unspecific, often unattached, but just barely submerged discontent that in some inchoate way women relate to being female. It has not escaped most women's attention that their femaleness defines much of who they can be. Restrictions, conflicting demands, intolerable but necessarily tolerated work, the accumulation of constant small irritations and indignities of everyday existence have often been justified on the basis of sex. Consciousness raising coheres and claims these impressions.

Feminists tend to believe that most if not all women resent women's status on some level of their being; even women's defense of their status can be a response to that status. Why some women take the step of identifying their situation with their status as women, transforming their discontents into grievances, is a crucial unanswered question of feminism (or, for that matter, of marxism). What brings people to be conscious of their oppression as common rather than remaining on the level of bad feelings, to see their group identity as a systematic necessity that benefits another group, is the first question of organizing. The fact that consciousness-raising groups were there presupposes the discovery that they were there to make. But what may have begun as a working assumption becomes a working discovery: women are a group, in the sense that a shared reality of treatment exists sufficient to provide a basis for identification—at least enough to begin talking about it in a group of women. This often pre-articulate consensus shapes a procedure, the purpose of which becomes to unpack the concrete moment-to-moment meaning of being a woman in a society that men dominate, by looking at how women see their everyday experience in it. Women's lives are discussed in all their momentous triviality, that is, as they are lived through. The technique explores the social world each woman inhabits through her speaking of it, through comparison with other women's experiences, and through women's experiences of each other in the group itself. Metaphors of hearing and speaking commonly evoke the transformation women experience from silence to voice. As Toni McNaron put it, "within every story I have ever heard from a woman, I have found some voice of me. The details are of course unique to the speaker—they are our differences. But the meaning which they make is common to us all. I will not understand what is common without hearing the details which reveal it to me."[2] The particularities become facets of the collective understanding within which differences constitute rather than undermine collectivity.

The fact that men were not physically present was usually considered necessary to the process. Although the ways of seeing that women have learned in relation to men were very much present or there would be little to discuss, men's temporary concrete absence helped women feel more free of the immediate imperative to compete for male attention and approval, to be passive or get intimidated, or to support men's version of reality. It made speech possible. With these constraints at some remove, women often found that the group confirmed awarenesses they had hidden, including from themselves. Subjects like sexuality, family, body, money, and power could be discussed more openly. The pain of women's roles and women's stake in them could be confronted critically, without the need every minute to reassure men that these changes were not threatening to them or to defend women's breaking of roles as desirable. The all-woman context valued women to each other as sources of insight, advice, information, stimulation, and problems. By providing room for women to be close, these groups demonstrated how far women were separated and how that separation deprived women of access to the way their treatment is systematized. "People who are without names, who do not know themselves, who have no culture, experience a kind of paralysis of consciousness. The first step is to connect and learn to trust one another."[3] This context for serious confrontation also revealed how women had been trivialized to each other. Pamela Allen called these groups "free space."[4] She meant a respectful context for interchange within which women could articulate the inarticulate, admit the inadmissible. The point of the process was not so much that hitherto-undisclosed facts were unearthed or that denied perceptions were corroborated or even that reality was tested, although all these happened. It was not only that silence was broken and that speech occurred. The point was, and is, that this process moved the reference point for truth and thereby the definition of reality as such. Consciousness raising alters the terms of validation by creating community through a process that redefines what counts as verification. This process gives both content and form to women's point of view.[5]

Concretely, consciousness-raising groups often focused on specific incidents and internal dialogue: what happened today, how did it make you feel, why did you feel that way, how do you feel now? Extensive attention was paid to small situations and denigrated pursuits that made up the common life of women in terms of energy, time, intensity, and definition—prominently, housework and sexuality. Women said things like this:

> I am nothing when I am by myself. In myself, I am nothing. I only know I exist because I am needed by someone who is real, my husband, and by my children. My husband goes out into the real world. Other people recognize him as real, and take him into account. He affects other people and events. He does things and changes things and they

are different afterwards. I stay in my imaginary world in this house, doing jobs that I largely invent, and that no-one cares about but myself. I do not change things. The work I do changes nothing; what I cook disappears, what I clean one day must be cleaned again the next. I seem to be involved in some sort of mysterious process.[6]

Intercourse was interrogated: how and by whom it is initiated, its timing, woman's feelings during and after, its place in relationships, its meaning, its place in being a woman.[7] Other subjects included interactions in routine situations like walking down the street, talking with bus drivers, interacting with cocktail waitresses. Women's stories—work and how they came to do it; children; sexual history, including history of sexual abuse—were explored. Adrienne Rich reflects the process many women experienced and the conclusion to which many women came:

> I was looking desperately for clues, because if there were no clues then I thought I might be insane. I wrote in a notebook about this time: "Paralyzed by the sense that there exists a mesh of relationships—e.g., between my anger at the children, my sensual life, pacifism, sex (I mean sex in its broadest significance, not merely sexual desire)—an interconnectedness which, if I could see it, make it valid, would give me back myself, make it possible to function lucidly and passionately. Yet I grope in and out among these dark webs." I think I began at this point to feel that politics was not something "out there" but something "in here" and of the essence of my condition.[8]

Woman's self-concept emerged: who she thinks she is, how she was treated in her family, who they told her she was (the pretty one, the smart one), how she resisted, how that was responded to, her feelings now about her life and herself, her account of how she came to feel that way, whether other group members experience her the way she experiences herself, how she carries her body and delivers her mannerisms, the way she presents herself and interacts in the group. Contradictions between messages tacitly conveyed and messages explicitly expressed inspired insightful and shattering criticism, as with women who behave seductively while complaining that men accost them. Complicity in oppression acquires concrete meaning as women emerge as shapers of reality as well as shaped by it. A carefully detailed and critically reconstructed composite image is built of women's experienced meaning of "being a woman." From women's collective perspective, a woman embodies and expresses a moment-to-moment concept of herself in the way she walks down the street, structures a household, pursues her work and friendships, shares her sexuality—a certain concept of how she has survived and who she survives as. A minute-by-minute moving picture is created of women becoming, refusing, sustaining their condition.

Interactions usually overlooked as insignificant if vaguely upsetting proved good subjects for detailed scrutiny. A woman mentions the way a man on the subway looked at her. How did this make her feel? Why does she feel so degraded? so depressed? Why can the man make her hate her body? How much of this feeling comes from her learned distrust of how men use her sexually? Does this show up in other areas of her life? Do other women feel this way? What form of power does this give the man? Do all men have, or exercise, such power? Could she have done anything at the time? Can the group do anything now? Women learn that the entire structure of sexual domination, the tacit relations of deference and command, can be present in a passing glance.

Realities hidden under layers of valued myth were unmasked simply by talking about what happens every day, such as the hard physical labor performed by the average wife and mother, the few women who feel strictly vaginal orgasms and the many who pretend they do. Women confronted collectively the range of overt violence represented in the life experience of their group of women, women who might previously have appeared "protected." They found fathers who raped them; boyfriends who shot at them; doctors who aborted them when they weren't pregnant or sterilized them "accidentally"; psychoanalysts who so-called seduced them, committing them to mental hospitals when they exposed them; mothers who committed suicide or lived to loathe themselves more when they failed; employers who fired them for withholding sexual favors or unemployment offices that refused benefits when they quit, finding their reason personal and uncompelling. Women learned that men see and treat women from their angle of vision, and they learned the content of that vision.

These details together revealed and documented the kind of world women inhabit socially and some of what it feels like for them to inhabit it, how women are systematically deprived of a self and how that process of deprivation constitutes socialization to femininity. In consciousness raising, women become aware of this reality as at once very specific—a woman's social condition and self-concept as it is lived through by her—and as a social reality in which all women more or less participate, however diversely, and in which all women can be identified. Put another way, although a woman's specific race or class or physiology may define her among women, simply being a woman has a meaning that decisively defines all women socially, from their most intimate moments to their most anonymous relations. This social meaning, which is unattached to any actual anatomical differences between the sexes, or to any realities of women's response to it, pervades everyday routine to the point that it becomes a reflex, a habit. Sexism is seen to be all of a piece and so much a part of the omnipresent background of life that a massive effort of collective concentration is required even to discern that it has edges. Consciousness raising is such an effort. Taken in this way, consciousness means a good deal more than a set of ideas. It constitutes a lived knowing of the social reality of being female.

What women become conscious of—the substance of radical feminist analysis—is integral to this process. Perhaps most obviously, it becomes difficult to take seriously accounts of women's roles or personal qualities based on nature or biology, except as authoritative appeals that have shaped women according to them. Combing through women's lives event by event, detail by detail, it is no mystery that women are who they are, given the way they have been treated. Patterns of treatment that would create feelings of incapacity in anybody are seen to connect seamlessly with acts of overt discrimination to deprive women of tools and skills, creating by force the status they are supposed to be destined for by anatomy. Heterosexuality, supposed natural, is found to be forced on women moment to moment. Qualities pointed to as naturally and eternally feminine—nurturance, intuition, frailty, quickness with their fingers, orientation to children—or characteristics of a particular subgroup of women—such as married women's supposed talent for exacting, repetitive, simple tasks, or Black women's supposed interest in sex—look simply like descriptions of the desired and required characteristics of particular occupants of women's roles. Meredith Tax summarized this insight: "We didn't get this way by heredity or by accident. We have been molded into these deformed postures, pushed into these service jobs, made to apologize for existing, taught to be unable to do anything requiring any strength at all, like opening doors or bottles. We have been told to be stupid, to be silly."[9]

If such qualities are biological imperatives, women conform to them remarkably imperfectly. When one gets to know women close up and without men present, it is remarkable the extent to which their so-called biology, not to mention their socialization, has failed. The discovery that these apparently unchangeable dictates of the natural order are powerful social conventions often makes women feel unburdened, since individual failures no longer appear so individualized. Women become angry as they see women's lives as one avenue after another foreclosed by gender.

More than their content, it is the relation to lived experience which is new about these insights. It is one thing to read a nineteenth-century tract describing a common problem of women. It is quite another for women to hear women speak the pain they feel, wonder what they have to fall back on, know they need a response, recognize the dilemmas, struggle with the same denial that the pain is pain, that it is also one's own, that women are real. Susan Griffin expressed it. "We do not rush to speech. We allow ourselves to be moved. We do not attempt objectivity . . . We said we had experienced this ourselves. I felt so much for her then, she said, with her head cradled in my lap, she said, I knew what to do. We said we were moved to see her go through what we had gone through. We said this gave us some knowledge."[10]

It was common for women in consciousness-raising groups to share radical changes in members' lives, relationships, work, life goals, and sexuality. This process created bonds and a different kind of knowledge, collective knowledge built on moving and being moved, on changing and being changed. As an experience, it went beyond empirical information that women are victims of social inequality. It built an experienced sense of how it came to be this way and that it can be changed. Women experienced the walls that have contained them as walls—and sometimes walked through them. For instance, when they first seriously considered never marrying or getting a divorce, women often discovered their economic dependency, having been taught to do little they can sell or having been paid less than men who sell comparable work. Why? To understand the precise causation would be to identify the supportive dynamics of male supremacy and capitalism. But an equivalency, at least, was clear: women's work is defined as inferior work, and inferior work is defined as work for women. Inferior work is often considered appropriate for women by the same standards that define it as inferior, and by the same standards that define "women's work" as inferior work—its pay, status, interest or complexity, contacts with people, its relation to cleanliness or care of bodily needs. Inextricably, women may find themselves inwardly dependent as well: conditioned not to think for themselves, to think that without a man they are nothing, or to think that they are less "woman" when without one. The point is not how well women conform to this standard but that there is such a standard and women do not create it. The power dynamic behind these facts is brought into the open when women break out, from the panic they feel at the thought and from the barriers they encounter when they try. It becomes clear, from one horror story after another, that men's position of power over women is a major part of what defines men as men to themselves, and women as women to themselves. Challenge to that power is taken as a threat to male identity and self-definition. Men's reaction of threat is also a challenge to women's self-definition, which has included supporting men, making men feel masculine, and episodically being treated better as a reward. Men's response to women's redefinition as in control is often to show women just how little control they have by threatening women's material or physical survival or their physical or sexual or emotional integrity. Women learn they have learned to "act independently in a dependent fashion."[11] And sometimes they find ways to resist all of this.

This place of consciousness in social construction is often most forcefully illustrated in the least materially deprived women, because the contrast between their economic conditions and their feminist consciousness can be so vivid:

> As suburban women, we recognize that many of us live in more economic and material comfort than our urban sisters, but we have come to realize through the women's movement, feminist ideas and consciousness raising, that this comfort only hides our essential powerlessness and oppression. We live in comfort only to the extent that our homes, clothing, and the services we receive feed and prop the status and egos of the men who support us. Like dogs on a leash, our own status and power will reach as far as our husbands and their income and prestige will allow. As human beings, as individuals, we in fact

own very little and should our husbands leave us or us them, we will find ourselves with the care and responsibility of children without money, jobs, credit or power. For this questionable condition, we have paid the price of isolation and exploitation by the institutions of marriage, motherhood, psychiatry and consumerism. Although our life styles may appear materially better, we are, as all women, dominated by men at home, in bed, and on the job, emotionally, sexually, domestically and financially.[12]

Women found they face these conditions sharply through nonmarriage or divorce or on becoming openly lesbian. Women who do not need men for sexual fulfillment can suddenly be found "incompetent" on their jobs when their bosses learn of their sexual preference. Similarly, when a women's health clinic is opened, and women handle their own bodies, male-controlled hospitals often deny admitting privileges, threatening every woman who attends the clinic. These conditions arise when women suggest that if housework is so fulfilling men should have the chance to do it themselves: it is everybody's job, women just blame themselves or do it when it is not done or done well. Always in the background, often not very far, is the sanction of physical intimidation, not because men are stronger but because they are willing and able to use their strength with relative social impunity; or not because they use it, but because they do not have to. In addition, identity invalidation is a form of power a man has for the price of invoking it: you are an evil woman, you are a whore (you have sex on demand), you are a failure as a woman (you do not have sex on demand) Women learn they have to become people who respond to these appeals on some level because they are backed up by material indulgences and deprivations. The understanding that a social group that is accorded, possesses, and uses such tools over others to its own advantage is powerful and that it exercises a form of social control or authority becomes not a presupposition or rhetorical hyperbole but a substantiated conclusion.

Perhaps the most pervasive realization of consciousness raising was that men as a group benefit from these same arrangements by which women are deprived. Women see that men derive many advantages from women's roles, including being served and kept in mind, supported and sustained, having their children cared for and their sexual needs catered to, and being kept from the necessity of doing jobs so menial they consider them beneath them unless there is no other job (or a woman) around. But the major advantage men derive, dubious though it may seem to some, is the process, the value, the mechanism by which their interest itself is enforced and perpetuated and sustained: power. Power in its socially male form. It is not only that men treat women badly, although often they do, but that it is their choice whether or not to do so. This understanding of power is one of the key comprehensions of feminism. The reality it points to, because it is everywhere and relatively invariant, appears to be nowhere separable from the whole, from the totality it defines.

Women, it is said, possess corresponding power. Through consciousness raising, women found that women's so-called power was the other side of female powerlessness. A woman's supposed power to deny sex is the underside of her actual lack of power to stop it. Women's supposed power to get men to do things for them by nagging or manipulating is the other side of the power they lack to have their every need anticipated, to carry out the task themselves, to be able to deliver upon sharing the responsibility equally, or to invoke physical fear to gain compliance with their desires without even having to mention it. Once the veil is lifted, once relations between the sexes are seen as power relations, it becomes impossible to see as simply unintended, well-intentioned, or innocent the actions through which women are told every day what is expected and when they have crossed some line. From the male point of view, no injury may be meant. But women develop an incisive eye for routines, strategems, denials, and traps that operate to keep women in place and to obscure the recognition that it is a place at all. Although these actions may in some real way be unintentional, they are taken, in some other real way, as meant. [13]

These discussions explored the functioning of sex roles in even one's closest "personal" relations, where it was thought women were most "ourselves," hence most free. Indeed, the reverse often seemed to be the case. The measure of closeness often seemed to be the measure of the oppression. When shared with other women, one's most private events often came to look the most stereotypical, the most for the public. Each woman, in her own particular, even chosen, way reproduces in her most private relations a structure of dominance and submission which characterizes the entire public order. The impact of this insight can be accounted for in part by the fact that it is practiced on the level of group process, so that what could be a sociopsychological or theoretical insight becomes a lived experience. That is, through making public, through discussing in the group, what had been private, for example sexual relations, it was found that the split between public and private, at least in the context of relations between the sexes, made very little sense, except as it functioned ideologically to keep each woman feeling alone, particularly in her experiences of sexual violation.

> After sharing, we *know* that women suffer at the hands of a male supremacist society and that this male supremacy intrudes into every sphere of our existence, controlling the ways in which we are allowed to make our living and the ways in which we find fulfillment in personal relationships. We know that our most secret, our most private problems are grounded in the way that women are treated, in the way women are allowed to live [14]

The analysis that the personal is the political came out of consciousness raising. It has four interconnected facets. First, women as a group are dominated by men as a group, and therefore as individuals. Second, women are subordinated in society, not by personal nature or by biology. Third, the gender division, which includes the sex division of labor which keeps women in high-heeled low-status jobs, pervades and determines even women's personal feelings in relationships. Fourth, since a woman's problems are not hers individually but those of women as a whole, they cannot be addressed except as a whole. In this analysis of gender as a nonnatural characteristic of a division of power in society, the personal becomes the political.

Pervasively implicit in these substantive insights is feminism's method of knowing about the world in its epistemological and political ramifications. Consciousness raising is a face-to-face social experience that strikes at the fabric of meaning of social relations between and among women and men by calling their givenness into question and reconstituting their meaning in a transformed and critical way. The most apparent quality of this method is its aim of grasping women's situation as it is lived through. The process identifies the problem of women's subordination as a problem that can be accessed through women's consciousness, or lived knowing, of her situation. This implicitly posits that women's social being is in part constituted or at least can be known through women's lived-out view of themselves. Consciousness raising attacks this problem by unraveling and reordering what every woman "knows" because she has lived it, and in so doing forms and reforms, recovers and changes, its meaning. This is accomplished through using the very instrument—women experiencing how they experience themselves—that is the product of the process to be understood. The apparent circularity of this as a theory of knowing about the world is not a barrier to analysis, but rather the core of the method, the way it breaks the circularity of that which it is attempting to understand in order to change. The seemingly self-enclosed character of feminist consciousness and the community it inhabits by creating it is, in reality, the opposite of solipsism: what it sees is that it is male reality that is self-enclosed. Feminism only seems to be circular from the point of view of the existing epistemology because that is the relation of a new paradigm to the old one:

> Like the choice between competing political institutions, that between competing paradigms proves to be a choice between incompatible modes of community life. Because it has that character, the choice is not and cannot be determined merely by the evaluative procedures characteristic of normal science, for these depend in part upon a particular paradigm, and that paradigm is at issue. When paradigms enter, as they must, into a debate about paradigm choice, their role is necessarily circular. Each group uses its own paradigm to argue in that paradigm's defense. [15]

Theories of right knowing are epistemologies. An epistemology is a story of a relation between knower and known. In the history of thought, this relation has been variously cast as a relation between subject and object, value and fact, phenomena and noumena, mind and matter, world and representation, text or evidence and interpretation, and other polarities and antinomies. The point of such distinctions is to establish an account of how knowing connects with what one purports to know. One purpose of this has been to establish an authoritative account of the real in order to expose errors and delusions conclusively in an agreed-upon way. The point is to establish world in mind. Science, for example, seeks empirical certainty over opinion or fiction or delusion or faith. All approaches to knowledge set up modes by which to tell whether what one thinks is real, is real. This connection embodies what is called methodology; adherence to it defines what is called rationality. Method thus puts into operation a way of acquiring that knowledge that a particular epistemological stance approves as real.

Scientific epistemology defines itself in the stance of "objectivity," whose polar opposite is subjectivity. Socially, men are considered objective, women subjective. Objectivity as a stance toward the world erects two tests to which its method must conform: distance and aperspectivity. To perceive reality accurately, one must be distant from what one is looking at and view it from no place and at no time in particular, hence from all places and times at once. This stance defines the relevant world as that which can be objectively known, as that which can be known in this way. An epistemology decisively controls not only the form of knowing but also its content by defining how to proceed, the process of knowing, and by confining what is worth knowing to that which can be known in this way.

The posture scientific epistemology takes toward its world defines the basic epistemic question as a problem of the relation between knowledge—where knowledge is defined as a replication or reflection or copy of reality—and objective reality, defined as that world which exists independent of any knower or vantage point, independent of knowledge or the process of coming to know, and, in principle, knowable in full. For science, the tests of reality are replicability and measurability, the test of true meaning is intersubjective communicability, the test of rationality is formal (axiomatic) logical consistency, and the test of usefulness, as in technology, is whether it can be done.

Social science attempts to view the social world objectively, as physical science has viewed the physical world. One effect has been to uncover many roots of what has previously been taken as the simply given. That which previously was used as explanation becomes that which is to be explained. The scientifically real is found to embody many determinants that science sees as getting in the way of knowing social reality, to the extent they can be accounted for by that reality. In this perspective, for example, psychology traditionally constructs problems of personality, development, and psychosis as intervening within the knower between knowledge and reality, producing distortions from some combination of the person's "nature" and "nurture." Thus Piaget's stages of cognitive development can be viewed as progressive stages of epistemological growth, cognitively grasping the world at a given developmental stage.[16] There is seldom any questioning of the objective "out there" reality of the world the child is attempting to come to know, the possibly distinct and changing object world the child inhabits.

Consistent with this approach, social science attacks the problem of its own knowing largely in terms of the limitations on the "in here" of the knower, with concern for how these limits can be overcome, exorcised, or contained.[17] Its model of knowledge posits a mind needing to overstep its determinants in order to get outside itself in order to get at the facts. Otherwise, it is thought, the mind will only propagate and project its delusions, its determinants, the limitations of its experiences, onto social reality, remaining forever trapped within itself. The movement to uncover the sources of social experience has thus also been a movement that has devalued these sources by regarding them as barriers or distortions between the knower and the known. If social knowledge can be interpreted in terms of the social determinants of the knower, it is caused. Therefore, its truth value, in this definition of tests for truth, is undercut. If it has a time or place—or gender—it becomes doubtful because situated.

Feminist method as practiced in consciousness raising, taken as a theory of knowing about social being, pursues another epistemology. Women are presumed able to have access to society and its structure because they live in it and have been formed by it, not in spite of those facts. Women can know society because consciousness is part of it, not because of any capacity to stand outside it or oneself. This stance locates the position of consciousness, from which one knows, in the standpoint and time frame of that attempting to be known. The question is not whether objective reality exists but whether that concept accesses the is-ness of the world. Feminist epistemology asserts that the social process of being a woman is on some level the same process as that by which woman's consciousness becomes aware of itself as such and of its world. Mind and world, as a matter of social reality, are taken as interpenetrated. Knowledge is neither a copy nor a miscopy of reality, neither representative nor misrepresentative as the scientific model would have it, but a response to living in it. Truth is in a sense a collective experience of truth, in which "knowledge" is assimilated to consciousness, a consciousness that exists as a reality in the world, not merely in the head. This epistemology does not at all deny that a relation exists between thought and some reality other than thought, or between human activity (mental or otherwise) and the products of that activity. Rather, it redefines the epistemological issue from being the scientific one, the relation between knowledge and objective reality, to a problem of the relation of consciousness to social being. This move contextualizes verification, rendering epistemology, in the words of Jane Flax, "the study of the life situation of consciousness, an inquiry which is ultimately political and historical."[18]

An epistemology preempts the definition of reality when its criteria for conclusiveness become taken for granted, as constituting "reality itself," as rules or standards in terms of which other forms of knowing are tested. For science, these criteria are distance and aperspectivity. Though apparently general, and asserted by science as not constructs of reality but ways of getting at it, they have specific social roots and implications. These include devaluing as biased and unreliable the view from the inside and within the moment, and the perspective from the bottom of the social order. For science not only etches itself on the world through its technology, making the world a scientific place in which to live, but also propagates itself through its picture of social reality. This picture exists complete with those categories that a scientific epistemology can perceive as real. Social science provides no account of this prior picture of social reality upon which its "empirically derived" explanations are then superimposed, which its data then "confirm." Because social science is crippled by its mythos as distanced and aperspectival, it cannot give an account of the social reality it approaches because it cannot give an account of its approach.

The social power of science creates a reality that conforms to its image. Conflicting views of reality, although they retain a subcultural or subconscious life and power, are authoritatively defined as unreal or irrational. Sanctions behind the ruling reality construction range from whatever happens inside people who never seem to have conscious thoughts of different ways of being, to bad grades in school, jailing, and mental hospitalization for those who do. The choice of an epistemology is, in Kuhn's words, "like the choice between competing political institutions"[19] because it *is* a choice of political institution—one that women never chose.

Consciousness raising discovered that one form of the social existence of male power is inside women. In this form, male power becomes self-enforcing. Women become "thingified in the head."[20] Once incarnated, male superiority tends to be reaffirmed and reinforced in what can be seen as well as in what can be done. So male power both is and is not illusory. As it justifies itself, namely as natural, universal, unchangeable, given, and morally correct, it is illusory; but the fact that it is powerful is no illusion. Power is a social relation. Given the imperatives of women's lives, the necessity to avoid punishment—from self-rejection to involuntary incarceration to suicide—it is not irrational for women to see themselves in a way that makes their necessary compliance tolerable, even satisfying. Living each day reconvinces everyone, women and men alike, of male hegemony, which is hardly a myth, and of women's innate inferiority and men's innate superiority, a myth that each day's reliving makes difficult to distinguish meaningfully from reality.

The deepest paradox of consciousness raising and its most potent contribution is that it affirms that there both is and can be another reality for women by doing nothing but examining the current society's deadest ends. Effectively, the process redefines women's feelings of discontent as indigenous to their situation rather than to themselves as crazy, maladjusted, hormonally imbalanced, bitchy, or ungrateful. It is validating to comprehend oneself as devalidated rather that as invalid. Women's feelings are interpreted as appropriate responses to their conditions. This analysis need not posit that feelings are asocial or universally correct as a representation of experience. Nor does it mean that women who feel what they are supposed to feel validate the society that forces them to feel that way. The distinction between "in here" and "out there" made in society through scientific objectivity is, however, seen to operate as a legitimating ideology that supports men's views of what women should think and be by powerfully stigmatizing as irrational and unreal women's feelings of rage and rebellion, by individualizing them, and by keeping the "privacy" (that is, isolation) of home and sexual life from being comprehended as gender's collective realities.

Of course, objective data do document the difficulties and inequities of woman's situation. Whether such data can scientifically conclusively demonstrate that women are oppressed, deprived of power, and objectified is something else again. Certainly a good deal of men's tyranny over women can be observed through data, experiments, and research; in this form it can be communicated to people who do not experience it. Many things can be known in this way. Yet seemingly regardless of objective conditions this knowing does not move people to see their own or others' condition as lacking in power—and for good reason. Knowing these facts as object removes it. Nor does it show that it is unnecessary or changeable, except speculatively, because what is not there is not considered real. Women's situation cannot be truly known for what it is, in the feminist sense, without knowing that it can be other than it is. By operating as legitimating ideology, the scientific standard for verifying reality can reinforce a growing indignation, but it cannot create feminism that was not already there. Knowing objective facts does not do what consciousness does. Patterns of abuse can be made to look more convincing without the possibility of change seeming even a little more compelling. Viewed as object reality, the more inequality is pervasive, the more it is simply "there." And the more real it looks, the more it looks like the truth.

As a way of knowing about social conditions, consciousness raising by contrast shows women their situation in a way that affirms they can act to change it. Consciousness raising socializes women's knowing. It produces an analysis of woman's world which is not objective in the positivistic sense of being a perfect reflection of reality conceived as abstract object; it is certainly not distanced or aperspectival. It is collective and critical. It embodies shared feelings, comprehensions, and experiences of women as products of their conditions, through being critical of their condition together. In so doing, it builds a community frame of reference which recasts the perceived content of social life as it alters the relation between the "I," the "other," and the "we." Consciousness raising, through socializing women's knowing, transforms it, creating a shared reality that "clears a space in the world" within which women can begin to move.[21] Seen as method, this process gives the resulting analysis its ground as well as its concreteness, specificity, and historicity.

Consciousness raising can also affirm that although women are deprived of power, within the necessity of their compliance is a form of power which they possess but have not yet seized. Mostly, women comply. Women learn they are defined in terms of subordinate roles; failing to challenge these roles confirms male supremacy in a way it needs. Daily social actions are seen to cooperate with and conform to a principle. They are not random, natural, socially neutral, or without meaning beyond themselves. They are not freely willed, but they are actions nonetheless. From seeing that such actions have meaning for maintaining and constantly reaffirming the structure of male supremacy at their expense, women can come to see the possibility, even the necessity, of acting differently. Women can act because they have been acting all along. Although it is one thing to act to preserve power relations and quite another to act to challenge them, once it is seen that these relations require daily acquiescence, acting on different principles, even in very small ways, seems not quite so impossible.

Consciousness raising also affirms that women can know because it does not place correct knowledge beyond them. Women need not stand outside experience to validly comprehend it. The instrument of social perception is created by the social process by which women are controlled. But this apparent paradox is not a solipsistic circle or a subjectivist retreat. Realizing that women largely recognize themselves in sex-stereotyped terms, really do feel the needs they have been encouraged to feel, do feel fulfilled in the expected ways, often actually choose what has been prescribed, makes possible the realization that women at the same time do not recognize themselves in, do not feel, and have not chosen this place.

Thus feminism recognizes that cognitive judgments need not be universally agreed upon to be true. It redefines validity as nonuniversal but nevertheless correct, rather than (as does relativism, for instance) undercutting the ability to cognitively judge. The account of error, of women's nonfeminist perception of their situation, is that the perception is probably as justified by aspects of the woman's experience as a feminist perception would be.[22] This is a problem for the account only if one argues that *only* authoritative or universal truth is truth or that feminist consciousness is inevitable. In contrast to science, consciousness raising does not devalue the roots of social experience as it uncovers them, nor does it set up rules for certainty. It allows a critical embrace of who one has been made by society rather than demanding a removal of all that one is before one can understand one's situation. The process affirms a product of the determinants—self as knower of one's condition—while building a criticism of the conditions that have produced one as one is. It also makes everyone a theorist.

Feminism locates the relation of woman's consciousness to her life situation in the relation of two moments: being shaped in the image of one's oppression, yet struggling against it. In so doing, women struggle against the world in themselves as well as toward a future. The real question, both for explanation and for organizing, is what is the relation between the first process, woman becoming her role, and the second, her rejection of it?

What is the feminist account of how women can come to reject the learning portrayed as so encompassing? The analysis of how one gets to be the way one is does not readily explain how some come to reject it, much less the view that one must and can change it into something specifically envisioned. What accounts for some women's turning upon their conditioning? In other words, what is the relationship between consciousness and material conditions for feminism? A theory that explains how some women come to be critical does not explain why others, who are for all purposes of the analysis identical, are not critical. Yet an explanation of why many women do not even seem to notice their oppression fails to interpret, except as exceptions, those who do.

Feminism, through consciousness raising, has grasped the completeness of the incursion into who one really becomes through growing up female in a male-dominated society. This effect can be understood as a distortion of self. It is not only one's current self one is understanding, but the self that understands what one has become *as* a distortion. On one level, this is exactly right. On another level, it exposes a dilemma: understanding women's conditions leads to the conclusion that women are damaged. If the reality of this damage is accepted, women are in fact not full people in the sense men are allowed to become. So on what basis can a demand for equal treatment be grounded? If women are what they are made, are determined, women must create new conditions, take control of their determinants. But how does one come to know this? On the other hand, if women go beyond the prescribed limitations on the basis (presumably) of something outside their conditions, such as being able to see the injustice or damage of inequality, what is the damage of inequality? The early twentieth-century feminist movement may have run aground on its version of this rock.

A similar tension arises in marxist theory, if in a slightly different way. Attempting to account for the consciousness of the proletariat is very difficult to the extent consciousness is historicized and the ruling ideology reifies class relations. How can consciousness be alienated, hence ideological, as a result of capitalist social relations and yet be aware of the necessity to revolutionize this system? Capitalist social relations distort cognition; yet it is precisely the relation to the mode of production under capitalism that gives the point of view of the proletariat (through its material position and its struggle against it) its revolutionary potential and makes the old society the midwife of the new. If one substitutes "knowledge of the truth about their social condition" for "science" (which is what Marx often seemed to mean by the term), Marx's description of proletarian consciousness at certain historical times could describe women's consciousness today:

> But in the measure that history moves forward, and with it the struggle of the proletariat assumes clearer outlines, they no longer need to seek science in their minds; they have only to take note of what is happening before their eyes and to become its mouthpiece . . . From this moment, science, which is a product of this historical movement, has associated itself consciously with it, has ceased to become doctrinaire and has become revolutionary.[23]

The question then becomes not whether such knowledge is possible, but whether women are such a people and now is such a time.

Consciousness raising has revealed that male power is real. It is just not the only reality, as it claims to be. Male power is a myth that makes itself true. To raise consciousness is to confront male power in its duality: as at once total on one side and a delusion on the other. In consciousness raising, women learn they have learned that men are everything, women their negation, but the sexes are equal. The content of the message is revealed as true and false at the same time; in fact, each part reflects the other transvalued. If "Men are all, women their negation" is taken as social criticism rather than as simple description, it becomes clear for the first time that women are men's equals, everywhere in chains. The chains become visible, the civil inferiority—the inequality—the product of subjection and a mode of its enforcement. Reciprocally, the moment it is seen that this life as we know it is not equality, that the sexes are not socially equal, womanhood can no longer be defined in terms of lack of maleness, as negativity. For the first time, the question of what a woman is seeks its ground in and of a world understood as neither of its making nor in its own image, and finds, within a critical embrace of woman's fractured and alien image, the shadow world women have made and a vision of the possibility of equality. As critique, women's communality describes a fact of male supremacy, a fact of sex "in itself": no woman escapes the meaning of being a woman within a gendered social system, and sex inequality is not only pervasive but may be universal (in the sense of never having not been in some form), though "intelligible only in . . . locally specific forms."[24] For women to become a sex "for itself"[25] is to move community to the level of vision.

# 6 | *Method and Politics*

It is quite true that there are no limits to masculine egotism in ordinary life. In order to change the conditions of life we must learn to see them through the eyes of women.

—Leon Trotsky

On principle it is quite wrong to try founding a theory on observable magnitudes alone. In reality, the very opposite happens. It is the theory which decides what we can observe.

—Albert Einstein

The detached observer is as much entangled as the active participant.

—Theodor Adorno

A science needs points of view . . .

—Karl Popper

*M*ethod organizes the apprehension of truth. It determines what counts as evidence and defines what is taken as verification. Operatively, it determines what a theory takes to be real. "Method is not neutral; it establishes the criteria by which one judges the validity of conclusions, and consequently carries with it not simply technical skills but deeper philosophical commitments and implications."[1] With theories of the organization of social life, method in this broader sense—approaches to searching for and apprehending the real—both produces and proceeds from substantive conclusions on questions like relevance (what questions count? what evidence supports answers?), structure (what is connected with what, and how?), and reliability (when is information worthy of belief?). On this level, no matter how open to the world a method is, it is always to some degree tautologous with its discoveries.

In the Western philosophical tradition, method has sought authority: how to produce an account of knowledge which is certain, which ends speculation and precludes skepticism, which has power that no one else can as powerfully contest. The search has been for an approach to the real on which to base arguments and conclusions that will make one's point of view unquestionable and unanswerable, immortal and definitive and the last word, regardless of time, place, or person. Its thrust has been to end diversity of viewpoint, so that there can be no valid disagreement over what knowing is right knowing.[2] Its history is the history of an attempt to exert such power over reality as comes from methodological hegemony over the means of knowing, validating only those ways of proceeding which advance the project of producing what it regards as requisite certainty. Objectivity has been its answer, its standard, its holy grail. When it speaks and there is silence, it imagines it has found it.

Marxism and feminism, as critiques of the real, seek both an account of their approach to reality which differs from the dominant account and a lever for change. How can what they know be so different from the authoritative version and still be right? How can their account of the way power produces both perspective and reality be true, knowable without change, yet capable of producing change? With marxism and feminism, as with other theories that are critical of society's organization, method serves to locate and identify the problem each theory addresses, the social reality giving rise to that problem, and the approach to solving it. Looked at in this way, work and sexuality as concepts derive their meaning and primacy from the way each theory approaches, grasps, interprets, and inhabits its world. There is a relationship between how and what a theory sees. It would be distorted to imagine a marxist method without class, a feminist method without sex. Yet attempts to synthesize marxism and feminism have not confronted each theory on the level of method.[3] Rather than considering which came (or comes) first, sex or class, the more fundamental task for theory is to explore the methods, the approaches to reality, that found and made these categories meaningful in the first place.

Marxist method is not monolithic. Beginning with Marx, it has divided between an epistemology that embraces its own historicity and one that claims a reality beyond history. In the first tendency, all thought, including social analysis, is seen as ideological in the sense of being shaped by social being, the conditions of which are external to no theory. Its project for theory is to create what Lukács described as "a theory of theory and a consciousness of consciousness."[4] Theory is a social activity engaged in the life situation of consciousness.[5] In the second tendency, theory is acontextual to the extent that it is accurate. Real processes and thought processes are distinct; being has primacy over knowledge. The real can be unified with knowledge of the real, as in dialectical materialism, only because they have previously been separated.[6] Theory as a form of thought is methodologically set apart both from the illusions endemic to social reality—ideology—and from reality itself. Reality is a world defined as thinglike, independent of both theory and ideology. Ideology means thought that is socially determined without being conscious of its determinations. Situated thought is as likely to produce "false consciousness" as access to truth. Theory by definition is, by contrast, nonideological. Since ideology is intrinsically interested, theory must be disinterested in order to penetrate the justifications and legitimations of the status quo. As Louis Althusser warned, "We know that a 'pure' science only exists on condition that it continually frees itself from ideology which occupies it, haunts it, or lies in wait for it."[7] The theorist must, in this sense, be classless. When this attempt succeeds, society is seen "from the point of view of class exploitation."[8] This second tendency, which better describes Engels than Marx, best grounds the marxist claim to be scientific. A theory that embraced its own historicity might see such an imperative as itself historically contingent. The first approach grounds its claim to capture as thought the flux of history. The second has become the dominant tradition; the first is more hospitable to feminism.

Feminism has not been perceived as having a method, or even a central argument. It has been perceived not as a systematic analysis but as a loose collection of complaints and issues that, taken together, describe rather than explain the misfortunes of the female sex.[9] The challenge is to demonstrate that feminism systematically converges upon a central explanation of sex inequality through an approach distinctive to its subject yet applicable to the whole of social life, including class.

Under the rubric of feminism, woman's situation has been explained as a consequence of biology[10] or of reproduction and mothering, social organizations of biology[11] as caused by the marriage law[12]—or, as an extension, as caused by the patriarchal family, becoming society as a "patriarchy."[13] Or, it has been explained as a consequence of artificial gender roles and their attendant attitudes.[14] Informed by these attempts, but conceiving nature, law, the family, and roles as consequences, not as foundations, feminism fundamentally identifies sexuality as the primary social sphere of male power. The centrality of sexuality emerges not from Freudian conceptions, nor from Lacanian roots,[15] but from consciousness raising and other feminist practice on diverse issues, including rape, incest, battery, sexual harassment, abortion, prostitution, and pornography. In these areas, feminist efforts aim to confront and change women's lives concretely. Taken together, they are producing a feminist political theory centering upon sexuality: its social determination, daily construction, birth-to-death expression, and male control.

Feminist inquiry into these specific issues began with a broad unmasking through consciousness raising of the attitudes that legitimate and hide women's status, the daily practices and ideational envelope that contain woman's body: notions that women desire and provoke rape, that girls' experiences of incest are fantasies, that career women plot and advance by sexual parlays, that prostitutes are lustful, that wife beating expresses the intensity of love. Beneath each idea were revealed bare coercion and broad connections to women's social definition as a sex. Research on sex roles, pursuing Simone de Beauvoir's insight that "one is not born, one rather becomes a woman,"[16] her understanding that society reduces woman's cultural place to the natural order and thereby eliminates women's capacity for freedom, disclosed an elaborate process of how and what one learns to become a woman. Gender, cross-culturally, was found to be a learned trait, an acquired characteristic, an assigned status, with qualities that vary independent of biology and an ideology that attributes them to nature.

The discovery that the female archetype is the feminine stereotype exposed "woman" as a social construction. Contemporary industrial society's version of her is docile, soft, passive, nurturant, vulnerable, weak, narcissistic, childlike, incompetent, masochistic, and domestic, made for childcare, home care, and husband care. Conditioning to these values permeates the upbringing of girls and the images for emulation thrust upon women. Women who resist or fail, including those who never did fit—such as Black and working-class women who cannot survive if they are soft and weak and incompetent;[17] assertively self-respecting women; women with ambitions in the world, meaning ambitions of male dimensions—are considered less female, lesser women. Women who comply or succeed are elevated as models, tokenized if they succeed on male terms or portrayed as consenting to their natural place and dismissed as having participated if they complain.

If the literature on sex roles and the investigations of particular issues are read in light of each other, each element of the female gender stereotype is revealed as, in fact, sexual. Vulnerability means the appearance/reality of easy sexual access; passivity means receptivity and disabled resistance, enforced by trained physical weakness; softness means pregnability by something hard. Incompetence seeks help as vulnerability seeks shelter, inviting the embrace that becomes the invasion, trading exclusive access for protection . . . from that same access. Domesticity nurtures the consequent progeny, proof of potency, and ideally waits at home dressed in Saran Wrap.[18] Woman's infantilization evokes pedophilia; fixation on dismembered body parts (the breast man, the leg man) evokes fetishism; idolization of vapidity, necrophilia. Narcissism ensures that woman identifies with the image of herself man holds up: "Hold still, we are going to do your portrait, so that you can begin looking like it right away."[19] Masochism means that pleasure in violation becomes her sensuality. Lesbians can so violate the sexuality implicit in female gender stereotypes as not to be considered women at all, or lesbian existence must be suppressed to reaffirm the stereotypes.

Socially, femaleness means femininity, which means attractiveness to men, which means sexual attractiveness, which means sexual availability on male terms. What defines woman as such is what turns men on, and everything any kind of woman is, does. Virtuous girls, virginal, are "attractive," up on those pedestals from which they must be brought down; unvirtuous girls, whores, are "provocative," so deserve whatever they get. Gender socialization is the process through which women come to identify themselves as such sexual beings, as beings that exist for men, specifically for male sexual use. It is that process through which women internalize (make their own) a male image of their sexuality as their identity as women, and thus make it real in the world.

> The overall objective of female conditioning is to make women perceive themselves and their lives through male eyes and so to secure their unquestioning acceptance of a male-defined and male-derived existence. The overall objective of male conditioning is to make men perceive themselves and their lives through their own eyes and so to prepare them for an existence in and on their own terms.[20]

This is not just an illusion. Feminist inquiry into women's own experience of sexuality requires revision of previous views of sexual issues and transforms the concept of sexuality itself—its determinants and its role in society and politics. According to this revision, one "becomes a woman"—acquires and identifies with the status of the female—not so much through physical maturation or inculcation into appropriate role behavior as through the experience of sexuality: a complex unity of physicality, emotionality, identity, and status affirmation, in which sexual intercourse is central. Sex as gender and sex as sexuality are thus defined in terms of each other, but it is sexuality that determines gender, not the other way around. This, the central but never stated insight of Kate Millett's *Sexual Politics,* resolves the linguistic duality in the meaning of the term *sex* itself.

First sexual intercourse is a commonly definitive experience of gender definition. For many women, it is a rape. It may occur in the family, instigated by a father or older brother who decided to "make a lady out of my sister."[21] Women's sex/gender initiation may be abrupt and anomic: "When she was 15 she had an affair with a painter. He fucked her and she became a woman."[22] Simone de Beauvoir implied a similar point when she said: "It is at her first abortion that a woman begins to 'know.' "[23] What women learn in order to "have sex," in order to "become women"—woman as gender—comes through the experience of, and is a condition for, "having sex"— woman as sexual object for man, the use of women's sexuality by men. Indeed, to the extent sexuality is social, women's sexuality is its use, just as femaleness is its alterity.

Many issues that appear sexual from this standpoint have not been seen as such, nor have they been seen as defining a politics. Incest, for example, is commonly seen as a question of distinguishing the real evil, a crime against the family, from girlish seductiveness or fantasy. Contraception and abortion have been framed as matters of reproduction and fought out as proper or improper social constraints on nature. Or they are seen as private, the issue being state intervention in intimate relations. Sexual harassment was a nonissue, even a nonexperience; once defined and raised as an issue, it was made a problem of distinguishing personal relationships or affectionate flirtation from abuse of position, position meaning place in a work hierarchy. Lesbians, when visible at all, have been seen as either perverted or not, to be tolerated or not. Pornography has been considered a question of freedom to speak and depict the erotic, as against the obscene or the violent. Prostitution has been understood either as mutual lust and degradation or as an equal exchange of sexual need for economic need. The issue in rape has been whether the intercourse was provoked/mutually desired, or whether it was forced: was it sex or was it violence? Across and beneath these issues, sexuality itself has been divided into parallel provinces: traditionally, into religion or biology; in modern transformation, into morality or psychology. Almost never politics.

In a feminist perspective, the formulation of each issue, in the terms just described, expresses ideologically the same interest that the problem it formulates expresses concretely: the interest from the male point of view. Women experience the sexual events these issues codify as a cohesive whole within which each resonates. The defining theme of that whole is the male pursuit of control over women's sexuality— men not as individuals or as biological beings, but as a gender group characterized by maleness as socially constructed, of which this pursuit is definitive. For example, women who need abortions see contraception as a struggle not only for control over the biological products of sexual expression but also over the social rhythms and mores of sexual intercourse. These norms often appear hostile to women's self-protection even when the technology is at hand. As an instance of such norms, women notice that sexual harassment looks a great deal like ordinary heterosexual initiation under conditions of gender inequality. Few women are in a position to refuse unwanted sexual initiatives. That consent rather than nonmutality is the line between rape and intercourse further exposes the inequality in normal social expectations. So does the substantial amount of male force allowed in the focus on the woman's resistance, resistance that tends to be disabled by women's socialization to passivity. Rape in marriage expresses the male sense of entitlement to access to women they annex; incest extends it to the children. Pornography becomes difficult to distinguish from art and ads once it is clear that what is degrading to women is the same as what is compelling to the consumer. Pimps sell unilateral sex by selling women to men through prostitution or pornography. That most of these issues codify behavior that is neither countersystemic nor exceptional is supported by women's experience as victims: these behaviors are either not illegal or are illegal but effectively permitted on a large scale. As women's experience blurs the lines between deviance and normalcy, it obliterates the distinction between abuses of women and the social definition of what a woman is.

These investigations reveal rape, incest, sexual harassment, pornography, and prostitution[24] as not primarily abuses of physical force, violence, authority, or economics, although they are that. They are abuses of women; they are abuses of sex. They need not and do not rely for their coerciveness upon forms of enforcement other than the sexual; that those forms of enforcement, at least in this context, are themselves sexualized is closer to the truth. They are not the erotization of something else, like power; eroticism itself exists in this form. Nor are they perversions of art and morality. They are art and morality from the male point of view. They are sexual because they express the relations, values, feelings, norms, and behaviors of the culture's sexuality, in which considering things like rape, pornography, incest, prostitution, or lesbianism deviant, perverse, or blasphemous is part of their excitement potential. That these behaviors are illegal makes them be considered repressed. This is largely what makes it possible for the desire to do them, which is in fact the rush of power to express itself, to be experienced as the desire for freedom.

Sexuality, then, is a form of power. Gender, as socially constructed, embodies it, not the reverse. Women and men are divided by gender, made into the sexes as we know them, by the social requirements of its dominant form, heterosexuality, which institutionalizes male sexual dominance and female sexual submission.[25] If this is true, sexuality is the linchpin of gender inequality.

Feminism has a theory of power: sexuality is gendered as gender is sexualized. Male and female are created through the erotization of dominance and submission. The man/woman difference and the dominance/submission dynamic define each other. This is the social meaning of sex and the distinctively feminist account of gender inequality. Sexual objectification, the central process within this dynamic, is at once epistemological and political.[26] The feminist theory of knowledge is inextricable from the feminist critique of power because the male point of view forces itself upon the world as its way of apprehending it.

The perspective from the male standpoint enforces woman's definition, encircles her body, circumlocutes her speech, and describes her life. The male perspective is systemic and hegemonic. Male is a social and political concept, not a biological attribute, having nothing whatever to do with inherency, preexistence, nature, essence, inevitability, or body as such. Indeed, it is more epistemological than ontological in a way that undercuts the distinction itself, given male power to conform being with perspective. Thus the perspective from the male standpoint is not always each man's opinion or even some aggregation or sum of men's opinions, although most men adhere to it, nonconsciously and without considering it a point of view, as much because it makes sense of their experience (the male experience) as because it is in their interest. It is rational for them. Because it is the dominant point of view and defines rationality, women are pushed to see reality in its terms, although this denies their vantage point as women in that it contradicts at least some of their lived experience, particularly the experience of violation through sex. But, largely, the content of the signification "woman" from the male point of view is the content of women's lives.

Each sex has its role, but their stakes and power are not equal. If the sexes are unequal, and perspective participates in situation, there is no ungendered reality or ungendered perspective. And they are connected. In this context, objectivity—the nonsituated, universal standpoint, whether claimed or aspired to—is a denial of the existence or potency of sex inequality that tacitly participates in constructing reality from the dominant point of view. Objectivity, as the epistemological stance of which objectification is the social process, creates the reality it apprehends by defining as knowledge the reality it creates through its way of apprehending it. Sexual metaphors for knowing are no coincidence. In the Bible, to know a woman is to have sex with her; you acquire carnal knowledge. Many scholarly metaphors elaborate the theme of violating boundaries to appropriate from inside to carry off, the classic meaning of rape.[27] At least since Plato's cave, this appropriation has been achieved first visually, visual metaphors for

knowing have been prioritized as a method of verification,[28] giving
visual objectification, as in pornography, particular potency.[29] The
solipsism of this approach does not undercut its sincerity, but it is
interest that precedes method.

Feminism criticizes this male totality without an account of
women's capacity to do so or to imagine or realize a more whole truth.
Feminism affirms women's point of view, in large part, by revealing,
criticizing, and explaining its impossibility. This is not a dialectical
paradox. It is a methodological expression of women's situation, in
which the struggle for consciousness is a struggle for world: for a
sexuality, a history, a culture, a community, a form of power, an
experience of the sacred. If women had consciousness or world, sex
inequality would be harmless, or all women would be feminist. Yet
women have something of both, or there would be no such thing as
feminism. Why can women know that this—life as we have known
it—is not all, not enough, not ours, not just? Now, why don't all
women?

Feminism aspires to represent the experience of all women as
women see it, yet criticizes antifeminism and misogyny, including by
women. Not all women agree with the feminist account of women's
situation, nor do all feminists agree with any single rendition of
feminism. Authority of interpretation—here, the claim to speak for all
women—is always fraught because authority is the issue male method
intended to settle. Consider the accounts of their own experience given
by right-wing women and lesbian sadomasochists. How can male
supremacy be diminishing to women when women embrace and
defend their place in it? How can dominance and submission violate
women when women eroticize it? Now what is women's point of view?
Most responses simply regard some women's views as "false
consciousness"[30] or embrace any version of women's experience which
a biological female claims. Neither an objectivist dismissal nor a
subjectivist retreat addresses the issue. Treating some women's views
as merely wrong, because they are unconscious conditioned reflections
of oppression and thus complicitous in it, posits objective ground.
Just as science devalues experience in the process of uncovering its
roots, this approach criticizes the substance of a view because it can be
accounted for by its determinants. Most things can. Both feminism
and antifeminism respond to the condition of women, so feminism is
not exempt from devaluation on the same account. The "false

consciousness" approach begs the question by taking women's self-reflections as evidence of their stake in their oppression, when the women whose self-reflections are at issue are questioning whether their condition is oppressed at all. The subjectivist approach proceeds as if women were free, or at least had considerable latitude to make or choose the meanings of their situation. Both responses arise because of an unwillingness to dismiss some women as simply deluded while granting other women the ability to see the truth. But they do nothing but answer determinism with transcendence, traditional marxism with traditional liberalism, dogmatism with tolerance. The first approach claims authority on the basis of its removal from the observed and also has no account, other than its alleged lack of involvement, of its own ability to provide an account of its own standpoint. The second approach tends to assume that women have power and are free in exactly the ways feminism has found they are not. The way in which the subject/object split undermines the feminist project here is that the "false consciousness" approach cannot explain experience as it is experienced by those who experience it, and its alternative can only reiterate the terms of that experience.

The practice of a politics of all women in the face of its theoretical impossibility in traditional terms is creating a new process of theorizing and a new form of theory. Although feminism emerges from women's particular experience, it is not subjective or partial, for no interior ground and few if any aspects of life are free of male power. Nor is feminism objective, abstract, or universal. It claims no external ground or unsexed sphere of generalization or abstraction beyond male power, nor transcendence of the specificity of each of its manifestations. How is it possible to have an engaged truth that does not simply reiterate its determinations? *Dis*engaged truth reiterates *its* determinations. Choice of method is choice of determinants—a choice that, for women as such, has been unavailable because of the subordination of women. Feminism does not begin with the premise that it is unpremised. It does not aspire to persuade an unpremised audience, because there is no such audience. Its project is to uncover and claim as valid the experience of women, the major content of which is the devaluation of women's experience.

This defines the task of feminism not only because male dominance is perhaps the most pervasive and tenacious system of power in history, but because it is metaphysically nearly perfect. Its point of view is the standard for point-of-viewlessness, its particularity the meaning of universality. Its force is exercised as consent, its authority as participation, its supremacy as the paradigm of order, its control as the definition of legitimacy. In the face of this, feminism claims the voice of women's silence, the sexuality of women's eroticized desexualization, the fullness of "lack," the centrality of women's marginality and exclusion, the public nature of privacy, the presence of women's absence. This approach is more complex than transgression, more transformative than transvaluation, deeper than mirror-imaged resistance, more affirmative than the negation of negativity. It is neither materialist nor idealist; it is feminist. Neither the transcendence of liberalism nor the determination of materialism works for women. Idealism is too unreal; women's inequality is enforced, so it cannot simply be thought out of existence, certainly not by women. Materialism is too real; women's inequality has never not existed, so women's equality never has. That is, the equality of women to men will not be scientifically provable until it is no longer necessary to do so. Women's situation offers no outside to stand on or gaze at, no inside to escape to, too much urgency to wait, no place else to go, and nothing to use but the twisted tools that have been shoved down our throats. There is no Archimedean point—or, men are their own Archimedean point, which makes it not very Archimedean. If feminism is revolutionary, this is why.

Feminism has been widely thought to contain tendencies of liberal feminism, radical feminism, and socialist feminism. But just as socialist feminism has often amounted to traditional marxism— usually Engels, applied to women—liberal feminism has been liberalism applied to women. Radical feminism is feminism. Radical feminism—after this, feminism unmodified—is methodologically post-marxist. It moves to resolve the marxist-feminist problematic on the level of method, furthering the project Sartre identified in which philosophy conserves, absorbs, and surpasses marxism so that it "cease[s] to be a particular inquiry and become[s] the foundation of all inquiry."[31] Because feminist method emerges from the concrete conditions of all women as a sex, it dissolves the individualist, naturalist, idealist, moralist structure of liberalism, the politics of which science is the epistemology. Where liberal feminism sees sexism primarily as an illusion or myth to be dispelled, an inaccuracy to be corrected, feminism sees the male point of view as fundamental to the male power to create the world in its own image, the image of its desires, not just as its delusory end product. Feminism distinctively as such comprehends that what counts as truth is produced in the interest of those with power to shape reality, and that this process is as pervasive as it is necessary as it is changeable. Unlike the scientific strain in marxism and the Kantian imperative in liberalism, which in this context share most salient features, feminism neither claims universality nor, failing that, reduces to relativity. It does not seek a generality that subsumes its particulars or an abstract theory for a science of sexism. It rejects the approach of control over nature (including women) analogized to control over society (also including women) which has grounded the "science of society" project as the paradigm for political knowledge since (at least) Descartes.

In this theory, a women is identified as a being who identifies and is identified as one whose sexuality exists for someone else, who is socially male. What is termed women's sexuality is the capacity to arouse desire in that someone. If what is sexual about a woman is what the male point of view requires for excitement, for arousal and satisfaction, have male requirements so usurped its terms as to have become them? Considering women's sexuality in this way forces confrontation with whether there is, in the possessive sense of "women's," any such thing. Is women's sexuality its absence? If being for another is women's sexual construction, it can be no more escaped by separatism, men's temporary concrete absence, than it can be eliminated or qualified by sexual permissiveness, which, in this context, looks like women emulating male roles. As Susan Sontag put it:

> The question is: what sexuality are women to be liberated to enjoy? Merely to remove the onus placed upon the sexual expressiveness of women is a hollow victory if the sexuality they become freer to enjoy remains the old one that converts women into objects . . . This already "freer" sexuality mostly reflects a spurious idea of freedom: the right of each person, briefly, to exploit and dehumanize someone else. Without a change in the very norms of sexuality, the liberation of women is a meaningless goal. Sex as such is not liberating for women. Neither is more sex.[32]

Does removing or revising gender constraints upon sexual expression change or even challenge its norms? This question ultimately is one of social determination in the broadest sense: its mechanism, permeability, specificity, and totality. When women engage in ritualized sexual dominance and submission with each other, does that express the male supremacist structure or subvert it? (If Blacks owned Black slaves, would that express the white supremacist structure or subvert it?) The answer for gender depends upon whether one has a social or biological definition of gender and sexuality. Lesbian sex, simply as sex between women, given a social definition of gender and sexuality, does not by definition transcend the erotization of dominance and submission and their social equation with masculinity and femininity.[33] The aphorism "Feminism is the theory; lesbianism is the practice"[34] accepts a simplistic view of the relation between theory and practice. Feminism reconceptualizes the connection between being and thinking such that it may be more accurate to say that feminism provides the epistemology of which lesbianism is an ontology. But on a deeper level of feminism, the epistemology/ontology distinction collapses altogether. What is a purely ontological category, a category of "being" free of social perception? Surely not the self/other distinction. Ultimately, the feminist approach turns social inquiry into a political hermeneutics: inquiry into situated meaning, in which the inquiry itself participates. A feminist political hermeneutics would be a theory of the answer to the question, "What does it mean?" that would comprehend that the first question to address is, "To whom?" within a context that comprehends gender as a social division of power.[35]

If women are socially defined such that female sexuality cannot be lived or spoken or felt or even somatically sensed apart from its enforced definition, so that it is its own lack, then there is no such thing as a woman as such; there are only walking embodiments of men's projected needs. Under male supremacy, asking whether there is, socially, a female sexuality is the same as asking whether women exist. Methodologically, the concept that the personal is political is the feminist answer to this question. Relinquishing all instinctual, natural, transcendental, and divine authority, this concept grounds women's sexuality on purely relational terrain, anchoring women's power and accounting for women's discontent in the same world they stand against. The personal as political is not a simile, not a metaphor, and not an analogy. It does not mean that what occurs in personal life is similar to, or comparable with, what occurs in the public arena. It is not an application of categories from public life to the private world, as when Engels (followed by Bebel) says that in the family the husband is the bourgeois and the wife represents the proletariat.[36] Nor is it an equation of two spheres that remain analytically distinct, as when Wilhelm Reich interpreted state behavior in sexual terms,[37] or a one-way infusion of one sphere into the other, as when Harold Lasswell interpreted political behavior as the displacement of personal problems into public objects.[38] It means that women's distinctive experience as women occurs within that sphere that has been socially lived as the personal—private, emotional, interiorized, particular, individuated, intimate—so that what it is to know the politics of woman's situation is to know women's personal lives, particularly women's sexual lives.

The substantive principle governing the authentic politics of women's personal lives is pervasive powerlessness to men, expressed and reconstituted daily as sexuality. To say that the personal is political means that gender as a division of power is discoverable and verifiable through women's intimate experience of sexual objectification, which is definitive of and synonymous with women's lives as gender female. Thus, to feminism, the personal is epistemologically the political, and its epistemology is its politics. Feminism, on this level, is the theory of women's point of view. It is the theory of Judy Grahn's "common woman" speaking Adrienne Rich's "common language."[39] Consciousness raising understood as process rather than as thing is its quintessential expression.

Feminism does not appropriate an existing method—such as scientific method—and apply it to a different sphere of society to reveal its preexisting political aspect. Consciousness raising not only comes to know different things as politics; it comes to know them in a different way. Women's experience of politics, of life as sex object,[40] gives rise to its own method of appropriating that reality: feminist method. As its own kind of social analysis, within yet outside the male paradigm, as women's lives are, feminist method has a distinctive theory of the relation between method and truth, the individual and her social surroundings, the presence and place of the natural and spiritual in culture and society, and social being and causality itself. Having been objectified as sexual beings while stigmatized as ruled by subjective passions, women reject the distinction between knowing subject and known object—the division between subjective and objective postures—as the means to comprehend social life. Disaffected from objectivity, having been its prey, but excluded from its world through relegation to subjective inwardness, women's interest lies in overthrowing *the distinction itself*. A feminism that seeks only to affirm subjectivity as the equal of objectivity, or to create for itself a subject rather than an object status, seeks to overturn hierarchy while leaving difference, the difference hierarchy has created, intact.

Proceeding connotatively and analytically at the same time, consciousness raising is at once commonsense expression and critical articulation of concepts. Taking situated feelings and common (both ordinary and shared) detail as the matter of political analysis, it explores terrain that is most damaged, most contaminated, yet therefore most one's own, most intimately known, most open to reclamation. The process can be described as a collective "sympathetic internal experience of the gradual construction of [the] system according to its inner necessity,"[41] as a strategy for deconstructing it.

Through consciousness raising, women grasp the collective reality of women's condition from within the perspective of that experience, not from outside it. The claim that a sexual politics exists and is socially fundamental is grounded in the claim of feminism *to* women's perspective, not apart from it. Its claim to women's perspective is its claim to truth.[42] In its account of itself, women's point of view contains a duality analogous to that of the marxist proletariat: determined by the reality the theory explodes, it thereby claims special access to that reality. Feminism does not see its view as subjective, partial, or undetermined but as a critique of the purported generality, disinterestedness, and universality of previous accounts. These have not so much been half right as they have invoked a wrong because partial whole. Feminism not only challenges masculine partiality but questions the universality imperative itself. Aperspectivity is revealed as a strategy of male hegemony.[43]

"Representation of the world," Beauvoir wrote, "like the world itself, is the work of men; they describe it from their own point of view, which they confuse with absolute truth."[44] The parallel between representation and construction should be sustained: men create the world from their own point of view, which then becomes the truth to be described. This is a closed system, not anyone's confusion. Power to create the world from one's point of view, particularly from the point of view of one's pleasure, is power in its male form.[45] The male epistemological stance, which corresponds to the world it creates, is objectivity: the ostensibly noninvolved stance, the view from a distance and from no particular perspective, apparently transparent to its reality. It does not comprehend its own perspectivity, does not recognize what it sees as subject like itself, or that the way it apprehends its world is a form of its subjugation and presupposes it. The objectively knowable is object. Woman through male eyes is sex object, that by which man knows himself at once as man and as subject. What is objectively known corresponds to the world and can be verified by being pointed to (as science does) because the world itself is controlled from the same point of view.

Combining, like any form of power, legitimation with force, male power extends beneath the representation of reality to its construction: it makes women (as it were) and so verifies (makes true) who women "are" in its view, simultaneously confirming its way of being and its vision of truth, as it creates the social reality that supports both. This works much like the way the social relations of production operate as epistemology, presenting the commodity form as objective thing rather than as congealed labor: "It is a definite social relation between men, that assumes, in their eyes, the fantastic form of a relation between things."[46] Except here the person is the product. This location situates women very differently from men with regard to epistemic problems. Men's power to force the world to be any way their mind can invent means that they are forever wondering what is really going on out there. Did their mind invent reality or discover it? Lesek Kolakowski, a contemporary marxist, says that because man's knowing the world comes from relating to it as an object of his needs, "we can say that in all the universe man cannot find a well so deep that, leaning over it, he does not discover at the bottom his own face."[47] As liberal theory has looked for the truth of women in the mirror of nature, left theory has looked for the truth of women in the mirror of social materiality. In nature, liberalism discovered the female; in society, the left discovered the feminine. Having located a ground for women's condition within women's inequality, these theories speak feminism in the liberal voice, feminism in the left voice. Feminism unmodified reveals their nature and their society to be mirrors of each other: the male gender looking at itself looking at itself. In other words, men have Cartesian doubt for good reason.[48] As Carolyn Porter has observed of Heisenbergian uncertainty, a contemporary form of this anxiety, "indeterminacy constitutes a scandal for science precisely because it reconstitutes the objective world as one including the subject."[49] Feminism is surely that kind of scandal for a reality that is constituted by men as they apprehend it.[50]

Women, however, have the opposite problem from Descartes. The objective world is not a reflection of women's subjectivity, if indeed women—subjected, defined by subjectivism, and not having been permitted to be a subject—can be said to possess a subjectivity. Epistemologically speaking, women know the male world is out there because it hits them in the face. No matter how they think about it, try to think it out of existence or into a different shape, it remains independently real, keeps forcing them into certain molds. No matter what they think or do, they cannot get out of it. It has all the indeterminacy of a bridge abutment hit at sixty miles per hour. Making a similar point on the real existence of the human world, Sartre noted in criticizing "the so-called 'positivism' which imbues today's Marxist" that "a positivist who held on to his teleological color blindness in practical life would not live very long."[51]

The eroticism that corresponds to the male side of this epistemology (or, perhaps better, the epistemology that corresponds to this eroticism), its sexual ontology, is "the use of things to experience self."[52] Women are the things and men are the self. The eroticism that corresponds to the female side of this epistemology, its sexual ontology, is, as a woman coerced into pornography put it, "You do it, you do it, and you do it; then you become it."[53] The fetish speaks feminism. Objectification makes supremacist sexuality a material reality of women's lives, not just a psychological, attitudinal, or ideological one. It obliterates the mind/matter distinction that such a division is premised upon. Like the value of a commodity, women's sexual desirability is fetishized: it is made to appear a quality of the object itself, spontaneous and inherent, independent of the social relation that creates it, uncontrolled by the force that requires it. It helps if the object cooperates: hence, the vaginal orgasm;[54] hence, faked orgasms altogether.[55] Women's sexualness, like male prowess, is no less real for being mythic. It is embodied. Commodities do have value, too, but only in the system that fetishizes them. Women's bodies possess no less real desirability—or, probably, desire. Sartre exemplifies the problem on the epistemological level: "But if I desire a house, or a glass of water, or a woman's body, how could this body, this glass, this piece of property reside in my desire and how can my desire be anything but the consciousness of these objects as desirable?"[56] Indeed. Objectivity is the methodological stance of which objectification is the social process. Sexual objectification is the primary process of the subjection of women. It unites act with word, construction with expression, perception with enforcement, myth with reality. Man fucks woman; subject verb object.

Are objectification and alienation distinguishable in this analysis? Objectification in marxist materialism is thought to be the foundation of human freedom, the work process whereby a subject becomes embodied in products and relationships.[57] Alienation is the socially contingent distortion of that process, a reification of products and relations which prevents them from being, and from being seen as, dependent on human agency.[58] But from the point of view of the object, objectification *is* alienation. For women, there is no distinction between objectification and alienation because women have not authored objectifications, they have been them. Women have been the nature, the matter, the acted upon to be subdued by the acting subject seeking to embody himself in the social world. Reification, similarly, is not merely an illusion to the reified; it is also their social reality. The alienated who can grasp self only as other is no different from the objectified who can grasp self only as thing. To be man's other *is* to be his thing. The problem of how the object can know herself as such is the same as how the alienated can know its own alienation. This, in turn, poses the problem of feminism's account of women's consciousness.

How can woman, as created, "thingified in the head,"[59] complicit in the body, see her condition as such? In order to account for women's consciousness, much less propagate it, feminism must grasp that male power produces the world before it distorts it. Women's complicity in their condition does not contradict its fundamental unacceptability if women have little choice but to become persons who then freely choose women's roles. For this reason, the reality of women's oppression is, finally, neither demonstrable nor refutable empirically. Until this problem is confronted on the level of method, criticism of what exists can be undercut by pointing to the reality to be criticized. Women's bondage, degradation, damage, complicity, and inferiority—together with the possibility of resistance, movement, or exceptions—will operate as barriers to consciousness rather than as means of access to what women need to become conscious of in order to change.

If this analysis is correct, to be realistic about sexuality socially is to see it from the male point of view, and to be feminist is to do so with a critical awareness that that is what one is doing. Because male power creates the reality of the world to which feminist insights, when accurate, refer, feminist theory will simply capture that reality but expose it as specifically male for the first time. For example, men say all women are whores; feminism observes that men have the power to make prostitution women's definitive condition. Men define women as sexual beings; feminism comprehends that femininity is sexual. Men see rape as intercourse; feminism observes that men make much intercourse rape.[60] Men say women desire to be degraded; feminism sees female masochism as the ultimate success of male supremacy and puzzle (and marvel) over its failures. The feminist use of the verb "to be" is this kind of "is."

Feminism has unmasked maleness as a form of power that is both omnipotent and nonexistent, an unreal thing with very real consequences. Zora Neale Hurston captured its two-sidedness: "The town had a basketfull of feelings good and bad about Joe's positions and possessions, but none had the temerity to challenge him. They bowed down to him rather, because he was all of these things, and then again he was all of these things because the town bowed down."[61] "Positions and possessions" and rulership create each other in relation. To answer an old question—how is value created and distributed?—Marx needed to create a new account of the social world. To answer an equally old question, or rather to question an equally old reality—what explains the inequality of women to men? or, how does gender become domination and domination become sex? or, what is male power?—feminism needs to create an entirely new account of the political world. Feminism thus stands in relation to marxism as marxism does to classical political economy: its final conclusion and ultimate critique. Compared with marxism, the place of thought and things in method and reality is reversed in a transformation and seizure of power which penetrates subject with object and theory with practice. In a dual motion, feminism turns marxism inside out and on its head.

# 7 | *Sexuality*

then she says (and this is what I live through over
    and over)—she says: *I do not know if sex is an
    illusion*
*I do not know*
*who I was when I did those things*
*or who I said I was*
*or whether I willed to feel*
*what I had read about*
*or who in fact was there with me*
*or whether I knew, even then*
*that there was doubt about these things*
                        —Adrienne Rich, "Dialogue"

I had always been fond of her in the most innocent, asexual
way. It was as if her body was always entirely hidden behind
her radiant mind, the modesty of her behavior, and her taste
in dress. She had never offered me the slightest chink
through which to view the glow of her nakedness. And now
suddenly the butcher knife of fear had slit her open. She was
as open to me as the carcass of a heifer slit down the middle
and hanging on a hook. There we were . . . and suddenly I
felt a violent desire to make love to her. Or to be more exact,
a violent desire to rape her.
                        —Milan Kundera, *The Book of
                        Laughter and Forgetting*

[S]he had thought of something, something about the body,
about the passions which it was unfitting for her as a woman
to say. Men, her reason told her, would be shocked . . .
telling the truth about my own experiences as a body, I do
not think I solved. I doubt that any woman has solved it yet.
The obstacles against her are still immensely powerful—and
yet they are very difficult to define.
                        —Virginia Woolf, "Professions for
                        Women"

What is it about women's experience that produces a distinctive perspective on social reality? How is an angle of vision and an interpretive hermeneutics of social life created in the group, women? What happens to women to give them a particular interest in social arrangements, something to have a consciousness of? How are the qualities we know as male and female socially created and enforced on an everyday level? Sexual objectification of women—first in the world, then in the head, first in visual appropriation, then in forced sex, finally in sexual murder[1]—provides answers.

Male dominance is sexual. Meaning: men in particular, if not men alone, sexualize hierarchy; gender is one. As much a sexual theory of gender as a gendered theory of sex, this is the theory of sexuality that has grown out of consciousness raising. Recent feminist work, both interpretive and empirical, on rape, battery, sexual harassment, sexual abuse of children, prostitution and pornography, support it.[2] These practices, taken together, express and actualize the distinctive power of men over women in society; their effective permissibility confirms and extends it. If one believes women's accounts of sexual use and abuse by men;[3] if the pervasiveness of male sexual violence against women substantiated in these studies is not denied, minimized, or excepted as deviant or episodic;[4] if the fact that only 7.8 percent of women in the United States are not sexually assaulted or harassed in their lifetimes is considered not ignorable or inconsequential;[5] if the women to whom it happens are not considered expendable; if violation of women is understood as sexualized on some level—then sexuality itself can no longer be regarded as unimplicated. Nor can the meaning of practices of sexual violence be categorized away as violence not sex. The male sexual role, this information and analysis taken together suggest, centers on aggressive intrusion on those with less power. Such acts of dominance are experienced as sexually arousing, as sex itself.[6] They therefore are. The new knowledge on the sexual violation of women by men thus frames an inquiry into the place of sexuality in gender and of gender in sexuality.

A feminist theory of sexuality based on these data locates sexuality within a theory of gender inequality, meaning the social hierarchy of men over women. To make a theory feminist, it is not enough that it be authored by a biological female, nor that it describe female sexuality as different from (if equal to) male sexuality, or as if sexuality in women ineluctably exists in some realm beyond, beneath, above, behind—in any event, fundamentally untouched and unmoved by— an unequal social order. A theory of sexuality becomes feminist methodologically, meaning feminist in the post-marxist sense, to the extent it treats sexuality as a social construct of male power: defined by men, forced on women, and constitutive of the meaning of gender. Such an approach centers feminism on the perspective of the subordi- nation of women to men as it identifies sex—that is, the sexuality of dominance and submission—as crucial, as a fundamental, as on some level definitive, in that process. Feminist theory becomes a project of analyzing that situation in order to face it for what it is, in order to change it.

Focusing on gender inequality without a sexual account of its dynamics, as most work has, one could criticize the sexism of existing theories of sexuality and emerge knowing that men author scripts to their own advantage, women and men act them out; that men set conditions, women and men have their behavior conditioned; that men develop developmental categories through which men develop, and women develop or not; that men are socially allowed selves hence identities with personalities into which sexuality is or is not well integrated, women being that which is or is not integrated, that through the alterity of which a self experiences itself as having an identity; that men have object relations, women are the objects of those relations; and so on. Following such critique, one could attempt to invert or correct the premises or applications of these theories to make them gender neutral, even if the reality to which they refer looks more like the theories—once their gender specificity is revealed—than it looks gender neutral. Or, one could attempt to enshrine a distinctive "women's reality" as if it really were permitted to exist as something more than one dimension of women's response to a condition of powerlessness. Such exercises would be revealing and instructive, even deconstructive, but to limit feminism to correcting sex bias by acting in theory as if male power did not exist in fact, including by valorizing in writing what women have had little choice but to be limited to becoming in life, is to limit feminist theory the way sexism limits women's lives: to a response to terms men set.

A distinctively feminist theory conceptualizes social reality, including sexual reality, on its own terms. The question is, what are they? If women have been substantially deprived not only of their own experience but of terms of their own in which to view it, then a feminist theory of sexuality which seeks to understand women's situation in order to change it must first identify and criticize the construct "sexuality" as a construct that has circumscribed and defined experience as well as theory. This requires capturing it in the world, in its situated social meanings, as it is being constructed in life on a daily basis. It must be studied in its experienced empirical existence, not just in the texts of history (as Foucault does), in the social psyche (as Lacan does), or in language (as Derrida does). Sexual meaning is not made only, or even primarily, by words and in texts. It is made in social relations of power in the world, through which process gender is also produced. In feminist terms, the fact that male power has power means that the interests of male sexuality construct what sexuality as such means, including the standard way it is allowed and recognized to be felt and expressed and experienced, in a way that determines women's biographies, including sexual ones. Existing theories, until they grasp this, will not only misattribute what they call female sexuality to women as such, as if it were not imposed on women daily; they will also participate in enforcing the hegemony of the social construct "desire," hence its product, "sexuality," hence its construct "woman," on the world.

The gender issue, in this analysis, becomes the issue of what is taken to be "sexuality"; what sex means and what is meant by sex, when, how, with whom, and with what consequences to whom. Such questions are almost never systematically confronted, even in discourses that purport feminist awareness. What sex is—how it comes to be attached and attributed to what it is, embodied and practiced as it is, contextualized in the ways it is, signifying and referring to what it does—is taken as a baseline, a given, except in explanations of what happened when it is thought to have gone wrong. It is as if "erotic," for example, can be taken as having an understood referent, although it is never defined, except to imply that it is universal yet individual, ultimately variable and plastic, essentially indefinable but overwhelmingly positive. "Desire," the vicissitudes of which are endlessly extolled and philosophized in culture high and low, is not seen as fundamentally problematic or as calling for explanation on the concrete, interpersonal operative level, unless (again) it is supposed to be there and is not. To list and analyze what seem to be the essential elements for male sexual arousal, what has to be there for the penis to work, seems faintly blasphemous, like a pornographer doing market research. Sex is supposed both too individual and too universally transcendent for that. To suggest that the sexual might be continuous with something other than sex itself—something like politics—is seldom done, is treated as detumescent, even by feminists. It is as if sexuality comes from the stork.

Sexuality, in feminist light, is not a discrete sphere of interaction or feeling or sensation or behavior in which preexisting social divisions may or may not be played out. It is a pervasive dimension of social life, one that permeates the whole, a dimension along which gender occurs and through which gender is socially constituted; it is a dimension along which other social divisions, like race and class, partly play themselves out. Dominance eroticized defines the imperatives of its masculinity, submission eroticized defines its femininity. So many distinctive features of women's status as second class—the restriction and constraint and contortion, the servility and the display, the self-mutilation and requisite presentation of self as a beautiful thing, the enforced passivity, the humiliation—are made into the content of sex for women. Being a thing for sexual use is fundamental to it. This approach identifies not just a sexuality that is shaped under conditions of gender inequality but reveals this sexuality itself to be the dynamic of the inequality of the sexes. It is to argue that the excitement at reduction of a person to a thing, to less than a human being, as socially defined, is its fundamental motive force. It is to argue that sexual difference is a function of sexual dominance. It is to argue a sexual theory of the distribution of social power by gender, in which this sexuality that is sexuality is substantially what makes the gender division be what it is, which is male dominant, wherever it is, which is nearly everywhere.

Across cultures, in this perspective, sexuality is whatever a given culture or subculture defines it as. The next question concerns its relation to gender as a division of power. Male dominance appears to exist cross-culturally, if in locally particular forms. Across cultures, is whatever defines women as "different" the same as whatever defines women as "inferior" the same as whatever defines women's "sexuality"? Is that which defines gender inequality as merely the sex difference also the content of the erotic, cross-culturally? In this view, the feminist theory of sexuality is its theory of politics, its distinctive contribution to social and political explanation. To explain gender inequality in terms of "sexual politics"[7] is to advance not only a political theory of the sexual that defines gender but also a sexual theory of the political to which gender is fundamental.

In this approach, male power takes the social form of what men as a gender want sexually, which centers on power itself, as socially defined. In capitalist countries, it includes wealth. Masculinity is having it; femininity is not having it. Masculinity precedes male as femininity precedes female, and male sexual desire defines both. Specifically, "woman" is defined by what male desire requires for arousal and satisfaction and is socially tautologous with "female sexuality" and "the female sex." In the permissible ways a woman can be treated, the ways that are socially considered not violations but appropriate to her nature, one finds the particulars of male sexual interests and requirements. In the concomitant sexual paradigm, the ruling norms of sexual attraction and expression are fused with gender identity formation and affirmation, such that sexuality equals heterosexuality equals the sexuality of (male) dominance and (female) submission.

Post-Lacan, actually post-Foucault, it has become customary to affirm that sexuality is socially constructed.[8] Seldom specified is what, socially, it is constructed of, far less who does the constructing or how, when, or where.[9] When capitalism is the favored social construct, sexuality is shaped and controlled and exploited and repressed by capitalism; not, capitalism creates sexuality as we know it. When sexuality is a construct of discourses of power, gender is never one of them; force is central to its deployment but through repressing it, not through constituting it; speech is not concretely investigated for its participation in this construction process. Power is everywhere therefore nowhere, diffuse rather than pervasively hegemonic. "Constructed" seems to mean influenced by, directed, channeled, as a highway constructs traffic patterns. Not: Why cars? Who's driving? Where's everybody going? What makes mobility matter? Who can own a car? Are all these accidents not very accidental? Although there are partial exceptions (but disclaimers notwithstanding) the typical model of sexuality which is tacitly accepted remains deeply Freudian[10] and essentialist: sexuality is an innate sui generis primary natural prepolitical unconditioned[11] drive divided along the biological gender line, centering on heterosexual intercourse, that is, penile intromission, full actualization of which is repressed by civilization. Even if the sublimation aspect of this theory is rejected, or the reasons for the repression are seen to vary (for the survival of civilization or to maintain fascist control or to keep capitalism moving), sexual expression is implicitly seen as the expression of something that is to a significant extent pre-social and is socially denied its full force. Sexuality remains largely pre-cultural and universally invariant, social only in that it needs society to take socially specific forms. The impetus itself is a hunger, an appetite founded on a need; what it is specifically hungry for and how it is satisfied is then open to endless cultural and individual variance, like cuisine, like cooking.

Allowed/not allowed is this sexuality's basic ideological axis. The fact that sexuality is ideologically bounded is known. That these are its axes, central to the way its "drive" is driven, and that this is fundamental to gender and gender is fundamental to it, is not.[12] Its basic normative assumption is that whatever is considered sexuality should be allowed to be "expressed." Whatever is called sex is attributed a normatively positive valence, an affirmative valuation. This *ex cathedra* assumption, affirmation of which appears indispensable to one's credibility on any subject that gets near the sexual, means that sex as such (whatever it is) is good—natural, healthy, positive, appropriate, pleasurable, wholesome, fine, one's own, and to be approved and expressed. This, sometimes characterized as "sex-positive," is, rather obviously, a value judgment.

Kinsey and his followers, for example, clearly thought (and think) the more sex the better. Accordingly, they trivialize even most of those cases of rape and child sexual abuse they discern as such, decry women's sexual refusal as sexual inhibition, and repeatedly interpret women's sexual disinclination as "restrictions" on men's natural sexual activity, which left alone would emulate (some) animals.[13] Followers of the neo-Freudian derepression imperative have similarly identified the frontier of sexual freedom with transgression of social restraints on access, with making the sexually disallowed allowed, especially male sexual access to anything. The struggle to have everything sexual allowed in a society we are told would collapse if it were, creates a sense of resistance to, and an aura of danger around, violating the powerless. If we knew the boundaries were phony, existed only to eroticize the targeted transgressable, would penetrating them feel less sexy? Taboo and crime may serve to eroticize what would otherwise feel about as much like dominance as taking candy from a baby. Assimilating actual powerlessness to male prohibition, to male power, provides the appearance of resistance, which makes overcoming possible, while never undermining the reality of power, or its dignity, by giving the powerless actual power. The point is, allowed/not allowed becomes the ideological axis along which sexuality is experienced when and because sex— gender and sexuality—is about power.

.One version of the derepression hypothesis that purports feminism is: civilization having been male dominated, female sexuality has been repressed, not allowed. Sexuality as such still centers on what would otherwise be considered the reproductive act, on intercourse: penetration of the erect penis into the vagina (or appropriate substitute orifices), followed by thrusting to male ejaculation. If reproduction actually had anything to do with what sex was for, it would not happen every night (or even twice a week) for forty or fifty years, nor would prostitutes exist. "We had sex three times" typically means the man entered the woman three times and orgasmed three times. Female sexuality in this model refers to the presence of this theory's "sexuality," or the desire to be so treated, in biological females; "female" is somewhere between an adjective and a noun, half possessive and half biological ascription. Sexual freedom means women are allowed to behave as freely as men to express this sexuality, to have it allowed, that is (hopefully) shamelessly and without social constraints to initiate genital drive satisfaction through heterosexual intercourse.[14] Hence, the liberated woman. Hence, the sexual revolution.

The pervasiveness of such assumptions about sexuality throughout otherwise diverse methodological traditions is suggested by the following comment by a scholar of violence against women:

If women were to escape the culturally stereotyped role of disinterest in and resistance to sex and to take on an assertive role in expressing their own sexuality, rather than leaving it to the assertiveness of men, it would contribute to the reduction of rape . . . First, and most obviously, voluntary sex would be available to more men, thus reducing the "need" for rape. Second, and probably more important, it would help to reduce the confounding of sex and aggression.[15]

In this view, somebody must be assertive for sex to happen. Voluntary sex—sexual equality—means equal sexual aggression. If women freely expressed "their own sexuality," more heterosexual intercourse would be initiated. Women's "resistance" to sex is an imposed cultural stereotype, not a form of political struggle. Rape is occasioned by women's resistance, not by men's force; or, male force, hence rape, is created by women's resistance to sex. Men would rape less if they got more voluntarily compliant sex from women. Corollary: the force in rape is not sexual to men.

Underlying this quotation lurks the view, as common as it is tacit, that if women would just accept the contact men now have to rape to get—if women would stop resisting or (in one of the pornographers' favorite scenarios) become sexual aggressors—rape would wither away. On one level, this is a definitionally obvious truth. When a woman accepts what would be rape if she did not accept it, what happens is sex. If women were to accept forced sex as sex, "voluntary sex would be available to more men." If such a view is not implicit in this text, it is a mystery how women equally aggressing against men sexually would eliminate, rather than double, the confounding of sex and aggression. Without such an assumption, only the confounding of sexual aggression with gender would be eliminated. If women no longer resisted male sexual aggression, the confounding of sex with aggression would, indeed, be so epistemologically complete that it would be eliminated. No woman would ever be sexually violated, because sexual violation would be sex. The situation might resemble the one evoked by a society categorized as "rape-free" in part because the men assert there is no rape there: "our women never resist."[16] Such pacification also occurs in "rape-prone" societies like the United States, where some force may be perceived as force, but only above certain threshold standards.[17]

While intending the opposite, some feminists have encouraged and participated in this type of analysis by conceiving rape as violence, not sex.[18] While this approach gave needed emphasis to rape's previously effaced elements of power and dominance, it obscured its elements of sex. Aside from failing to answer the rather obvious question, if it is violence not sex, why didn't he just hit her? this approach made it impossible to see that violence is sex when it is practiced as sex.[19] This is obvious once what sexuality is, is understood as a matter of what it means and how it is interpreted. To say rape is violence not sex preserves the "sex is good" norm by simply distinguishing forced sex as "not sex," whether it means sex to the perpetrator or even, later, to the victim, who has difficulty experiencing sex without reexperiencing the rape. Whatever is sex cannot be violent; whatever is violent cannot be sex. This analytic wish-fulfillment makes it possible for rape to be opposed by those who would save sexuality from the rapists while leaving the sexual fundamentals of male dominance intact.

While much previous work on rape has analyzed it as a problem of inequality between the sexes but not as a problem of unequal sexuality on the basis of gender,[20] other contemporary explorations of sexuality that purport to be feminist lack comprehension either of gender as a form of social power or of the realities of sexual violence. For instance, the editors of *Powers of Desire* take sex "as a central form of expression, one that defines identity and is seen as a primary source of energy and pleasure."[21] This may be how it "is seen," but it is also how the editors, operatively, see it. As if women choose sexuality as definitive of identity. As if it is as much a form of women's "expression" as it is men's. As if violation and abuse are not equally central to sexuality as women live it.

The *Diary* of the Barnard conference on sexuality pervasively equates sexuality with "pleasure." "Perhaps the overall question we need to ask is: how do women . . . negotiate sexual pleasure?"[22] As if women under male supremacy have power to. As if "negotiation" is a form of freedom. As if pleasure and how to get it, rather than dominance and how to end it, is the "overall" issue sexuality presents feminism. As if women do just need a good fuck. In these texts, taboos are treated as real restrictions —as things that really are not allowed— instead of as guises under which hierarchy is eroticized. The domain of the sexual is divided into "restriction, repression, and danger" on the one hand and "exploration, pleasure, and agency" on the other.[23] This division parallels the ideological forms through which dominance and submission are eroticized, variously socially coded as heterosexuality's male/female, lesbian culture's butch/femme, and sadomasochism's top/bottom.[24] Speaking in role terms, the one who pleasures in the illusion of freedom and security within the reality of danger is the "girl"; the one who pleasures in the reality of freedom and security within the illusion of danger is the "boy." That is, the *Diary* uncritically adopts as an analytic tool the central dynamic of the phenomenon it purports to be analyzing. Presumably, one is to have a sexual experience of the text.

The terms of these discourses preclude or evade crucial feminist questions. What do sexuality and gender inequality have to do with each other? How do dominance and submission become sexualized, or, why is hierarchy sexy? How does it get attached to male and female? Why does sexuality center on intercourse, the reproductive act by physical design? Is masculinity the enjoyment of violation, femininity the enjoyment of being violated? Is that the social meaning of intercourse? Do "men love death"?[25] Why? What is the etiology of heterosexuality in women? Is its pleasure women's stake in subordination?

Taken together and taken seriously, feminist inquiries into the realities of rape, battery, sexual harassment, incest, child sexual abuse, prostitution, and pornography answer these questions by suggesting a theory of the sexual mechanism. Its script, learning, conditioning, developmental logos, imprinting of the microdot, its deus ex machina, whatever sexual process term defines sexual arousal itself, is force, power's expression. Force is sex, not just sexualized; force is the desire dynamic, not just a response to the desired object when desire's expression is frustrated. Pressure, gender socialization, withholding benefits, extending indulgences, the how-to books, the sex therapy are the soft end; the fuck, the fist, the street, the chains, the poverty are the hard end. Hostility and contempt, or arousal of master to slave, together with awe and vulnerability, or arousal of slave to master— these are the emotions of this sexuality's excitement. "Sadomasochism is to sex what war is to civil life: the magnificent experience," wrote Susan Sontag.[26] "[I]t is hostility—the desire, overt or hidden, to harm another person—that generates and enhances sexual excitement," wrote Robert Stoller.[27] Harriet Jacobs, a slave, speaking of sex with a white master, wrote, "It seems less demeaning to give one's self, than to submit to compulsion."[28] It is clear from the data that the force in sex and the sex in force is a matter of simple empirical description—unless one accepts that force in sex is not force anymore, it is just sex; or, if whenever a woman is forced it is what she really wants, or it or she does not matter; or, unless prior aversion or sentimentality substitutes what one wants sex to be, or will condone or countenance as sex, for what is actually happening.

To be clear: what is sexual is what gives a man an erection. Whatever it takes to make the penis shudder and stiffen with the experience of its potency is what sexuality means culturally. Whatever else does this, fear does, hostility does, hatred does, the helplessness of a child or a student or an infantilized or restrained or vulnerable woman does, revulsion does, death does. Hierarchy, a constant creation of person/thing, top/bottom, dominance/subordination relations, does. What is understood as violation, conventionally penetration and intercourse, defines the paradigmatic sexual encounter. The scenario of sexual abuse is: you do what I say. These textualities and these relations, situated within as well as creating a context of power in which they can be lived out, become sexuality. All this suggests that what is called sexuality is the dynamic of control by which male dominance—in forms that range from intimate to institutional, from a look to a rape—eroticizes and thus defines man and woman, gender identity and sexual pleasure. It is also that which maintains and defines male supremacy as a political system. Male sexual desire is thereby simultaneously created and serviced, never satisfied once and for all, while male force is romanticized, even sacralized, potentiated and naturalized, by being submerged into sex itself.

In contemporary philosophical terms, nothing is "indeterminate" in the post-structuralist sense here; it is all too determinate.[29] Nor does its reality provide just one perspective on a relativistic interpersonal world that could mean anything or its opposite.[30] The reality of pervasive sexual abuse and its erotization does not shift relative to perspective, although whether or not one will see it or accord it significance may. Interpretation varies relative to place in sexual abuse, certainly; but the fact that women are sexually abused as women, located in a social matrix of sexualized subordination, does not go away because it is often ignored or authoritatively disbelieved or interpreted out of existence. Indeed, some ideological supports for its persistence rely precisely upon techniques of social indeterminacy: no language but the obscene to describe the unspeakable; denial by the powerful casting doubt on the facticity of the injuries; actually driving its victims insane. Indeterminacy, in this light, is a neo-Cartesian mind game that raises acontextualized interpretive possibilities that have no real social meaning or real possibility of any, thus dissolving the ability to criticize the oppressiveness of actual meanings without making space for new ones. The feminist point is simple. Men are women's material conditions. If it happens to women, it happens.

Women often find ways to resist male supremacy and to expand their spheres of action. But they are never free of it. Women also embrace the standards of women's place in this regime as "our own" to varying degrees and in varying voices—as affirmation of identity and right to pleasure, in order to be loved and approved and paid, in order just to make it through another day. This, not inert passivity, is the meaning of being a victim.[31] The term is not moral: who is to blame or to be pitied or condemned or held responsible. It is not prescriptive: what we should do next. It is not strategic: how to construe the situation so it can be changed. It is not emotional: what one feels better thinking. It is descriptive: who does what to whom and gets away with it.

Thus the question Freud never asked is the question that defines sexuality in a feminist perspective: what do men want? Pornography provides an answer. Pornography permits men to have whatever they want sexually. It is their "truth about sex."[32] It connects the centrality of visual objectification to both male sexual arousal and male models of knowledge and verification, objectivity with objectification. It shows how men see the world, how in seeing it they access and possess it, and how this is an act of dominance over it. It shows what men want and gives it to them. From the testimony of the pornography, what men want is: women bound, women battered, women tortured, women humiliated, women degraded and defiled, women killed. Or, to be fair to the soft core, women sexually accessible, have-able, there for them, wanting to be taken and used, with perhaps just a little light bondage. Each violation of women—rape, battery, prostitution, child sexual abuse, sexual harassment—is made sexuality, made sexy, fun, and liberating of women's true nature in the pornography. Each specifically victimized and vulnerable group of women, each tabooed target group—Black women, Asian women, Latin women, Jewish women, pregnant women, disabled women, retarded women, poor women, old women, fat women, women in women's jobs, prostitutes, little girls—distinguishes pornographic genres and subthemes, classified according to diverse customers' favorite degradation. Women are made into and coupled with anything considered lower than human: animals, objects, children, and (yes) other women. Anything women have claimed as their own—motherhood, athletics, traditional men's jobs, lesbianism, feminism—is made specifically sexy, dangerous, provocative, punished, made men's in pornography.

Pornography is a means through which sexuality is socially constructed, a site of construction, a domain of exercise. It constructs women as things for sexual use and constructs its consumers to desperately want women to desperately want possession and cruelty and dehumanization./Inequality itself, subjection itself, hierarchy itself, objectification itself, with self-determination ecstatically relinquished, is the apparent content of women's sexual desire and desirability. "The major theme of pornography as a genre," writes Andrea Dworkin, "is male power."[33]/Women are in pornography to be violated and taken, men to violate and take them, either on screen or by camera or pen, on behalf of the viewer./Not that sexuality in life or in media never expresses love and affection; only that love and affection are not what is sexualized in this society's actual sexual paradigm, as pornography testifies to it. Violation of the powerless, intrusion on women, is. The milder forms, possession and use, the mildest of which is visual objectification, are. This sexuality of observation, visual intrusion and access, of entertainment, makes sex largely a spectator sport for its participants.

If pornography has not become sex to and from the male point of view, it is hard to explain why the pornography industry makes a known ten billion dollars a year selling it as sex mostly to men; why it is used to teach sex to child prostitutes, to recalcitrant wives and girlfriends and daughters, to medical students, and to sex offenders; why it is nearly universally classified as a subdivision of "erotic literature"; why it is protected and defended as if it were sex itself.[34] And why a prominent sexologist fears that enforcing the views of feminists against pornography in society would make men "erotically inert wimps."[35] No pornography, no male sexuality.

A feminist critique of sexuality in this sense is advanced in Andrea Dworkin's *Pornography: Men Possessing Women*. Building on her earlier identification of gender inequality as a system of social meaning,[36] an ideology lacking basis in anything other than the social reality its power constructs and maintains, she argues that sexuality is a construct of that power, given meaning by, through, and in pornography. In this perspective, pornography is not harmless fantasy or a corrupt and confused misrepresentation of otherwise natural healthy sex, nor is it fundamentally a distortion, reflection, projection, expression, representation, fantasy, or symbol of it.[37] Through pornography, among other practices, gender inequality becomes both sexual and socially real. Pornography "reveals that male pleasure is inextricably tied to victimizing, hurting, exploiting." "Dominance in the male system is pleasure." Rape is "the defining paradigm of sexuality," to avoid which boys choose manhood and homophobia.[38]

Women, who are not given a choice, are objectified; or, rather, "the object is allowed to desire, if she desires to be an object."[39] Psychology sets the proper bounds of this objectification by terming its improper excesses "fetishism," distinguishing the uses from the abuses of women.[40] Dworkin shows how the process and content of women's definition as women, as an under-class, are the process and content of their sexualization as objects for male sexual use. The mechanism is (again) force, imbued with meaning because it is the means to death;[41] and death is the ultimate sexual act, the ultimate making of a person into a thing.

Why, one wonders at this point, is intercourse "sex" at all? In pornography, conventional intercourse is one act among many; penetration is crucial but can be done with anything; penis is crucial but not necessarily in the vagina. Actual pregnancy is a minor subgeneric theme, about as important in pornography as reproduction is in rape. Thematically, intercourse is incidental in pornography, especially when compared with force, which is primary. From pornography one learns that forcible violation of women is the essence of sex. Whatever is that and does that is sex. Everything else is secondary. Perhaps the reproductive act is considered sexual because it is considered an act of forcible violation and defilement of the female distinctively as such, not because it "is" sex a priori.

To be sexually objectified means having a social meaning imposed on your being that defines you as to be sexually used, according to your desired uses, and then using you that way. Doing this is sex in the male system. Pornography is a sexual practice of this because it exists in a social system in which sex in life is no less mediated than it is in representation. There is no irreducible essence, no "just sex." If sex is a social construct of sexism, men have sex with their image of a woman. Pornography creates an accessible sexual object, the possession and consumption of which is male sexuality, to be possessed and consumed as which is female sexuality. This is not because pornography depicts objectified sex, but because it creates the experience of a sexuality which is itself objectified./The appearance of choice or consent, with their attribution to inherent nature, is crucial in concealing the reality of force. Love of violation, variously termed female masochism and consent, comes to define female sexuality,[42] legitimating this political system by concealing the force on which it is based./

In this system, a victim, usually female, always feminized, is "never forced, only actualized."[43] Women whose attributes particularly fixate men—such as women with large breasts—are seen as full of sexual desire. Women men want, want men. Women fake vaginal orgasms, the only "mature" sexuality, because men demand that women enjoy vaginal penetration.[44] Raped women are seen as asking for it: if a man wanted her, she must have wanted him. Men force women to become sexual objects, "that thing which causes erection, then hold themselves helpless and powerless when aroused by her."[45] Men who sexually harass say women sexually harass them. They mean they are aroused by women who turn them down. This elaborate projective system of demand characteristics—taken to pinnacles like fantasizing a clitoris in a woman's throat[46] so that men can enjoy forced fellatio in real life, assured that women do too—is surely a delusional structure deserving of serious psychological study. Instead, it is women who resist it who are studied, seen as in need of explanation and adjustment, stigmatized as inhibited and repressed and asexual. The assumption that in matters sexual women really want what men want from women, makes male force against women in sex invisible. It makes rape sex./Women's sexual "reluctance, dislike, and frigidity," women's puritanism and prudery in the face of this sex, is "the silent rebellion of women against the force of the penis . . . an ineffective rebellion, but a rebellion nonetheless."[47]

Nor is homosexuality without stake in this gendered sexual system. Putting to one side the obviously gendered content of expressly adopted roles, clothing, and sexual mimicry, to the extent the gender of a sexual object is crucial to arousal, the structure of social power which stands behind and defines gender is hardly irrelevant, even if it is rearranged. Some have argued that lesbian sexuality—meaning here simply women having sex with women, not with men—solves the problem of gender by eliminating men from women's voluntary sexual encounters.[48] Yet women's sexuality remains constructed under conditions of male supremacy; women remain socially defined as women in relation to men; the definition of women as men's inferiors remains sexual even if not heterosexual, whether men are present at the time or not. To the extent gay men choose men because they are men, the meaning of masculinity is affirmed as well as undermined. It may also be that sexuality is so gender marked that it carries dominance and submission with it, whatever the gender of its participants.

Each structural requirement of this sexuality as revealed in pornography is professed in recent defenses of sadomasochism, described by proponents as that sexuality in which "the basic dynamic . . . is the power dichotomy."[49] Exposing the prohibitory underpinnings on which this violation model of the sexual depends, one advocate says: "We select the most frightening, disgusting or unacceptable activities and transmute them into pleasure." The relational dynamics of sadomasochism do not even negate the paradigm of male dominance, but conform precisely to it: the ecstasy in domination ("I like to hear someone ask for mercy or protection"); the enjoyment of inflicting psychological as well as physical torture ("I want to see the confusion, the anger, the turn-on, the helplessness"); the expression of belief in the inferior's superiority belied by the absolute contempt ("the bottom must be my superior . . . playing a bottom who did not demand my respect and admiration would be like eating rotten fruit"); the degradation and consumption of women through sex ("she feeds me the energy I need to dominate and abuse her"); the health and personal growth rationale ("it's a healing process"); the anti-puritan radical therapy justification ("I was taught to dread sex . . . It is shocking and profoundly satisfying to commit this piece of rebellion, to take pleasure exactly as I want it, to exact it like tribute"); the bipolar doublethink in which the top enjoys "sexual service" while "the will to please is the bottom's source of pleasure." And the same bottom line of all top-down sex: "I want to be in control." The statements are from a female sadist. The good news is, it is not biological.

As pornography connects sexuality with gender in social reality, the feminist critique of pornography connects feminist work on violence against women with its inquiry into women's consciousness and gender roles. It is not only that women are the principal targets of rape, which by conservative definition happens to almost half of all women at least once in their lives. It is not only that over one-third of all women are sexually molested by older trusted male family members

or friends or authority figures as an early, perhaps initiatory, interpersonal sexual encounter. It is not only that at least the same
percentage, as adult women, are battered in homes by male intimates.
It is not only that about one-fifth of American women have been or are
known to be prostitutes, and most cannot get out of it. It is not only
that 85 percent of working women will be sexually harassed on the
job, many physically, at some point in their working lives.[50] All this
documents the extent and terrain of abuse and the effectively
unrestrained and systematic sexual aggression by less than one-half of
the population against the other more than half. It suggests that it is
basically allowed.

It does not by itself show that availability for this treatment defines
the identity attributed to that other half of the population; or, that
such treatment, all this torment and debasement, is socially considered
not only rightful but enjoyable, and is in fact enjoyed by the dominant
half; or, that the ability to engage in such behaviors defines the
identity of that half. And not only of that half. Now consider the
content of gender roles. All the social requirements for male sexual
arousal and satisfaction are identical with the gender definition of
"female." All the essentials of the male gender role are also the
qualities sexualized as "male" in male dominant sexuality. If gender is
a social construct, and sexuality is a social construct, and the question
is, of what is each constructed, the fact that their contents are
identical—not to mention that the word *sex* refers to both—might be
more than a coincidence.

As to gender, what is sexual about pornography is what is unequal
about social life. To say that pornography sexualizes gender and
genders sexuality means that it provides a concrete social process
through which gender and sexuality become functions of each other.
Gender and sexuality, in this view, become two different shapes taken
by the single social equation of male with dominance and female with
submission. Feeling this as identity, acting it as role, inhabiting and
presenting it as self, is the domain of gender. Enjoying it as the erotic,
centering upon when it elicits genital arousal, is the domain of
sexuality. Inequality is what is sexualized through pornography; it is
what is sexual about it. The more unequal, the more sexual. The
violence against women in pornography is an expression of gender
hierarchy, the extremity of the hierarchy expressed and created
through the extremity of the abuse, producing the extremity of the

male sexual response. Pornography's multiple variations on and departures from the male dominant/female submissive sexual/gender theme are not exceptions to these gender regularities. They affirm them. The capacity of gender reversals (dominatrixes) and inversions (homosexuality) to stimulate sexual excitement is derived precisely from their mimicry or parody or negation or reversal of the standard arrangement. This affirms rather than undermines or qualifies the standard sexual arrangement as the standard sexual arrangement, the definition of sex, the standard from which all else is defined, that in which sexuality as such inheres.

Such formal data as exist on the relationship between pornography and male sexual arousal tend to substantiate this connection between gender hierarchy and male sexuality. Normal men viewing pornography over time in laboratory settings become more aroused to scenes of rape than to scenes of explicit but not expressly violent sex, even if (especially if?) the woman is shown as hating it.[51] As sustained exposure perceptually inures subjects to the violent component in expressly violent sexual material, its sexual arousal value remains or increases. "On the first day, when they see women being raped and aggressed against, it bothers them. By day five, it does not bother them at all, in fact, they enjoy it."[52] Sexual material that is seen as nonviolent, by contrast, is less arousing to begin with and becomes progressively less arousing over time, after which exposure to sexual violence is sexually arousing.[53] Viewing sexual material containing express aggression against women makes normal men more willing to aggress against women.[54] It also makes them see a female rape victim as less human, more objectlike, less worthy, less injured, and more to blame for the rape. Sexually explicit material that is not seen as expressly violent but presents women as hysterically responsive to male sexual demands, in which women are verbally abused, dominated and degraded, and treated as sexual things, makes men twice as likely to report willingness to sexually aggress against women than they were before exposure. So-called nonviolent materials like these make men see women as less than human, as good only for sex, as objects, as worthless and blameworthy when raped, as really wanting to be raped, and as unequal to men.[55] As to material showing violence only, it might be expected that rapists would be sexually aroused to scenes of violence against women, and they are.[56] But many normal male subjects, too, when seeing a woman being aggressed against by a man, perceive the interaction to be sexual even if no sex is shown.[57]

Male sexuality is apparently activated by violence against women and expresses itself in violence against women to a significant extent. If violence is seen as occupying the most fully achieved end of a dehumanization continuum on which objectification occupies the least express end, one question that is raised is whether some form of hierarchy —the dynamic of the continuum—is currently essential for male sexuality to experience itself. If so, and if gender is understood to be a hierarchy, perhaps the sexes are unequal so that men can be sexually aroused. To put it another way, perhaps gender must be maintained as a social hierarchy so that men will be able to get erections; or, part of the male interest in keeping women down lies in the fact that it gets men up. Maybe feminists are considered castrating because equality is not sexy.

Recent inquiries into rape support such suspicions. Men often rape women, it turns out, because they want to and enjoy it. The act, including the dominance, is sexually arousing, sexually affirming, and supportive of the perpetrator's masculinity. Many unreported rapists report an increase in self-esteem as a result of the rape.[58] Indications are that reported rapists perceive that getting caught accounts for most of the unpleasant effects of raping.[59] About one-third of all men say they would rape a woman if they knew they would not get caught.[60] That the low conviction rate may give them confidence is supported by the prevalence rate.[61] Some convicted rapists see rape as an "exciting" form of interpersonal sex, a recreational activity or "adventure," or as a means of revenge or punishment on all women or some subgroup of women or an individual woman. Even some of those who did the act out of bad feelings make it clear that raping made them feel better. "Men rape because it is rewarding to do so."[62] If rapists experience rape as sex, does that mean there can be nothing wrong with it?

Once an act is labeled rape there is an epistemological problem with seeing it as sex.[63] Indeed, this is a major social function served by labeling acts rape. Rape becomes something a rapist does, as if he were a separate species. But no personality disorder distinguishes most rapists from normal men.[64] Psychopaths do rape, but only about 5 percent of all known rapists are diagnosed psychopathic.[65] In spite of the numbers of victims, the normalcy of rapists, and even given the fact that most women are raped by men they know (making it most unlikely that a few lunatics know around half of the women in the United States), rape remains considered psychopathological and therefore not about sexuality.

Add this to rape's pervasiveness and permissibility, together with the belief that it is both rare and impermissible. Combine this with the similarity between the patterns, rhythms, roles, and emotions, not to mention acts, which make up rape (and battery) on the one hand and intercourse on the other. All this makes it difficult to sustain the customary distinctions between pathology and normalcy, parophilia and nomophilia, violence and sex, in this area. Some researchers have previously noticed the centrality of force to the excitement value of pornography but have tended to put it down to perversion. Robert Stoller, for example, observes that pornography today depends upon hostility, voyeurism, and sadomasochism and calls perversion "the erotic form of hatred."[66] If the perverse in this context is seen not as the other side of a bright normal/abnormal line but as an undiluted expression of a norm that permeates many ordinary interactions, hatred of women—that is, misogyny—becomes a dynamic of sexual excitement itself.

Compare victims' reports of rape with women's reports of sex. They look a lot alike.[67] Compare victims' reports of rape with what pornography says is sex. They look a lot alike.[68] In this light, the major distinction between intercourse (normal) and rape (abnormal) is that the normal happens so often that one cannot get anyone to see anything wrong with it. Which also means that anything sexual that happens often and one cannot get anyone to consider wrong is intercourse, not rape, no matter what was done. The distinctions that purport to divide this territory look more like the ideological supports for normalizing the usual male use and abuse of women as "sexuality" through authoritatively pretending that whatever is exposed of it is deviant. This may have something to do with the conviction rate in rape cases (making all those unconvicted men into normal men, and all those acts into sex). It may have something to do with the fact that most convicted rapists, and many observers, find rape convictions incomprehensible.[69] And with the fact that marital rape is considered by many to be a contradiction in terms ("But if you can't rape your wife, who can you rape?").[70] And with the fact that so many rape victims have trouble with sex afterward.[71]

What effect does the pervasive reality of sexual abuse of women by men have on what are deemed the more ordinary forms of sexual interaction? How do these material experiences create interest and point of view? Consider women. Recall that more than one-third of all girls experience sex, perhaps are sexually initiated, under conditions that even this society recognizes are forced or at least unequal.[72] Perhaps they learn this process of sexualized dominance as sex. Top-down relations feel sexual. Is sexuality throughout life then ever not on some level a reenactment of, a response to, that backdrop? Rape, adding more women to the list, can produce similar resonance. Sexually abused women—most women—seem to become either sexually disinclined or compulsively promiscuous or both in series, trying to avoid the painful events, or repeating them over and over almost addictively, or both, in an attempt to reacquire a sense of control or to make them come out right. Women also widely experience sexuality as a means to male approval; male approval translates into nearly all social goods. Violation can be sustained, even sought out, to this end. Sex can, then, be a means of trying to feel alive by redoing what has made one feel dead, of expressing a denigrated self-image seeking its own reflection in self-action in order to feel fulfilled, or of keeping up one's stock with the powerful.

Many women who have been sexually abused (like many survivors of concentration camps and ritual torture) report having distanced and split themselves as a conscious strategy for coping with the abuse. With women, this dissociation often becomes a part of their sexuality per se and of their experience of the world, especially their experience of men. Women widely report having this sensation during sex. Not feeling pain, including during sex, has a similar etiology. As one pornography model put it,

O: I had quite a bit of difficulty as a child. I was suicidal for a time, because I never felt attached to my body. I just felt completely detached from my body; I felt like a completely separate entity from it. I still see my body as a tool, something to be used.

DR: Give me an example of how today you sense not being attached to your body.

O: I don't feel pain.

DR: What do you mean, literally?

O: I really don't feel pain . . .

DR:    When there is no camera and you are having sexual relations, are you still on camera?

O:    Yes. I'm on camera 24 hours a day . . .

DR:    Who are you?

O:    Who? Olympia Dancing-Doll: The Sweet with the Super-Supreme.

DR:    What the hell is that?

O:    That's the title of my act . . .

DR:    [pointing to her] This is a body. Is it your body?

O:    Yes.

DR:    Are you your body?

O:    No. I'm not my body, but it is my body.[73]

Women often begin alienating themselves from their body's self-preserving reactions under conditions under which they cannot stop the pain from being inflicted, and then find the deadening process difficult to reverse. Some then seek out escalating pain to feel sexual or to feel alive or to feel anything at all. One particularly devastating and confusing consequence of sexual abuse for women's sexuality—and a crisis for consciousness—occurs when one's body experiences abuse as pleasurable. Feeling loved and aroused and comforted during incest, or orgasm during rape, are examples. Because body is widely regarded as access to unmediated truth in this culture, women feel betrayed by their bodies and seek mental justifications (Freudian derepression theory provides an excellent one) for why their body's reactions are their own true reactions, and their values and consciousness (which interprets the event as a violation) are socially imposed. That is, they come to believe they really wanted the rape or the incest and interpret violation as their own sexuality.[74]

Interpreting women's responses to pornography, in which there is often a difference between so-called objective indices of arousal, such as vaginal secretions, and self-reported arousal, raises similar issues. Repression is the typical explanation.[75] It seems at least as likely that women disidentify with their bodies' conditioned responses. Not to be overly behavioral, but does anyone think Pavlov's dogs were really hungry every time they salivated at the sound of the bell? If it is possible that hunger is inferred from salivation, perhaps humans experience[76] sexual arousal from pornographic cues and, since sexuality is social, that is sexual arousal. Identifying that as a conditioned response to a set of social cues, conditioned to what it is for political reasons, is not the same as considering the response proof of sexual truth simply because it physically happens. Further, research shows that sexual fetishism can be experimentally induced readily in "normal" subjects.[77] If this can be done with sexual responses that the society does not condone out front, why is it so unthinkable that the same process might occur with those sexual responses it does?

If the existing social model and reality of sexuality center on male force, and if that sex is socially learned and ideologically considered positive and is rewarded, what is surprising is that not all women eroticize dominance, not all love pornography, and many resent rape. As Valerie Heller has said of her use in incest and pornography, both as a child and as an adult, "I believed I existed only after I was turned on, like a light switch by another person. When I needed to be nurtured I thought I wanted to be used . . . Marks and bruises and being used was the way I measured my self worth. You must remember that I was taught that because men were fucking my body and using it for their needs it meant I was loved."[78] Given the pervasiveness of such experiences, the truly interesting question becomes why and how sexuality in women is ever other than masochistic.

All women live in sexual objectification the way fish live in water. Given the statistical realities, all women live all the time under the shadow of the threat of sexual abuse. The question is, what can life as a woman mean, what can sex mean, to targeted survivors in a rape culture? Given the statistical realities, much of women's sexual lives will occur under post-traumatic stress. Being surrounded by pornography—which is not only socially ubiquitous but often directly used as part of sex[79]—makes this a relatively constant condition. Women cope with objectification through trying to meet the male standard, and measure their self-worth by the degree to which they succeed. Women seem to cope with sexual abuse principally by denial or fear. On the denial side, immense energy goes into defending sexuality as just fine and getting better all the time, and into trying to make sexuality feel all right, the way it is supposed to feel. Women who are compromised, cajoled, pressured, tricked, blackmailed, or outright forced into sex (or pornography) often respond to the unspeakable humiliation, coupled with the sense of having lost some irreplaceable integrity, by claiming that sexuality as their own. Faced with no alternatives, the strategy to acquire self-respect and pride is: I chose it.

Consider the conditions under which this is done. This is a culture in which women are socially expected—and themselves necessarily expect and want—to be able to distinguish the socially, epistemologically, indistinguishable. Rape and intercourse are not authoritatively separated by any difference between the physical acts or amount of force involved but only legally, by a standard that centers on the man's interpretation of the encounter. Thus, although raped women, that is, most women, are supposed to be able to feel every day and every night that they have some meaningful determining part in having their sex life—their life, period—not be a series of rapes, the most they provide is the raw data for the man to see as he sees it. And he has been seeing pornography. Similarly, "consent" is supposed to be the crucial line between rape and intercourse, but the legal standard for it is so passive, so acquiescent, that a woman can be dead and have consented under it. The mind fuck of all of this makes liberalism's complicitous collapse into "I chose it" feel like a strategy for sanity. It certainly makes a woman at one with the world.

On the fear side, if a woman has ever been beaten in a relationship, even if "only once," what does that do to her everyday interactions, or her sexual interactions, with that man? With other men? Does her body ever really forget that behind his restraint he can do that any time she pushes an issue, or for no reason at all? Does her vigilance ever really relax? If she tried to do something about it, as many women do, and if nothing was done, as it usually is not, does she ever forget that that is what can be done to her at any time and nothing will be done about it? Does she smile at men less—or more? If she writes at all, does she imitate men less—or more? If a woman has ever been raped, ever, does a penis ever enter her without some body memory, if not a flashback then the effort of keeping it back; or does she hurry up or keep trying, feeling something gaining on her, trying to make it come out right? If a woman has ever been raped, does she ever fully regain the feeling of physical integrity, of self-respect, of having what she wants count somewhere, of being able to make herself clear to those who have not gone through what she has gone through, of living in a fair society, of equality?

Given the effects of learning sexuality through force or pressure or imposition; given the constant roulette of sexual violence; given the daily sexualization of every aspect of a woman's presence—for a woman to be sexualized means constant humiliation or threat of it, being invisible as human being and center stage as sex object, low pay, and being a target for assault or being assaulted. Given that this is the situation of all women, that one never knows for sure that one is not next on the list of victims until the moment one dies (and then, who knows?), it does not seem exaggerated to say that women are sexual, meaning that women exist, in a context of terror. /Yet most professionals in the area of sexuality persist in studying the inexplicabilities of what is termed female sexuality acontextually, outside the context of gender inequality and its sexual violence—navel gazing, only slightly further down.[80]

The general theory of sexuality emerging from this feminist critique does not consider sexuality to be an inborn force inherent in individuals, nor cultural in the Freudian sense, in which sexuality exists in a cultural context but in universally invariant stages and psychic representations. It appears instead to be culturally specific, even if so far largely invariant because male supremacy is largely universal, if always in specific forms. Although some of its abuses (like prostitution) are accentuated by poverty, it does not vary by class, although class is one hierarchy it sexualizes. Sexuality becomes, in this view, social and relational, constructing and constructed of power. Infants, though sensory, cannot be said to possess sexuality in this sense because they have not had the experiences (and do not speak the language) that give it social meaning. Since sexuality is its social meaning, infant erections, for example, are clearly sexual in the sense that this society centers its sexuality on them, but to relate to a child as though his erections mean what adult erections have been conditioned to mean is a form of child abuse. Such erections have the meaning they acquire in social life only to observing adults.

When Freud changed his mind and declared that women were not telling the truth about what had happened to them when they said they were abused as children, he attributed their accounts to "fantasy."[81] This was regarded as a theoretical breakthrough. Under the aegis of Freud, it is often said that victims of sexual abuse imagine it, that it is fantasy, not real, and their sexuality caused it. The feminist theory of sexuality suggests that it is the doctors who, because of their sexuality, as constructed, imagine that sexual abuse is a fantasy when it is real—real both in the sense that the sex happened and in the sense that it was abuse./Pornography is also routinely defended as "fantasy," meaning not real. But it is real: the sex that makes it is real and is often abuse, and the sex that it makes is sex and is often abuse./ Both the psychoanalytic and the pornographic "fantasy" worlds are what men imagine women imagine and desire because they are what men, raised on pornography, imagine and desire about women. Thus is psychoanalysis used to legitimate pornography, calling it fantasy, and pornography used to legitimate psychoanalysis, to show what women really want. Psychoanalysis and pornography, seen as epistemic sites in the same ontology, are mirrors of each other, male supremacist sexuality looking at itself looking at itself.

Perhaps the Freudian process of theory-building occurred like this: men heard accounts of child abuse, felt aroused by the account, and attributed their arousal to the child who is now a woman. Perhaps men respond sexually when women give an account of sexual violation because sexual words are a sexual reality, in the same way that men respond to pornography, which is (among other things) an account of the sexual violation of a woman. Seen in this way, much therapy as well as court testimony in sexual abuse cases is live oral pornography. Classical psychoanalysis attributes the connection between the experience of abuse (hers) and the experience of arousal (his) to the fantasy of the girl child. When he does it, he likes it, so when she did it, she must have liked it, or she must have thought it happened because she as much enjoys thinking about it happening to her as he enjoys thinking about it happening to her. Thus it cannot be abusive to her. Because he wants to do it, she must want it done.

Feminism also doubts the mechanism of repression in the sense that unconscious urges are considered repressed by social restrictions. Male sexuality is expressed and expressed and expressed, with a righteousness driven by the notion that something is trying to keep it from expressing itself. Too, there is a lot of doubt both about biology and about drives. Women are less repressed than oppressed, so-called women's sexuality largely a construct of male sexuality searching for someplace to happen, repression providing the reason for women's inhibition, meaning unwillingness to be available on demand. In this view, one function of the Freudian theory of repression (a function furthered rather than qualified by neo-Freudian adaptations) is ideologically to support the freeing of male sexual aggression while delegitimating women's refusal to respond.

There may be a feminist unconscious, but it is not the Freudian one. Perhaps equality lives there. Its laws, rather than a priori, objective, or universal, might as well be a response to the historical regularities of sexual subordination, which under bourgeois ideological conditions require that the truth of male dominance be concealed in order to preserve the belief that women are sexually self-acting: that women want it. The feminist psychic universe certainly recognizes that people do not always know what they want, have hidden desires and inaccessible needs, lack awareness of motivation, have contorted and opaque interactions, and have an interest in obscuring what is really going on. But this does not essentially conceal that what women really want is more sex. It is true, as Freudians have persuasively observed, that many things are sexual that do not present themselves as such. But in ways Freud never dreamed.

At risk of further complicating the issues, perhaps it would help to think of women's sexuality as women's like Black culture is Blacks'. it is, and it is not. The parallel cannot be precise in part because, owing to segregation, Black culture developed under more autonomous conditions than women, intimately integrated with men by force, have had. Still, both can be experienced as a source of strength, joy, expression, and as an affirmative badge of pride.[82] Both remain nonetheless stigmatic in the sense of a brand, a restriction, a definition as less. This is not because of any intrinsic content or value, but because the social reality is that their shape, qualities, texture, imperative, and very existence are a response to powerlessness. They exist as they do because of lack of choice. They are created out of social conditions of oppression and exclusion. They may be part of a strategy for survival or even of change. But, as is, they are not the whole world, and it is the whole world that one is entitled to. This is why interpreting female sexuality as an expression of women's agency and autonomy, as if sexism did not exist, is always denigrating and bizarre and reductive, as it would be to interpret Black culture as if racism did not exist. As if Black culture just arose freely and spontaneously on the plantations and in the ghettos of North America, adding diversity to American pluralism.

So long as sexual inequality remains unequal and sexual, attempts to value sexuality as women's, possessive as if women possess it, will remain part of limiting women to it, to what women are now defined as being. Outside of truly rare and contrapuntal glimpses (which most people think they live almost their entire sex life within), to seek an equal sexuality without political transformation is to seek equality under conditions of inequality. Rejecting this, and rejecting the glorification of settling for the best that inequality has to offer or has stimulated the resourceful to invent, are what Ti-Grace Atkinson meant to reject when she said: "I do not know any feminist worthy of that name who, if forced to choose between freedom and sex, would choose sex. She'd choose freedom every time."[83]

# III. THE STATE

A nation and a woman are not forgiven the unguarded hour in which the first adventurer that came along could violate them.

—Karl Marx

The repossession by women of our bodies will bring far more essential change to human society than the seizing of the means of production by workers. The female body has been both territory and machine, virgin wilderness to be exploited and assembly-line turning out life. We need to imagine a world in which every woman is the presiding genius of her own body. In such a world, women will truly create new life, bring forth not only children (if and as we choose) but the visions, and the thinking, necessary to sustain, console and alter human existence—a new relationship to the universe. Sexuality, politics, intelligence, power, motherhood, work, community, intimacy will develop new meanings. Thinking itself will be transformed. This is where we have to begin.

—Adrienne Rich

# 8 | *The Liberal State*

> The difference between the judges and Sir Isaac [Newton] is that a mistake by Sir Isaac in calculating the orbit of the earth would not send it spinning around the sun with an increased velocity . . . while if the judges . . . come to a wrong result, it is none the less law.
> —John Chipman Gray (1909)

> Political revolutions aim to change political institutions in ways that those institutions themselves prohibit.
> —Thomas Kuhn (1962)

*F*eminism has no theory of the state. Just as feminism has a theory of power but lacks a specific theory of its state form, marxism has a theory of value which (through the organization of work in production) becomes class analysis, but also a problematic theory of the state. Marx himself did not address the state much more explicitly than he addressed women. Women were substratum, the state epiphenomenon.[1] He termed the state "a concentrated expression of economics,"[2] a reflection of the real action, which occurred elsewhere; it was "the official résumé of society,"[3] a unity of ruptures; it, or its "executive," was "but a committee for managing the common affairs of the whole bourgeoisie."[4] Engels frontally analyzed women and the state, and together. But just as he presumed the subordination of women in every attempt to reveal its roots, he presupposed something like the state, or statelike society, in every attempt to find its origins.[5]

Marx tended to use the term *political* narrowly to refer to the state or its laws, criticizing as exclusively political interpretations of the state's organization or behavior which took them as sui generis, as if they were to be analyzed apart from economic conditions. He termed "political power" as embodied in the modern state "the official expression of antagonism in civil society."[6] Changes on this level could, therefore, emancipate the individual only within the framework of the existing social order, termed "civil society."[7] Revolution on this level was "partial, merely political revolution."[8] Accordingly, until recently, most marxist theory has tended to consider as political that which occurs between classes and the state as the instrument of the economically dominant class.[9] That is, it has interpreted the political in terms of the marxist view of social inequality and the state in terms of the class that controls it. The marxist theory of social inequality has been its theory of politics. The state as such was not seen as furthering particular interests through its form. This theory does not so much collapse the state into society (although it goes far in that direction) as conceive the state as determined by the totality of social relations of which the state is one determined and determining part—without specifying which, or how much, is which.

After 1848, having seen the bourgeoisie win revolutions but then not exercise state power directly, Marx tried to understand how states could plainly serve the bourgeoisie's interest yet not represent it as a class.[10] His attempts form the basis for much contemporary marxist work that has tried to grasp the specificity of the institutional state: how it wields class power or operates within class strictures or supplements or moderates class rule or transforms class society or responds to approach by a left aspiring to rulership or other changes. While much liberal theory has seen the state as emanating power, and traditional marxism has seen the state as expressing power constituted elsewhere, recent marxism, much of it structuralist, has tried to analyze state power as specific to the state as a form, yet integral to a determinate social whole understood in class terms.

Politics becomes "an autonomous phenomenon that is constrained by economics but not reducible to it."[11] This state is found "relatively autonomous"; that is, the state, expressed through its functionaries, has a definite class character, is definitely capitalist or socialist, but also has its own interests, which are to some degree independent of those of the ruling class and even of the class structure.[12] The state as such, in this view, has a specific power and interest, termed "the political," such that class power, class interest expressed by and in the state, and state behavior, though inconceivable in isolation from one another, are nevertheless not linearly linked or strictly coextensive. Thus Jon Elster argues that Marx saw that the bourgeoisie perceived their interests best furthered "if they remain outside politics."[13] Much of this work locates "the specificity of the political" in a mediate "region" between the state and its own ground of power (which alone, as in the liberal conception, would set the state above or apart from class) and the state as possessing no special supremacy or priority in terms of power, as in the more orthodox marxist view.[14] For Nicos Poulantzas, for example, the "specific autonomy which is characteristic of the function of the state . . . is the basis of the specificity of the political"[15]—whatever that means.

The idea that the state is relatively autonomous, a kind of first among equals of social institutions, has the genius of appearing to take a stand on the issue of reciprocal constitution of state and society while straddling it.[16] Is the state essentially autonomous of class but partly determined by it, or is it essentially determined by class but not exclusively so? Is it relatively constrained within a context of freedom or relatively free within a context of constraint?[17] As to who or what fundamentally moves and shapes the realities and instrumentalities of domination, and where to go to do something about it, what qualifies what is as ambiguous as it is crucial. When this work has investigated law as a particular form of state expression, it has served to relieve the compulsion to find all law—directly or convolutedly, nakedly or clothed in unconscious or devious rationalia—to be simply "bourgeois," without undercutting the notion that it, with all state emanations, is determinately driven by interest.[18]

Feminism has not confronted, on its own terms, the relation between the state and society within a theory of social determination specific to sex. As a result, it lacks a jurisprudence, that is, a theory of the substance of law, its relation to society, and the relationship between the two. Such a theory would comprehend how law works as a form of state power in a social context in which power is gendered. It would answer the questions: What is state power? Where, socially, does it come from? How do women encounter it? What is the law for women? How does law work to legitimate the state, male power, itself? Can law do anything for women? Can it do anything about women's status? Does how the law is used matter?

In the absence of answers, feminist practice has oscillated between a liberal theory of the state on the one hand and a left theory of the state on the other. Both theories treat law as the mind of society: disembodied reason in liberal theory, reflection of material interest in left theory. In liberal moments, the state is accepted on its own terms as a neutral arbiter among conflicting interests. The law is actually or

potentially principled, meaning predisposed to no substantive outcome, or manipulable to any ends, thus available as a tool that is not
fatally twisted. Women implicitly become an interest group within
pluralism, with specific problems of mobilization and representation,
exit and voice, sustaining incremental gains and losses. In left
moments, the state becomes a tool of dominance and repression, the
law legitimating ideology, use of the legal system a form of utopian
idealism or gradualist reform, each apparent gain deceptive or
cooptive, and each loss inevitable.

Liberalism applied to women has supported state intervention on
behalf of women as abstract persons with abstract rights, without
scrutinizing the content and limitations of these notions in terms of
gender. Marxism applied to women is always on the edge of
counseling abdication of the state as an arena altogether—and with it
those women whom the state does not ignore or who are in no position
to ignore it. As a result, feminism has been left with these tacit
alternatives: either the state is a primary tool of women's betterment
and status transformation, without analysis (hence strategy) of it as
male; or women are left to civil society, which for women has more
closely resembled a state of nature. The state, and with it the law, have
been either omnipotent or impotent: everything or nothing. The
feminist posture toward the state has therefore been schizoid on issues
central to women's status. Rape, abortion, pornography, and sex
discrimination are examples.[19] To grasp the inadequacies for women of
liberalism on the one hand and marxism on the other is to begin to
comprehend the role of the liberal state[20] and liberal legalism[21] within
a post-marxist feminism of social transformation.

Gender is a social system that divides power. It is therefore a
political system. That is, over time, women have been economically
exploited, relegated to domestic slavery, forced into motherhood,
sexually objectified, physically abused, used in denigrating entertainment, deprived of a voice and authentic culture, and disenfranchised
and excluded from public life. Women, by contrast with comparable
men, have systematically been subjected to physical insecurity;
targeted for sexual denigration and violation; depersonalized and
denigrated; deprived of respect, credibility, and resources; and
silenced—and denied public presence, voice, and representation of
their interests. Men as men have generally not had these things done
to them; that is, men have had to be Black or gay (for instance) to have
these things done to them as men. Men have done these things to

women. Even conventional theories of power—the more individuated, atomistic, and decisional approaches of the pluralists, as well as
the more radical theories, which stress structural, tacit, contextual,
and relational aspects of power—recognize such conditions as defining positions of power and powerlessness.[22] If one defines politics
with Harold Lasswell, who defines a political act as "one performed in power perspectives,"[23] and with Robert Dahl, who defines a political system as "any persistent pattern of human relationships that involves, to a significant extent, power, rule, or authority,"[24] and
with Kate Millett, who defines political relationships as "power
structured relationships,"[25] the relation between women and men
is political.

Unlike the ways in which men systematically enslave, violate,
dehumanize, and exterminate other men, expressing political inequalities among men, men's forms of dominance over women have been
accomplished socially as well as economically, prior to the operation of
law, without express state acts, often in intimate contexts, as everyday
life. So what is the role of the state in sexual politics? Neither
liberalism nor marxism grants women, as such, a specific relation to
the state. Feminism has described some of the state's treatment of the
gender difference but has not analyzed the state's role in gender
hierarchy. What, in gender terms, are the state's norms of account-
ability, sources of power, real constituency? Is the state to some degree
autonomous of the interests of men or an integral expression of them?
Does the state embody and serve male interests in its form, dynamics,
relation to society, and specific policies? Is the state constructed upon
the subordination of women? If so, how does male power become state
power? Can such a state be made to serve the interests of those upon
whose powerlessness its power is erected? Would a different relation
between state and society, such as may exist under socialism, make a
difference? If not, is masculinity inherent in the state form as such, or
is some other form of state, or some other way of governing,
distinguishable or imaginable? In the absence of answers to these
questions, feminism has been caught between giving more power to
the state in each attempt to claim it for women and leaving unchecked
power in the society to men. Undisturbed, meanwhile, like the
assumption that women generally consent to sex, is the assumption
that women consent to this government. The question for feminism is:
what is this state, from women's point of view?

The state is male in the feminist sense:[26] the law sees and treats women the way men see and treat women. The liberal state coercively and authoritatively constitutes the social order in the interest of men as a gender—through its legitimating norms, forms, relation to society, and substantive policies. The state's formal norms recapitulate the male point of view on the level of design. In Anglo-American jurisprudence, morals (value judgments) are deemed separable and separated from politics (power contests), and both from adjudication (interpretation). Neutrality, including judicial decision making that is dispassionate, impersonal, disinterested, and precedential, is considered desirable and descriptive.[27] Courts, forums without predisposition among parties and with no interest of their own, reflect society back to itself resolved. Government of laws, not of men, limits partiality with written constraints and tempers force with reasonable rule-following.

At least since Langdell's first casebook in 1871, this law has aspired to be a science of rules and a science with rules, a science of the immanent generalization subsuming the emergent particularity, of prediction and control of social regularities and regulations, preferably codified. The formulaic "tests" of "doctrine" aspire to mechanism, classification to taxonomy, legislators to Linnaeus. Courts intervene only in properly "factualized" disputes,[28] cognizing social conflicts as if collecting empirical data; right conduct becomes rule-following.[29] But these demarcations between morals and politics, science and politics, the personality of the judge and the judicial role, bare coercion and the rule of law, tend to merge in women's experience.[30] Relatively seamlessly they promote the dominance of men as a social group through privileging the form of power—the perspective on social life—which feminist consciousness reveals as socially male. The separation of form from substance, process from policy, adjudication from legislation, judicial role from theory or practice, echoes and reechoes at each level of the regime its basic norm: objectivity.

Formally, the state is male in that objectivity is its norm. Objectivity is liberal legalism's conception of itself. It legitimates itself by reflecting its view of society, a society it helps make by so seeing it, and calling that view, and that relation, rationality. Since rationality is measured by point-of-viewlessness, what counts as reason is that which corresponds to the way things are. Practical rationality, in this approach, means that which can be done without changing anything. In this framework, the task of legal interpretation becomes

"to perfect the state as mirror of the society."[31] Objectivist epistemology is the law of law. It ensures that the law will most reinforce
existing distributions of power when it most closely adheres to its own
ideal of fairness. Like the science it emulates, this epistemological
stance cannot see the social specificity of reflexion as method or its
choice to embrace that which it reflects. Such law not only reflects a
society in which men rule women; it rules in a male way insofar as "the
phallus means everything that sets itself up as a mirror."[32] Law, as
words in power, writes society in state form and writes the state onto
society. The rule form, which unites scientific knowledge with state
control in its conception of what law is, institutionalizes the objective
stance as jurisprudence.

The state is male jurisprudentially, meaning that it adopts the
standpoint of male power on the relation between law and society.
This stance is especially vivid in constitutional adjudication, thought
legitimate to the degree it is neutral on the policy content of
legislation. The foundation for its neutrality is the pervasive assumption that conditions that pertain among men on the basis of gender
apply to women as well—that is, the assumption that sex inequality
does not really exist in society. The Constitution—the constituting
document of this state society—with its interpretations assumes that
society, absent government intervention, is free and equal; that its
laws, in general, reflect that; and that government need and should
right only what government has previously wronged. This posture is
structural to a constitution of abstinence: for example, "Congress shall
make no law abridging the freedom of . . . speech." Those who have
freedoms like equality, liberty, privacy, and speech socially keep them
legally, free of governmental intrusion. No one who does not already
have them socially is granted them legally.

In this light, once gender is grasped as a means of social
stratification, the status categories basic to medieval law, thought to
have been superseded by liberal regimes in aspirational nonhierarchical
constructs of abstract personhood, are revealed deeply unchanged.
Gender as a status category was simply assumed out of legal existence,
suppressed into a presumptively pre-constitutional social order
through a constitutional structure designed not to reach it. Speaking
descriptively rather than functionally or motivationally, the strategy is
first to constitute society unequally prior to law; then to design the
constitution, including the law of equality, so that all its guarantees

apply only to those values that are taken away by law; then to construct legitimating norms so that the state legitimates itself through noninterference with the status quo. Then, so long as male dominance is so effective in society that it is unnecessary to impose sex inequality through law, such that only the most superficial sex inequalities become *de jure,* not even a legal guarantee of sex equality will produce social equality.

The posture and presumptions of the negative state, the view that government best promotes freedom when it stays out of existing social arrangements, reverberates throughout constitutional law. Doctrinally, it is embodied in rubrics like the "state action" requirement of equal protection law, in the law of freedom of speech, and in the law of privacy. The "state action" requirement restricts the Constitution to securing citizens' equality rights only from violations by governments, not by other citizens. The law of the First Amendment secures freedom of speech only from governmental deprivation. In the law of privacy, governmental intervention itself is unconstitutional.[33]

In terms of judicial role, these notions are defended as the "passive virtues":[34] courts should not (and say they do not) impose their own substantive views on constitutional questions. Judges best vindicate the Constitution when they proceed as if they have no views, when they reflect society back to itself from the angle of vision at which society is refracted to them. In this hall of mirrors, only in extremis shall any man alter what any other man has wrought. The offspring of proper passivity is substancelessness. Law produces its progeny immaculately, without messy political intercourse.

Philosophically, this posture is expressed in the repeated constitutional invocation of the superiority of "negative freedom"—staying out, letting be—over positive legal affirmations. Negative liberty gives one the right to be "left to do or be what [he] is able to do or be, without interference from other persons." The state that pursues this value promotes freedom when it does not intervene in the social status quo. Positive freedom, freedom to do rather than to keep from being done to, by distinction, gives one the right to "control or . . . determine someone to do, or be, this rather than that."[35] If one group is socially granted the positive freedom to do whatever it wants to another group, to determine that the second group will be and do this rather than that, no amount of negative freedom legally guaranteed to the second group will make it the equal of the first. For women, this has meant that civil society, the domain in which women are distinctively subordinated and deprived of power, has been placed beyond reach of legal guarantees. Women are oppressed socially, prior to law, without express state acts, often in intimate contexts. The negative state cannot address their situation in any but an equal society—the one in which it is needed least.

This posture is enforced through judicial methodology, the formative legal experience for which is *Lochner v. New York,* a case that arose out of the struggle of the working class to extract livable working conditions from a capitalist state through legislated reform.[36] Invalidating legislation that would have restricted the number of hours bakers could work on grounds of freedom of contract, the Supreme Court sided with capitalism over workers. The dissenters' view, ultimately vindicated, was that the majority had superimposed its own views on the Constitution; they, by contrast, would passively reflect the Constitution by upholding the legislation. Soon after, in *Muller v. Oregon,* the Supreme Court upheld restrictive hours legislation for women only.[37] The opinion distinguished *Lochner* on the basis that women's unique frailty, dependency, and breeding capacity placed her "at a disadvantage in the struggle for subsistence." A later ruling, *West Coast Hotel v. Parrish,* generally regarded as ending the *Lochner* era, also used women as a lever against capitalism. Minimum-wage laws were upheld for women because "the exploitation of a class of workers who are in an unequal position with respect to bargaining power and are thus relatively defenseless against the denial of a living wage . . . casts a direct burden for their support upon the community."[38]

Concretely, it is unclear whether these special protections, as they came to be called, helped or hurt women.[39] These cases did do something for some workers (female) concretely; they also demeaned all women ideologically. They did assume that women were marginal and second-class members of the workforce; they probably contributed to keeping women marginal and second-class workers by keeping some women from competing with men at the male standard of exploitation. This benefited both male workers and capitalists. These rulings supported one sector of workers against all capitalists by benefiting male workers at the expense of female workers. They did help the working class by setting precedents that eventually supported minimum-wage and maximum-hours laws for all workers.[40] They were a victory against capitalism and for sexism, for some women perhaps at the expense of all women (maybe including those they helped), for the working class perhaps at women's expense, at least so long as they were "women only."

The view of women in *Muller* and *West Coast Hotel* was that of the existing society: demeaning, paternalistic, and largely unrealistic; as with most pedestalization, its concrete benefits were equivocal at best.[41] The view of workers in *Lochner* left capitalism unchecked and would have precluded most New Deal social reforms men wanted. (Protecting all workers was not considered demeaning by anyone.) For these reasons, these cases have come to stand for a critique of substantivity in adjudication as such. But their methodological solution—judicial neutrality—precludes from constitutional relief groups who are socially abject and systematically excluded from the usual political process. Despite universal rejections of "Lochnering," this substantive approach in neutral posture has continued to be incorporated in constitutional method, including in the law of equality. If over half the population has no voice in the Constitution, why is upholding legislation to give them a voice impermissibly substantive and activist, while striking down such legislation is properly substanceless and passive? Is permitting such an interpretation of, for example, the equality principle in a proper case activism, while not permitting it is properly nonsubstantive? Overruling *Lochner* was at least as judicially active as *Lochner* itself was. Further, why are legislation and adjudication regarded as exercises of state power, but passivity in the face of social inequality—even under a constitutional equality principle—is not? The result is, substantivity and activism are hunted down, flailed, and confined, while their twins, neutrality and passivity, roam at large.

To consider the "passive virtues" of judicial restraint as a tool for social change suggests that change for workers was constitutional only because workers were able to get power in legislatures. To achieve such changes by constitutional principle before achieving them socially and politically would be to engage in exactly the kind of substantive judicial activism that those who supported the changes said they opposed. The reasoning was: if courts make substantive decisions, they will express their prejudices, here, exploitive of workers, demeaning and unhelpful of women. The alternatives have been framed, then, as substantive adjudication that demeans and deprives on the one hand, or as substanceless adjudication that, passively virtuous, upholds whatever power can get out of the political process as it is.

The underlying assumption of judicial neutrality is that a status quo exists which is preferable to judicial intervention—a common law status quo, a legislative status quo, an economic status quo, or a gender status quo. For women, it also tends to assume that access to the conventional political realm might be available in the absence of legal rights. At the same time it obscures the possibility that a substantive approach to women's situation could be adequate to women's distinctive social exploitation—ground a claim to civil equality, for example—and do no more to license judicial arbitrariness than current standards do. From women's point of view, adjudications are already substantive; the view from nowhere already has content. *Lochner* saw workers legally the way capitalists see workers socially: as free agents, bargaining at arm's length. *Muller* saw women legally the way men see women socially: as breeders, marginal workers, excludable. If one wants to claim no more for a powerless group than what can be extracted under an established system of power, one can try to abstract them into entitlement by blurring the lines between them and everyone else. Neutrality as pure means makes some sense. If, however, the claim is against the definition and distribution of power itself, one needs a critique not so much of the substantivity of cases like *Lochner* and *Muller*, but of their substance. Such a critique must also include that aspect of the liberal tradition in which one strategy for dominance has been substancelessness.[42]

If the content of positive law is surveyed more broadly from women's point of view, a pattern emerges. The way the male point of view frames an experience is the way it is framed by state policy. Over and over again, the state protects male power through embodying and ensuring existing male control over women at every level—cushioning, qualifying, or *de jure* appearing to prohibit its excesses when necessary to its normalization. *De jure* relations stabilize de facto relations. Laws that touch on sexuality provide illustrations of this argument. As in society, to the extent possession is the point of sex, rape in law is sex with a woman who is not yours, unless the act is so as to make her yours. Social and legal realities are consistent and mutually determinate: since law has never effectively interfered with men's ability to rape women on these terms, it has been unnecessary to make this an express rule of law. Because part of the kick of pornography involves eroticizing the putatively prohibited, obscenity law putatively prohibits pornography enough to maintain its desirability without ever making it unavailable or truly illegitimate. Because the stigma of prostitution is the stigma of sexuality is the stigma of the female gender, prostitution may be legal or illegal, but so long as women are unequal to men and that inequality is sexualized, women will be bought and sold as prostitutes, and law will do nothing about it.

Women as a whole are kept poor, hence socially dependent on men, available for sexual or reproductive use. To the extent that abortion exists to control the reproductive consequences of intercourse, hence to facilitate male sexual access to women, access to abortion will be controlled by "a man or The Man."[43] So long as this is effectively done socially, it is unnecessary to do it by law. Law need merely stand passively by, reflecting the passing scene. The law of sex equality stays as far away as possible from issues of sexuality. Rape, pornography, prostitution, incest, battery, abortion, gay and lesbian rights: none have been sex equality issues under law.[44] In the issues the law of sex discrimination does treat, male is the implicit reference for human, maleness the measure of entitlement to equality. In its mainstream interpretation, this law is neutral: it gives little to women that it cannot also give to men, maintaining sex inequality while appearing to address it. Gender, thus elaborated and sustained by law, is maintained as a division of power. The negative state views gender and sexual relations as neutrally as *Lochner* viewed class relations.

The law on women's situation produced in this way views women's situation from the standpoint of male dominance. It assumes that the conditions that pertain among men on the basis of sex—consent to sex, comparative privacy, voice in moral discourse, and political equality on the basis of gender—apply to women. It assumes on the epistemic level that sex inequality in society is not real. Rape law takes women's usual response to coercion—acquiescence, the despairing response of hopelessness to unequal odds—and calls that consent. Men coerce women; women "consent." The law of privacy treats the private sphere as a sphere of personal freedom. For men, it is. For women, the private is the distinctive sphere of intimate violation and abuse, neither free nor particularly personal. Men's realm of private freedom is women's realm of collective subordination. The law of obscenity treats pornography as "ideas."[45] Whether or not ideas are sex for men, pornography certainly is sex for men. From the standpoint of women, who live the sexual abuse in pornography as everyday life, pornography is reality. The law of obscenity treats regulation of pornography from the standpoint of what is necessary to protect it: as regulation of morals, as some men telling other men what they may not see and do and think and say about sex. From the standpoint of women, whose torture pornography makes entertainment, pornography is the essence of a powerless condition, its effective protection by the state the essence of sexual politics. Obscenity law's "moral ideas" are a political reality of women's subordination. Just as, in male law, public oppression masquerades as private freedom and coercion is guised as consent, in obscenity law real political domination is presented as a discourse in ideas about virtue and vice.

Rape law assumes that consent to sex is as real for women as it is for men. Privacy law assumes that women in private have the same privacy men do. Obscenity law assumes that women have the access to speech men have. Equality law assumes that women are already socially equal to men. Only to the extent women have already achieved social equality does the mainstream law of equality support their inequality claims. The laws of rape, abortion, obscenity, and sex discrimination show how the relation between objectification, understood as the primary process of the subordination of women, and the power of the state is the relation between the personal and the political at the level of government. These laws are not political because the state is presumptively the sphere of politics. They are integral to sexual politics because the state, through law, institutionalizes male power over women through institutionalizing the male point of view in law. Its first state act is to see women from the standpoint of male dominance; its next act is to treat them that way. This power, this state, is not a discrete location, but a web of sanctions throughout society which "control[s] the principal means of coercion" that structures women's everyday lives.[46] The Weberian monopoly on the means of legitimate coercion, thought to distinguish the state as an entity, actually describes the power of men over women in the home, in the bedroom, on the job, in the street, throughout social life. It is difficult, actually, to find a place it does not circumscribe and describe. Men are sovereign in society in the way Austin describes law as sovereign: a person or group whose commands are habitually obeyed and who is not in the habit of obeying anyone else.[47] Men are the group that has had the authority to make law, embodying H. L. A. Hart's "rule of recognition" that, in his conception, makes law authoritative.[48] Distinctively male values (and men) constitute the authoritative interpretive community that makes law distinctively lawlike to the likes of Ronald Dworkin.[49] If one combines "a realistic conception of the state with a revolutionary theory of society,"[50] the place of gender in state power is not limited to government, nor is the rule of law limited to police and courts. The rule of law and the rule of men are one thing, indivisible, at once official and unofficial—officially circumscribed, unofficially not. State power, embodied in law, exists throughout society as male power at the same time as the power of men over women throughout society is organized as the power of the state.

Perhaps the failure to consider gender as a determinant of state behavior has made the state's behavior appear indeterminate. Perhaps the objectivity of the liberal state has made it appear autonomous of class. Including, but beyond, the bourgeois in liberal legalism, lies what is male about it. However autonomous of class the liberal state may appear, it is not autonomous of sex. Male power is systemic. Coercive, legitimated, and epistemic, it *is* the regime.

# 9 | *Rape: On Coercion and Consent*

Negotiations for sex are not carried on like those for the rent of a house. There is often no definite state on which it can be said that the two have agreed to sexual intercourse. They proceed by touching, feeling, fumbling, by signs and words which are not generally in the form of a Roman stipulation.

— Honoré, twentieth-century British
legal scholar and philosopher

Rape is an extension of sexism in some ways, and that's an extension of dealing with a woman as an object . . . Stinky [her rapist] seemed to me as though he were only a step further away, a step away from the guys who sought me on the streets, who insist, my mother could have died, I could be walking down the street and if I don't answer their rap, they got to go get angry and get all hostile and stuff as though I walk down the street as a . . . . that my whole being is there to please men in the streets. But Stinky only seemed like someone who had taken it a step further . . . he felt like an extension, he felt so common, he felt so ordinary, he felt so familiar, and it was maybe that what frightened me the most was that how similar to other men he seemed. They don't come from Mars, folks.

— Carolyn Craven, reporter

If you're living with a man, what are you doing running around the streets getting raped?

— Edward Harrington, defense
attorney in New Bedford gang
rape case

*I*f sexuality is central to women's definition and forced sex is central to sexuality, rape is indigenous, not exceptional, to women's social condition. In feminist analysis, a rape is not an isolated event or moral transgression or individual interchange gone wrong but an act of terrorism and torture within a systemic context of group subjection, like lynching. The fact that the state calls rape a crime opens an inquiry into the state's treatment of rape as an index to its stance on the status of the sexes.

Under law, rape is a sex crime that is not regarded as a crime when it looks like sex. The law, speaking generally, defines rape as intercourse with force or coercion and without consent.[1] Like sexuality under male supremacy, this definition assumes the sadomasochistic definition of sex: intercourse with force or coercion can be or become consensual. It assumes pornography's positive-outcome-rape scenario: dominance plus submission is force plus consent. This equals sex, not rape. Under male supremacy, this is too often the reality. In a critique of male supremacy, the elements "with force and without consent" appear redundant. Force is present because consent is absent.

Like heterosexuality, male supremacy's paradigm of sex, the crime of rape centers on penetration.[2] The law to protect women's sexuality from forcible violation and expropriation defines that protection in male genital terms. Women do resent forced penetration. But penile invasion of the vagina may be less pivotal to women's sexuality, pleasure or violation, than it is to male sexuality. This definitive element of rape centers upon a male-defined loss. It also centers upon one way men define loss of exclusive access. In this light, rape, as legally defined, appears more a crime against female monogamy (exclusive access by one man) than against women's sexual dignity or intimate integrity. Analysis of rape in terms of concepts of property, often invoked in marxian analysis to criticize this disparity, fail to encompass the realities of rape.[3] Women's sexuality is, socially, a thing to be stolen, sold, bought, bartered, or exchanged by others. But women never own or possess it, and men never treat it, in law or in life, with the solicitude with which they treat property. To be property would be an improvement. The moment women "have" it—"have sex" in the dual gender/sexuality sense—it is lost as theirs.

To have it is to have it taken away. This may explain the male incomprehension that, once a woman has had sex, she loses anything when subsequently raped. To them women have nothing to lose. It is true that dignitary harms, because nonmaterial, are ephemeral to the legal mind. But women's loss through rape is not only less tangible; it is seen as unreal. It is difficult to avoid the conclusion that penetration itself is considered a violation from the male point of view, which is both why it is the centerpiece of sex and why women's sexuality, women's gender definition, is stigmatic. The question for social explanation becomes not why some women tolerate rape but how any women manage to resent it.

Rape cases finding insufficient evidence of force reveal that acceptable sex, in the legal perspective, can entail a lot of force. This is both a result of the way specific facts are perceived and interpreted within the legal system and the way the injury is defined by law. The level of acceptable force is adjudicated starting just above the level set by what is seen as normal male sexual behavior, including the normal level of force, rather than at the victim's, or women's, point of violation.[4] In this context, to seek to define rape as violent not sexual is as understandable as it is futile. Some feminists have reinterpreted rape as an act of violence, not sexuality, the threat of which intimidates all women.[5] Others see rape, including its violence, as an expression of male sexuality, the social imperatives of which define as well as threaten all women.[6] The first, epistemologically in the liberal tradition, comprehends rape as a displacement of power based on physical force onto sexuality, a preexisting natural sphere to which domination is alien. Susan Brownmiller, for example, examines rape in riots, wars, pogroms, and revolutions; rape by police, parents, prison guards; and rape motivated by racism. Rape in normal circumstances, in everyday life, in ordinary relationships, by men as men, is barely mentioned.[7] Women are raped by guns, age, white supremacy, the state—only derivatively by the penis. The view that derives most directly from victims' experiences, rather than from their denial, construes sexuality as a social sphere of male power to which forced sex is paradigmatic. Rape is not less sexual for being violent. To the extent that coercion has become integral to male sexuality, rape may even be sexual to the degree that, and because, it is violent.

The point of defining rape as "violence not sex" has been to claim an ungendered and nonsexual ground for affirming sex (heterosexuality) while rejecting violence (rape). The problem remains what it has always been: telling the difference. The convergence of sexuality with violence, long used at law to deny the reality of women's violation, is recognized by rape survivors with a difference: where the legal system has seen the intercourse in rape, victims see the rape in intercourse. The uncoerced context for sexual expression becomes as elusive as the physical acts come to feel indistinguishable. Instead of asking what is the violation of rape, their experience suggests that the more relevant question is, what is the nonviolation of intercourse? To know what is wrong with rape, know what is right about sex. If this, in turn, proves difficult, the difficulty is as instructive as the difficulty men have in telling the difference when women see one. Perhaps the wrong of rape has proved so difficult to define because the unquestionable starting point has been that rape is defined as distinct from intercourse,[8] while for women it is difficult to distinguish the two under conditions of male dominance.

In the name of the distinction between sex and violence, reform of rape statutes has sought to redefine rape as sexual assault.[9] Usually, assault is not consented to in law; either it cannot be consented to, or consensual assault remains assault.[10] Yet sexual assault consented to is intercourse, no matter how much force was used. The substantive reference point implicit in existing legal standards is the sexually normative level of force. Until this norm is confronted as such, no distinction between violence and sexuality will prohibit more instances of women's experienced violation than does the existing definition. Conviction rates have not increased under the reform statutes.[11] The question remains what is seen as force, hence as violence, in the sexual arena.[12] Most rapes, as women live them, will not be seen to violate women until sex and violence are confronted as mutually definitive rather than as mutually exclusive. It is not only men convicted of rape who believe that the only thing they did that was different from what men do all the time is get caught.

Consent is supposed to be women's form of control over intercourse, different from but equal to the custom of male initiative. Man proposes, woman disposes. Even the ideal it is not mutual. Apart from the disparate consequences of refusal, this model does not envision a situation the woman controls being placed in, or choices she frames. Yet the consequences are attributed to her as if the sexes began at arm's length, on equal terrain, as in the contract fiction. Ambiguous cases of consent in law are archetypically referred to as "half won arguments in parked cars."[13] Why not half lost? Why isn't half enough? Why is it an argument? Why do men still want "it," feel entitled to "it," when women do not want them? The law of rape presents consent as free exercise of sexual choice under conditions of equality of power without exposing the underlying structure of constraint and disparity. Fundamentally, desirability to men is supposed a woman's form of power because she can both arouse it and deny its fulfillment. To woman is attributed both the cause of man's initiative and the denial of his satisfaction. This rationalizes force. Consent in this model becomes more a metaphysical quality of a woman's being than a choice she makes and communicates. Exercise of women's so-called power presupposes more fundamental social powerlessness.[14]

The law of rape divides women into spheres of consent according to indices of relationship to men. Which category of presumed consent a woman is in depends upon who she is relative to a man who wants her, not what she says or does. These categories tell men whom they can legally fuck, who is open season and who is off limits, not how to listen to women. The paradigm categories are the virginal daughter and other young girls, with whom all sex is proscribed, and the whorelike wives and prostitutes, with whom no sex is proscribed. Daughters may not consent; wives and prostitutes are assumed to, and cannot but.[15] Actual consent or nonconsent, far less actual desire, is comparatively irrelevant. If rape laws existed to enforce women's control over access to their sexuality, as the consent defense implies, no would mean no, marital rape would not be a widespread exception,[16] and it would not be effectively legal to rape a prostitute.

All women are divided into parallel provinces, their actual consent counting to the degree that they diverge from the paradigm case in their category. Virtuous women, like young girls, are unconsenting, virginal, rapable. Unvirtuous women, like wives and prostitutes, are consenting, whores, unrapable. The age line under which girls are presumed disabled from consenting to sex, whatever they say, rationalizes a condition of sexual coercion which women never outgrow. One day they cannot say yes, and the next day they cannot say no. The law takes the most aggravated case for female powerlessness based on gender and age combined and, by formally prohibiting all sex as rape, makes consent irrelevant on the basis of an assumption of powerlessness. This defines those above the age line as powerful, whether they actually have power to consent or not. The vulnerability girls share with boys—age—dissipates with time. The vulnerability girls share with women—gender—does not. As with protective labor laws for women only, dividing and protecting the most vulnerable becomes a device for not protecting everyone who needs it, and also may function to target those singled out for special protection for special abuse. Such protection has not prevented high rates of sexual abuse of children and may contribute to eroticizing young girls as forbidden.

As to adult women, to the extent an accused knows a woman and they have sex, her consent is inferred. The exemption for rape in marriage is consistent with the assumption underlying most adjudications of forcible rape: to the extent the parties relate, it was not really rape, it was personal.[17] As marital exemptions erode, preclusions for cohabitants and voluntary social companions may expand. As a matter of fact, for this purpose one can be acquainted with an accused by friendship or by meeting him for the first time at a bar or a party or by hitchhiking. In this light, the partial erosion of the marital rape exemption looks less like a change in the equation between women's experience of sexual violation and men's experience of intimacy, and more like a legal adjustment to the social fact that acceptable heterosexual sex is increasingly not limited to the legal family. So although the rape law may not now always assume that the woman consented simply because the parties are legally one, indices of closeness, of relationship ranging from nodding acquaintance to living together, still contraindicate rape. In marital rape cases, courts look for even greater atrocities than usual to undermine their assumption that if sex happened, she wanted it.[18]

This approach reflects men's experience that women they know do meaningfully consent to sex with them. *That* cannot be rape; rape must be by someone else, someone unknown. They do not rape women they know. Men and women are unequally socially situated with regard to the experience of rape. Men are a good deal more likely to rape than to be raped. This forms their experience, the material conditions of their epistemological position. Almost half of all women, by contrast, are raped or victims of attempted rape at least once in their lives. Almost 40 percent are victims of sexual abuse in childhood.[19] Women are more likely to be raped than to rape and are most often raped by men whom they know.[20]

Men often say that it is less awful for a woman to be raped by someone she is close to: "The emotional trauma suffered by a person victimized by an individual with whom sexual intimacy is shared as a normal part of an ongoing marital relationship is not nearly as severe as that suffered by a person who is victimized by one with whom that intimacy is not shared."[21] Women often feel as or more traumatized from being raped by someone known or trusted, someone with whom at least an illusion of mutuality has been shared, than by some stranger. In whose interest is it to believe that it is not so bad to be raped by someone who has fucked you before as by someone who has not? Disallowing charges of rape in marriage may, depending upon one's view of normalcy, "remove a substantial obstacle to the resumption of normal marital relationships."[22] Note that the obstacle is not the rape but the law against it. Apparently someone besides feminists finds sexual victimization and sexual intimacy not all that contradictory under current conditions. Sometimes it seems as though women and men live in different cultures.

Having defined rape in male sexual terms, the law's problem, which becomes the victim's problem, is distinguishing rape from sex in specific cases. The adjudicated line between rape and intercourse commonly centers on some assessment of the woman's "will." But how should the law or the accused know a woman's will? The answer combines aspects of force with aspects of nonconsent with elements of resistance, still effective in some states.[23] Even when nonconsent is not a legal element of the offense, juries tend to infer rape from evidence of force or resistance. In Michigan, under its reform rape law, consent was judicially held to be a defense even though it was not included in the statute.[24]

The deeper problem is that women are socialized to passive receptivity; may have or perceive no alternative to acquiescence; may prefer it to the escalated risk of injury and the humiliation of a lost fight; submit to survive. Also, force and desire are not mutually exclusive under male supremacy. So long as dominance is eroticized, they never will be. Some women eroticize dominance and submission; it beats feeling forced. Sexual intercourse may be deeply unwanted, the woman would never have initiated it, yet no force may be present. So much force may have been used that the woman never risked saying no. Force may be used, yet the woman may prefer the sex—to avoid more force or because she, too, eroticizes dominance. Women and men know this. Considering rape as violence not sex evades, at the moment it most seems to confront, the issue of who controls women's sexuality and the dominance/submission dynamic that has defined it. When sex is violent, women may have lost control over what is done to them, but absence of force does not ensure the presence of that control. Nor, under conditions of male dominance, does the presence of force make an interaction nonsexual. If sex is normally something men do to women, the issue is less whether there was force than whether consent is a meaningful concept.[25]

To explain women's gender status on a rape theory, Susan Brownmiller argues that the threat of rape benefits all men.[26] How is unspecified. Perhaps it benefits them sexually, hence as a gender: male initiatives toward women carry the fear of rape as support for persuading compliance, the resulting appearance of which has been considered seduction and termed consent. Here the victims' perspective grasps what liberalism applied to women denies: that forced sex as sexuality is not exceptional in relations between the sexes but constitutes the social meaning of gender. "Rape is a man's act, whether it is a male or a female man and whether it is a man relatively permanently or relatively temporarily; and being raped is a woman's experience, whether it is a female or a male woman and whether it is a woman relatively permanently or relatively temporarily."[27] To be rapable, a position that is social not biological, defines what a woman is.

Marital rape and battery of wives have been separated by law. A feminist analysis suggests that assault by a man's fist is not so different from assault by a penis, not because both are violent but because both are sexual. Battery is often precipitated by women's noncompliance with gender requirements.[28] Nearly all incidents occur in the home, most in the kitchen or bedroom. Most murdered women are killed by their husbands or boyfriends, usually in the bedroom. The battery cycle accords with the rhythms of heterosexual sex.[29] The rhythm of lesbian sadomasochism is the same.[30] Perhaps violent interchanges, especially between genders, make sense in sexual terms.

The larger issue raised by sexual aggression for the interpretation of the relation between sexuality and gender is: what is heterosexuality? If it is the erotization of dominance and submission, altering the participants' gender does not eliminate the sexual, or even gendered, content of aggression. If heterosexuality is males over females, gender matters independently. Arguably, heterosexuality is a fusion of the two, with gender a social outcome, such that the acted upon is feminized, is the "girl" regardless of sex, the actor correspondingly masculinized. Whenever women are victimized, regardless of the biology of the perpetrator, this system is at work. But it is equally true that whenever powerlessness and ascribed inferiority are sexually exploited or enjoyed—based on age, race, physical stature or appearance or ability, or socially reviled or stigmatized status—the system is at work.

Battery thus appears sexual on a deeper level. Stated in boldest terms, sexuality is violent, so perhaps violence is sexual. Violence against women is sexual on both counts, doubly sexy. If this is so, wives are beaten, as well as raped, as women—as the acted upon, as gender, meaning sexual, objects. It further follows that acts by anyone which treat a woman according to her object label, woman, are in a sense sexual acts. The extent to which sexual acts are acts of objectification remains a question of one's account of women's freedom to live their own meanings as other than illusions, of individuals' ability to resist or escape, even momentarily, prescribed social meanings short of political change. Clearly, centering sexuality upon genitality distinguishes battery from rape at exactly the juncture that both existing law, and seeing rape as violence not sex, do.

Most women get the message that the law against rape is virtually unenforceable as applied to them. Women's experience is more often delegitimated by this than the law is. Women, as realists, distinguish between rape and experiences of sexual violation by concluding that they have not "really" been raped if they have ever seen or dated or slept with or been married to the man, if they were fashionably dressed or not provably virgin, if they are prostitutes, if they put up with it or tried to get it over with, if they were force-fucked for years. The implicit social standard becomes: if a woman probably could not prove it in court, it was not rape.

The distance between most intimate violations of women and the legally perfect rape measures the imposition of an alien definition. From women's point of view, rape is not prohibited; it is regulated. Even women who know they have been raped do not believe that the legal system will see it the way they do. Often they are not wrong. Rather than deterring or avenging rape, the state, in many victims' experiences, perpetuates it. Women who charge rape say they were raped twice, the second time in court. Under a male state, the boundary violation, humiliation, and indignity of being a public sexual spectacle makes this more than a figure of speech.[31]

Rape, like many other crimes, requires that the accused possess a criminal mind (*mens rea*) for his acts to be criminal. The man's mental state refers to what he actually understood at the time or to what a reasonable man should have understood under the circumstances. The problem is that the injury of rape lies in the meaning of the act to its victim, but the standard for its criminality lies in the meaning of the act to the assailant. Rape is only an injury from women's point of view. It is only a crime from the male point of view, explicitly including that of the accused.

The crime of rape is defined and adjudicated from the male standpoint, presuming that forced sex is sex and that consent to a man is freely given by a woman. Under male supremacist standards, of course, they are. Doctrinally, this means that the man's perceptions of the woman's desires determine whether she is deemed violated. This might be like other crimes of subjective intent if rape were like other crimes. With rape, because sexuality defines gender norms, the only difference between assault and what is socially defined as a noninjury is the meaning of the encounter to the woman. Interpreted this way, the legal problem has been to determine whose view of that meaning constitutes what really happened, as if what happened objectively exists to be objectively determined. This task has been assumed to be separable from the gender of the participants and the gendered nature of their exchange, when the objective norms and the assailant's perspective are identical.

As a result, although the rape law oscillates between subjective tests and objective standards invoking social reasonableness, it uniformly presumes a single underlying reality, rather than a reality split by the divergent meanings inequality produces. Many women are raped by men who know the meaning of their acts to their victims perfectly well and proceed anyway.[32] But women are also violated every day by men who have no idea of the meaning of their acts to the women. To them it is sex. Therefore, to the law it is sex. That becomes the single reality of what happened. When a rape prosecution is lost because a woman fails to prove that she did not consent, she is not considered to have been injured at all. It is as if a robbery victim, finding himself unable to prove he was not engaged in philanthropy, is told he still has his money. Hermeneutically unpacked, the law assumes that, because the rapist did not perceive that the woman did not want him, she was not violated. She had sex. Sex itself cannot be an injury. Women have sex every day. Sex makes a woman a woman. Sex is what women are for.

Men set sexual mores ideologically and behaviorally, define rape as they imagine women to be sexually violated through distinguishing that from their image of what they normally do, and sit in judgment in most accusations of sex crimes. So rape comes to mean a strange (read Black) man who does not know his victim but does know she does not want sex with him, going ahead anyway. But men are systematically conditioned not even to notice what women want. Especially if they consume pornography, they may have not a glimmer of women's indifference or revulsion, including when women say no explicitly. Rapists typically believe the woman loved it. "Probably the single most used cry of rapist to victim is 'You bitch . . . slut . . . you know you want it. You all want it' and afterward, 'there now, you really enjoyed it, didn't you?' "[33] Women, as a survival strategy, must ignore or devalue or mute desires, particularly lack of them, to convey the impression that the man will get what he wants regardless of what they want. In this context, to measure the genuineness of consent from the individual assailant's point of view is to adopt as law the point of view which creates the problem. Measuring consent from the socially reasonable, meaning objective man's, point of view reproduces the same problem under a more elevated label.[34]

Men's pervasive belief that women fabricate rape charges after consenting to sex makes sense in this light. To them, the accusations are false because, to them, the facts describe sex. To interpret such events as rapes distorts their experience. Since they seldom consider that their experience of the real is anything other than reality, they can only explain the woman's version as maliciously invented. Similarly, the male anxiety that rape is easy to charge and difficult to disprove, also widely believed in the face of overwhelming evidence to the contrary, arises because rape accusations express one thing men cannot seem to control: the meaning to women of sexual encounters.

Thus do legal doctrines, incoherent or puzzling as syllogistic logic, become coherent as ideology. For example, when an accused wrongly but sincerely believes that a woman he sexually forced consented, he may have a defense of mistaken belief in consent or fail to satisfy the mental requirement of knowingly proceeding against her will.[35] Sometimes his knowing disregard is measured by what a reasonable man would disregard. This is considered an objective test. Sometimes the disregard need not be reasonable so long as it is sincere. This is considered a subjective test. A feminist inquiry into the distinction between rape and intercourse, by contrast, would inquire into the meaning of the act from women's point of view, which is neither. What is wrong with rape in this view is that it is an act of subordination of women to men. It expresses and reinforces women's inequality to men. Rape with legal impunity makes women second-class citizens.

This analysis reveals the way the social conception of rape is shaped to interpret particular encounters and the way the legal conception of rape authoritatively shapes that social conception. When perspective is bound up with situation, and situation is unequal, whether or not a contested interaction is authoritatively considered rape comes down to whose meaning wins. If sexuality is relational, specifically if it is a power relation of gender, consent is a communication under conditions of inequality. It transpires somewhere between what the woman actually wanted, what she was able to express about what she wanted, and what the man comprehended she wanted.

Discussing the conceptually similar issue of revocation of prior consent, on the issue of the conditions under which women are allowed to control access to their sexuality from one penetration to the next, one commentator notes: "Even where a woman revokes prior consent, such is the male ego that, seized of an exaggerated assessment of his sexual prowess, a man might genuinely believe her still to be consenting; resistance may be misinterpreted as enthusiastic coopera-tion; protestations of pain or disinclination, a spur to more sophisti-cated or more ardent love-making; a clear statement to stop, taken as referring to a particular intimacy rather than the entire per-formance."[36] This vividly captures common male readings of women's indications of disinclination under many circumstances[37] and the perceptions that determine whether a rape occurred. The specific defense of mistaken belief in consent merely carries this to its logical apex. From whose standpoint, and in whose interest, is a law that allows one person's conditioned unconsciousness to contraindicate another's violation? In conceiving a cognizable injury from the viewpoint of the reasonable rapist, the rape law affirmatively rewards men with acquittals for not comprehending women's point of view on sexual encounters.

Whether the law calls this coerced consent or defense of mistaken belief in consent, the more the sexual violation of women is routine, the more pornography exists in the world the more legitimately, the more beliefs equating sexuality with violation become reasonable, and the more honestly women can be defined in terms of their fuckability. It would be comparatively simple if the legal problem were limited to avoiding retroactive falsification of the accused's state of mind. Surely there are incentives to lie. The deeper problem is the rape law's assumption that a single, objective state of affairs existed, one that merely needs to be determined by evidence, when so many rapes involve honest men and violated women. When the reality is split, is the woman raped but not by a rapist? Under these conditions, the law is designed to conclude that a rape did not occur. To attempt to solve this problem by adopting reasonable belief as a standard without asking, on a substantive social basis, to whom the belief is reasonable and why—meaning, what conditions make it reasonable —is one-sided: male-sided.[38] What is it reasonable for a man to believe concerning a woman's desire for sex when heterosexuality is compulsory? What is it reasonable for a man (accused or juror) to believe concerning a woman's consent when he has been viewing positive-outcome-rape pornography?[39] The one whose subjectivity becomes the objectivity of "what happened" is a matter of social meaning, that is, a matter of sexual politics. One-sidedly erasing women's violation or dissolving presumptions into the subjectivity of either side are the alternatives dictated by the terms of the object/subject split, respectively. These alternatives will only retrace that split to women's detriment until its terms are confronted as gendered to the ground.

# 10 | *Abortion: On Public and Private*

> In a society where women entered sexual intercourse willingly, where adequate contraception was a genuine social priority, there would be no "abortion issue" . . . Abortion is violence . . . It is the offspring, and will continue to be the accuser of a more pervasive and prevalent violence, the violence of rapism.
>
> —Adrienne Rich, *Of Woman Born*

$M$ost women who seek abortions became pregnant while having sexual intercourse with men. Most did not mean or wish to conceive. In women's experience, sexuality and reproduction are inseparable from each other and from gender. The abortion debate, by contrast, has centered on separating control over sexuality from control over reproduction, and on separating both from gender. Liberals have supported the availability of the abortion choice as if the woman just happened on the fetus,[1] usually on the implicit view that reproductive control is essential to sexual freedom and economic independence. The political right imagines that the intercourse that precedes conception is usually voluntary, only to urge abstinence, as if sex were up to women. At the same time, the right defends male authority, specifically including a wife's duty to submit to sex. Continuing this logic, many opponents of state funding of abortions would permit funding of abortions when pregnancy results from rape or incest.[2] They make exceptions for those special occasions on which they presume women did not control sex. Abortion's proponents and opponents share a tacit assumption that women significantly control sex.

Feminist investigations suggest otherwise. Sexual intercourse, still the most common cause of pregnancy, cannot simply be presumed coequally determined. Women feel compelled to preserve the appearance—which, acted upon, becomes the reality—of male direction of sexual expression, as if it were male initiative itself that women want, as if it were that which women find arousing. Men enforce this. It is much of what men want in a woman, what pornography eroticizes and prostitutes provide. Rape—that is, intercourse with force that is recognized as force—is adjudicated not according to the power or force that the man wields, but according to indices of intimacy between the parties. The more intimate one is with one's accused rapist, the less likely a court is to find that what happened was rape. Often indices of intimacy include intercourse itself. If "no" can be taken as "yes," how free can "yes" be?

Under these conditions, women often do not use birth control because of its social meaning, a meaning women did not create. Using contraception means acknowledging and planning the possibility of intercourse, accepting one's sexual availability, and appearing nonspontaneous. It means appearing available to male incursions. It also means that one must want to have sex. A good user of contraception can be presumed sexually available and, among other consequences, raped with relative impunity. (Doubters should consider rape cases in which the fact that a woman had a diaphragm in is taken as an indication that what happened to her was intercourse, not rape.) Studies of abortion clinics show that women who repeatedly seek abortions, especially the repeat offenders high on the list of the right's villains—their best case for opposing abortion as female sexual irresponsibility—when asked why, say something like the sex just happened. Every night for two and a half years.[3] Can a woman be presumed to control access to her sexuality if she feels unable to interrupt intercourse to insert a diaphragm? Or worse, cannot even want to, aware that she risks a pregnancy she knows she does not want? Would she stop the man for any other reason, such as, for instance, the real taboo—lack of desire? If not, how is sex, hence its consequences, meaningfully voluntary for women? Norms of sexual rhythm and romance which are felt to be interrupted by women's needs are constructed against women's interests. Sex does not look a lot like freedom when it appears normatively less costly for women to risk an undesired, often painful, traumatic, dangerous, sometimes illegal, and potentially life-threatening procedure than to protect oneself in advance. Yet abortion policy has never been explicitly approached in the context of how women get pregnant; that is, as a consequence of intercourse under conditions of gender inequality; that is, as an issue of forced sex.

Several important explorations are bracketed by this approach. The first is, what are babies to men? On one level, men respond to women's right to abort as if confronting the possibility of their own potential nonexistence—at women's hands, no less. On another level, men's issues of potency, of continuity as a compensation for mortality, of the thrust to embody themselves or their own image in the world, underlie their relation to babies (and much else). The second bracketed issue is one that, unlike the first, has been discussed extensively in the abortion debate: the moral rightness of abortion. The abortion choice should be available and must be women's, but not because the fetus is not a form of life. Why should women not make life-or-death decisions? The problem has been that if the fetus has *any* standing in the debate, it has more weight than women do. Women's embattled need to survive in a world hostile to their survival has largely precluded exploration of these issues. That is, the perspective from which feminists have addressed abortion has been shaped and constrained by the very conditions of sex inequality which have made abortion access the problem it is. Women have not been able to risk thinking about these issues on their own terms because the terms have not been theirs—in sex, in social life, or in court.

In 1973 the Supreme Court found that a statute that made criminal all abortions except those to save the life of the mother violated the constitutional right to privacy.[4] The privacy right had been previously created as a constitutional principle in a case that decriminalized the prescription and use of contraceptives.[5] In other words, courts use the privacy rubric to connect contraception with abortion through privacy in the same way that feminism does through sexuality. In *Roe*, the right to privacy was found "broad enough to encompass a woman's decision whether or not to terminate her pregnancy." In 1981 three justices observed in a dissent: "In the abortion context, we have held that the right to privacy shields the woman from undue state intrusion in and external scrutiny of her very personal choice."[6]

In 1981 the Supreme Court decided in *Harris v. McRae* that this right to privacy did not mean that federal Medicaid programs had to cover medically necessary abortions. Privacy, the Court had said, was guaranteed for "a woman's decision whether or not to terminate her pregnancy." The government was then permitted to support one decision and not another: to fund continuing conceptions and not to fund discontinuing them. Asserting that decisional privacy was nevertheless constitutionally intact, the Court stated that "although the government may not place obstacles in the path of a woman's exercise of her freedom of choice, it need not remove those not of its own creation."[7] It is apparently a very short step from that in which the government has a duty *not* to intervene, to that in which it has *no* duty to intervene. Citing *Harris,* the Court found this was no step at all in a case that held state child protection officials were not, absent discrimination, legally responsible for a child who was permanently injured through an abusive situation of which they were aware: "while the State may have been aware of the dangers that Joshua faced in the free world, it played no part in their creation, nor did it do anything to render him any more vulnerable to them."[8] The world without state intervention, the world of state inaction, the private world of Joshua's abuse and poor women's unfunded abortions, is "the free world." For those who use and abuse women and children, it is.

Regarded as the outer edge of limits on government, the idea of privacy embodies a tension between precluding public exposure or governmental intrusion on the one hand, and autonomy in the sense of protecting personal self-action on the other. This is a tension, not just two facets of one right. The liberal state resolves this tension by identifying the threshold of the state at its permissible extent of penetration into a domain that is considered free by definition: the private sphere. By this move the state secures "an inviolable personality" by ensuring "autonomy of control over the intimacies of personal identity."[9] The state does this by centering its self-restraint on body and home, especially bedroom. By staying out of marriage and the family—essentially meaning sexuality, that is, hetero-sexuality—from contraception through pornography to the abortion decision, the law of privacy proposes to guarantee individual bodily integrity, personal exercise of moral intelligence, and freedom of intimacy.[10] But have women's rights of access to those values been guaranteed? The law of privacy instead translates traditional liberal values into individual rights as a means of subordinating those rights to specific social imperatives.[11] In particular, the logic of the grant of the abortion right is consummated in the funding decision, enforcing male supremacy with capitalism, translating the ideology of the private sphere into the individual woman's legal right to privacy as a means of subordinating women's collective needs to the imperatives of male supremacy.

Here, as in other areas of law, the way the male point of view constructs a social event or legal need will be the way that social event or legal need is framed by state policy. To the extent possession is the point of sex, illegal rape will be sex with a woman who is not yours unless the act makes her yours. If part of the thrill of pornography involves eroticizing the putatively prohibited, illegal pornography—obscenity—will be prohibited enough to keep pornography desirable without ever making it truly illegitimate or unavailable. If, from the male standpoint, male is the implicit definition of human, maleness will be the implicit standard by which sex equality is measured in discrimination law, from which women will be "different." In parallel terms, reproduction is sexual. Men control sexuality. The state supports the interest of men as a group. So why was abortion legalized? Why were women given even that much control? It is not an accusation of bad faith to answer that the interests of men as a social group converge with the definition of justice embodied in law through the male point of view. The abortion right frames the ways men arrange among themselves to control the reproductive consequences of intercourse. The availability of abortion enhances the availability of intercourse.

Since Freud, the social problem posed by sexuality has been understood as the problem of the innate desire for sexual pleasure being repressed by the constraints of civilization. In this context, inequality arises as an issue only in women's repressive socialization to passivity and coolness (so-called frigidity or desexualization) and in the disparate consequences of biology, pregnancy. Who defines what is sexual, what sexuality therefore is, to whom what stimuli are erotic and why, and who defines the conditions under which sexuality is expressed—these issues have not even been available for consideration. Civilization's answer to these questions has fused women's reproductivity with their attributed sexuality in its definition of what a woman is. Women are defined as women by the uses, sexual and reproductive, to which men wish to put them.

In this context it becomes clear why the struggle for reproductive freedom has never included a woman's right to refuse sex. In the concept of sexual liberation which has undergirded the politics of choice, sexual equality has been a struggle for women to have sex with

men on the same terms as men: "without consequences." Meaning, no
children. In this sense the abortion right has been sought as freedom
from the unequal reproductive consequences of sexual expression, with
sexuality centered on heterosexual genital intercourse. It has been as if
biological organisms, rather than social relations, reproduced the
species. But if one's concern is not how more people can get more sex,
but who defines sexuality—both pleasure and violation—and therefore
who defines women, the abortion right is situated within a very
different problematic: the social and political inequality of the sexes.
This repositioning of the issue requires reformulating the problem of
sexuality from the repression of drives by civilization to the oppression
of women by men.

Even before *Roe v. Wade,* arguments for abortion under the rubric of
feminism have rested upon the right to control one's own body, gender
neutral.[12] This argument has been appealing for the same reasons it is
inadequate: socially, women's bodies have not been theirs; women
have not controlled their meanings and destinies. Feminists have tried
to assert that control without risking pursuit of the idea that
something more than women's bodies might be at stake, something
closer to a net of relations in which women are gendered and
unequal.[13] Some feminists have noticed that women's right to decide
has become merged with an overwhelmingly male professional's right
not to have his judgment second-guessed by the government.[14] But
whatever their underlying politics, most abortion advocates, at least
since 1971, have argued in rigidly and rigorously gender-neutral
terms.

For instance, Judith Jarvis Thomson's argument that an abducted
woman had no obligation to be a celebrated violinist's life support
system was to mean that women have no obligation to support a
fetus.[15] No woman who needs an abortion—no woman, period—is
valued, no potential a woman's life might hold is cherished, like a
gender-neutral famous violinist's unencumbered possibilities. The
problems of gender are underlined in this analogy rather than solved
or even addressed. The origin of the hypothetical in force gives the
conclusion much of its moral weight. But the parallel would begin the
abortion problem in rape, perhaps confining abortions to instances in
which force is recognized as force, like rape or incest. The applicability
of the origin in force to the normal abortion is neither embraced nor
disavowed, although the argument was intended to justify the normal

abortion. The parable is constructed to begin the debate after sex occurred but requires discussion of the relation of intercourse to rape to make sense of its application. Because this issue has been studiously avoided in the abortion context, the unequal and liberal basis on which woman's private personhood is constructed has been obscured.

Abortion promises women sex with men on the same terms on which men have sex with women. So long as women do not control access to their sexuality, this facilitates women's heterosexual availability. In other words, under conditions of gender inequality, sexual liberation in this sense does not so much free women sexually as it frees male sexual aggression. The availability of abortion removes the one real consequence men could not easily ignore, the one remaining legitimated reason that women have had for refusing sex besides the headache. As Andrea Dworkin puts it, analyzing male ideology on abortion: "Getting laid was at stake."[16]

Privacy doctrine is an ideal vehicle for this process. The liberal ideal of the private holds that, so long as the public does not interfere, autonomous individuals interact freely and equally. Privacy is the ultimate value of the negative state. Conceptually, this private is hermetic. It means that which is inaccessible to, unaccountable to, unconstructed by, anything beyond itself. By definition, it is not part of or conditioned by anything systematic outside it. It is personal, intimate, autonomous, particular, individual, the original source and final outpost of the self, gender neutral. It is defined by everything that feminism reveals women have never been allowed to be or to have, and by everything that women have been equated with and defined in terms of men's ability to have. To complain in public of inequality within the private contradicts the liberal definition of the private. In the liberal view, no act of the state contributes to shaping its internal alignments or distributing its internal forces, so no act of the state should participate in changing it. Its inviolability by the state, framed as an individual right, presupposes that the private is not already an arm of the state. In this scheme, intimacy is implicitly thought to guarantee symmetry of power. Injuries arise through violation of the private sphere, not within and by and because of it.

In private, consent tends to be presumed. Showing coercion is supposed to void this presumption. But the problem is getting anything private to be perceived as coercive. In law, the private is fundamentally an angle of vision, a way of seeing from the point of view of power, attached later to a place or quality of being. It sees so as to surround power with a sacred circle of impunity. Private is what men call the damage they want to be permitted to do as far as their arms extend to whomever they do not want permitted to fight back. Epistemically, in gender terms, it means that male force is invisible. When aggression occurs, what is seen is consent. Privacy seems to stick to white upper-class men and follow them into the world, forfeited only under unusual conditions, while consent seems to stick to women. As interpretation, when what men do is private, their aggression is not seen at all, and women are seen to consent to it. It is not that this is never overcome, but rather that there is something there that must be overcome in order for force to be seen as force.

This epistemic problem explains why privacy doctrine is most at home at home, the place women experience the most force, in the family, and why it centers on sex. Why a person would "allow" force in private (the "why doesn't she leave" question raised to battered women) is a question given its insult by the social meaning of the private as a sphere of choice. For women the measure of the intimacy has been the measure of the oppression. This is why feminism has had to explode the private. This is why feminism has seen the personal as the political. The private is public for those for whom the personal is political. In this sense, for women there is no private, either normatively or empirically. Feminism confronts the fact that women have no privacy to lose or to guarantee. Women are not inviolable. Women's sexuality is not only violable, it is—hence, women are—seen in and as their violation. To confront the fact that women have no privacy is to confront the intimate degradation of women as the public order. The doctrinal choice of privacy in the abortion context thus reaffirms and reinforces what the feminist critique of sexuality criticizes: the public/private split. The political and ideological meaning of privacy as a legal doctrine is continuous with the concrete consequences of the public/private split for the lives of women. In this light, the abortion funding ruling appears consistent with the larger meaning of the original granting of the abortion right.

The right to privacy looks like a sword in men's hands presented as a shield in women's. Freedom from public intervention coexists uneasily with any right that requires social preconditions to be meaningfully delivered. For example, if inequality is socially pervasive and enforced, equality will require intervention, not abdication, to be meaningful. But the right to privacy is not thought to require social change. It is not even thought to require any social preconditions, other than nonintervention by the public. The point for the abortion cases is not that indigency—the specific barrier to effective choice in *Harris v. McRae*—is well within the public power to remedy, nor that the state is hardly exempt in issues of the distribution of wealth. The point is that *Roe v. Wade* presumes that government nonintervention in the private sphere promotes a woman's freedom of choice. When the alternative is jail, there is much to be said for this presumption. But the *McRae* result sustains the meaning of privacy in *Roe:* women are guaranteed by the public no more than what they can get in private—what they can extract through their intimate associations with men. Women with privileges, including class privileges, get rights.

Women were granted the abortion right as a private privilege, not as a public right. Women got control over reproduction which is controlled by "a man or The Man,"[17] an individual man or the doctors or the government. Abortion was not so much decriminalized as it was legalized. In *Roe v. Wade,* the government set the stage for the conditions under which women got this right. Most of the control that women won out of legalization has gone directly into the hands of men—husbands, doctors, or fathers—and what remains in women's hands is now subject to attempted reclamation through regulation.[18] This, surely, must be what is meant by reform.

It is not inconsistent, then, that, framed as a privacy right, a woman's decision to abort would have no claim on public support and would genuinely not be seen as burdened by that deprivation.[19] State intervention would have admitted that the private sphere, left alone, is a sphere of preclusion of procreative choice, of inequality, in need of rectification. State intervention would have provided a choice women did not have in private, would have contradicted the male-supremacist structure of the private; the *McRae* result confirmed that structure. Privacy conceived as a right from public intervention and disclosure is the opposite of the relief that *McRae* sought for welfare women. What they got was privacy constructed from the point of view with the power to make procreative choices without governmental intervention—that is, the liberal construct of choice, from the male point of view. The women in *McRae,* women whose sexual refusal has counted for particularly little, needed something positive, not abdication, to make their privacy effective. The logic of the Court's response resembles the logic by which women are supposed to consent to sex: preclude the alternatives, then call the one remaining option "her choice." Women's alternatives are precluded prior to the reach of the legal doctrine by conditions of sex, race, and class—the very conditions the privacy frame leaves tacit and guarantees.

Liberalism converges with the left at this edge of the feminist critique of male power. Herbert Marcuse speaks of "philosophies which are 'political' in the widest sense—affecting society as a whole, demonstrably transcending the sphere of privacy."[20] This formulation does and does not describe the feminist political, because "women both have and have not had a common world."[21] Women share isolation in the home and degradation in intimacy. The private sphere, which confines and separates women, is therefore a political sphere, a common ground of women's inequality. Rather than transcending the private as a predicate to politics, feminism politicizes it. For women, epistemically and daily, the private necessarily transcends the private. If the most private also most "affects society as a whole," the separation between public and private collapses as anything other than potent ideology in life and in law, enforced on women's lives. If marxists treated sex the way they treat class, this analysis would be understood. For example, Schlomo Avineri observes that a person's private status is determined in modern society by property relations (that is, by "civil society"), which relations are no longer private but determine politics. Politics remains a rationalization of property relations, as it was for Marx, but what was private is nonetheless political.[22] The failure of marxism adequately to address intimacy on the one hand, government on the other, is the same failure as the indistinguishability of marxism from liberalism on questions of sexual politics.

When the law of privacy restricts intrusions into intimacy, it bars changes in control over that intimacy. The existing distribution of power and resources within the private sphere are precisely what the law of privacy exists to protect. In one remarkable if subliminal admission that male power by men in the family is coextensive with state power, the Supreme Court held that a state could not grant biological fathers the right to veto abortions in the first trimester because, given *Roe*, the state did not have this power.[23] Observe that the very things feminism regards as central to the subjection of women—the very place, the body; the very relations, heterosexual; the very activities, intercourse and reproduction; and the very feelings, intimate—form the core of privacy doctrine's coverage. Privacy law assumes women are equal to men in there. Through this perspective, the legal concept of privacy can and has shielded the place of battery, marital rape, and women's exploited domestic labor. It has preserved the central institutions whereby women are deprived of identity, autonomy, control, and self-definition. It has protected a primary activity through which male supremacy is expressed and enforced. Just as pornography is legally protected as individual freedom of expression—without any questions about whose freedom and whose expression and at whose expense—abstract privacy protects abstract autonomy, without inquiring into whose freedom of action is being sanctioned, at whose expense, from whose point of view.

To fail to recognize the meaning of the private in the ideology and reality of women's subordination by seeking protection behind a right to that privacy is to cut women off from collective verification and state support in the same act. When women are segregated in private, separated from each other one at a time, a right *to* that privacy isolates women at once from each other and from public recourse. This right to privacy is a right of men "to be let alone"[24] to oppress women one at a time. It embodies and reflects the private sphere's existing definition of womanhood. This instance of liberalism—defined from the male standpoint as if it had no particularity and applied to women as if they were persons, gender neutral[25]—reinforces the division between public and private which is very particular and not gender neutral. It is an ideological division that covers up male power, lies about women's shared experience, and mystifies the unity among the spheres of women's violation. It polices the division between public and private, an at once epistemic and material division that keeps the private in male hands, beyond public redress, and depoliticizes women's subjection within it. Privacy law keeps some men out of the bedrooms of other men.

# 11 | *Pornography: On Morality and Politics*

Pornosec, the subsection of the Fiction Department which turned out cheap pornography for distribution among the proles . . . nicknamed Muck House by the people who worked it . . . produce[d] booklets in sealed packets with titles like "Spanking Stories" or "One Night in a Girls' School," to be bought furtively by proletarian youths who were under the impression that they were buying something illegal.

—George Orwell, *1984*

Silence is a woman's ornament.

—Sophocles

*P*ossession and use of women through the sexualization of intimate intrusion and access to them is a central feature of women's social definition as inferior and feminine. Visual and verbal intrusion, access, possession, and use is predicated upon and produces physical and psychic intrusion, access, possession, and use. In contemporary industrial society, pornography is an industry that mass produces sexual intrusion on, access to, possession and use of women by and for men for profit. It exploits women's sexual and economic inequality for gain. It sells women to men as and for sex. It is a technologically sophisticated traffic in women.

This understanding of the reality of pornography must contend not only with centuries of celebratory intellectual obfuscation.[1] It must contend with a legal tradition of neutralization through abstraction from the realities of power, a tradition that has authoritatively defined pornography as not about women as such at all, but about sex, hence about morality, and as not about acts or practices, but about ideas. Uncovering gender in this area of law reveals women to be most invisible when most exposed and most silent when used in defense of speech. In both pornography and the law of obscenity, women are seen only as sex and heard only when mouthing a sexual script. When pornography and the law of pornography are investigated together, it becomes clear that pornography is to women's status, hence its critique is to feminism, as its preservation is to male supremacy in its liberal legal guise.

The law of obscenity[2] is the state's approach to addressing the pornography problem, which it construes as an issue of regulation of expression under the First Amendment.[3] Nudity, explicitness, excess of candor, arousal or excitement, prurience, unnaturalness—these qualities raise concerns under obscenity law when sex is depicted or portrayed. Abortion or birth control information or treatments for "restoring sexual virility" (whose, do you suppose?) have also been covered.[4] Sex forced on real women so that it can be sold at a profit to be forced on other real women; women's bodies trussed and maimed and raped and made into things to be hurt and obtained and accessed and this presented as the nature of women; the coercion that is visible and the coercion that has become invisible—this and more grounds the feminist concern with pornography. Obscenity as such probably does little harm.[5] Pornography contributes causally to attitudes and behaviors of violence and discrimination which define the treatment and status of half the population.[6]

Obscenity law is concerned with morality, meaning good and evil, virtue and vice. The concerns of feminism with power and powerlessness are first political, not moral. From the feminist perspective, obscenity is a moral idea; pornography is a political practice. Obscenity is abstract; pornography is concrete. Obscenity conveys moral condemnation as a predicate to legal condemnation. Pornography identifies a political practice that is predicated on power and powerlessness—a practice that is, in fact, legally protected. The two concepts represent two entirely different things.

In accounting for gender inequality as part of the socially constructed relationship between power—the political—on the one hand and knowledge of truth and reality—the epistemological—on the other, the classic description Justice Stewart once offered of the obscenity standard, "I know it when I see it,"[7] becomes even more revealing than it is usually taken to be. Taken as a statement that connects epistemology with power, if one asks, from the point of view of women's experience, does he know what women know when we see what we see, one has to doubt it, given what is on the newsstands. How does his point of view keep what is there, there? To liberal critics, his admission exposed the relativity, the partiality, the insufficient abstractness of the obscenity standard. Not to be emptily universal, to leave your concreteness showing, is a sin among men. Their problem with Justice Stewart's formulation is that it implies that anything, capriciously, could be suppressed. In fact, almost nothing is. The meaning of what his view permits, as it turns out, is anything but capricious. It is entirely systematic and determinate. His statement is precisely descriptively accurate; its candor is why it has drawn so much criticism.[8] He admitted what courts do epistemologically all the time. In so doing, he both did it and gave it the stature of doctrine (if only dictum). That is, he revealed that the obscenity standard—and it is not unique—is built on what the male standpoint sees. The problem is, so is pornography. In this way, the law of obscenity reproduces the pornographic point of view of women on the level of constitutional jurisprudence.

Pornography, in the feminist view, is a form of forced sex, a practice of sexual politics, an institution of gender inequality.[9] In this perspective, pornography, with the rape and prostitution in which it participates, institutionalizes the sexuality of male supremacy, which fuses the erotization of dominance and submission with the social construction of male and female. Gender is sexual. Pornography constitutes the meaning of that sexuality. Men treat women as whom they see women as being. Pornography constructs who that is. Men's power over women means that the way men see women defines who women can be. Pornography is that way.[10] In this light, obscenity law can be seen to treat morals from the male point of view, meaning the standpoint of male dominance. The feminist critique of pornography, by contrast, proceeds from women's point of view, meaning the standpoint of the subordination of women to men.

One can be for or against this pornography without getting beyond liberalism. The critical yet formally liberal view of Susan Griffin, for example, conceptualizes eroticism as natural and healthy but corrupted and confused by "the pornographic mind."[11] Pornography distorts

Eros, which preexists and persists, despite male culture's pornographic "revenge" upon it. Eros is, unaccountably, still there. Pornography mistakes it, mis-images it, misrepresents it. There is no critique of reality here, only objections to how it is seen; no critique of that reality that pornography imposes on women's real lives, those lives that are so seamlessly consistent with the pornography that it can be credibly defended by saying it is only a mirror of reality.

Contrast this with the feminist analysis of pornography by Andrea Dworkin, in which sexuality itself is a social construct, gendered to the ground. Male dominance here is not an artificial overlay upon an underlying inalterable substratum of uncorrupted essential sexual being. Sexuality free of male dominance will require change, not reconceptualization, transcendence, or excavation. Pornography is not imagery in some relation to a reality elsewhere constructed. It is not a distortion, reflection, projection, expression, fantasy, representation, or symbol either. It is sexual reality. Andrea Dworkin's *Pornography* presents a sexual theory of gender inequality of which pornography is a core constitutive practice. The way pornography produces its meaning constructs and defines men and women as such. Gender is what gender means. [12] It has no basis in anything other than the social reality its hegemony constructs. The process that gives sexuality its male supremacist meaning is therefore the process through which gender inequality becomes socially real.

In this analysis, the liberal defense of pornography as human sexual liberation, as derepression—whether by feminists, marxists, or neo-Freudians—is a defense not only of force and sexual terrorism, but of the subordination of women. [13] Sexual liberation in the liberal sense frees male sexual aggression in the feminist sense. What in the liberal view looks like love and romance looks a lot like hatred and torture to the feminist. Pleasure and eroticism become violation. Desire appears as lust for dominance and submission. The vulnerability of women's projected sexual availability is victimization. The acting that women are allowed is asking to be acted upon. Play conforms to scripted roles, fantasy expresses ideology not exemption from it, and admiration of natural physical beauty becomes objectification.

The experience of the (overwhelmingly) male audiences who consume pornography is therefore not fantasy or simulation or catharsis but sexual reality: the level of reality on which sex itself largely operates. [14] To understand this does not require noticing that women in pornography are real women to whom something real is being done.[15] It does not even require inquiring into the systematic infliction of pornographic sexuality upon women, although it helps.[16] The aesthetic of pornography itself, the way it provides what those who consume it want, is itself the evidence. Pornography turns a woman into a thing to be acquired and used.[17] When uncensored explicit— that is, the most pornographic—pornography tells all, all means what a distanced detached observer would report about who did what to whom. This is the turn-on. Why does having sex as object, observing sex objectively presented, cause the male viewer to experience his own sexuality? Because his eroticism is, socially, a watched thing.[18]

If objectivity is the epistemological stance of which objectification is the social process, the way the perceptual posture of a material position is embodied as a social form of power, the most sexually potent depictions and descriptions would be the most objective blow-by-blow re-presentations. Pornography participates in its audience's eroticism because it creates an accessible sexual object, the possession and consumption of which is male sexuality, to be consumed and possessed as which is female sexuality. In this sense, sex in life is no less mediated than it is in art. Men have sex with their image of a woman. Escalating explicitness, "exceeding the bounds of candor," is the aesthetic of pornography not because the materials depict objectified sex but because they create the experience of a sexuality which is itself objectified.[19] It is not that life and art imitate each other; in sexuality, they are each other.

The law of obscenity has literally nothing in common with this feminist critique. Men's obscenity is not women's pornography. Obscenity is more concerned with whether men blush, pornography with whether women bleed—both producing a sexual rush. One commentator has said, "Obscenity is not suppressed primarily for the protection of others. Much of it is suppressed for the purity of the 'consumer.' Obscenity, at bottom, is not a crime. Obscenity is a sin."[20] This is literally accurate. A sin is an idea that something is bad. Men are turned on by obscenity, including by its suppression, in the same way they are by sin. Animated by morality from the male standpoint, in which violation—of women and rules—is eroticized, obscenity law proceeds according to the interest of male power, robed in gender-neutral good and evil.

Morality in its specifically liberal form animates the organization of state power on the pornography issue. Its approach is premised upon a set of parallel distinctions which can be consistently traced through obscenity law. Although the posture this law adopts toward the problem it envisions has shifted over time, its fundamental norms remain consistent: public is opposed to private, ethics is opposed to morality, and factual is opposed to valued determinations. These distinctions are supposed gender neutral but are implicitly, socially, gender based: female is private, moral, valued, subjective; male is public, ethical, factual, objective.[21] To construe concern with pornography in these socially "feminine" terms, under male dominance, is to preclude legitimate state intervention. If such gendered concepts are constructs of the male experience, imposed from the male standpoint on society as a whole, liberal morality is an expression of male supremacist politics. That is, discourse conducted in terms of good and evil which does not expose the gendered foundations of these concepts proceeds oblivious to—and serves to disguise the presence and interest of—the position of power which underlies, and is furthered by, that discourse.

Obscenity law proposes to control what and how sex can be publicly shown. In practice, its standard centers upon the same features that feminism and pornography both reveal as key to male sexuality: the erect penis and penetration.[22] Historically, obscenity law was vexed by restricting such portrayals while protecting great literature. (Nobody considered protecting women.) Solving this problem by exempting works of perceived value, obscenity restrictions relaxed—some might say collapsed—revealing a significant shift in the last decade.[23] Under the old law, pornography was publicly repudiated yet privately consumed and actualized: do anything to women with impunity in private behind a veil of public denial and civility. Under the new law, in a victory for Freudian derepression, pornography is publicly celebrated.[24] The old private rules have become the new public rules. Women were sex and are still sex. Greater efforts of brutality have become necessary to eroticize the taboo—each taboo being a hierarchy in disguise—since the frontier of the taboo keeps vanishing as one crosses it. Put another way, more and more violence has become necessary to keep the progressively desensitized consumer aroused to the illusion that sex (and he) is daring and dangerous. Making sex with the powerless "not allowed" is a way of keeping "getting it" defined as an act of power, an assertion of hierarchy, which keeps it sexy in a sexual system in which hierarchy is sexy. In addition, pornography has become ubiquitous. Sexual terrorism has become democratized. Pornography has become truly available to women for the first time in history. Among other effects, this central mechanism of sexual subordination, this means of systematizing the definition of women as a sexual class, has now become available to its victims for scrutiny and analysis as an open public system, not just as a private secret abuse.[25] Hopefully, this was a mistake.

In obscenity law, the state has been perfected as the mirror of society. In pornography, women are sex. In obscenity law, women are sex. In pornography, women's bodies are dirty. In obscenity law, obscenity is filth. In pornography, the more explicit the sex, the more pornographic. In obscenity law, the more explicit the sex, the more obscene. In pornography, sex is a dirty secret. Obscenity law sees it, therefore helps keep it, that way. Pornography sees nothing wrong with what it does to women. Neither does obscenity law. Pornography is socially decried but socially permitted. Obscenity is the legal device through which it is legally repudiated but legally permitted.

On a deeper level, male morality sees that which maintains its power as good, that which undermines or qualifies it or questions its absoluteness as evil. Differences in the law over time—such as the liberalization of obscenity doctrine—reflect either changes in which group of men has power or shifts in perceptions of the best strategy for maintaining male supremacy—probably some of both. But it must be made to work. The outcome, descriptively analyzed, is that obscenity law prohibits what it sees as immoral, which from women's standpoint tends to be relatively harmless, while protecting what it sees as moral, which is often damaging to women. So it, too, is a politics, only covertly so. What male morality finds evil, meaning threatening to its power, feminist politics tends to find comparatively harmless. What feminist politics identifies as central in women's subordination—the erotization of dominance and submission—male morality tends to find relatively harmless or defend as affirmatively valuable, hence as protected speech.

In 1973, obscenity under law came to mean that which "the average person applying contemporary standards, would find that, taken as a whole, appeals to the prurient interest; that [which] depicts or describes, in a patently offensive way, sexual conduct as defined by the applicable state law; and that which, taken as a whole, lacks serious literary, artistic, political, or scientific value."[26] Feminism doubts whether "the average person," gender neutral, exists; has more questions about the content and process of definition of community standards than about deviations from them; wonders why prurience counts but powerlessness does not, why sensibilities are better protected from offense than women are from exploitation; defines sexuality, hence its violation and expropriation, more broadly than does any state law; and wonders why a body of law which cannot in practice tell rape from intercourse should be entrusted with telling pornography from anything less. In feminist perspective, one notices that although the law of obscenity says that sex on streetcorners is not supposed to be legitimated "by the fact that the persons are simultaneously engaged in a valid political dialogue,"[27] the requirement that the work be considered "as a whole" legitimates something very like that on the level of publications such as *Playboy*,[28] even though experimental evidence is beginning to support what victims have long known: legitimate settings diminish the injury perceived to be done to the women whose trivialization and objectification it contextualizes.[29] Besides, if a woman is subjected, why should it matter that the work has other value?[30] Perhaps what redeems a work's value among men enhances its injury to women. Existing standards of literature, art, science, and politics are, in feminist light, remarkably consonant with pornography's mode, meaning, and message. Finally and foremost, a feminist approach reveals that although the content and dynamic of pornography concerns women—the sexuality of women, women as sexuality—in the same way that the vast majority of "obscenities" refer specifically to women's bodies, women's invisibility has been such that the law of obscenity has never even considered pornography a women's issue.[31]

To appeal to "prurient interest" means to give a man an erection.[32] Men are scared to make it possible for some men to tell other men what they can and cannot have sexual access to, because men have power. Men believe that if you do not let them have theirs, they might not let you have yours. This is why the indefinability of pornography—all the "one man's this is another man's that"—is so central to pornography's definition.[33] It is not because all men are such great liberals, but because those other men might be able to do to them whatever *they* can do to *them,* which may explain why the liberal principle is what it is.

What this frame on the issue obscures, because the fought-over are invisible, is that the fight over a definition of pornography is a fight among men over the terms of access to women, hence over the best means to guarantee male power as a system. The tacit questions become: Whose sexual practices threaten this system? Are they men whose sexual access can be sacrificed in the interest of maintaining it for the rest? Public sexual access by men to anything other than women is far less likely to be protected speech. This is not to say that male sexual access to anything—children, other men, women with women, objects, animals—is not the real rule. The issue is rather how public, hence how express in law, that system will be.

In this light, the "prurient interest" prong of the obscenity standard has a built-in bind. To find prurience as a fact, someone has to admit sexual arousal by the materials;[34] but male sexual arousal signals the importance of protection. Men put themselves in this position and then wonder why they cannot agree. Sometimes it seems that what is obscene is what does not turn on the Supreme Court, or what revolts them more, which is rare, since revulsion is eroticized. Sometimes it seems that what is obscene is what turns on those men whom the men in power think they can afford to ignore. Sometimes it seems that what is obscene is what makes dominant men see themselves as momentary potential targets of male sexual aggression. Sometimes it seems that anything can be done to a woman, but obscenity is sex that makes male sexuality look bad.[35]

Courts' difficulties in framing workable standards to separate "prurient" from other sexual interest, commercial exploitation from art or advertising, sexual speech from sexual conduct, and obscenity from great literature make the feminist point. These lines have proved elusive in law because they do not exist in life. Commercial sex resembles art because both exploit women's sexuality. The liberal slippery slope is the feminist totality. Politically speaking, whatever obscenity may do, pornography converges with more conventionally acceptable depictions and descriptions just as rape does with intercourse, because both are acts within the same power relation. Just as it is difficult to distinguish literature or art against a background, a standard, of objectification, it is difficult to discern sexual freedom against a background, a standard, of sexual coercion. This does not mean that it cannot be done. It means that legal standards will be practically unenforceable, will reproduce this problem rather than solve it, until they address its fundamental issue—gender inequality—directly.

To define the pornographic as the "patently offensive" further misconstrues its harm. Pornography is not bad manners or poor choice of audience; obscenity is. Pornography is also not an idea; obscenity is. The legal fiction whereby the obscene is "not speech" has deceived few;[36] it has effectively avoided the need to adjudicate pornography's social etiology. But obscenity law got one thing right: pornography is more actlike than thoughtlike. The fact that pornography, in a feminist view, furthers the idea of the sexual inferiority of women, a political idea, does not make pornography a political idea. That one can express the idea a practice expresses does not make that practice an idea. Pornography is not an idea any more than segregation or lynching are ideas, although both institutionalize the idea of the inferiority of one group to another. The law considers obscenity deviant, antisocial. If it causes harm, it causes antisocial acts, acts against the social order.[37] In a feminist perspective, pornography is the essence of a sexist social order, its quintessential social act.

If pornography is an act of male supremacy, its harm is the harm of male supremacy made difficult to see because of its pervasiveness, potency, and success in making the world a pornographic place. Specifically, the harm cannot be discerned from the objective standpoint because it is so much of "what is." Women live in the world pornography creates, live its lie as reality. As Naomi Scheman has said, "lies are what we have lived, not just what we have told, and no story about correspondence to what is real will enable us to distinguish the truth from the lie."[38] So the issue is not what the harm of pornography is, but how the harm of pornography is to become visible. As compared with what? To the extent pornography succeeds in constructing social reality, it becomes invisible as harm.

The success, therefore the harm, of pornography, is invisible to the male state in its liberal guise and so has been defined out of the customary approach taken to, and the dominant values underlying, the First Amendment. The theory of the First Amendment under which most pornography is protected from governmental restriction proceeds from liberal assumptions[39] that do not apply to the situation of women. First Amendment theory, like virtually all liberal legal theory, presumes the validity of the distinction between public and private: the "role of law [is] to mark and guard the line between the sphere of social power, organized in the form of the state, and the arena of private right."[40] On this basis, courts distinguish between obscene billboards ("thrust upon the unwilling viewer") and the private possession of obscenity at home.[41] The problem is that not only the public but also the private is a "sphere of social power" of sexism. On paper and in life, pornography is thrust upon unwilling women in their homes.[42] The distinction between public and private does not cut the same for women as for men.[43] As a result, it is men's right to inflict pornography upon women in private that is protected.

The liberal theory underlying First Amendment law proceeds on the belief that free speech, including pornography, helps discover truth. Censorship, in its view, restricts society to partial truths. Laissez-faire might be an adequate theory of the social preconditions for knowledge in a nonhierarchical society. In a society of gender inequality, the speech of the powerful impresses its view upon the world, concealing the truth of powerlessness under a despairing acquiescence that provides the appearance of consent and makes protest inaudible as well as rare. Pornography can invent women because it has the power to make its vision into reality, which then passes, objectively, for truth. So while the First Amendment supports pornography on the belief that consensus and progress are facilitated by allowing all views, however divergent and unorthodox, it fails to notice that pornography (like the racism, including anti-Semitism, of the Nazis and the Klan) is not at all divergent or unorthodox. It is the ruling ideology. Feminism, the dissenting view, is suppressed by pornography. Thus, while defenders of pornography argue that allowing all speech, including pornography, frees the mind to fulfill itself, pornography freely enslaves women's minds and bodies inseparably, normalizing the terror that enforces silence on women's point of view.

In liberalism, speech must never be sacrificed for other social goals.[44] But liberalism has never understood this reality of pornography: the free so-called speech of men silences the free speech of women. It is the same social goal, just other people. This is what a real inequality, a real conflict, a real disparity in social power looks like. First, women do not simply have freedom of speech on a social level. The most basic assumption underlying First Amendment adjudication is that, socially, speech is free. The First Amendment itself says, "Congress shall make no law . . . abridging the freedom of speech." Free speech exists. The problem for government is to avoid constraining that which, if unconstrained by government, is free. This tends to presuppose that whole segments of the population are not systematically silenced socially, prior to government action. Second, the law of the First Amendment comprehends that freedom of expression, in the abstract, is a system but fails to comprehend that sexism (and racism), in the concrete, are also systems. As a result, it cannot grasp that the speech of some silences the speech of others in a way that is not simply a matter of competition for airtime. That pornography chills women's expression is difficult to demonstrate empirically because silence is not eloquent. Yet on no more of the same kind of evidence, the argument that suppressing pornography might chill legitimate speech has supported its protection.

First Amendment logic has difficulty grasping harm that is not linearly caused in the "John hit Mary" sense. The idea is that words or pictures can be harmful only if they produce harm in a form that is considered an action. Words work in the province of attitudes, actions in the realm of behavior. Words cannot constitute harm in themselves—never mind libel, invasion of privacy, blackmail, bribery, conspiracy, most sexual harassment, and most discrimination. What is saying "yes" in Congress—a word or an act? What is saying "Kill" to a trained guard dog? What is its training? What is saying "You're fired" or "We have enough of your kind around here"? What is a sign that reads "Whites Only?" What is a real estate advertisement that reads "Churches Nearby?" What is a "Help Wanted—Male" ad? What is a letter that states: "Constituent interests dictate that the understudy to my administrative assistant be a man"? What is "Sleep with me and I'll give you an 'A' "? These words, printed or spoken, are so far from legally protecting the cycle of events they actualize that they are regarded as evidence that acts occurred, in some cases as actionable in themselves.[45] Is a woman raped by an attitude or a behavior? Which is sexual arousal? Which is cross burning? The difficulty of the distinction in the abstract has not prevented the law from acting when the consequences were seen to matter. When words are tantamount to acts, they are treated as acts.

The ascendancy of the positivistic idea of causality as used in First Amendment absolutism,[46] which in pure form would prohibit all restrictions by government on everything classified as expression, dates from around the time when it was believed conclusively proved that it is impossible to prove conclusively that pornography causes harm.

This notion of causality did not first appear in this law at this time, however.[47] As Judge Jerome Frank said in a footnote in *Roth,* "According to Judge Bok, an obscenity statute may be validly enforced when there is proof of a causal relation between a particular book and undesirable conduct. Almost surely, such proof cannot ever be adduced."[48] Criticizing old ideas of atomic physics in light of Einstein's theory of relativity, Werner Heisenberg stated the conditions that must exist for a causal relation to make sense. "To co-ordinate a definite cause to a definite effect has sense only when both can be observed without introducing a foreign element disturbing their interrelation. The law of causality, because of its very nature, can only be defined for isolated systems."[49] Among the influences that disturb the isolation of systems are observers.

The law of obscenity has never been required to show a causal relation between the obscene and anything else, by this standard or any other. Underlying the adoption of such a causality standard in debates on the merits of state intervention in the pornography area is a rather hasty analogy between the regularities of physical and social systems, an analogy that has seldom been explicitly justified or even updated as the physical sciences have altered their epistemological foundations. Social systems are not isolated systems. Experimental research, in which it has been scientifically shown that pornography has harmful effects, minimizes what will always be "foreign elements" at some cost of simulating social reality. Yet whenever field experiments are done for verisimilitude, it is said that the interactions are insufficiently isolated to prove pure causality. If pornography is systemic, it may not be isolable from the system in which it exists.[50] This does not mean that no harm exists. It does mean that because the harm is so pervasive, it cannot be sufficiently isolated to be perceived as existing according to this model of causality, a model that is neither the existing legal standard, the only scientific standard, a standard used in other policy areas (like the relation between smoking and cancer or driving drunk and having accidents). Nor is it a social or political standard in which the experiences of victims have any weight. In other words, if pornography is seen as harmful only if it causes harm by this model, and if pornography's harm cannot be isolated from society's organization itself, its harm will not be perceptible within the episteme.

The dominant view is that pornography must cause harm just as car accidents cause harm, or its effects are not cognizable as harm. The trouble with this individuated, atomistic, linear, exclusive, isolated, narrowly tortlike—in a word, postivistic—conception of injury is that the way pornography targets and defines women for abuse and discrimination does not work like this. It does hurt individuals, just not as individuals in a one-at-a-time sense, but as members of the group women. Individual harm is caused one woman and not another essentially as one number rather than another is caused in roulette; but on a group basis, the harm is absolutely selective and systematic. Its causality is essentially collective and totalistic and contextual. To reassert atomistic linear causality as a sine qua non of injury—you cannot be harmed unless you are harmed through this etiology—is to refuse to respond to the true nature of this specific kind of harm. Such refusals call for explanation. Morton Horowitz has written that the issue of causality in tort law is "one of the pivotal ideas in a system of legal thought that sought to separate private law from politics and to insulate the legal system from the threat of redistribution."[51] Perhaps causality in the law of obscenity is an attempt to privatize the injury pornography does to women in order to insulate the same system from the threat of gender equality.

Women are known to be brutally coerced into pornographic performances. But so far it is only with children, usually male children, that courts see that the speech of pornographers was once someone else's life.[52] Courts and commissions and legislatures and researchers have searched largely in vain for the injury of pornography in the mind of the (male) consumer or in "society," or in empirical correlations between variations in levels of "anti-social" acts and liberalization in obscenity laws.[53] Speech can be regulated "in the interests of unwilling viewers, captive audiences, young children, and beleaguered neighborhoods,"[54] but the normal level of sexual force—force that is not seen as force because it is inflicted on women and called sex—has never been a policy issue in the pornography area. Until the last few years experimental research never approached the question of whether pornographic stimuli might support sexual aggression against women or whether violence per se might be sexually stimulating or have sexual sequelae.[55] Research is just beginning on the consequences for women of sexual depictions that show consensual dominance and submission.[56] We know the least about the impact of female-only nudity, depictions of specific acts like penetration, or sex that appears mutual in a social context of gender inequality. We know even less about why sex—that is, women—*must,* seemingly, be experienced through a traffic in pictures and words.

Beyond offensiveness or prurience, to say that pornography is "dehumanizing" is an attempt to articulate its harm. But "human being" is a social concept with many possible meanings. If one looks at liberal meanings of personhood through a feminist political analysis of what pornography does to women, the inadequacy of the liberal dehumanization critique becomes clear. In a feminist perspective, pornography dehumanizes women in a culturally specific and empirically descriptive—not liberal moral—sense. In the same act, pornography dispossesses women of the same power of which it possesses men: the power of sexual, hence gender, definition. The power to tell one who one is and the power to treat one accordingly. Perhaps a human being, for gender purposes, is someone who controls the social definition of sexuality.

By distinction, a person in one Kantian view is a free and rational agent whose existence is an end in itself, as opposed to instrumental.[57] In pornography, women exist for the end of male pleasure. Kant sees "human" as characterized by universal abstract rationality, with no component of individual or group differences, and as a "bundle of rights."[58] Pornography purports to define what a woman is. It does this on a group basis, including when it raises individual qualities to sexual stereotypes, as in the strategy of *Playboy's* "Playmate of the Month." Perhaps pornography derives much of its sexual power, as well as part of its justification, from the implicit assumption that the Kantian notion of person actually describes the condition of women in this society, so that if we are there, we are freely and rationally there, when the fact is that women—in pornography and in part because of pornography—have no such rights.

Other views of the person include one of Wittgenstein's statements that the best picture of the human soul is the human body.[59] Apparently this depends upon what picture of the human body one has in mind. Marx's work offers various concepts of personhood deducible from his critique of various forms of productive organization. Whatever material conditions the society values defines a person there, so that in a bourgeois society, a person might be a property owner.[60] But women are the property that constitute the personhood, understood as the masculinity, of men under capitalism. Thinking further in marxian terms, one wonders whether women in pornography are more properly fetishes or objects. Does pornography more attribute lifelikeness to that which is dead—as in fetishism—or make deathlike that which is alive—as in objectification? Probably this depends upon whether, socially speaking, women are more dead than alive.

In Hume's concept of a person as a bundle or collection of sense perceptions, such that the feeling of self-identity over time is a persistent illusion,[61] one finds a view of the human that coincides with the view of women in pornography. The empiricist view of person is the pornographic view of women. No critique of dominance or subjection, certainly not of objectification, can be grounded in a vision of reality in which all sense perceptions are just sense perceptions. This is one way an objectivist epistemology supports the unequal holding and wielding of power in a society in which the persistent illusion of selfhood of half the population is materially supported and maintained at the expense of the other half. Those who are socially allowed a self are also allowed the luxury of postulating its illusoriness and having that called a philosophical position. Whatever self they ineluctably have, they do not lose by saying it is an illusion. On this level, taken as high male ideology, much of Western culture becomes descriptive even if not particularly explanatory. Thus Hume defines the human in the same terms feminism uses to define women's dehumanization: for women in pornography, the self is, precisely, a persistent illusion.

According to moral philosopher Bernard Williams, being human ordinarily entails valuing self-respect and feeling pain.[62] As principal author of the *Williams Report* on obscenity in England, Williams found women deprived of neither quality in or by pornography. Of course, how self is defined, what respect attaches to, stimuli of pleasure, and to an extent stimuli and thresholds of pain are cultural variables. Women in pornography are turned on by being put down and feel pain as pleasure. We want it, we beg for it, we get it. To argue that this is dehumanizing is not to take respect as an ahistorical absolute or to treat pain as socially or personally invariant or uniformly negative. Rather, it is to say that the acceptance of the social definition of these values—the acceptance of self-respect and the avoidance of pain as values—permits the erotization of their negative—debasement and torture—in pornography. It is only to the extent that each of these values is socially accepted as human within a given culture that their negation becomes a quality of sex and is eroticized in and as "woman." Only when self-respect is accepted as human does debasement become sexy and female; only when the avoidance of pain is accepted as human does torture become sexy and female. In this way, women's sexuality as expressed in pornography precisely negatives her status as human. But there is more: exactly what is defined as degrading to a human being, however that is socially defined, is exactly what is sexually arousing to the male point of view in the pornography, just as the one to whom it is done is the girl regardless of sex. In this way, it is specifically women whom pornography identifies with and by sexuality—a painful, debasing sexuality of torture, a sexuality of humiliation and use—as the erotic is equated with the dehumanizing.

To define the pornographic as that which is violent, not sexual, as liberal moral analyses tend to, is to trivialize and evade the essence of this critique while seeming to express it. As with rape, where the issue is not the presence or absence of force but what sex is as distinct from coercion, the question for pornography is what eroticism is distinct from the subordination of women. This is not a rhetorical question. Under male dominance, whatever sexually arouses a man is sex. In pornography, the violence is the sex. The inequality is sex. The humiliation is sex. The debasement is sex. The intrusion is sex. Pornography does not work sexually without gender hierarchy. If there is no inequality, no violation, no dominance, no force, there is no sexual arousal. Obscenity law does the pornographers a real favor by obscuring this, pornography's central dynamic, under the coy gender-neutral abstraction of "prurient interest" while adding the dominance interest of state prohibition.

Calling rape and pornography violent, not sexual (the banner of much antirape and antipornography work), is an attempt to protest that women do not find rape pleasurable or pornography stimulating while avoiding claiming this rejection as women's point of view. The concession to the objective stance, the attempt to achieve credibility by covering up the specificity of viewpoint, not only abstracts from women's experience; it lies about it. Women and men both know men find rape sexual and pornography erotic. It therefore is. Women and men both know that sexuality is commonly violent without being any the less sexual. To deny this sets up the situation so that when women are aroused by sexual violation, experience it as women's sexuality, the feminist analysis is seen to be contradicted. But it is not contradicted, it is proved. The male supremacist definition of female sexuality as lust for self-annihilation has won. It would be surprising, feminist analysis would be wrong, and sexism would be trivial if this were merely exceptional.[63] To reject forced sex in the name of women's point of view requires an account of women's experience of being violated by the same acts both sexes have learned as natural and fulfilling and erotic when no critique, no alternatives, and few transgressions have been permitted.

The depersonalization critique and the "violence not sex" critique expose a double standard of sex and of personhood but do not attack the masculinity of the standards for personhood and for sex which pornography sets. The critiques are thus useful, to some extent deconstructive, but beg the deeper questions of the place of pornography in sexuality and of sexuality in the construction of women's definition and status. They act as if women can be "persons" by interpretation—as if the concept is not, in every socially real way, defined by and in terms of and reserved for men, and as if sexuality is not itself a construct of male power. To do this is to act as if pornography did not exist or were impotent. Deeper than the personhood question or the violence question is the question of the mechanism of social causation by which pornography constructs women and sex, defining what "woman" means and what sexuality is in terms of each other, hence excluding women's social reality from the substantive definition of personhood.

The law of obscenity at times says that sexual expression is only talk, and therefore cannot be intrinsically harmful. Yet somehow pornographic talk is vital to protect. If pornography is a practice of gender inequality, especially to the degree that pornography works on the ideological level and gender *is* an ideology, if pornography is sex and gender is sexual, the question of the relation between pornography and life is nothing less than the question of the dynamic of the subordination of women to men. If "objectification . . . is never trivial," girls *are* ruined by books.[64] Consciousness of this process—connecting thought and life, mind and body with social power, point of view with politics—has been obstructed by fear of repressive state use of any critique of any form of expression, by the power of pornographers to create a climate hostile to inquiry into their power and profits, and by the power of pornography to create women in its image of their use.

Because obscenity law so evades the reality of pornography, it is difficult to show that the male state, hegemonically liberal whether in the hands of conservatives or of liberals, actually protects pornography. The deception that the state is hostile to sexual derepression and eager to repress pornography, the fantasy that an authoritarian state restricts pornography rather than protects it, lay clearly exposed when the courts were confronted with the real damage pornography does to women's status and treatment as the basis for making it civilly actionable to its victims. The courts accepted the harm but held the pornography more important than those it harms—hence protected it as speech. In *American Bookseller Assn. Inc. v. Hudnut* the Seventh Circuit Court of Appeals held that an ordinance that makes the injuries of pornography actionable as sex inequality is unconstitutional under the First Amendment because it prohibits expression of a point of view.[65]

Acts became ideas and politics became morals as the court transformed coercion, force, assault, and trafficking in subordination into "thought control" and second-class citizenship on the basis of gender into "ideas that can be expressed about sexuality."[66] Obscenity law, which is based upon nothing but value judgments about morality, was presented as the standard for constitutional point-of-viewlessness. The court saw legal intervention against acts (most of which are already crimes) as "point of view" discrimination without doubting the constitutionality of state intervention against obscenity, which has no connection with acts and is expressly defined on the basis of point of view about sex. The court saw civil action by individual women as censorship threatening freedom, yet saw no threat to freedom and no censorship in criminal prosecutions of obscenity. When is a point of view not a point of view? When it is yours—especially when your words, like those of the pornographers, are words in power. In the epistemologically hermetic doublethink of the male point of view, prohibiting advances toward sex equality under law is state neutrality. From the male standpoint, it looks neutral because the state mirrors the inequality of the social world. Under the aegis of this neutrality, state protection of pornography becomes official policy.[67]

The law of pornography thus has the same surface theme and the same underlying theme as pornography itself. Superficially both involve morality: rules made and transgressed for purposes of sexual arousal. Actually, both are about power: the equation between the erotic and the control of women by men, *women* made and transgressed for purposes of sexual arousal. It seems essential to the kick of pornography that it be to some degree against the rules, but never truly unavailable or truly illegitimate. Thus obscenity law, like the law of rape, preserves both the value and the ability to get what it purports to devalue and restrict access to by prohibition. Obscenity law helps keep pornography sexy by putting state power—force, hierarchy—behind its purported prohibition on what men can have sexual access to. The law of obscenity is to pornography as pornography is to sex: a map that purports to be a mirror, a practice that pretends to represent a practice, a legitimation and authorization and set of directions and guiding controls that project themselves onto social reality, while purporting merely to reflect an image of what is already there. Pornography presents itself as fantasy or illusion or idea, which can be good or bad as it is accurate or inaccurate while it actually, hence accurately, distributes power. Liberal morality cannot deal with illusions that constitute reality because its theory of reality, lacking a substantive critique of the distribution of social power, cannot get behind the empirical word, truth by correspondence. On the surface, both pornography and the law of obscenity are about sex. But it is the status of women that is at stake.

# 12 | Sex Equality: On Difference and Dominance

> There is one thing of which one can say neither that it is one meter long nor that it is not one meter long, and that is the standard meter in Paris.
>
> —Ludwig Wittgenstein

> The measure of man is man.
>
> —Pythagoras

> [Men] think themselves superior to women, but they mingle that with the notion of equality between men and women. It's very odd.
>
> —Jean-Paul Sartre

*I*nequality because of sex defines and situates women as women. If the sexes were equal, women would not be sexually subjected. Sexual force would be exceptional, consent to sex could be commonly real, and sexually violated women would be believed. If the sexes were equal, women would not be economically subjected, their desperation and marginality cultivated, their enforced dependency exploited sexually or economically. Women would have speech, privacy, authority, respect, and more resources than they have now. Rape and pornography would be recognized as violations, and abortion would be both rare and actually guaranteed.

In the United States, it is acknowledged that the state is capitalist; it is not acknowledged that it is male. The law of sex equality, constitutional by interpretation and statutory by joke, erupts through this fissure, exposing the sex equality that the state purports to guarantee.[1] If gender hierarchy and sexuality are reciprocally constituting—gender hierarchy providing the eroticism of sexuality and sexuality providing an enforcement mechanism for male dominance over women—a male state would predictably not make acts of sexual dominance actionable as gender inequality. Equality would be kept as far away from sexuality as possible. In fact, sexual force is not conventionally recognized to raise issues of sex inequality, either against those who commit the acts or against the state that condones them. Sexuality is regulated largely by criminal law, occasionally by tort law, neither on grounds of equality.[2] Reproductive control, similarly, has been adjudicated primarily as an issue of privacy. It is as if a vacuum boundary demarcates sexual issues on the one hand from the law of equality on the other. Law, structurally, adopts the male point of view: sexuality concerns nature not social arbitrariness, interpersonal relations not social distributions of power, the sex difference not sex discrimination.

Sex discrimination law, with mainstream moral theory, sees equality and gender as issues of sameness and difference. According to this approach, which has dominated politics, law, and social perception, equality is an equivalence not a distinction, and gender is a distinction not an equivalence. The legal mandate of equal treatment—both a systemic norm and a specific legal doctrine—becomes a matter of treating likes alike and unlikes unlike, while the sexes are socially defined as such by their mutual unlikeness. That is, gender is socially constructed as difference epistemologically, and sex discrimination law bounds gender equality by difference doctrinally. Socially, one tells a woman from a man by their difference from each other, but a woman is legally recognized to be discriminated against on the basis of sex only when she can first be said to be the same as a man. A built-in tension thus exists between this concept of equality, which presupposes sameness, and this concept of sex, which presupposes difference. Difference defines the state's approach to sex equality epistemologically and doctrinally. Sex equality becomes a contradiction in terms, something of an oxymoron. The deepest issues of sex inequality, in which the sexes are most constructed as socially different, are either excluded at the threshold or precluded from coverage once in. In this way, difference is inscribed on society as the meaning of gender and written into law as the limit on sex discrimination.

In sex discrimination law, sex inequality in life becomes "sex classification" in law, each category defined by its difference from the other. A classification in law or in fact is or is not a sex-based discrimination depending upon the accuracy of its "fit"[3] with gender and upon the validity of its purpose for government or business. A classification, in the classic formulation of the "rational relation" test, "must be reasonable, not arbitrary, and must rest upon some ground of difference having a fair and substantial relation to the object of the legislation, so that all persons similarly circumstanced shall be treated alike."[4] Under the equal protection clause of the Fourteenth Amendment, the line drawn by a rule or practice being challenged as discriminatory is required to track the gender line more closely than this. To be nondiscriminatory, the relation between gender and the line's proper objectives must be more than rational but need not be perfect. In what has been termed "intermediate scrutiny"—a judicial standard of care for women only—gender lines are scrutinized more carefully than most, but not as strictly as some.[5] They are not prohibited absolutely, as they would have been under the dominant interpretation of the Equal Rights Amendment (ERA).[6] Seen on this doctrinal continuum, which scrutinizes the correlation between gender lines and the purposes of drawing them, the ERA was not a new departure but a proposal to take the standard equal protection approach to its conclusion.

Equality is comparative in sex discrimination law. Sex in law is compared with sex in life, and women are compared with men. Relevant empirical similarity to men is the basis for the claim to equal treatment for women. For differential treatment to be discriminatory, the sexes must first be "similarly situated" by legislation, qualifications, circumstance, or physical endowment.[7] This standard applies to sex the broader legal norm of neutrality, the law's version of objectivity. To test for gender neutrality, reverse the sexes and compare. To see if a woman was discriminated against on the basis of sex, ask whether a similarly situated man would be or was so treated. Relevant difference supports different treatment, no matter how categorical, disadvantageous, or cumulative. Accurate reflections of situated disparities are thus rendered either noncomparable or rational, therefore differences not inequalities for legal purposes. In this view, normative equality derives from and refers to empirical equivalence. Situated differences produce differentiated outcomes without necessarily involving discrimination.

In this mainstream epistemologically liberal approach,[8] the sexes are by nature biologically different, therefore socially properly differentiated for some purposes. Upon this natural, immutable, inherent, essential, just, and wonderful differentiation, society and law are thought to have erected some arbitrary, irrational, confining, and distorting distinctions. These are the inequalities the law against sex discrimination targets. As one scholar has put it, "any prohibition against sexual classifications must be flexible enough to accommodate two legitimate sources of distinctions on the basis of sex: biological differences between the sexes and the prevailing heterosexual ethic of American society."[9] The proposed federal ERA's otherwise uncompromising prohibition on sex-based distinctions provides parallel exceptions for "unique physical characteristics" and "personal privacy."[10] Laws or practices that express or reflect sex "stereotypes," understood as inaccurate overgeneralized attitudes often termed "archaic" or "outmoded," are at the core of this definition of discrimination.[11] Mistaken illusions about real differences are actionable, but any distinction that can be accurately traced to biology or heterosexuality is not a discrimination but a difference.

From women's point of view, gender is more an inequality of power than a differentiation that is accurate or inaccurate. To women, sex is a social status based on who is permitted to do what to whom; only derivatively is it a difference. For example, one woman reflected on her gender: "I wish I had been born a doormat, or a man."[12] Being a doormat is definitely different from being a man. Differences between the sexes do descriptively exist. But the fact that these are a woman's realistic options, and that they are so limiting, calls into question the perspective that considers this distinction a "difference." Men are not called different because they are neither doormats nor women, but a woman is not socially permitted to be a woman and neither doormat nor man.

From this perspective, considering gender a matter of sameness and difference covers up the reality of gender as a system of social hierarchy, as an inequality. The differences attributed to sex become lines that inequality draws, not any kind of basis for it. Social and political inequality begins indifferent to sameness and difference. Differences are inequality's post hoc excuse, its conclusory artifact, its outcome presented as its origin, its sentimentalization, its damage that is pointed to as the justification for doing the damage after the damage has been done, the distinctions that perception is socially organized to notice because inequality gives them consequences for social power. Gender might not even code as difference, might not mean distinction epistemologically, were it not for its consequences for social power. Distinctions of body or mind or behavior are pointed to as cause rather than effect, with no realization that they are so deeply effect rather than cause that pointing to them at all is an effect. Inequality comes first; difference comes after. Inequality is material and substantive and identifies a disparity; difference is ideational and abstract and falsely symmetrical. If this is so, a discourse and a law of gender that center on difference serve as ideology to neutralize, rationalize, and cover disparities of power, even as they appear to criticize or problematize them. Difference is the velvet glove on the iron fist of domination. The problem then is not that differences are not valued; the problem is that they are defined by power. This is as true when difference is affirmed as when it is denied, when its substance is applauded or disparaged, when women are punished or protected in its name.

Doctrinally speaking, two alternative paths to sex equality for women exist within the mainstream approach to sex discrimination, paths that follow the lines of the sameness/difference tension. The leading one is: be the same as men. This path is termed "gender neutrality" doctrinally and the single standard philosophically. It is testimony to how substance becomes form in law that this rule is considered formal equality. Because it mirrors the values of the social world, it is considered abstract, meaning transparent to the world and lacking in substance. Also for this reason it is considered to be not only *the* standard, but *a* standard at all. Legally articulated as conforming normative standards to existing reality, as law reflecting life, the strongest doctrinal expression of sameness would prohibit taking gender into account in any way, with exceptions for "real differences." This is so far the leading rule that the words "equal to" are code for, or/and equivalent to, the words "the same as"—with the referent for both unspecified.

To women who want equality yet find themselves "different," the doctrine provides an alternative route: be different from men. This equal recognition of difference is termed the special benefit rule or special protection rule legally, the double standard philosophically. It is in rather bad odor, reminiscent of women's exclusion from the public sphere and of protective labor laws.[13] Like pregnancy, which always brings it up, it is something of a doctrinal embarrassment. Considered an exception to true equality and not really a rule of law at all, it is the one place where the law of sex discrimination admits it is recognizing something substantive. Together with the Bona Fide Occupational Qualification (BFOQ) and the exception for unique physical characteristics under ERA policy, compensatory legislation, and sex-conscious relief in particular litigation, affirmative action is thought to live here.[14] Situated differences can produce different treatment—indulgences *or* deprivations. This equality law is agnostic as to which.

The philosophy underlying the sameness/difference approach applies liberalism to women. Sex is a natural difference, a division, a distinction, beneath which lies a stratum of human commonality, sameness.[15] The moral thrust of the sameness branch of the doctrine conforms normative rules to empirical reality by granting women access to what men have: to the extent women are no different from men, women deserve what men have. The differences branch, which is generally regarded as patronizing and unprincipled but necessary to avoid absurdity, exists to value or compensate women for what they are or have become distinctively as women—by which is meant, unlike men, or to leave women as "different" as equality law finds them.

Most scholarship on sex discrimination law concerns which of these paths to sex equality is preferable in the long run or more appropriate to any particular issue, as if they were all there is.[16] As a prior matter, however, treating issues of sex equality as issues of sameness and difference is to take a particular approach. This approach is here termed the sameness/difference approach because it is obsessed with the sex difference. Its main theme is: "we're the same, we're the same, we're the same." Its counterpoint theme (in a higher register) goes: "but we're different, but we're different, but we're different." Its story is: on the first day, difference was; on the second day, a division was created upon it; on the third day, occasional dominance arose. Division may be rational or irrational. Dominance either seems or is justified or unjustified. Difference *is*.

Concealed is the substantive way in which man has become the measure of all things. Under the sameness rubric, women are measured according to correspondence with man, their equality judged by proximity to his measure. Under the difference rubric, women are measured according to their lack of correspondence from man, their womanhood judged by their distance from his measure. Gender neutrality is the male standard. The special protection rule is the female standard. Masculinity or maleness is the referent for both. Approaching sex discrimination in this way, as if sex questions were difference questions and equality questions were sameness questions, merely provides two ways for the law to hold women to a male standard and to call that sex equality.

Sameness/difference doctrine has mediated what women have gotten as women from this state under the rubric of sex discrimination. It does address a very important problem: how to get women access to everything women have been excluded from, while also valuing everything that women are or have been allowed to become or have developed as a consequence of their struggle either not to be excluded from most of life's pursuits or to be taken seriously under the terms that have been permitted to be women's terms. It negotiates what women have managed in relation to men. Its guiding impulse is: we are as good as you. Anything you can do, we can do. Just get out of the way. It has improved elite access to employment and education— the public pursuits, including academic and professional and blue-collar work—to the military, and more than nominal access to athletics.[17] It has moved to alter the dead ends that were all women were seen as good for, and what passed for lack of physical training, which was serious training in passivity and enforced weakness. The military draft has presented the sameness route to equality in all its simple dignity and complex equivocality: as citizens, women should have to risk being killed just like men.[18] Citizenship is whole. The consequences of women's resistance to its risks should count as men's count.[19]

The sameness standard has mostly gotten men the benefit of those few things women have historically had—for all the good they did. Under gender neutrality, the law of custody and divorce has shifted once again, giving men what is termed an equal chance at custody of children and at alimony.[20] Men often look like better parents under gender-neutral rules like level of income and presence of nuclear family, because men make more money and (as it is termed) initiate the building of family units. They also have greater credibility and authority in court. Under gender neutrality, men are in effect granted a preference as parents because society advantages them before they get to court. But law is prohibited from taking that preference into account because that would mean taking gender into account, which would be sex discrimination. Nor are the group realities that make women more in need of alimony permitted to matter, because only individual factors, gender-neutrally considered, may matter. So the fact that women will live their lives, as individuals, as members of the group women, with women's chances in a sex-discriminatory society, may not count or it is sex discrimination. The equality principle in this form mobilizes the idea that the way to get things for women is to get them for men. Men have gotten them. Women have lost their children and financial security and still have not gained equal pay or equal work, far less equal pay for equal work, and are close to losing separate enclaves like women's schools through this approach.[21]

What this doctrine apparently means by sex inequality is not what happens to women, and what it means by sex equality is only getting things for women that can also be gotten for men. The law of sex discrimination seems to be looking only for those ways women are kept down which have *not* wrapped themselves up as a difference, whether original, imposed, or imagined. As to original differences: what to do about the fact that women have an ability men still lack, gestating children in utero? Pregnancy is therefore a difference, yet it does not define a perfect gender line because not all women become pregnant.[22] Gender here is first defined biologically—to encompass that which affects all women and only women—and then the most biological of differences, pregnancy, is excluded because it is not biological (that is, 100 percent) enough. Besides, pregnancy is a difference, on the basis of which differentiations can be made without being discriminatory. Pregnancy is both too gendered and not gendered enough, so women can safely not be compensated for job absences, guaranteed jobs on return, and so on. Gender neutrality suggests, indeed, that it may be sex discrimination to give women what they need because only women need it. It would certainly be considered special protection. But it is not, in this approach, sex discrimination *not* to give only women what they need, because then only women will not get what they need.[23] On this logic, sex discrimination law prohibits virtually nothing that socially disadvantages women and only women. Other than *de jure,* sex discrimination is a null set.

Consider imposed differences: what to do about the fact that most women are segregated into low-paying jobs where there are no men? Arguing that the structure of the marketplace will be subverted if comparable worth is put into effect (an interesting comment on the radical potential of a reform with much in common with "wages for housework" proposals),[24] difference doctrine says that because there is no man to set a standard from which women's treatment is a deviation, there is no sex discrimination, only a sex difference. Never mind that there is no man to compare with because no man would do that job if he had a choice, and because he is a man, he does, so he does not. Straightforward cases of sex discrimination run aground on the same rock. For example, in *Sears v. EEOC,* the Equal Employment Opportunities Commission argued that massive statistical disparities between women and men in some categories of better-paying jobs showed sex discrimination by Sears. One expert, Alice Kessler Harris, assuming women's sameness with men in the name of feminism, supported them, saying that whenever women were permitted to be exceptions, they were. Defendant Sears argued that women were different from men, did not necessarily want the same things men want, such as better-paying jobs. Another expert, Rosalind Rosenberg, arguing women's differences from men in the name of feminism, supported them. Given that the women in the data overwhelmingly divided on gender lines, and that neither the doctrinal assumptions nor the sex inequality of the job definitions was challenged, not to mention the social sexism that constructs what people "want," the argument on women's differences won, and women lost.[25]

Now consider de facto discrimination, the so-called subtle reaches of the imposed category. Most jobs require that a qualified gender-neutral person not be the primary caretaker of the worker's preschool child.[26] Pointing out that this fact raises a concern of gender in a society in which women are expected to care for young children is taken as day one of taking gender into account in the structuring of jobs. To do that would violate the rule against not noticing situated differences based on gender. So it is never clear that day one of taking gender into account in job structuring was the day the job was structured with the expectation that its occupant would not have primary childcare responsibilities.

Imaginary sex differences, such as those between equally qualified male and female applicants for estate administration,[27] sex discrimination doctrine can handle. But if women were not taught to read and write (as was once the case, the women are still a majority of the world's illiterates), the gender difference between women and men in estate administration would not be imaginary. Such a society would be in even greater need of a law against sex inequality, yet this doctrine would be incapable of addressing it as an inequality problem. Illusions and mistakes sex discrimination law can deal with. Realities are another thing entirely. The result is, due to sex inequality, even when women are "similarly situated" to men they are often not seen as such. The deeper problem is, due to sex inequality, they are seldom permitted to become "similarly situated" to men.

This law takes the same approach to the social reality of sex inequality that the ideology of sex inequality takes to social life, and considers itself legitimate because the two correspond. For this reason, sex equality law is always being undermined by the problem it is trying to solve. It cannot recognize, for instance, that men do not have to be the same as anyone to be entitled to most benefits. It cannot recognize that every quality that distinguishes men from women is already affirmatively compensated in society's organization and values, so that it implicitly defines the standards it neutrally applies. Men's physiology defines most sports, their health needs largely define insurance coverage, their socially designed biographies defined work-place expectations and successful career patterns, their perspectives and concerns define quality in scholarship, their experiences and obsessions define merit, their military service defines citizenship, their presence defines family, their inability to get along with each other—their wars and rulerships—defines history, their image defines god, and their genitals define sex. These are the standards that are presented as gender neutral. For each of men's differences from women, what amounts to an affirmative action plan is in effect, otherwise known as the male-dominant structure and values of American society. But whenever women are found different from men and insist on not having it held against them, every time a difference is used to keep women second class and equality law is brought in as redress, the doctrine has a paradigm trauma.

Clearly, there are many differences between women and men. Systematically elevating one-half of a population and denigrating the other half would not likely produce a population in which everyone is the same. What sex equality law fails to notice is that men's differences from women are equal to women's differences from men. Yet the sexes are not equally situated in society with respect to their relative differences. Hierarchy of power produces real as well as fantasied differences, differences that are also inequalities. The differences are equal. The inequalities, rather obviously, are not.

Missing in sex equality law is what Aristotle missed in his empiricist notion that equality means treating likes alike and unlikes unlike.[28] No one has seriously questioned it since. Why should one have to be the same as a man to get what a man gets simply because he is one? Why does maleness provide an original entitlement, unquestioned on the basis of its gender, while women who want to make a case of unequal treatment in a world men have made in their image (this is really the part Aristotle missed)[29] have to show in effect that they are men in every relevant respect, unfortunately mistaken for women on the basis of an accident of birth?

The women that gender neutrality benefits, and there are some, expose this method in highest relief. They are mostly women who have achieved a biography that somewhat approximates the male norm, at least on paper. They are the qualified, the least of sex discrimination's victims. When they are denied a man's chance, it looks the most like sex bias. The more unequal society gets, the fewer such women are permitted to exist. The more unequal society gets, the less likely this sex equality doctrine is to be able to do anything about it, because unequal power creates both the appearance and the reality of sex differences along the same lines as it creates sex inequalities.

The special benefits side of the sameness/difference approach has not compensated women for being second class. Its double standard does not give women the dignity of the single standard, nor does it suppress the gender of its referent: female. The special benefits rule is the only place in mainstream sex equality doctrine where one can identify as a woman and not have that mean giving up all claim to equal treatment. But it comes close. Originally, women were permitted to be protected in the workforce, with dubious benefit.[30] Then, under its double standard, women who stood to inherit something when their husbands died were allowed to exclude a small percentage of inheritance tax, Justice Douglas waxing eloquent about the difficulties of all women's economic situation.[31] If women are going to be stigmatized as different, the compensation should at least fit the disparity. Women have also gotten three more years than men get before being advanced or kicked out of the military hierarchy. This is to compensate them for being precluded from combat, the usual way to advance.[32] Making exceptions for women, as if they are a special case, often seems preferable to correcting the rule itself, even when women's "specialness" is dubious or shared or statutorily created.

Excluding women is always an option if sex equality feels in tension with the pursuit itself. For example, women have been excluded from contact jobs in male-only prisons in the name of "their very womanhood" because they might get raped, the Court taking the viewpoint of the reasonable rapist on women's employment opportunities.[33] The conditions that create women's rapability are not seen as susceptible to legal change, nor is predicating women's employment upon their inevitability seen as discriminatory. Apparently, rapability is a difference. Women have also been protected out of hazardous jobs because they did not wish to be sterilized, or the employer did not want to run that risk. The job has health hazards, and somebody who might be a real person some day and therefore could sue—a fetus—might be hurt if potentially fertile women were given jobs that would subject their bodies to possible harm.[34] Fertile women are apparently not real persons and therefore cannot sue either for the hazard to their health or for the lost employment opportunity—although only women are treated in this way. Men, it seems, are never excludable as such, even when their fertility (as with health hazards) or their lives (as with combat) are threatened, even though only men are being harmed.

These two routes to sex equality, the sameness route and the difference route, divide women according to their relations with men and according to their proximity to a male standard. Women who step out of women's traditional relations with men and become abstract persons—exceptional to women's condition rather than receiving the protections of it—are seen as seeking to be like men. They are served equality with a vengeance. If they win, they receive as relief the privilege of meeting the male standard, of paying the price of admission which men are trained for as men and are supposed to pay, even if regularly they do not. Women who assert claims under the difference route, claims in traditional role terms, may, if they win, be protected, or they may be left in sex-specific disadvantage. Different situations may justify different treatment—better or worse.

The result of gender neutrality is that at the same time that very few women gain access to the preconditions effectively to assert equality on male terms, women created in society's traditional mold lose the guarantees of those roles to men asserting sex equality. Women asking courts to enforce the guarantees that have been part of the bargain of women's roles receive less and less, while also not receiving the benefits of the social changes that would qualify them for rights on the same terms as men. This is not a transitional problem. Abstract equality necessarily reinforces the inequalities of the status quo to the extent that it evenly reflects an unequal social arrangement. The law of sex discrimination has largely refused to recognize that it is women who are unequal to men, and has called this refusal the equality principle.

Because, in this doctrine, equality of rights rests upon a claim to similarity, and gender is actually a hierarchy, men who fail as men readily qualify for women's special treatment, while few women attain the prerequisites to claim equality with men. Many of the doctrinally definitive sex discrimination cases that have reached the Supreme Court since 1971 have been brought by men seeking access to the few benefits women had.[35] Many have won, while women plaintiffs seeking opportunities previously reserved for men lose and lose and lose, and usually do not even get to the Supreme Court.[36] As a result of men's easier downward mobility combined with men's comparatively greater access to resources and credibility, access men almost never lose, sex discrimination law's compensatory, preferential, or protective rationales on women's behalf have most often been articulated in the context of challenges by men to sex-specific provisions that cushion or qualify but do not change women's status. As often they reinforce it in backhanded ways. One such case upheld a male-only statutory rape law against a sex equality challenge on the grounds that only women get pregnant, ignoring that young men also get raped, that the youngest raped women do not get pregnant, and that women over the age of majority get raped as well as pregnant. Because rape was not recognized as an act of sex inequality, the Court preserved young men as sexual actors, even with adult women, and divided the female population into categories of accessibility to forced sex. The age line kept little girls sexually taboo and thus sexually targeted, by definition unable to consent. Girls one day older and women were left effectively consenting, presumed equals unless proved otherwise.[37]

Another case preserved the male-only draft, forcing only men to risk their lives in combat, and, with it, men as society's primary combatants, its legitimate violence in their hands.[38]

Granted, some widowers are like most widows: poor because their spouse has died. Some husbands are like most wives: dependent on their spouse. A few fathers, like most mothers, are primary caretakers. But to occupy these positions is consistent with female gender norms; most women share them. The gender-neutral approach to sex discrimination law obscures, and the protectionist rationale declines to change, the fact that women's poverty and consequent financial dependence on men (whether in marriage, welfare, the workplace, or prostitution), forced motherhood, and sexual vulnerability substantively constitute their social status *as women,* as members of their gender. That some men at times find themselves in similar situations does not mean that they occupy that status as men, as members of their gender. They do so as exceptions, both in norms and in numbers. Unlike women, men are not poor or primary caretakers of children on the basis of sex.

The standards of sex discrimination law are for society's exceptions. To claim that they are situated similarly to men, women must be exceptions. They must be able to claim all that sex inequality has, in general, systematically taken from women: financial independence, job qualifications, business experience, leadership qualities, assertiveness and confidence, a sense of self, peer esteem, physical stature, strength or prowess, combat skills, sexual impregnability, and, at all stages of legal proceedings, credibility. Taking the sexes "as individuals," meaning one at a time, as if they do not belong to genders, perfectly obscures these collective realities and substantive correlates of gender group status behind the mask of recognition of individual rights. It is the woman who has largely escaped gender inequality who is best able to claim she has been injured by it. It seems a woman must already be equal before she can complain of inequality.

Sex discrimination law requires that women either be gender objects or emulate maleness to qualify as subject. These criteria interestingly parallel the two-pronged "passionlessness" that Nancy Cott identifies as women's side of the bargain under which women were historically allowed access to this form of institutional equality at all. "Passionlessness"—sexual acted-uponness as female gender definition—was the price of women's admission to Victorian moral equality.[39] Passionless women merit equal protection (equal treatment, separate version female) or qualified permission to be second-class men (equal treatment, version male). Passionateness would merely break the rule, disentitling the women to moral equality but leaving passionlessness standing as the rule for women. Nonpassionless women—perhaps self-acting, self-defined, self-respecting, not sexually defined, and resisting sex inequality from that position—simply do not exist in these terms. If gender status is sexually based, sexual equality would be real equality. In this light, this form of sexual objectification as the price for equality looks like inequality as the price for equality, and the bourgeois bargain—the terms on which women as a gender were admitted to abstract personhood and individuality in the first place— is revealed to have had a sexual price.

Under sex equality law, to be human, in substance, means to be a man. To be a person, an abstract individual with abstract rights, may be a bourgeois concept, but its content is male. The only way to assert a claim *as* a member of the socially unequal group women, as opposed to seeking to assert a claim as *against* membership in the group women, is to seek treatment on a sexually denigrated basis. Human rights, including "women's rights," have implicitly been limited to those rights that men have to lose. This may be in part why men persistently confuse procedural and abstract equality with substantive equality: for them, they are the same. Abstract equality has never included those rights that women as women most need and never have had. All this appears rational and neutral in law because social reality is constructed from the same point of view.

Stereotyping—inaccurate or exaggerated misreflections—is the archetypal liberal injury. It happens in the head or in symbolic social space. It freezes the process of objectification (of which it is a bona fide part) at its moment of inaccuracy, failing to grasp, thus being always potentially defeated by, images that become behaviorally and emotionally real. Most do. Taking, for example, job applicants on an individual basis obscures rather than relieves this fact, although it surely helps some individuals. That women and girls may not be physically strong, or do not appear physically intimidating compared with men and boys, may be consequences as much as causes of the social image of proper womanhood as weak and of manhood as strong. The issue is not simply one of rigid assumption of biological causality in the face of social variation to the contrary. It is a question of one's account of the reality of gender at the point of dismantling it. Power in society includes both legitimate force and the power to determine decisive socialization processes and therefore the power to produce reality. The distinction between women and men is not simply etched onto perceived reality, but superimposed on a picture that already exists in the mind because it exists in the social world. If a stereotype has a factual basis, if it is not merely a lie or a distortion but has become empirically real, it is not considered sex discriminatory. It is a difference. To criticize sexual objectification as a process of sex inequality, by contrast, is to see actual disparity as part of the injury of inequality through which stereotypes are made most deeply injurious at the point at which they become empirically real.

In cases in which sex-differential treatment is not facial, discrimination law is increasingly requiring a showing that discriminatory "motive" or "intent"[40] animated the challenged behavior. Much like the mental element in rape, this requirement defines the injury of sex discrimination from the standpoint of the perpetrator. If he did not mean harm, no harm was done. If the perpetrator did not intend his acts to be based on sex, they were not based on sex.[41] Discrimination is a moral lapse. Women know that much if not most sexism is unconscious, heedless, patronizing, well-meant, or profit-motivated. It is no less denigrating, damaging, or sex-specific for not being "on purpose."[42] Intent requires proof that defendants first know women's value but then choose to disregard it. But the point at which bigotry is most determinative is the point at which women are not seen as full human beings at all. Often members of both sexes value women's work less highly, on the basis only of their knowledge that a woman did the work. Yet, not knowing that one has sexist attitudes, or not knowing that they are influencing one's judgments, is legally taken as a reason that sex discrimination did not occur.

Similarly, burdens of proof effectively presume a non-sex-discriminatory universe, the one men largely occupy, to which plaintiffs are required to prove themselves and their situation exceptions. As a context within which to evaluate claims and weigh evidence, the doctrine permits women bringing cases to receive no benefit of a recognition that discrimination against women occurs. Defendants need only "articulate a legitimate and nondiscriminatory reason" for their actions[43] to recover the benefit of the assumption that the merit system generally works. This in spite of the evidence that women overwhelmingly are not advanced according to ability. This allocation of burden of proof is presented as neutral and unbiased and merely technical. Presuming that equality in general exists militates against finding inequality in particular cases as surely as presuming that inequality in general exists militates in favor of finding inequality in particular cases. Social inequality makes neutral ground unavailable: the law against it must assume that either equality or inequality is the social norm. Assuming that equality generally exists, and that each challenged instance is an exception, makes it almost impossible to produce equality by law.

Sex discrimination law is fundamentally undercut by its concepts of sex, of inequality, and of law. The underlying strategy is to conceive sex as a difference; to diagnose the evil of sex inequality as mistaken differences; to imagine that sex equality—the elimination of unreal differences—has been achieved; and to generate rules from this projected point as a strategy for reaching it. Its reflective method—law mirrors the reality of sex, the reality of sex inequality—embodies this strategy. To suppose that legally assuming the situation really *is* equal in order to make it so is the sentimentality of liberalism. The distanced aperspectivity that achieves the sought-after blindness to sex differences also achieves blindness to sex inequality. Such an approach cannot distinguish separatism from segregation, nondiscrimination from forced integration, or diversity from assimilation. It also misdiagnoses the stake the dominant have in maintaining the situation, because neither it nor they know they are dominant. Ronald Dworkin, for example, defines the equality standard of liberalism as one that "imposes no sacrifice or constraint on any citizen in virtue of an argument that the citizen could not accept without abandoning his sense of equal worth,"[44] He seems not to recognize that the inferiority of women is necessary, substantively, to masculine self worth in unequal societies, indeed that this is part of the reason sex inequality persists.

All these doctrines—the intent requirement, the allocations of burden of proof, but most fundamentally the requirement of similar situation across the gender line—authoritatively deny that social reality is split by sex inequality. This denial, which makes sense from the male point of view, merges the legal standard for a cognizable inequality with objectivity as an epistemological stance. Objectivity assumes that equally competent observers similarly situated see, or at least report seeing, the same thing. Feminism radically questions whether the sexes are ever, under current conditions, similarly situated even when they inhabit the same conditions. (It questions some standards for competence as well.) The line between subjective and objective perception which is supposed to divide the idiosyncratic, nonreplicable, religious, partial, and unverifiable—the unscientific— from the real presumes the existence of a single object reality and its noncontingence upon angle of perception. But if women's condition exists, there are (at least) two *object* realms of social meaning. Women's point of view is no more subjective than men's if women inhabit a sex-discriminatory object reality.

In this analysis, social circumstances, to which gender is central, produce distinctive interests, hence perceptions, hence meanings, hence definitions of rationality. This observation neither reduces gender to thinking differently, rightness to relative subjectivity, nor principle to whose ox is gored. It does challenge the view that neutrality, specifically gender neutrality as an expression of objectivity, is adequate to the nonneutral objectified social reality women experience. If differentiation were the problem, gender neutrality would make sense as an approach to it. Since hierarchy is the problem, it is not only inadequate, it is perverse. In questioning the principledness of neutral principles,[45] this analysis suggests that current law to rectify sex inequality is premised upon, and promotes, its continued existence.

The analytical point of departure and return of sex discrimination law is thus the liberal one of gender differences, understood rationally or irrationally to create gender inequalities. The feminist issue, by contrast, is gender hierarchy, which not only produces inequalities but shapes the social meaning, hence legal relevance, of the sex difference. To the extent that the biology of one sex is a social disadvantage, while the biology of the other is not, or is a social advantage, the sexes are equally different but not equally powerful. The issue becomes the social meaning of biology, not any facticity or object quality of biology itself. Similarly, both sexes possess a sexuality that occupies a place in "the heterosexual ethic." To the extent that the sexuality of one sex is a social stigma, target, and provocation to violation, while the sexuality of the other is socially a source of pleasure, adventure, power (indeed, the social definition of potency), and a focus for deification, entertainment, nurturance, and derepression, the sexuality of each is equally different, equally heterosexual or not, but not equally socially powerful. The relevant issue is the social meaning of the sexuality and gender of women and men, not their sexuality or gender "itself"—if such a distinction can be made. To limit efforts to end gender inequality at the point where biology or sexuality is encountered, termed differences, without realizing that these exist in law or society only in terms of their specifically sexist social meanings, amounts to conceding that gender inequality may be challenged so long as the central epistemological pillars of gender as a system of power are permitted to remain standing.

So long as this is the way these issues are framed, women's demands for sex equality will appear to be demands to have it both ways: the same when women are the same as men, different when different. But this is the way men have it: equal and different too. The same as women when they are the same and want to be, and different from women when they are different or want to be, which usually they do. Equal and different too would be parity. But under male supremacy, while being told women get it both ways—the specialness of the pedestal and an even chance at the race, the ability to be a woman and a person, too—few women get much benefit of either. The sameness route ignores the fact that the indices or injuries of sex or sexism often ensure that simply being a woman may mean seldom being in a position sufficiently similar to a man's to have unequal treatment attributed to sex bias. The difference route incorporates and reflects rather than alters the substance of women's inferior status, presenting a protection racket as equal protection of the laws. In this way, the legal forms available for urging the injuries of sex inequality obscure the gender of this equality's reference point while effectively precluding complaint for women's sex-specific grievances.

When sameness is the standard for equality, a critique of gender hierarchy looks like a request for special protection in disguise. In fact, it envisions a change that would make a simple equal chance possible for the first time. To define the reality of gender as difference and the warrant of equality as sameness not only guarantees that sex equality will never be achieved; it is wrong on both counts. Sex in nature is not a bipolarity, it is a continuum; society makes it into a bipolarity. Once this is done, to require that one be the same as those who set the standard—those from whom one is already socially defined as different—simply means that sex equality is conceptually designed in law never to be achieved. Those who most need equal treatment will be the *least* similar, socially, to those whose situation sets the standard against which their entitlement to equal treatment is measured. The deepest problems of sex inequality do not find women "similarly situated" to men. Practices of inequality need not be intentionally discriminatory. The status quo need only be reflected unchanged. As a strategy for maintaining social power, descriptively speaking, first structure social reality unequally, and then require that entitlement to alter it be grounded on a lack of distinction in situation; first structure perception so that different equals inferior, and then require that discrimination be activated by evil minds who *know* that they are treating equals as less, in a society in which, epistemologically speaking, most bigots will be sincere.

The mainstream law of equality assumes that society is already fundamentally equal. It gives women legally no more than they already have socially, and little it cannot also give men. Actually doing anything for women under sex equality law is thus stigmatized as special protection or affirmative action rather than simply recognized as nondiscrimination or equality for the first time. So long as sex equality is limited by sex difference—whether valued or negated, staked out as a ground for feminism or occupied as the terrain of misogyny—women will be born, degraded, and die. Protection will be a dirty word and equality will be a special privilege.

[R]evolutions are not made by laws.
                    —Karl Marx, *Capital* (1867)

Time works changes, brings into existence new conditions
and purposes. Therefore a principle to be vital must be
capable of wider application than the mischief which gave it
birth. This is particularly true of constitutions . . . [In
interpreting] a constitution, therefore, our contemplation
cannot be only of what has been but of what may be.
                    —Justice McKenna, Weems v.
                    United States, 217 U.S. 349, 373
                    (1910)

There are those who hold that only in a change of heart on
the part of individuals separately [will] structural changes
. . . necessarily rise. On the other hand, some contend . . .
that unconscious, partially non-intentional and impersonal
prejudices are historically rooted and built into many of our
modes of behaviour and our institutions . . . Here, a change
in structure (law) would help bring about, re-enforce or
cooperate with a change of heart. They go together. Hard
hearts seem often to go with hard heads, and soft hearts with
soft ones; but then, too, we encounter hard hearts with soft
heads. What we need are soft hearts with hard heads . . .
We cannot wait for changes of heart—usually they take time
and much pain, and generally the law has a wonderful effect
on the head.
                    —Patrick Lawlor, Q.C., "Group
                    Defamation" (1984)

# 13 | *Toward Feminist Jurisprudence*

Happy above all Countries is our Country where that equality
is found, without destroying the necessary subordination.
—Thomas Lee Shippen (1788)

If I fight, some day some woman will win.
—Michelle Vinson (1987)

A jurisprudence is a theory of the relation between life
and law. In life, "woman" and "man" are widely
experienced as features of being, not constructs of perception, cultural
interventions, or forced identities. Gender, in other words, is lived as
ontology, not as epistemology. Law actively participates in this
transformation of perspective into being. In liberal regimes, law is a
particularly potent source and badge of legitimacy, and site and cloak
of force. The force underpins the legitimacy as the legitimacy conceals
the force. When life becomes law in such a system, the transformation
is both formal and substantive. It reenters life marked by power.

In male supremacist societies, the male standpoint dominates civil
society in the form of the objective standard—that standpoint which,
because it dominates in the world, does not appear to function as a
standpoint at all. Under its aegis, men dominate women and children,
three-quarters of the world. Family and kinship rules and sexual mores
guarantee reproductive ownership and sexual access and control to men
as a group. Hierarchies among men are ordered on the basis of race and
class, stratifying women as well. The state incorporates these facts of
social power in and as law. Two things happen: law becomes
legitimate, and social dominance becomes invisible. Liberal legalism
is thus a medium for making male dominance both invisible and
legitimate by adopting the male point of view in law at the same time
as it enforces that view on society.

Through legal mediation, male dominance is made to seem a feature of life, not a one-sided construct imposed by force for the advantage of a dominant group. To the degree it succeeds ontologically, male dominance does not look epistemological: control over being produces control over consciousness, fusing material conditions with consciousness in a way that is inextricable short of social change. Dominance reified becomes difference. Coercion legitimated becomes consent. Reality objectified becomes ideas; ideas objectified become reality. Politics neutralized and naturalized becomes morality. Discrimination in society becomes nondiscrimination in law. Law is a real moment in the social construction of these mirror-imaged inversions as truth. Law, in societies ruled and penetrated by the liberal form, turns angle of vision and construct of social meaning into dominant institution. In the liberal state, the rule of law—neutral, abstract, elevated, pervasive—both institutionalizes the power of men over women and institutionalizes power in its male form.

From a feminist perspective, male supremacist jurisprudence erects qualities valued from the male point of view as standards for the proper and actual relation between life and law. Examples include standards for scope of judicial review, norms of judicial restraint, reliance on precedent, separation of powers, and the division between public and private law. Substantive doctrines like standing, justiciability, and state action adopt the same stance. Those with power in civil society, not women, design its norms and institutions, which become the status quo. Those with power, not usually women, write constitutions, which become law's highest standards. Those with power in political systems that women did not design and from which women have been excluded write legislation, which sets ruling values. Then, jurisprudentially, judicial review is said to go beyond its proper scope—to delegitimate courts and the rule of law itself—when legal questions are not confined to assessing the formal correspondence between legislation and the constitution, or legislation and social reality, but scrutinize the underlying substance. Lines of precedent fully developed before women were permitted to vote, continued while women were not allowed to learn to read and write, sustained under a reign of sexual terror and abasement and silence and misrepresentation continuing to the present day are considered valid bases for defeating "unprecedented" interpretations or initiatives from women's point of view. Doctrines of standing suggest that because women's deepest injuries are shared in some way by most or all women, no individual woman is differentially injured enough to be able to sue for women's deepest injuries.

Structurally, only when the state has acted can constitutional equality guarantees be invoked.[1] But no law gives men the right to rape women. This has not been necessary, since no rape law has ever seriously undermined the terms of men's entitlement to sexual access to women. No government is, yet, in the pornography business. This has not been necessary, since no man who wants pornography encounters serious trouble getting it, regardless of obscenity laws. No law gives fathers the right to abuse their daughters sexually. This has not been necessary, since no state has ever systematically intervened in their social possession of and access to them. No law gives husbands the right to batter their wives. This has not been necessary, since there is nothing to stop them. No law silences women. This has not been necessary, for women are previously silenced in society—by sexual abuse, by not being heard, by not being believed, by poverty, by illiteracy, by a language that provides only unspeakable vocabulary for their most formative traumas, by a publishing industry that virtually guarantees that if they ever find a voice it leaves no trace in the world. No law takes away women's privacy. Most women do not have any to take, and no law gives them what they do not already have. No law guarantees that women will forever remain the social unequals of men. This is not necessary, because the law guaranteeing sex equality requires, in an unequal society, that before one can be equal legally, one must be equal socially. So long as power enforced by law reflects and corresponds –in form and in substance– to power enforced by men over women in society, law is objective, appears principled, becomes just the way things are. So long as men dominate women effectively enough in society without the support of positive law, nothing constitutional can be done about it.

Law from the male point of view combines coercion with authority, policing society where its edges are exposed: at points of social resistance, conflict, and breakdown. Since there is no place outside this system from a feminist standpoint, if its solipsistic lock could be broken, such moments could provide points of confrontation, perhaps even openings for change. The point of view of a total system emerges as particular only when confronted, in a way it cannot ignore, by a demand from another point of view. This is why epistemology must be controlled for ontological dominance to succeed, and why conscious-ness raising is subversive. It is also why, when law sides with the powerless, as it occasionally has,[2] it is said to engage in something other than law—politics or policy or personal opinion—and to delegitimate itself.[3] When seemingly ontological conditions are challenged from the collective standpoint of a dissident reality, they become visible as epistemological. Dominance suddenly appears no longer inevitable. When it loses its ground it loosens its grip.

Thus, when the Supreme Court held that racial segregation did not violate equality rights, it said that those who felt that to be segregated on the basis of race implied inferiority merely chose to place that construction upon it. The harm of forced separation was a matter of point of view.[4] When the Supreme Court later held that racial segregation violated equality rights, it said that segregation generated a feeling of inferiority in the hearts and minds of Black children which was unlikely ever to be undone. Both Courts observed the same reality: the feelings of inferiority generated by apartheid. *Plessy* saw it from the standpoint of white supremacy; *Brown* saw it from the standpoint of the Black challenge to white supremacy, envisioning a social equality that did not yet exist. Inequality is difficult to see when everything tells the unequal that the status quo is equality—for them. To the Supreme Court, the way Black people saw their own condition went from being sneered at as a point of view within their own control, a self-inflicted epistemological harm, to being a constitutional measure of the harm a real social condition imposed upon them. Consciousness raising shifts the episteme in a similar way, exposing the political behind the personal, the dominance behind the submission, partici-pating in altering the balance of power subtly but totally. The question is, what can extend this method to the level of the state for women?

To begin with, why law? Marx saw the modern state as "the official expression of antagonism in civil society."[5] Because political power in such a state could emancipate the individual only within the frame-work of the existing social order, law could emancipate women to be equal only within "the slavery of civil society."[6] By analogy, women would not be freed from forced sex, but freed to engage in it and initiate it. They would not be freed from reproductive tyranny and exploitation, but freed to exercise it. They would not be liberated from the dialectic of economic and sexual dominance and submission, but freed to dominate. Depending upon the substantive analysis of civil dominance, either women would dominate men, or some women (with all or some men) would dominate other women. In other words, the liberal vision of sex equality would be achieved. Feminism unmodified, methodologically postmarxist feminism, aspires to better.

From the feminist point of view, the question of women's collective reality and how to change it merges with the question of women's point of view and how to know it. What do women live, hence know, that can confront male dominance? What female ontology can confront male epistemology; that is, what female epistemology can confront male ontology? What point of view can question the code of civil society? The answer is simple, concrete, specific, and real: women's social inequality with men on the basis of sex, hence the point of view of women's subordination to men. Women are not permitted fully to know what sex equality would look like, because they have never lived it. It is idealist, hence elitist, to hold that they do. But they do not need to. They know inequality because they have lived it, so they know what removing barriers to equality would be. Many of these barriers are legal; many of them are social; most of them exist at an interface between law and society.

Inequality on the basis of sex, women share. It is women's collective condition. The first task of a movement for social change is to face one's situation and name it. The failure to face and criticize the reality of women's condition, a failure of idealism and denial, is a failure of feminism in its liberal forms. The failure to move beyond criticism, a failure of determinism and radical paralysis, is a failure of feminism in its left forms. Feminism on its own terms has begun to give voice to and describe the collective condition of women as such, so largely comprised as it is of all women's particularities. It has begun to uncover the laws of motion of a system that keeps women in a condition of imposed inferiority. It has located the dynamic of the social definition of gender in the sexuality of dominance and subordination, the sexuality of inequality: sex as inequality and inequality as sex. As sexual inequality is gendered as man and women, gender inequality is sexualized as dominance and subordination. The social power of men over women extends through laws that purport to protect women as part of the community, like the rape law; laws that ignore women's survival stake in the issue, like the obscenity law, or obscure it, like the abortion law; and laws that announce their intent to remedy that inequality but do not, like the sex equality law. This law derives its authority from reproducing women's social inequality to men in legal inequality, in a seamless web of life and law.

Feminist method adopts the point of view of women's inequality to men. Grasping women's reality from the inside, developing its specificities, facing the intractability and pervasiveness of male power, relentlessly criticizing women's condition as it identifies with all women, it has created strategies for change, beginning with consciousness raising. On the level of the state, legal guarantees of equality in liberal regimes provide an opening. Sex inequality is the true name for women's social condition. It is also, in words anyway, illegal sometimes. In some liberal states, the belief that women already essentially have sex equality extends to the level of law. From a perspective that understands that women do *not* have sex equality, this law means that, once equality is meaningfully defined, the law cannot be applied without changing society. To make sex equality meaningful in law requires identifying the real issues, and establishing that sex inequality, once established, matters.

Sex equality in law has not been meaningfully defined for women, but has been defined and limited from the male point of view to correspond with the existing social reality of sex inequality. An alternative approach to this mainstream view threads through existing law. It is the reason sex equality law exists at all. In this approach, inequality is a matter not of sameness and difference, but of dominance and subordination. Inequality is about power, its definition, and its maldistribution. Inequality at root is grasped as a question of hierarchy, which—as power succeeds in constructing social perception and social reality—derivatively becomes categorical distinctions, differences. Where mainstream equality law is abstract, this approach is concrete; where mainstream equality law is falsely universal, this approach remains specific.[7] The goal is not to make legal categories that trace and trap the status quo, but to confront by law the inequalities in women's condition in order to change them.

This alternate approach centers on the most sex-differential abuses of women as a gender, abuses that sex equality law in its sameness/difference obsession cannot confront. It is based on the reality that feminism, beginning with consciousness raising, has most distinctively uncovered, a reality about which little systematic was known before 1970: the reality of sexual abuse. It combines women's sex-based destitution and enforced dependency and permanent relegation to disrespected and starvation-level work—the lived meaning of class for women—with the massive amount of sexual abuse of girls apparently endemic to the patriarchal family, the pervasive rape and attempted rape about which nothing is done, the systematic battery of women in homes, and prostitution—the fundamental condition of women—of which the pornography industry is an arm. Keeping the reality of gender in view makes it impossible to see gender as a difference, unless this subordinated condition of women is that difference. This reality has called for a new conception of the problem of sex inequality, hence a new legal conception of it, both doctrinally and jurisprudentially.

Experiences of sexual abuse have been virtually excluded from the mainstream doctrine of sex equality because they happen almost exclusively to women and because they are experienced as sex. Sexual abuse has not been seen to raise sex *equality* issues because these events happen specifically and almost exclusively to women as women. Sexuality is socially organized to require sex inequality for excitement and satisfaction. The least extreme expression of gender inequality, and the prerequisite for all of it, is dehumanization and objectification. The most extreme is violence. Because sexual objectification and sexual violence are almost uniquely done to women, they have been systematically treated as the sex difference, when they represent the socially situated subjection of women to men. The whole point of women's social relegation to inferiority as a gender is that this is not generally done to men. The systematic relegation of an entire people to a condition of inferiority is attributed to them, made a feature of theirs, and read out of equality demands and equality law, when it is termed a "difference." This condition is ignored entirely, with all the women who are determined by it, when only features women share with the privileged group are allowed to substantiate equality claims.

It follows that seeing sex equality questions as matters of reasonable or unreasonable classification of relevant social characteristics expresses male dominance in law. If the shift in perspective from gender as difference to gender as dominance is followed, gender changes from a distinction that is ontological and presumptively valid to a detriment that is epistemological and presumptively suspect. The given becomes the contingent. In this light, liberalism, purporting to discover gender, has discovered male and female in the mirror of nature; the left has discovered masculine and feminine in the mirror of society. The approach from the standpoint of the subordination of women to men, by contrast, criticizes and claims the specific situation of women's enforced inferiority and devaluation, pointing a way out of the infinity of reflections in law-and-society's hall of mirrors where sex equality law remains otherwise trapped.

Equality understood substantively rather than abstractly, defined on women's own terms and in terms of women's concrete experience, is what women in society most need and most do not have. Equality is also what society holds that women have already, and therefore guarantees women by positive law. The law of equality, statutory and constitutional, therefore provides a peculiar jurisprudential opportunity, a crack in the wall between law and society. Law does not usually guarantee rights to things that do not exist. This may be why equality issues have occasioned so many jurisprudential disputes about what law is and what it can and should do. Every demand from women's point of view looks substantive, just as every demand from women's point of view requires change. Can women, demanding actual equality through law, be part of changing the state's relation to women and women's relation to men?

The first step is to claim women's concrete reality. Women's inequality occurs in a context of unequal pay, allocation to disrespected work, demeaned physical characteristics, targeting for rape, domestic battery, sexual abuse as children, and systematic sexual harassment. Women are daily dehumanized, used in denigrating entertainment, denied reproductive control, and forced by the conditions of their lives into prostitution. These abuses occur in a legal context historically characterized by disenfranchisement, preclusion from property ownership, exclusion from public life, and lack of recognition of sex-specific injuries.[8] Sex inequality is thus a social and political institution.

The next step is to recognize that male forms of power over women are affirmatively embodied as individual rights in law. When men lose power, they feel they lose rights. Often they are not wrong. Examples include the defense of mistaken belief in consent in the rape law, which legally determines whether or not a rape occurred from the rapists' perspective; freedom of speech, which gives pimps rights to torture, exploit, use, and sell women to men through pictures and words, and gives consumers rights to buy them; the law of privacy, which defines the home and sex as presumptively consensual and protects the use of pornography in the home; the law of child custody, which purports gender neutrality while applying a standard of adequacy of parenting based on male-controlled resources and male-defined norms, sometimes taking children away from women but more generally controlling women through the threat and fear of loss of their children. Real sex equality under law would qualify or eliminate these powers of men, hence men's current "rights" to use, access, possess, and traffic women and children.

In this context, many issues appear as sex equality issues for the first time—sexual assault, for example. Rape is a sex-specific violation. Not only are the victims of rape overwhelmingly women, perpetrators overwhelmingly men, but also the rape of women by men is integral to the way inequality between the sexes occurs in life. Intimate violation with impunity is an ultimate index of social power. Rape both evidences and practices women's low status relative to men. Rape equates female with violable and female sexuality with forcible intrusion in a way that defines and stigmatizes the female sex as a gender. Threat of sexual assault is threat of punishment for being female. The state has laws against sexual assault but it does not enforce them. Like lynching at one time, rape is socially permitted, though formally illegal. Victims of sex crimes, mostly women and girls, are thus disadvantaged relative to perpetrators of sex crimes, largely men.

A systemic inequality between the sexes therefore exists in the social practice of sexual violence, subjection to which defines women's status, and victims of which are largely women, and in the operation of the state, which *de jure* outlaws sexual violence but de facto permits men to engage in it on a wide scale. Making sexual assault laws gender neutral does nothing to address this, nothing to alter the social equation of female with rapable, and may obscure the sex specificity of the problem. Rape should be defined as sex by compulsion, of which physical force is one form. Lack of consent is redundant and should not be a separate element of the crime.[9] Expanding this analysis would support as sex equality initiatives laws keeping women's sexual histories out of rape trials[10] and publication bans on victims' names and identities.[11] The defense of mistaken belief in consent—which measures whether a rape occurred from the standpoint of the (male) perpetrator—would violate women's sex equality rights by law because it takes the male point of view on sexual violence against women.[12] Similarly, the systematic failure of the state to enforce the rape law effectively or at all excludes women from equal access to justice, permitting women to be savaged on a mass scale, depriving them of equal protection and equal benefit of the laws.

Reproductive control, formerly an issue of privacy, liberty, or personal security, would also become a sex equality issue. The frame for analyzing reproductive issues would expand from focus on the individual at the moment of the abortion decision to women as a group at all reproductive moments. The social context of gender inequality denies women control over the reproductive uses of their bodies and places that control in the hands of men. In a context of inadequate and unsafe contraceptive technology, women are socially disadvantaged in controlling sexual access to their bodies through social learning, lack of information, social pressure, custom, poverty and enforced economic dependence, sexual force, and ineffective enforcement of laws against sexual assault. As a result, they often do not control the conditions under which they become pregnant. If intercourse cannot be presumed to be controlled by women, neither can pregnancy. Women have also been allocated primary responsibility for intimate care of children yet do not control the conditions under which they rear them, hence the impact of these conditions on their own lives.

In this context, access to abortion is necessary for women to survive unequal social circumstances. It provides a form of relief, however punishing, in a life otherwise led in conditions that preclude choice in ways most women have not been permitted to control. This approach also recognizes that whatever is done to the fetus is done to a woman. Whoever controls the destiny of a fetus controls the destiny of a woman. Whatever the conditions of conception, if reproductive control of a fetus is exercised by anyone but the woman, reproductive control is taken only from women, as women. Preventing a woman from exercising the only choice an unequal society leaves her is an enforcement of sex inequality. Giving women control over sexual access to their bodies and adequate support of pregnancies and care of children extends sex equality. In other words, forced maternity is a practice of sex inequality.[13] Because motherhood without choice is a sex equality issue, legal abortion should be a sex equality right. Reproductive technology, sterilization abuse, and surrogate motherhood, as well as abortion funding, would be transformed if seen in this light.

Pornography, the technologically sophisticated traffic in women that expropriates, exploits, uses, and abuses women, also becomes a sex equality issue. The mass production of pornography universalizes the violation of the women in it, spreading it to all women, who are then exploited, used, abused, and reduced as a result of men's consumption of it. In societies pervaded by pornography, all women are defined by it: this is what a woman wants, this is what a woman is. Pornography sets the public standard for the treatment of women in private and the limits of tolerance for what can be permitted in public, such as in rape trials. It sexualizes the definition of male as dominant and female as subordinate. It equates violence against women with sex and provides an experience of that fusion. It engenders rape, sexual abuse of children, battery, forced prostitution, and sexual murder.

In liberal legalism, pornography is said to be a form of freedom of speech. It seems that women's inequality is something pornographers want to say, and saying it is protected even if it requires doing it. Being the medium for men's speech supersedes any rights women have. Women become men's speech in this system. Women's speech is silenced by pornography and the abuse that is integral to it. From women's point of view, obscenity law's misrepresentation of the problem as moral and ideational is replaced with the understanding that the problem of pornography is political and practical. Obscenity law is based on the point of view of male dominance. Once this is exposed, the urgent issue of freedom of speech for women is not primarily the avoidance of state intervention as such, but getting equal access to speech for those to whom it has been denied. First the abuse must be stopped.[14] The endless moral debates between good and evil, conservative and liberal, artists and philistines, the forces of darkness and repression and suppression and the forces of light and liberation and tolerance, would be superseded by the political debate, the abolitionist debate: are women human beings or not? Apparently, the answer provided by legal mandates of sex equality requires repeating.

The changes that a sex equality perspective provides as an interpretive lens include the law of sex equality itself. The intent requirement would be eliminated. The state action requirement would weaken. No distinction would be made between nondiscrimination and affirmative action. Burdens of proof would presuppose inequality rather than equality as a factual backdrop and would be more substantively sensitive to the particularities of sex inequality. Comparable worth would be required. Statistical proofs of disparity would be conclusive. The main question would be: does a practice participate in the subordination of women to men, or is it no part of it? Whether statutes are sex specific or gender neutral would not be as important as whether they work to end or reinforce male supremacy, whether they are concretely grounded in women's experience of subordination or not. Discrimination law would not be confined to employment, education, and accommodation. Civil remedies in women's hands would be emphasized. Gay and lesbian rights would be recognized as sex equality rights. Since sexuality largely defines gender, discrimination based on sexuality is discrimination based on gender. Other forms of social discrimination and exploitation by men against women, such as prostitution and surrogate motherhood, would become actionable.

The relation between life and law would also change. Law, in liberal jurisprudence, objectifies social life. The legal process reflects itself in its own image, makes be there what it puts there, while presenting itself as passive and neutral in the process. To undo this, it will be necessary to grasp the dignity of women without blinking at the indignity of women's condition, to envision the possibility of equality without minimizing the grip of inequality, to reject the fear that has become so much of women's sexuality and the corresponding denial that has become so much of women's politics, and to demand civil parity without pretending that the demand is neutral or that civil equality already exists. In this attempt, the idealism of liberalism and the materialism of the left have come to much the same for women. Liberal jurisprudence that the law should reflect nature or society and left jurisprudence that all law does or can do is reflect existing social relations are two guises of objectivist epistemology. If objectivity is the epistemological stance of which women's sexual objectification is the social process, its imposition the paradigm of power in the male form, then the state appears most relentless in imposing the male point of view when it comes closest to achieving its highest formal criterion of distanced aperspectivity. When it is most ruthlessly neutral, it is most male; when it is most sex blind, it is most blind to the sex of the standard being applied. When it most closely conforms to precedent, to "facts," to legislative intent, it most closely enforces socially male norms and most thoroughly precludes questioning their content as having a point of view at all.

Abstract rights authoritize the male experience of the world. Substantive rights for women would not. Their authority would be the currently unthinkable: nondominant authority, the authority of excluded truth, the voice of silence. It would stand against both the liberal and left views of law. The liberal view that law is society's text, its rational mind, expresses the male view in the normative mode; the traditional left view that the state, and with it the law, is superstructural or ephiphenomenal, expresses it in the empirical mode. A feminist jurisprudence, stigmatized as particularized and protectionist in male eyes of both traditions, is accountable to women's concrete conditions and to changing them. Both the liberal and the left view rationalize male power by presuming that it does not exist, that equality between the sexes (room for marginal corrections conceded) is society's basic norm and fundamental description. Only feminist jurisprudence sees that male power does exist and sex equality does not, because only feminism grasps the extent to which antifeminism is misogyny and both are as normative as they are empirical. Masculinity then appears as a specific position, not just the way things are, its judgments and partialities revealed in process and procedure, adjudication and legislation.

Equality will require change, not reflection—a new jurisprudence, a new relation between life and law. Law that does not dominate life is as difficult to envision as a society in which men do not dominate women, and for the same reasons. To the extent feminist law embodies women's point of view, it will be said that its law is not neutral. But existing law is not neutral. It will be said that it undermines the legitimacy of the legal system. But the legitimacy of existing law is based on force at women's expense. Women have never consented to its rule—suggesting that the system's legitimacy needs repair that women are in a position to provide. It will be said that feminist law is special pleading for a particular group and one cannot start that or where will it end. But existing law is already special pleading for a particular group, where it has ended. The question is not where it will stop, but whether it will start for any group but the dominant one. It will be said that feminist law cannot win and will not work. But this is premature. Its possibilities cannot be assessed in the abstract but must engage the world. A feminist theory of the state has barely been imagined; systematically, it has never been tried.

# Notes

## 1. The Problem of Marxism and Feminism

1. Some contemporary French feminist theorists have used the term *desire* in a variety of ways. See, e.g., Hélène Cixous, "The Laugh of the Medusa: Viewpoint," trans. Kieth Cohen and Paula Cohen, *Signs: Journal of Women in Culture and Society* 1 (Summer 1976): 857–893; works by Xavière Gauthier, Luce Irigaray, and Annie LeClerc in *New French Feminisms: An Anthology,* ed. Elaine Marks and Isabelle de Courtivron (Amherst: University of Massachusetts Press, 1980). For the most part, the term is not used concretely, as I do here, but abstractly and conceptually, as most clearly exposed in Julia Kristeva, *Desire in Language* (New York: Columbia University Press, 1980), which is about semiotics in language. My sense of the term is also to be clearly distinguished from Gilles Deleuze and Felix Guattari, *Anti-Oedipus: Capitalism and Schizophrenia* (New York: Viking Press, 1977), and Guy Hocquenghem, *Homosexual Desire* (London: Allison & Busby, 1978). They do not problematize desire as such, but rather its repression, not seeing either that its determinants are gendered or that its so-called repression is essential to its existence as they know it.

2. I know no nondegraded English verb that elides the distinction between rape and intercourse, love and violation, the way this term does. Further, there is no other verb for the activity of sexual intercourse that would allow a construction parallel to "I am working," a phrase which could be applied to almost any activity that one considered to be work. Compared with work, sexuality is cabined off to the bedroom or the brothel. It is linguistically hermetic, creating the illusion that sexuality is a discrete activity rather than a mode or dimension of being which reaches throughout social life. This illusion of discreteness contributes to obscuring its pervasiveness. The lack of an active verb meaning "to act sexually" that envisions a woman's action is a linguistic expression of the realities of male dominance.

3. John Stuart Mill, *The Subjection of Women,* in *Essays on Sex Equality,* ed. Alice S. Rossi (Chicago: University of Chicago Press, 1970), pp. 184–185.

4. Feminists have previously observed the importance of consciousness raising without seeing it as method in the way developed here. See Pamela Allen, *Free Space: A Perspective on the Small Group in Women's Liberation* (New York: Times Change Press, 1970); Anuradha Bose, "Consciousness Raising," in *Mother Was*

*Not a Person,* ed. Margaret Anderson (Montreal: Content Publishing, 1972); Nancy McWilliams, "Contemporary Feminism, Consciousness-Raising, and Changing Views of the Political," in *Women in Politics,* ed. Jane Jaquette (New York: John Wiley & Sons, 1974); Joan Cassell, *A Group Called Women: Sisterhood and Symbolism in the Feminist Movement* (New York: David McKay, 1977); and Nancy Hartsock, "Fundamental Feminism: Process and Perspective," *Quest: A Feminist Quarterly* 2 (Fall 1975): 67–80.

5. Rosa Luxemburg, "Women's Suffrage and Class Struggle," in *Selected Political Writings,* ed. Dick Howard (New York: Monthly Review Press, 1971), pp. 219–220. It may or may not be true that women vote more conservatively than men on a conventional left–right spectrum. The suspicion that they do may have accounted for ambivalence of the left on women's suffrage as much as any principled view of the role of a reform like suffrage in a politics of radical change. Conservatives, however, were not prominent in fighting for women's right to vote.

6. Ibid., p. 220.

7. These observations have been complex and varied. Delia Davin, "Women in the Countryside of China," in *Women in Chinese Society,* ed. Margery Wolf and Roxane Witke (Stanford: Stanford University Press, 1974); Katie Curtin, *Women in China* (New York: Pathfinder Press, 1975); Judith Stacey, "When Patriarchy Kowtows: The Significance of the Chinese Family Revolution for Feminist Theory," *Feminist Studies* 2 (1975): 64–112; Julia Kristeva, *About Chinese Women* (New York: Urizen Books, 1977); Hilda Scott, *Does Socialism Liberate Women? Experiences from Eastern Europe* (Boston: Beacon Press, 1974); Margaret Randall, *Cuban Women Now* (Toronto: Women's Press, 1974) (an edited collection of Cuban women's own observations) and *Cuban Women Now: Afterword* (Toronto: Women's Press, 1974); Carollee Bengelsdorf and Alice Hageman, "Emerging from Underdevelopment: Women and Work in Cuba," in *Capitalist Patriarchy and the Case for Socialist Feminism,* ed. Zillah Eisenstein (New York: Monthly Review Press, 1979).

8. Barbara Ehrenreich, "What Is Socialist Feminism?" *WIN* (Women's International Network) *News,* June 3, 1976; reprinted in *Working Papers on Socialism and Feminism* (Chicago: New American Movement, n.d.).

9. Susan Brownmiller, quoted in Batya Weinbaum, *The Curious Courtship of Women's Liberation and Socialism* (Boston: South End Press, 1978), p. 7.

10. Stacey, "When Patriarchy Kowtows"; Janet Salaff and Judith Merkle, "Women and Revolution: The Lessons of the Soviet Union and China," *Socialist Revolution* 1, no. 4 (1970): 39–72; Linda Gordon, *The Fourth Mountain* (Cambridge, Mass.: Working Papers, 1973); Richard Stites, *The Women's Liberation Movement in Russia: Feminism, Nihilism, and Bolshevism* (Princeton: Princeton University Press, 1978), pp. 392–421.

11. Fidel Castro, "The New Role for Women in Cuban Society," in Linda Jenness, *Women and the Cuban Revolution* (New York: Pathfinder Press, 1970); but cf. his "Speech at Closing Session of the 2nd Congress of the Federation of Cuban Women," Nov. 29, 1974, *Cuba Review* 4 (December 1974): 17–23. Stephanie

Urdang, *A Revolution within a Revolution: Women in Guinea-Bissau* (Boston: New England Free Press, n.d.). This is the general position taken by official documents of the Chinese revolution, as collected by Elisabeth Croll, ed., *The Women's Movement in China: A Selection of Readings, 1949–1973,* Modern China Series, no. 6 (London: Anglo-Chinese Educational Institute, 1974). Mao Tse-tung recognized a distinctive domination of women by men (see discussion by Stuart Schram, *The Political Thought of Mao Tse-tung* [New York: Praeger Publishers, 1969], p. 257), but interpretations of his thought throughout the revolution saw issues of sex as bourgeois deviation (see Croll, pp. 19, 22, 32). The Leninist view which the latter documents seem to reflect is expressed in Clara Zetkin's account, "Lenin on the Woman Question," excerpted as an appendix in *The Woman Question: Selections from the Writings of Marx, Engels, Lenin, and Stalin* (New York: International Publishers, 1951), p. 89. Friedrich Engels implies a simultaneous or directly consequential transformation of the status of women with changes in relations of production; Friedrich Engels, *The Origin of the Family, Private Property, and the State,* ed. Eleanor Burke Leacock (New York: International Publishers, 1972) (hereafter cited as *Origin*). See Chapter 2.

12. See Robin Morgan, ed., *Sisterhood Is Global: The International Women's Movement Anthology* (Garden City, N.Y.: Doubleday/Anchor, 1984).

13. Sheila Rowbotham, *Hidden from History: Rediscovering Women in History from the Seventeenth Century to the Present* (New York: Random House, 1973); Mary Jo Buhle, "Women and the Socialist Party, 1901–1914," in *From Feminism to Liberation,* ed. Edith Hoshino Altbach (London: Schenkman, 1971); Robert Shaffer, "Women in the Communist Party, USA, 1930–1940," *Socialist Review* 45 (May–June 1979): 73–118. Contemporary attempts to create socialist-feminist groups and strategies are exemplified in position papers: Chicago Women's Liberation Union, "Socialist Feminism: A Strategy for the Women's Movement" (Mimeograph, Chicago, 1972); "The 'Principles of Unity' of the Berkeley-Oakland Women's Union," *Socialist Revolution* 4 (January–March 1974): 69–82; Lavender and Red Union, *The Political Perspective of the Lavender and Red Union* (Los Angeles: Fanshen Printing Collective, 1975). Rosalind Petchesky, "Dissolving the Hyphen: A Report on Marxist-Feminist Groups 1–5," in Eisenstein, *Capitalist Patriarchy,* pp. 373–389; and Red Apple Collective, "Women's Unions and Socialist Feminism," *Quest: A Feminist Quarterly* 4 (Summer 1977): 88–96, reflect on this process.

14. A wide variety of marxist approaches converge on this point. See Juliet Mitchell, *Woman's Estate* (New York: Random House, 1971), Sheila Rowbotham, *Women, Resistance, and Revolution: A History of Women and Revolution in the Modern World* (New York: Random House, 1972); Zillah Eisenstein, "Some Notes on the Relations of Capitalist Patriarchy," in Eisenstein, *Capitalist Patriarchy,* pp. 41–55; Eli Zaretsky, "Socialism and Feminism III: Socialist Politics and the Family," *Socialist Revolution* 4 (January–March 1974): 83–99; idem, "Capitalism, the Family, and Personal Life," ibid. 3 (January–April 1973): 69–126; idem, "Capitalism, the Family, and Personal Life, Part 2,"

ibid. (May–June 1973): 19–70; Virginia Held, "Marx, Sex, and the Transformation of Society," in *Women and Philosophy: Toward a Theory of Liberation,* ed. Carol C. Gould and Marx W. Wartofsky (New York: G. P. Putnam's Sons, 1976), pp. 168–184; Mihailo Marković, "Women's Liberation and Human Emancipation," ibid., pp. 145–167; Hal Draper, "Marx and Engels on Women's Liberation," in *Female Liberation,* ed. Roberta Salper (New York: Alfred A. Knopf, 1972), pp. 83–107.

15. Nancy Hartsock, "Feminist Theory and the Development of Revolutionary Strategy," in Eisenstein, *Capitalist Patriarchy,* p. 37.

16. This tendency, with important variations, is manifest in writings otherwise as diverse as Charnie Guettel, *Marxism and Feminism* (Toronto: Canadian Women's Education Press, 1974); Mary Alice Waters, "Are Feminism and Socialism Related?" in *Feminism and Socialism,* ed. Linda Jenness (New York: Pathfinder Press, 1972), pp. 18–26; Weather Underground, *Prairie Fire* (Underground, U.S.A.: Red Dragon Collective, 1975); Marjorie King, "Cuba's Attack on Women's Second Shift, 1974–1976," *Latin American Perspectives* 4 (Winter–Spring 1977): 106–119; Al Syzmanski, "The Socialization of Women's Oppression: A Marxist Theory of the Changing Position of Women in Advanced Capitalist Society," *Insurgent Sociologist* 6 (Winter 1976): 31–58; "The Political Economy of Women," *Review of Radical Political Economics* 4 (July 1972). See also Selma James, *Women, the Unions and Work, or What Is Not to Be Done* (Bristol: Falling Wall Press, 1976). This is true for "wages for housework" theory in that it sees women as exploited because they do work—housework.

17. *Origin;* Leon Trotsky, *Women and the Family,* trans. Max Eastman et al. (New York: Pathfinder Press, 1970); Evelyn Reed, *Woman's Evolution: From Matriarchal Clan to Patriarchal Family* (New York: Pathfinder Press, 1975); Lise Vogel, "The Earthly Family," *Radical America* 7 (July–October 1973): 9–50; Kollontai Collective, "The Politics of the Family: A Marxist View" (Paper presented at the Socialist Feminist Conference at Yellow Springs, Ohio, July 4–6, 1975); Linda Limpus, *Liberation of Women: Sexual Repression and the Family* (Boston: New England Free Press, n.d.); Marlene Dixon, "On the Super-Exploitation of Women," *Synthesis* 1, no. 4 (Spring 1977): 1–11; David P. Levine and Lynn S. Levine, "Problems in the Marxist Theory of the Family" (Photocopy, Department of Economics, Yale University, July 1978).

18. Juliet Mitchell, *Psychoanalysis and Feminism: Freud, Reich, Laing, and Women* (New York: Pantheon Books, 1974); Eli Zaretsky, "Male Supremacy and the Unconscious," *Socialist Revolution* 4 (January 1975): 7–56; Nancy Chodorow, *The Reproduction of Mothering: Psychoanalysis and the Sociology of Gender* (Berkeley: University of California Press, 1978). See also Herbert Marcuse, "Socialist Feminism: The Hard Core of the Dream," *Edcentric: A Journal of Educational Change,* November 1974, pp. 7–44.

19. Examples include: Nancy Hartsock, *Money, Sex, and Power* (Boston: Northeastern University Press, 1983); Political Economy of Women Group, "Women, the State, and Reproduction since the 1930s," in *On the Political Economy of*

*Women*, CSE Pamphlet no. 2 (London: Conference of Socialist Economists, 1977).

20. Henri Lefebvre, *Everyday Life in the Modern World* (Harmondsworth: Penguin Books, 1971); Bruce Brown, *Marx, Freud, and the Critique of Everyday Life: Toward a Permanent Cultural Revolution* (New York: Monthly Review Press, 1973).

21. Herbert Marcuse, *Eros and Civilization: A Philosophical Inquiry into Freud* (New York: Random House, 1955); Wilhelm Reich, *Sex-Pol: Essays, 1929–1934* (New York: Random House, 1972); Reimut Reiche, *Sexuality and Class Struggle* (London: New Left Books, 1970); Bertell Ollman, *Social and Sexual Revolution: Essays on Marx and Reich* (Boston: South End Press, 1979); Red Collective, *The Politics of Sexuality in Capitalism* (London: Red Collective, 1973).

22. Sheila Rowbotham, *Women's Liberation and the New Politics*, Spokesman Pamphlet no. 17 (Bristol: Falling Wall Press, 1971); Gayle Rubin, "'The Traffic in Women: Notes on the 'Political Economy' of Sex," in *Toward an Anthropology of Women*, ed. Rayna R. Reiter (New York: Monthly Review Press, 1975), pp. 157–210; Annette Kuhn and AnnMarie Wolpe, "Feminism and Materialism," in *Feminism and Materialism: Women and Modes of Production*, ed. Annette Kuhn and AnnMarie Wolpe (London: Routledge & Kegan Paul, 1978); Ann Foreman, *Femininity as Alienation: Women and the Family in Marxism and Psychoanalysis* (London: Pluto Press, 1977); Meredith Tax and Jonathan Schwartz, "The Wageless Slave and the Proletarian" (Mimeograph, 1972); Heidi I. Hartmann, "Capitalism, Patriarchy, and Job Segregation by Sex," *Signs: Journal of Women in Culture and Society* 1 (Spring 1976): 137–169, and "The Unhappy Marriage of Marxism and Feminism: Towards a More Progressive Union," *Capital and Class* 8 (Summer 1979): 1–33; Iris Young, "Beyond the Unhappy Marriage: A Critique of the Dual Systems Theory," in *Women and Revolution: A Discussion of the Unhappy Marriage and Marxism and Feminism*, ed. Lydia Sargent (Boston: South End Press, 1981), pp. 43–70; Linda Gordon, *Woman's Body, Woman's Right: A Social History of Birth Control in America* (New York: Grossman Publishers, 1976), pp. 403–418; idem, "The Struggle for Reproductive Freedom: Three Stages of Feminism," in Eisenstein, *Capitalist Patriarchy*, pp. 107–132; Charlotte Bunch and Nancy Myron, eds., *Class and Feminism* (Baltimore: Diana Press, 1974).

## 2. A Feminist Critique of Marx and Engels

1. This chapter does not address the ways in which Marx's theories of social life are, are not, or can be made applicable to women's experience or useful for women's liberation. It addresses what Marx and Engels explicitly said about women, women's status, and women's condition. This book treats the work of Marx as a whole, rather than dividing him into "old" and "young," but with the understanding that his work, like that of most people, did develop and change over time.

2. Karl Marx, *The German Ideology* (New York: International Publishers, 1972), p. 51. August Bebel, in his influential volume *Women under Socialism,* included sexuality in nature: "The satisfaction of the sexual instinct is as much a private concern as the satisfaction of any other natural instinct"; Lise Vogel, "The Earthly Family," *Radical America* 7 (July–October 1973): 4–5.

3. Karl Marx, *Capital,* 3 vols. (New York: International Publishers, 1967), 1:337 (hereafter cited as *Capital*).

4. *Capital,* 1:351, 352.

5. *Capital,* 1:42; see also 1:177–178.

6. *Capital,* 1:43.

7. Marx, *German Ideology,* p. 50.

8. *Capital,* 1:395, 397, 395.

9. *Capital,* 1:395, 398.

10. No distinction exists between these views of Marx and those of contemporary "pro-family" conservatives.

11. *Capital,* 1:399, 393–394.

12. Marx here appears to approve female protective laws, which have often seemed helpful but also detrimental in protecting women out of jobs they needed and wanted while failing to protect all workers from conditions that harmed them all. See also discussion in Chapter 8.

13. Karl Marx, *On the Jewish Question,* in *Karl Marx: Selected Writings,* ed. David McLellan (Oxford: Oxford University Press, 1977), p. 60.

14. Karl Marx, *Economic and Philosophic Manuscripts of 1844,* in ibid., p. 87.

15. Karl Marx and Friedrich Engels, *The Communist Manifesto,* in *Selected Works,* ed. V. Adoratsky, vol. 1 (New York: International Publishers, 1936), 224–225.

16. *Capital,* 1:402, 403.

17. In his discussion drawn from a parliamentary report on the employment of women as colliers in mines, Marx makes these points through quotations from interviews in which male miners find mining "degrading to the sex," injurious to women's ability to care for children, to their dress ("rather a man's dress . . . it drowns all sense of decency"), and to their own and their husbands' morality. Marx's only comment in his own voice is that the apparent concern of the questioners for these women is a cloak for their financial self-interest; *Capital,* 1:499–500. Actually, what the male miners say supports women's exclusion from this work—a viewpoint inconsistent with the motive of material interest Marx attributes to them. For example, they are asked, "Your feeling upon the whole subject is that the better class of colliers who desire to raise themselves and humanize themselves, instead of deriving help from the women, are pulled down by them?" "Yes . . ."; *Capital,* 1:489–490. One can only conclude that Marx is able to understand the concern of the bourgeois questioner as inimical to his own, so attributes it to material interest even when it conflicts with material interest. In fact, the exclusion of women from these jobs, whatever else it may reflect of humanitarianism, is in the material interest of male workers, converging with a denial of material self-interest by the bourgeois employer through an affirmation of his sexism.

18. *Capital,* 1:489–490, 377. This is attributed to the fact that under capitalism "the labourer exists for the process of production, and not the process of production for the labourer" (p. 377).

19. Karl Marx, "Chapitre de marriage," quoted in Juliet Mitchell, "Women: The Longest Revolution," in *From Feminism to Liberation,* ed. Edith Hoshino Altbach (London: Schenkman, 1971), p. 107 n. 9.

20. Marx, *The German Ideology* (Moscow: Progress Publishers, 1976), p. 194. See also Marx in *Marx: Selected Writings,* ed. McLellan: "The bourgeoisie has torn away from the family its sentimental veil, and has reduced the family relation to a mere money relation" (p. 224); and "On what foundation is the present family, the bourgeois family, based? On capital, on private gain. In its completely developed form this family exists only among the bourgeoisie. But this state of things finds its complement in the practical absence of the family among the proletarians, and in public prostitution" (p. 234).

21. *Origin.*

22. A diverse discussion that both illustrates and criticizes this impact is provided by Janet Sayers, Mary Evens, and Nanncke Redclift, eds., *Engels Revisited: New Feminist Essays* (London: Tavistock, 1987). The essay by Moira Maconachie, "Engels, Sexual Divisions, and the Family," pp. 98–112, criticizes Engels' naturalism.

23. Juliet Mitchell, *Woman's Estate* (New York: Random House, 1971); Gayle Rubin, "The Traffic in Women: Notes on the 'Political Economy' of Sex," in *Toward an Anthropology of Women,* ed. Rayna R. Reiter (New York: Monthly Review Press, 1975), p. 164.

24. Branka Magas, "Sex Politics: Class Politics," *New Left Review* 80 (March–April 1971): 69.

25. Karen Sachs, "Engels Revisited: Women, the Organization of Production, and Private Property," in *Woman, Culture, and Society,* ed. Michelle Z. Rosaldo and Louise Lamphere (Stanford: Stanford University Press, 1974), uses this approach.

26. Lenin, for example, says: "Notwithstanding all the liberating laws that have been passed, woman continues to be a domestic slave, because petty housework crushes, strangles, stultifies and degrades her, chains her to the kitchen and to the nursery, and wastes her labor on barbarously unproductive, petty, nerve-racking stultifying and crushing drudgery. The real emancipation of women, real communism, will begin only when a mass struggle (led by the proletariat which is in power) is started against this petty domestic economy, or rather when it is transformed on a mass scale into large-scale socialist economy"; V. I. Lenin, "Woman and Society," in *The Woman Question: Selections from the Writings of Marx, Engels, Lenin, and Stalin* (New York: International Publishers, 1951), p. 56.

27. Eli Zaretsky, "Socialism and Feminism III: Socialist Politics and the Family," *Socialist Revolution* 4 (January–March 1974): 85, 91, 96.

28. Examples of the unannotated use of a very common misinterpretation of Engels include Richard Edwards, Michael Reich, and Thomas Weiskopf, *The Capitalist*

*System: A Radical Analysis of American Society* (Englewood Cliffs, N.J.: Prentice-Hall, 1972), p. 325: "Male supremacy was probably the first form of oppression of one group in society by another; men were dominant over women in most precapitalist societies." The general theme of primitive sexual egalitarianism disrupted by the rise of private property is accepted by Evelyn Reed, *Woman's Evolution: From Matriarchal Clan to Patriarchal Family* (New York: Pathfinder Press, 1975); Eleanor Leacock, Introduction to *Origin;* and Heidi I. Hartmann, "Capitalism, Patriarchy, and Job Segregation by Sex," *Signs: Journal of Women in Culture and Society* 1 (Spring 1976): 137. It is interesting that the influence of Engels' theoretical approach seems quite independent of the data by Morgan on which it was purportedly based, data which have been rather widely discredited.

29. *Origin,* p. 129.
30. *Origin,* p. 120.
31. *Origin,* p. 129.
32. Wilhelm Reich, *Sex-Pol: Essays, 1929–1934* (New York: Random House, 1972), p. 182.
33. Kate Millett, *Sexual Politics* (Garden City, N.Y.: Doubleday, 1970), p. 120.
34. Susan Williams, *Lesbianism: A Socialist Feminist Perspective,* Radical Women Position Paper (Mimeograph, Seattle, April 1973), p. 3.
35. *Origin,* pp. 137, 134.
36. If this relation is understood as causal and not correlational, it could just as well mean that sex contradictions cause class contradictions. So Shulamith Firestone can refer to Engels when she argues that "beneath economics, reality is psychosexual," and proposes an analysis of the "psychosexual roots of class"; *The Dialectic of Sex: The Case for Feminist Revolution* (New York: Bantam Books, 1970), pp. 5, 11. Charlotte Bunch elaborates this argument as follows: "Class distinctions are an outgrowth of male domination as such, and not only divide women along economic lines but also serve to destroy vestiges of women's previous matriarchal strength"; Charlotte Bunch and Nancy Myron, eds., *Class and Feminism* (Baltimore: Diana Press, 1974), p. 8.
37. In a characteristic formulation, Engels writes that historical materialism is "that view of the course of history which seeks the ultimate cause and the great moving power of all important historical events in the economic development of society, in the changes in the modes of production and exchange, in the consequent division of society into distinct classes, and in the struggles of these classes against one another"; Friedrich Engels, *Socialism: Utopian and Scientific,* trans. E. Aveling (New York: International Publishers, 1935), p. 16.
38. *Origin,* p. 117.
39. The burden of maternity cannot be the answer, because a woman can as readily be kept pregnant by one man as by many.
40. *Origin,* pp. 118–119.
41. *Origin,* p. 118.
42. Karl Marx, *Wage-Labor and Capital* (New York: International Publishers, 1971), p. 28.

43. *Origin,* p. 113.
44. *Origin,* p. 119.
45. *Origin,* pp. 113–114.
46. *Origin,* pp. 172, 218, 222, 224–225.
47. *Origin,* p. 233.
48. This difference in treating the division of labor could be accounted for under capitalism by the tacit assumption that women's housework is not properly "production" because its dominant form is not commodities. But at the time of pairing marriage, housework was properly social production, yet the division of labor between women and men was somehow both nonexploitative and justifiable.
49. For pairing marriage places "by the side of the natural mother of the child . . . its natural and attested father with a better warrant of paternity, probably, than that of many a 'father' today"; *Origin,* p. 129.
50. *Origin,* pp. 128, 144.
51. Notes by Marx, quoted in *Origin,* p. 128.
52. *Origin,* p. 119.
53. Paraphrase of *Origin,* p. 138.
54. This ceases to be a problem with the introduction and generalization of money, as sheer exchange value can then be accumulated and commanded.
55. Without knowing the connection between the material relations and their imputed social meanings, one could equally well argue, "didn't the lust for property begin with man's lust to own 'his' children by owning their mother?" Barbara Deming, in Barbara Deming and Arthur Kinoy, *Women and Revolution: A Dialogue* (New York: National Interim Committee for a Mass Party of the People, April 1975) p. 32.
56. *Origin,* pp. 119–120.
57. Engels is clear, however, that he does not know "how and when this revolution took place"; *Origin,* p. 120.
58. *Origin,* p. 135. Since it costs money to enforce laws, legal requirements have little effect on workers' interpersonal relations; "here quite other personal and social conditions decide"; ibid.
59. *Origin,* p. 140. "Only now [in Roman times] were the conditions realized in which through monogamy—within it, parallel to it, or in opposition to it—the greatest moral advance we owe to it could have been achieved: modern individual sex love, which had hitherto been unknown to the entire world"; ibid., p. 140.
60. *Origin,* p. 135.
61. This position contrasts with the views of both Lenin and Trotsky, who thought that as the under-class, the proletariat would often contain society's most oppressive relations. See, e.g., Leon Trotsky, *Problems of Everyday Life and Other Writings on Culture and Science,* ed. G. R. Fidler et al. (New York: Pathfinder Press, 1973), pp. 78–87.
62. *Origin,* pp. 144–145. When private wealth disappears, will monogamy disappear? ". . . far from disappearing, it will, on the contrary, begin to be realized completely"; ibid., p. 139.

63. *Origin,* p. 139.

64. *Origin,* p. 139.

65. Some theorists on the left have tried to revive this failed account by arguing that both proletarian women and men are oppressed by the ruling class through imposed sex roles. Male workers' brutality toward their wives compensates for their powerlessness as workers. Why women are not brutal to men to compensate for their powerlessness as workers is never explained. It also follows that ruling-class men, who also learn sex roles, must both be oppressed by them and receive the benefits of them. This seems, in a feminist view, to be an attempt to define favored male groups out of the problem, evading the more straightforward and elegant feminist explanation: male power over women is a distinctive form of power that interrelates with the class structure but is neither derivative from nor a side effect of it. In this view, men oppress women to the extent that they can because it is in their interest and to their advantage to do so.

66. *Origin,* p. 137.

67. "With the patriarchal family and still more with the single monogamous family, a change came. Household management lost its public character. It no longer concerned society. It became a private service; the wife became the head servant, excluded from all participation in social production. Not until the coming of modern large-scale industry was the road to social production opened to her again—and then only to the proletarian wife"; *Origin,* p. 137.

68. This is what Lukács means by his criticism of "contemplative materialism": "Dialectics, [Engels] argues, is a continuous process of transition from one definition into the other. In consequence, a one-sided and rigid causality must be replaced by interaction. But he does not even mention the most vital inter-action, namely the dialectical relation between subject and object in the historical process, let alone give it the prominence it deserves. Yet without this factor dialectics ceases to be revolutionary, despite attempts (illusory in the last analysis) to retain 'fluid' concepts. For it implies a failure to recognize that in all meta-physics the object remains untouched and unaltered so that thought remains contemplative and fails to become practical; while for the dialectical method the central problem is to change reality. If this central function of the theory is disregarded, the virtues of forming 'fluid' concepts become altogether problem-atic: a purely 'scientific' matter. The theory might then be accepted or rejected in accordance with the prevailing state of science without any modification at all to one's basic attitudes, to the question of whether or not reality can be changed." Georg Lukács, *History and Class Consciousness: Studies in Marxist Dialectics,* trans. Rodney Livingstone (Cambridge, Mass: MIT Press, 1971), pp. 3–4.

### 3. A Marxist Critique of Feminism

1. Illuminating work has been done on the two tendencies by Alison Jaggar, *Feminist Politics and Human Nature* (Totowa, N.J.: Rowman and Allanheld,

1983, and by Zillah Eisenstein, *The Radical Future of Liberal Feminism* (New York: Longman, 1981), without suggesting that feminism divides liberal from radical along a formally marxist line.

2. Joan Cassell, *A Group Called Women: Sisterhood and Symbolism in the Feminist Movement* (New York: David McKay, 1977).

3. Toni A. H. McNaron, "Woman as Humanist?" (Paper presented to the Midwest Regional Association of Humanistic Psychologists, Minneapolis, June 4, 1977), p. 7.

4. John Stuart Mill, *Autobiography of John Stuart Mill,* ed. John Jacob Coss (New York: Columbia University Press, 1924), p. 162.

5. John Stuart Mill, *On Liberty* (Northbrook, Ill.: AHM Publishing, 1947), pp. 1, 5.

6. See, e.g., Kate Millett, *Sexual Politics* (Garden City, N.Y.: Doubleday, 1970): "Patriarchy's chief institution is the family" (p. 33).

7. John Stuart Mill, *The Subjection of Women,* in *Essays on Sex Equality,* ed. Alice S. Rossi (Chicago: University of Chicago Press, 1970), pp. 209, 218 (hereafter cited as *Subjection*).

8. *Subjection,* pp. 125, 130.

9. *Subjection,* p. 130.

10. *Subjection,* pp. 126, 142, 128, 181.

11. *Subjection,* pp. 217, 175, 242.

12. *Subjection,* pp. 195, 187–189.

13. *Subjection,* pp. 191, 192.

14. *Subjection,* p. 201.

15. *Subjection,* pp. 204, 212.

16. *Subjection,* p. 144; see also p. 185.

17. *Subjection,* p. 136.

18. *Subjection,* pp. 146, 161.

19. *Subjection,* pp. 209–210.

20. *Subjection,* p. 139.

21. *Subjection,* p. 141.

22. *Subjection,* pp. 152, 207, 153, 133.

23. Kent Harvey devised this analysis. Helpful feminist critiques of liberalism are anthologized in C. Pateman and E. Gross, eds., *Feminist Challenges: Social and Political Theory* (Boston: Northeastern University Press, 1986), pp. 63–124.

24. Anne Fausto-Sterling criticizes evidence and logic on biological determinants of gender in *Myths of Gender: Biological Theories about Women and Men* (New York: Basic Books, 1985). The target of her inquiry is the sociobiologists, but her demolition of their naturalism applies equally well to liberalism.

25. *Subjection* (subjection of women is "wrong in itself"), p. 125.

26. For example, Irwin Silber noted that "the ideas of contemporary feminism, although at this juncture emanating predominantly from the petty bourgeois intelligensia, have something useful to offer the working class movement . . . But it will take something stronger and more solidly based in reality than the aspirations of uppermiddle class women to offer an alternative that working

class women will find meaningful"; "Would Ms. America Change the Nature of the Pageant?" *Guardian,* September 19, 1973.

27. Although many feminist organizations lack an anticapitalist or class consciousness, I have not seen any empirical documentation supporting the assertion that feminists are predominantly from, or currently of, the middle class. My own experience in the women's movement is to the contrary.

28. August Bebel, *Women under Socialism,* trans. Daniel DeLeon (New York: New York Labor News Press, 1904), p. 121.

29. Karl Marx, *Early Writings,* ed. and trans. T. B. Bottomore (New York: McGraw-Hill, 1964), pp. 58–59.

30. Millett, *Sexual Politics,* p. 24.

31. Roxanne Dunbar, *Female Liberation as the Basis for Social Revolution* (Boston: New England Free Press, 1968).

32. Barbara Ehrenreich and Dierdre English, *Complaints and Disorders: The Sexual Politics of Sickness,* Glass Mountain Pamphlet no. 2 (New York: Feminist Press, 1973), p. 11.

33. Millett, *Sexual Politics,* p. 38.

34. Evelyn Reed, *Problems of Women's Liberation* (New York: Pathfinder Press, 1972), p. 74.

35. Sparticist League, *Women & Revolution: Journal of the Women's Commission of the Sparticist League* 7 (Autumn 1974): 15. See also Reed, *Problems,* p. 72, for a view by the Socialist Workers' Party which coincides with this approach.

36. The rest of this book discusses and expands on the radical feminist argument, which is not open to these criticisms.

37. Charnie Guettel, *Marxism and Feminism* (Toronto: Hunter Rose Company, 1974), p. 26.

38. Wally Seccombe, *The Housewife and Her Labour under Capitalism,* Red Pamphlet no. 8 (London: IMG Publications, 1975), p. 23; first published in *New Left Review* 83 (January–February 1974).

39. Branka Magas, "Sex Politics: Class Politics," *New Left Review* 80 (March–April 1971): 69.

40. Bebel, *Women under Socialism,* p. 210, exemplifies this position.

41. Karl Marx, *The Poverty of Philosophy* (New York: International Publishers, 1963), p. 115.

42. Marx, letter to P. V. Annenkov, in ibid., p. 181, is an example. Early on, Marx was equally critical of the reverse error, pure reflective materialism, criticizing pure fatalism as much as pure intention. He rejected the notion that people are simple products of their material conditions—the passive theory of mind—in his attack on the eighteenth-century materialism of Feuerbach: "The materialist doctrine concerning the changing of circumstances and upbringing forgets that circumstances are changed by men and that it is essential to educate the educator himself"; "Thesis III on Feuerbach," in *Karl Marx: Selected Writings,* ed. David McLellan (Oxford: Oxford University Press, 1977), p. 156.

43. Mary Daly, *Gyn/Ecology: The Metaethics of Radical Feminism* (Boston: Beacon Press, 1978), pp. 113–133. This is still an insightful and important work. The

formal idealism is almost eliminated in subsequent works by Daly, especially *Pure Lust: Elemental Feminist Philosophy* (Boston: Beacon Press, 1984), which treats women's consciousness in a complex, concrete, and constitutive way.

44. Susan Griffin, *Pornography and Silence: Culture's Revenge against Nature* (New York: Harper & Row, 1981), pp. 2–4, 251–265.

45. Carol Gilligan, *In a Different Voice* (Cambridge, Mass.: Harvard University Press, 1982).

46. For a subtle empirical treatment of some of these issues, see M. F. Belenky, B. M. Clinchy, N. R. Goldberger, and J. M. Tarule, *Women's Ways of Knowing: The Development of Self, Voice, and Mind* (New York: Basic Books, 1986). Gilligan is applied but also criticized: "In actuality, these women do not speak in a different voice. They have no voice at all. Conventional feminine goodness means being voiceless as well as selfless" (p. 167).

47. San Francisco Redstockings, "Our Politics Begin with Our Feelings," in *Masculine/Feminine: Readings in Sexual Mythology and the Liberation of Women,* ed. Betty Roszak and Theodore Roszak (New York: Harper & Row, 1969), pp. 285–290.

48. Marx, *Early Writings,* p. 158.

49. *Origin,* p. 221.

50. Seccombe, *The Housewife and Her Labour,* p. 22.

51. Ibid., pp. 27, 23 n. 33.

52. Ibid., p. 22.

53. Jill Johnston, "The Myth of Bonnies without Clydes: Lesbian Feminism and the Male Left," *Village Voice,* April 28, 1975, p. 14.

54. Marx, *Poverty of Philosophy,* p. 121.

55. Ibid., pp. 120–121.

56. Simone de Beauvoir, *The Second Sex,* ed. and trans. H. M. Parshley (New York: Alfred A. Knopf, 1970), p. 59.

57. Ibid.

58. Shulamith Firestone, *The Dialectic of Sex: The Case for Feminist Revolution* (New York: Bantam Books, 1970), pp. 5, 73.

59. Ibid., p. 238.

60. Susan Brownmiller, *Against Our Will: Men, Women, and Rape* (New York: Simon and Schuster, 1975), pp. 4, 6. The book, however, treated rape throughout as anything but a biological inevitability.

61. An astonishingly literal expression of the biological approach is provided by the Feminist Women's Health Center (FWHC). FWHC defines "control of our bodies" not only against male dominated professionals and institutions but also in part against women's bodies themselves. For example, the purpose of the technique of menstrual extraction is not birth control but "active and direct control of when and how we shall have our periods." This approach identifies the problem of lack of control as existing on the natural level, in women's menstrual periods themselves, rather than in the meaning or place society has given them. Women, tyrannized by their bodies, must wrest control from their bodies, rather than question why body needs social regulation. Anatomical

sisterhood suggests that when women have control over their bodies in this sense, they will have control over their lives. Carol Downer, *What Makes the Feminist Women's Health Center Feminist?* (n.p., 1974).

62. As Marx put it, the same men who establish their social relations through their material productivity also produce principles, ideas, and categories in conformity with their social relations. "These ideas, these categories, are as little eternal as the relations they express. They are *historical and transitory products*"; *Poverty of Philosophy,* pp. 109–110.

63. Jill Johnston, *Lesbian Nation: The Feminist Solution* (New York: Simon and Schuster, 1973), pp. 165–166.

64. Ibid., p. 152.

65. Juliet Mitchell, *Psychoanalysis and Feminism: Freud, Reich, Laing, and Women* (New York: Pantheon Books, 1974).

66. Beauvoir, *The Second Sex,* p. 57.

67. Nancy Chodorow, *The Reproduction of Mothering: Psychoanalysis and the Sociology of Gender* (Berkeley: University of California Press, 1978).

68. Dorothy Dinnerstein, *The Mermaid and the Minotaur: Sexual Arrangements and Human Malaise* (New York: Harper & Row, 1977). An apparent reversal, but actually an affirmation, of the biological definition of women was articulated by Jane Alpert. Alpert argued that women's biology is the ground for their liberation, not the source of their oppression. Calling her theory "mother right" (after Engels), Alpert argued that all women, whether or not they were actually mothers, possess by virtue of their biological potential for motherhood certain female personality characteristics, such as peacefulness, supportiveness, interpersonal sensitivity, emotional responsiveness, and nonaggression, which are undervalued and exploited by men in society but live on in women. Although, in this view, behavioral differences between the sexes arise from inherent biological differences, woman is not, as with Beauvoir and Firestone, tyrannized by her body, but by male society's negation and extraction of her natural attributes. For Alpert, biology as a category derives its meaning from a denial of any social basis to its meaning. Jane Alpert, unpublished interview with *off our backs* staff (Mimeograph, Washington, D.C., 1975).

69. Of course, when set in social context, biological critique need not be asocial: "Women are a colonized people, with our history, values, and cross-cultural culture having been taken from us—a gynocidal attempt manifest most blatantly in the patriarchy's seizure of our most basic and precious 'land,' our own bodies . . . Our ignorance about our own primary terrain, our bodies, is in the self-interest of patriarchy. We must begin, as women, to reclaim our land, and the most concrete place to begin is with our own flesh"; Robin Morgan in *Circle One: A Woman's Beginning Guide to Self Health and Sexuality,* ed. Elizabeth Campbell and Vicki Ziegler, 2d ed. (March 1975). Marxists like Guettel, however, criticize self-help: "The effort is a reaction to our exclusion, but its result is only to compound our misery. For example, do-it-yourself gynecology falls into the apolitical, indeed harmful self-help category. The alternate strategy would be attacking the chauvinism of current gynecologists,

working politically for improvement of hospital facilities, etc."; *Marxism and Feminism,* p. 45.

### 4. Attempts at Synthesis

1. The history of this concept in marxist theory is traced by Martin Jay, *Marxism and Totality: The Adventures of a Concept from Lukács to Habermas* (Berkeley: University of California Press, 1984). See also Georg Lukács, *History and Class Consciousness: Studies in Marxist Dialectics,* trans. Rodney Livingstone (Cambridge, Mass.: MIT Press, 1971), pp. 27–29.

2. Race and nation are analogous to sex in the place they occupy for, and the challenge they pose to, marxist theory, although they have historically received more attention.

3. In "The Tasks of the Proletariat in Our Revolution," in *The Collected Works of Lenin,* vol. 24 (New York: Pathfinder Press, 1900), 70, Lenin says: "Unless women are brought to take an independent part not only in political life generally, but also in daily and universal public service, it is no use talking about full and stable democracy, let alone socialism." See also V. I. Lenin, *Women and Society* (New York: International Publishers, 1938), and selections from it in *The Woman Question: Selections from the Writings of Marx, Engels, Lenin, and Stalin* (New York: International Publishers, 1951), particularly the appendix by Clara Zetkin, "Lenin on the Woman Question," in which she quotes Lenin in conversation: "The thesis must clearly point out that real freedom for women is possible only through communism. The inseparable connection between the social and human position of the woman, and private property in the means of production, must be strongly brought out. That will draw a clear and ineradicable line of distinction between our policy and feminism. And it will also supply the basis for regarding the woman question as a part of the social question, of the workers' problem, and so bind it firmly to the proletarian class struggle and the revolution" (p. 89).

4. See, e.g., Rosa Luxemburg, "Women's Suffrage and Class Struggle," in *Selected Political Writings,* ed. Dick Howard (New York: Monthly Review Press, 1971). Leon Trotsky also falls into this category, although his observations of women's status are more perceptive than either Lenin's or Luxemburg's. See his *Problems of Life* (London, 1953), e.g., p. 21. His most programmatic statement on the issue was made in a 1925 address, "The Protection of Motherhood and the Struggle for Culture," produced as a pamphlet, *Women and the Family by Leon Trotsky,* ed. Caroline Lund (New York: Pathfinder Press, 1970), pp. 31–45. See also his "To Build Socialism Means to Emancipate Women and Protect Mothers," in ibid., p. 45.

5. Ideological lines can cut very fine on the left. They also change often. The following examples do, however, illustrate some contemporary Marxist approaches of the "equation and collapse" tendency. The Sparticist League, a

Leninist group, states that "feminism is fundamentally counterposed to Marxism and therefore to the liberation of women"; *Women & Revolution: Journal of the Women's Commission of the Sparticist League* 7 (Autumn 1974): 15. The Revolutionary Union (later the Revolutionary Communist Party, formerly the Revolutionary Youth Movement [RYM] faction of Students for a Democratic Society [SDS]) glorifies the family unit—"for many working people, the family provides one of life's few bright spots" (*Revolution,* March 1974)—in order to collapse a feminist critique into an overriding socialist ideology. The Communist Labor Party, in many respects very different from the foregoing two groups, also tends to assume that women's status can be equated with class status, and when it diverges, it creates issues that are "too personal for us to comment on"; Nelson Perty, "Proletarian Morality," *Proletariat,* Spring 1974.

6. See *Capital,* 1:395, 398, 402, 498–499; but cf. pp. 489–499.

7. Louise W. Kneeland, "Feminism and Socialism," *New Review* 2 (August 1914): 442. Kneeland appears to have been the first to state this view in this form; it has since been ubiquitously repeated, truncated, rephrased and paraphrased.

8. Sheila Rowbotham, *Woman's Consciousness, Man's World* (Harmondsworth: Penguin, 1973), esp. pp. xiv, xvi, 57, 124.

9. *Origin;* August Bebel, *Woman under Socialism,* trans. Daniel DeLeon (New York: New York Labor News Press, 1904). This view finds contemporary expression in the work of Evelyn Reed: *Woman's Evolution: From Matriarchal Clan to Patriarchal Family* (New York: Pathfinder Press, 1975); *Problems of Women's Liberation* (New York: Pathfinder Press, 1972); "Women: Caste, Class or Oppressed Sex?" *International Socialist Review,* September 1970; and "Feminism and the 'Female Eunuch,' " *International Socialist Review,* July–August 1971.

10. Linda Jenness, *Women and the Cuban Revolution* (New York: Pathfinder Press, 1970); Elizabeth Stone, ed., *Women and the Cuban Revolution: Speeches and Documents* (New York: Pathfinder Press, 1981). See, e.g., Stephanie Urdang, *A Revolution within a Revolution: Women in Guinea Bissau* (Boston: New England Free Press, n.d.).

11. The Chinese situation is complex and changing. See Chapter 1, notes 7 and 11. The usual official view stresses the progress women have made and the barriers still to be overcome, stressing that the progress of socialism is the foundation of women's progress as women. See, e.g., Elizabeth Croll, ed., *The Women's Movement in China: A Selection of Readings, 1947–1973,* Modern China Series, no. 6 (London: Anglo-Chinese Educational Institute, 1974); Ruth Sidel, *Women and Child Care in China* (Baltimore: Penguin, 1973); Maud Russell, "Chinese Women: Liberated," *Far East Reporter,* n.d.; Editorial, "The Ongoing Revolution in Women's Liberation in the People's Republic of China," *Far East Reporter,* September 1977; Phyllis Andors, "Politics of Chinese Development: The Case of Women, 1960–1966," *Signs: Journal of Women in Culture and Society* 2 (Autumn 1976): 89–119.

12. Nancy Hartsock, "Feminist Theory and the Development of Revolutionary Strategy," in *Capitalist Patriarchy and the Case for Socialist Feminism,* ed. Zillah Eisenstein (New York: Monthly Review Press, 1979), p. 57.

13. Recent reissues of Alexandra Kollontai's work include *Sexual Relations and the Class Struggle: Love and the New Morality*, trans. Alix Holt (Bristol: Falling Wall Press, 1972); *Women Workers Struggle for their Rights*, trans. Celia Britton (Bristol: Falling Wall Press, 1973); and *Communism and the Family* (London: Pluto Press, April 1973). Regarding contemporary left groups, see Kathy McAfee and Myrna Wood, "Bread and Roses," in *From Feminism to Liberation*, ed. Edith Hoshino Altbach (London: Schenkman, 1971), pp. 21–38.

14. Some of the best work is by Eli Zaretsky: "Capitalism, the Family, and Personal Life," *Socialist Revolution* 3 (January–April 1973): 69–126; "Capitalism, the Family, and Personal Life: Part 2," ibid. (May–June 1973): 19–70; and "Socialism and Feminism III: Socialist Politics and the Family," ibid. 4 (January–March 1974): 83–99.

15. Shulamith Firestone, *The Dialectic of Sex: The Case for Feminist Revolution* (New York: Bantam Books, 1970).

16. Ginny Berson in *Class and Feminism*, ed. Charlotte Bunch and Nancy Myron (Baltimore: Diana Press, 1974), pp. 61–62.

17. Charlotte Perkins Gilman, *Women and Economics: A Study in the Economic Relation between Men and Women as a Factor in Social Revolution* (New York: Harper & Row, 1966), pp. 4–5, 220.

18. Margaret Benston, "The Political Economy of Women's Liberation," in Altbach, *From Feminism to Liberation*, pp. 199–210. Juliet Mitchell, "Women: The Longest Revolution," in ibid., pp. 93–124, takes a similar approach, extended and developed in her book *Woman's Estate* (New York: Random House, 1971).

19. Peggy Morton, "A Woman's Work Is Never Done," in Altbach, *From Feminism to Liberation*, pp. 211–228.

20. Mariarosa Dalla Costa and Selma James, *The Power of Women and the Subversion of the Community* (Bristol: Falling Wall Press, 1972). Sylvia Federici, "When Wages for Housework Becomes a Perspective," *Wages for Housework: Notebook #1* (Mimeograph, Philadelphia, 1975), pp. 12–18; idem, *Wages against Housework* (Bristol: Falling Wall Press, 1973). Nicole Cox and Sylvia Federici, *Counter-Planning from the Kitchen—Wages for Housework: A Perspective on Capital and the Left* (Bristol: Falling Wall Press, 1975).

21. Christine Delphy, *Close to Home: A Materialist Analysis of Women's Oppression* (Amherst: University of Massachusetts Press, 1984), esp. p. 174.

22. Lise Vogel, "The Earthly Family," *Radical America* 7 (July–October 1973): 28.

23. Zaretsky, "Socialism and Feminism III."

24. Carol Lopate, "Women and Pay for Housework," *Liberation* 18 (May–June 1974): 11.

25. Lotte Femminile, *A Programmatic Manifesto for the Struggle of Housewives in the Neighborhood* (Padua: Movimiento di Lotte Femminile, 1971).

26. See Zaretsky, "Socialism and Feminism III," p. 89.

27. Beth Ingber and the Cleveland Modern Times Group, "The Social Factory," *Falling Wall Review*, no. 5 (1976).

28. *Capital*, 1:39.

29. These propositions are synthesized from the following sources: Priscilla Allen

and Sylvina Schmidt, "In Defense of Feminism: A London Conference Report," in *Wages for Housework: Notebook #2* (Mimeograph, Philadelphia, 1975); Federici, "When Wages for Housework Becomes a Perspective"; Jackie Greenleaf, *Wages for Housework* (Mimeograph, Philadelphia, n.d.); Hodee Edwards, "Housework and Exploitation: A Marxist Analysis," *No More Fun and Games: A Journal of Female Liberation* 6 (July 1971): 92–100; Selma James, "Speech at the International House" and "When the Mute Speaks: The Work of Creating a Movement," in *Wages for Housework: Notebook #2;* Guliana Pompei, "Wages for Housework," in ibid.; Dalla Costa and James, *Power of Women;* Jean Gardiner, "Women's Domestic Labor," *New Left Review* 89 (January–February 1975); Wendy Edmond and Suzi Fleming, eds., *All Work and No Pay: Women, Housework and the Wages Due* (Bristol: Falling Wall Press, 1975); Wally Seccombe, *The Housewife and Her Labour under Capitalism,* Red Pamphlet 8 (London: IMG Publications, 1965); Jeanette Silviera, *The Housewife and Marxist Class Analysis* (Seattle, Wash.: printed privately, 1975); Cox and Federici, *Counter-Planning from the Kitchen;* Ira Gerstein, "Domestic Work and Capitalism," *Radical America* 7 (July–October 1973): 101–130; Joan Landes, "Wages for Housework: Subsidizing Capitalism?" *Quest: A Feminist Quarterly* 2 (Fall 1975); Ingber and Cleveland Modern Times Group, "The Social Factory."

30. Karl Marx, *Value, Price, and Profit,* in *Selected Works,* ed. V. Adoratsky, vol. 1 (New York: International Publishers, 1936), 305.

31. Marx, quoted and discussed in R. Meek, *Studies in the Labor Theory of Value* (London: Lawrence & Wishart, 1956), pp. 138–139.

32. Hegel is often referenced for this proposition. Hegel argued that the family is the repository of substantive ethical life, its basis being "love as the real, active and determining principle"; quoted in Schlomo Avineri, *The Social and Political Thought of Karl Marx* (Cambridge: Cambridge University Press, 1970), pp. 28–29.

33. Karl Marx and Friedrich Engels, *The Communist Manifesto,* in *Selected Works,* ed. Adoratsky, 1: 223–224. Schlomo Avineri criticizes Marx's "vicious, if not vulgar, attack on the bourgeois family in the Communist Manifesto"; *Social and Political Thought,* p. 90. Avineri continues: "The whole problem is to avoid romanticizing the family (or sex) and to reach at the same time a solution that will make the basic structural principle of sexual relations into a universal principle of social organization" (p. 91). From the feminist point of view, it already is.

34. S. Bowles, H. Gintis, P. Meyer, "The Long Shadow of Work: Education, the Family, and the Reproduction of the Social Division of Labor," *Insurgent Sociologist* 5 (Summer 1975): 18.

35. *Capital,* 3:830.

36. See generally Adam Smith, *The Wealth of Nations,* 2 vols. (New York: E. P. Dutton, 1960).

37. In *Karl Marx: Selected Writings,* ed. David McLellan (Oxford: Oxford University Press, 1977), 80–81.

38. Karl Marx, *Grundrisse: Foundations of the Critique of Political Economy,* trans.

Martin Nicolaus (New York: Vintage Books, 1973), p. 471 (hereafter cited as *Grundrisse*).

39. *Capital*, 3:819.
40. *Capital*, 1:167–168.
41. Karl Marx, *Value, Price, and Profit*, p. 312.
42. See David Ricardo, *The Principles of Political Economy and Taxation* (New York: E. P. Dutton, 1962).
43. "Just as, when we are considering commodities as values, we abstract from their different use-values, so it is with the labour represented by those values: we disregard the difference between its useful forms"; *Capital*, 1:12.
44. Karl Marx, *Introduction to a Critique of Political Economy* (New York: International Publishers, 1970), p. 299. See also *Capital*, 1:29.
45. *Capital*, 1:44.
46. *Capital*, 1:55–56.
47. It may be worth noting that *capitalists* are not indifferent to women's particularity, since at times they do not hire them, even when they could pay them less. Thus does misogyny sometimes outweigh the profit motive.
48. *Grundrisse*, p. 297.
49. *Grundrisse*, pp. 156–157.
50. *Grundrisse*, p. 241.
51. Ibid.
52. Adam Smith, *The Wealth of Nations*, 1:150.
53. *Capital*, 3:830.

## 5. Consciousness Raising

1. Sheila Rowbotham, *Woman's Consciousness, Man's World* (Harmondsworth: Penguin, 1973), p. 27.
2. Toni McNaron, *The Power of Person: Women Coming into Their Own* (Minneapolis: Women's Caucus of the National Association of Social Workers, 1982).
3. Rowbotham, *Woman's Consciousness*, p. 27.
4. Pamela Allen, *Free Space: A Perspective on the Small Group in Women's Liberation* (New York: Times Change Press, 1970).
5. In addition to the citations in Chapter 1, note 4, see Jo Freeman, *The Politics of Women's Liberation: A Case Study of an Emerging Social Movement and Its Relation to the Policy Process* (New York: David McKay, 1975), chap. 4; Carol Hanisch, *Notes from the Second Year* (New York: Radical Feminism, 1970), pp. 76–77. For possible parallels in Chinese "speak bitterness" sessions, see Richard H. Solomon, *Mao's Revolution and the Chinese Political Culture* (Berkeley: University of California Press, 1971), pp. 195–197, 209, 439, 441, 514, 523, 571.
6. Meredith Tax, "Woman and Her Mind: The Story of Everyday Life," in *Radical Feminism*, ed. Ann Koedt, Ellen Levine, and Anita Rapone (New York: Quadrangle Books, 1973), pp. 26–27.

7. An excellent example in writing, of which there are few, is Ingrid Bengis, *Combat in the Erogenous Zone: Writings on Love, Hate, and Sex* (New York: Alfred A. Knopf, 1973). See also Kate Millett, *Flying* (New York: Ballantine Books, 1974).

8. Adrienne Rich, "When We Dead Awaken: Writing as Re-Vision," in *On Lies, Secrets, and Silence: Selected Prose, 1966–1978* (New York: Norton, 1979), p. 44.

9. Tax, "Woman and Her Mind," pp. 26–27.

10. Susan Griffin, *Woman and Nature: The Roaring inside Her* (New York: Harper & Row, 1978), p. 197.

11. This is Steven Hymer's description of the results of Robinson Crusoe's socialization of Friday. Steven Hymer, "Robinson Crusoe and the Secret of Primitive Accumulation," *Monthly Review* 23 (September 1971): 16.

12. Westchester Radical Feminists, "Statement of Purpose, May, 1972," in Koedt, Levine, and Rapone, *Radical Feminism,* pp. 385–386.

13. Pat Mainardi, "The Politics of Housework," in *Sisterhood Is Powerful: An Anthology of Writings from the Women's Liberation Movement,* ed. Robin Morgan (New York: Random House, 1970), pp. 447–454, written in 1965, is an early and brilliant example of this perception.

14. Allen, *Free Space,* p. 27. See also Irene Peslikis, "Resistances to Consciousness," in Morgan, *Sisterhood Is Powerful,* pp. 337–339.

15. Thomas S. Kuhn, *The Structure of Scientific Revolutions,* 2d ed., vol. 2, no. 2 of *International Encyclopedia of Unified Science* (Chicago: University of Chicago Press, 1970), p. 94.

16. Jean Piaget, *The Moral Development of the Child* (New York: Collier Books, 1962).

17. See, e.g., Gunnar Myrdal, *Objectivity in Social Research* (New York: Pantheon Books, 1969). See also Stephen Toulmin, *Foresight and Understanding: An Inquiry into the Aims of Science* (New York: Harper & Row, 1963).

18. Jane P. Flax, "Epistemology and Politics: An Inquiry into Their Relation" (Ph.D. diss., Yale University, 1974), p. 19. For an illuminating discussion of Marx as a theory of "situated consciousness," see Lucio Colletti, *Marxism and Hegel,* trans. Laurence Graner (London: New Left Books, 1973), p. 204. The work of Berger and Luckmann is very helpful, although it does not go far enough and does not understand power; Peter Berger and Thomas Luckmann, *The Social Construction of Reality: A Treatise in the Sociology of Knowledge* (Garden City, N.Y.: Doubleday, 1966).

19. Kuhn, *Structure of Scientific Revolutions,* p. 94.

20. Rowbotham, *Woman's Consciousness,* p. 43.

21. Allen, *Free Space.*

22. For an illustration of this analysis put into practice, see Andrea Dworkin, *Right Wing Women* (New York: Perigee, 1983).

23. Karl Marx, *The Poverty of Philosophy* (New York: International Publishers, 1963), pp. 125–126.

24. Michelle Z. Rosaldo, "The Use and Abuse of Anthropology: Reflections on Feminism and Cross-Cultural Understanding," *Signs: Journal of Women in Culture and Society* 5 (Spring 1980): 417.

25. Marx discusses the in itself/for itself distinction in *Poverty of Philosophy*, p. 195, and in *The Eighteenth Brumaire of Louis Bonaparte*, in *Selected Works*. See L. Kolakowski, *Main Currents of Marxism*, trans. P. S. Falla, vol. 1 (Oxford: Clarendon Press, 1978), 356.

## 6. Method and Politics

1. Mary L. Shanley and Victoria Schuck, "In Search of Political Woman," *Social Science Quarterly* 55 (December 1975): 632–644.

2. This claim is illustrated and argued in this entire chapter. Useful investigations within different philosophical traditions which help support this observation are, e.g., Richard Rorty, *Philosophy and the Mirror of Nature* (Princeton: Princeton University Press, 1979): esp. 333–364 (on Kantian attempts to render all knowledge-claims commensurable and universality claims), and Karl R. Popper, *The Logic of Scientific Discovery* (New York: Harper & Row, 1959) (critique of positivism). For illustrations of linguistic philosophers attempting to come to grips with this problem, see Richard Rorty, ed., *The Linguistic Turn: Recent Essays in Philosophical Method* (Chicago: University of Chicago Press, 1967).

3. In one of the more conscious attempts, Nancy Hartsock proposes to create a feminist historical materialism, deciding that the material base for women's status is reproduction. This does not address either marxism or feminism on the level of method, but rather takes one physical object identified by feminism as important in women's condition and calls the resulting theory materialist because marxism is thought to center on the material; *Money, Sex, and Power* (Boston: Northeastern University Press, 1983).

4. Georg Lukács, "Class Consciousness," in *History and Class Consciousness: Studies in Marxist Dialectics*, trans. Rodney Livingstone (Cambridge, Mass.: MIT Press, 1971), p. 47.

5. See June P. Flax, "Epistemology and Politics: An Inquiry into Their Relation" (Ph.D. diss., Yale University, 1974).

6. Nicos Poulantzas, *Political Power and Social Classes*, trans. Timothy O'Hagan (London: Verso, 1978), p. 14.

7. Louis Althusser, *For Marx* (London: Verso, 1979), p. 170.

8. Louis Althusser, *Lenin and Philosophy*, trans. Ben Brewster (New York: Monthly Review Press, 1971), p. 8.

9. Since this sentence was first written in 1973, and first published in 1982, feminist philosophers have undertaken to redress this problem. See, e.g., S. Harding and M. Hintikka, eds., *Discovering Reality: Feminist Perspectives on Epistemology, Metaphysics, Methodology, and Philosophy of Science* (Dordrecht: D. Reidel, 1983). The statement remains true of the public perception of feminism, and the absence of concrete investigation of social life to ground philosophical method continues to undermine much feminist philosophy just

as surely as a lack of philosophical awareness undermines many concrete feminist investigations.

10. Simone de Beauvoir, *The Second Sex,* ed. and trans. H. M. Parshley (New York: Alfred A. Knopf, 1970), p. 59; Shulamith Firestone, *The Dialectic of Sex: The Case for Feminist Revolution* (New York: Bantam Books, 1970), p. 3; Susan Brownmiller, *Against Our Will: Men, Women, and Rape* (New York: Simon and Schuster, 1975), pp. 4, 6.

11. Adrienne Rich, *Of Woman Born: Motherhood as Experience and Institution* (New York: Norton, 1976); Nancy Chodorow, *The Reproduction of Mothering: Psychoanalysis and the Sociology of Gender* (Berkeley: University of California Press, 1978); Dorothy Dinnerstein, *The Mermaid and the Minotaur: Sexual Arrangements and Human Malaise* (New York: Harper & Row, 1977); Suzanne Arms, *Immaculate Deception: A New Look at Women and Childbirth in America* (Boston: Houghton Mifflin, 1975).

12. John Stuart Mill, *The Subjection of Women,* in *Essays on Sex Equality,* ed. Alice S. Rossi (Chicago: University of Chicago Press, 1970).

13. Kate Millett, *Sexual Politics* (Garden City, N.Y.: Doubleday, 1970), pp. 31, 32, 45.

14. Sandra L. Bem and Daryl J. Bem, "Case Study of Nonconscious Ideology: Training the Woman to Know Her Place," in *Beliefs, Attitudes, and Human Affairs,* ed. D. J. Bem (Belmont, Calif.: Brooks/Cole, 1970); Eleanor Emmons Maccoby and Carol Nagy Jacklin, *The Psychology of Sex Differences* (Stanford: Stanford University Press, 1974); and Shirley Weitz, *Sex Roles: Biological, Psychological, and Social Foundations* (New York: Oxford University Press, 1977).

15. Jacques Lacan, *Feminine Sexuality,* trans. Jacqueline Rose, ed. Juliet Mitchell and Jacqueline Rose (New York: Norton, 1982).

16. Beauvoir, *The Second Sex,* p. 249.

17. National Black Feminist Organization, "Statement of Purpose," *Ms.,* May 1974, p. 99: "The black woman has had to be strong, yet we are persecuted for having survived." Johnnie Tillmon, "Welfare Is a Women's Issue," *Liberation News Service,* February 26, 1972; reprinted in Rosalyn Baxandall, Linda Gordon, and Susan Reverby, eds., *America's Working Women: A Documentary History, 1600 to the Present* (New York: Random House, 1976), p. 355: "On TV a woman learns that human worth means beauty and that beauty means being thin, white, young and rich . . . In other words, an A.F.D.C. mother learns that being a 'real woman' means being all the things she isn't and having all the things she can't have."

18. Marabel Morgan, *The Total Woman* (Old Tappan, N.J.: Fleming H. Revell, 1973). "Total woman" makes blasphemous sexuality into a home art, redomesticating what prostitutes have marketed as forbidden.

19. Helène Cixous, "The Laugh of the Medusa: Viewpoint," trans. Keith Cohen and Paula Cohen, *Signs: A Journal of Women in Culture and Society* 1 (Summer 1976): 892.

20. Purple September Staff, "The Normative Status of Heterosexuality," in

*Lesbianism and the Women's Movement,* ed. Nancy Myron and Charlotte Bunch (Baltimore: Diana Press, 1975), pp. 80–81.

21. This phrase was used by an older brother in a child custody and divorce case, *Copeland v. Copeland,* on which I worked.

22. Andrea Dworkin, *The New Woman's Broken Heart* (Palo Alto, Calif.: Frog in the Well, 1980), p. 3.

23. Beauvoir, *The Second Sex.*

24. These issues are discussed in detail in Chapters 7, 9, 10, 11, and 12.

25. Ellen Morgan, *The Erotization of Male Dominance/Female Submission* (Pittsburgh: Know, 1975); Adrienne Rich, "Compulsory Heterosexuality and Lesbian Existence," *Signs: Journal of Women in Culture and Society* 5 (Summer 1980): 631–660.

26. This theme is concretely developed in Chapter 7.

27. One often hears of "a penetrating observation," "an incisive analysis," "piercing the veil." Mary Ellmann writes: "The male mind . . . is assumed to function primarily like a penis. Its fundamental character is seen to be aggression, and this quality is held essential to the highest or best working of the intellect"; *Thinking about Women* (New York: Harcourt, Brace, & World, 1968), p. 23.

28. See E. F. Keller and C. R. Grontkowski, "The Mind's Eye," in Harding and Hintikka, *Discovering Reality,* pp. 207–224.

29. Discussing photography generally, Susan Sontag observed: "The knowledge gained through still photographs will always be . . . a semblance of knowledge, a semblance of wisdom, as the act of taking pictures is a semblance of wisdom, a semblance of rape. The very muteness of what is, hypothetically, comprehensible in photographs is what constitutes their attraction and provocativeness"; *On Photography* (New York: Farrar, Straus and Giroux, 1980), p. 24.

30. As Marx once put it, "The reform of consciousness means nothing else than that we acquaint the world with its consciousness, that we wake the world up from the dream it is dreaming about itself, that we explain to the world the nature of its own actions"; letter to Arnold Ruge, September 1843, in Karl Marx, *The Early Texts,* ed. and trans. David McLellan (Oxford: Blackwell, 1971), p. 82.

31. Jean-Paul Sartre, *Search for a Method* (New York: Alfred A. Knopf, 1963), p. 181.

32. Susan Sontag, "The Third World of Women," *Partisan Review* 40 (1973): 188.

33. Butch/femme as *sexual,* not merely gender, role playing, together with parallels in lesbian sadomasochism's "top" and "bottom," suggests that sexual conformity extends far beyond gender object mores.

34. Attributed to Ti-Grace Atkinson by Anne Koedt, "Lesbianism and Feminism," in *Radical Feminism,* ed. Anne Koedt, Ellen Levine, and Anita Rapone (New York: Quadrangle Books, 1973) p. 246.

35. Useful general treatments of hermeneutical issues, which nevertheless proceed as if power, feminism, gender, or a specific problematic of women did not exist, include: Josef Bleicher, *Contemporary Hermeneutics: Hermeneutics as Method, Philosophy, and Critique* (London: Routledge & Kegan Paul, 1980); Hans-Georg Gadamer, *Philosophical Hermeneutics,* trans. David E. Linge (Berkeley: University

of California Press, 1976); Rosalind Coward and John Ellis, *Language and Materialism: Developments in Semiology and the Theory of the Subject* (London: Routledge & Kegan Paul, 1977).

36. *Origin;* August Bebel, *Women under Socialism,* trans. Daniel DeLeon (New York: New York Labor News Press, 1904).

37. Wilhelm Reich, *Sex-Pol: Essays, 1929–1934,* ed. Lee Baxandall (New York: Random House, 1972).

38. Harold Lasswell, *Psychoanalysis and Politics* (Chicago: University of Chicago Press, 1930).

39. Judy Grahn, *The Work of a Common Woman* (New York: St. Martin's Press, 1978), pp. 61–73. Adrienne Rich, "Origins and History of Consciousness," in *The Dream of a Common Language: Poems, 1974–1977* (New York: Norton, 1978), p. 7.

40. "A plain middle-aged woman, long a sufferer from cystitis, said on a television show recently in regard to sexual intercourse with her husband that because of the intense pain it caused her she 'got out of it' whenever she could. That illustrates what being a sex object means: that a woman has sexual obligations to perform which she has difficulty in escaping." This is certainly part of it. Power of Women Collective, "What Is a Sex Object?" *Socialist Woman* (London), 1975. See also Dana Densmore, "On the Temptation to Be a Beautiful Object," in *Toward a Sociology of Woman,* ed. C. Safilios-Rothschild (Lexington, Mass.: Xerox Publications, 1972), pp. 96–99; Rita Arditti, "Women as Objects: Science and Sexual Politics," *Science for the People* 6 (September 1974): 1–6; Charley Shively, "Cosmetics as an Act of Revolution," *Fag Rag* (Boston); reprinted in *Pink Triangles: Radical Perspectives on Gay Liberation,* ed. Pam Mitchell (Boston: Alyson, 1980), pp. 34–47. See Chapter 7.

41. The phrase is from Frederic Jameson, describing dialectical method in *Marxism and Form* (Princeton: Princeton University Press, 1971), p. xi.

42. This distinguishes both feminism and at least a strain in marxism from Freud: "My self-analysis is still interrupted and I have realized the reason. I can only analyze my self with the help of knowledge obtained objectively (like an outsider). Genuine self-analysis is impossible, otherwise there would be no [neurotic] illness"; Sigmund Freud, letter to Wilhelm Fliess, November 14, 1897, in *The Freud–Fliess Letters,* ed. Jeffrey Masson (Cambridge, Mass.: Harvard University Press, 1985), no. 71, p. 281. Thus, in a Freudian view, collective self-analysis could be collective neurosis because, although it is interpersonal, it is still an insider to its world. But who is to analyze men?

43. Feminist criticisms of objectivity include Julia Sherman and Evelyn Torton Beck, eds., *The Prism of Sex: Essays in the Sociology of Knowledge* (Madison: University of Wisconsin Press, 1977); Margrit Eichler, *The Double Standard: A Feminist Critique of Feminist Social Science* (New York: St. Martin's Press, 1980); Evelyn Fox Keller, "Gender and Science," *Psychoanalysis and Contemporary Thought* 1 (1978): 409–433; Adrienne Rich, "Toward a Woman-Centered

University," in *Woman and the Power to Change,* ed. Florence Howe (New York: McGraw-Hill, 1975).

44. Beauvoir, *The Second Sex,* p. 133. Beauvoir had not pursued the analysis to the point suggested here by 1979, either. See her "Introduction" in *New French Feminisms: An Anthology,* ed. Elaine Marks and Isabelle de Courtivron (Amherst: University of Massachusetts Press, 1980), pp. 41–56.

45. This is not to say that all men have power equally. For example, American Black men have substantially less of it. But to the extent they cannot create the world from their point of view, they experience themselves as unmanned, castrated. This observation supports rather than qualifies the sex specificity of the argument, without resolving the relationship between race and sex, or the relation of either to class. Attempts to confront the relation between race and sex which are at least sensitive to class issues include: Adrienne Rich, "Disloyal to Civilization: Feminism, Racism, and Gynephobia," in *On Lies, Secrets, and Silence: Selected Prose, 1966–1978* (New York: Norton, 1979); Selma James, *Sex, Race and Class* (Bristol: Falling Wall Press, 1967); R. Coles and J. H. Coles, *Women of Crisis* (New York: Dell/Delacorte Press, 1978); Socialist Women's Caucus of Louisville, *The Racist Use of Rape and the Rape Charge* (Louisville, Ky., [1977]); Angela Davis, "The Role of Black Women in the Community of Slaves," *Black Scholar* 3 (December 1971): 2–16; Karen Getman, "Sexual Control in the Slaveholding South: The Implementation and Maintenance of a Racial Caste System," 7 *Harvard Women's Law Journal* 115 (Spring 1984); E. V. Spelman, "Theories of Race and Gender/The Erasure of Black Women," *Quest: A Feminist Quarterly* 5 (1982): 36–62; Cherrie Moraga and Gloria Anzaldua, eds., *This Bridge Called My Back: Writings of Radical Women of Color* (Watertown, Mass.: Persephone Press, 1981).

46. *Capital,* 1:72. See also Alfred Sohn-Rethel's argument that the critique of the commodity holds the key to the historical explanation of the abstract conceptual mode of thinking, hence the division between intellectual and manual labor; *Intellectual and Manual Labor: A Critique of Epistemology* (London: Macmillan, 1978), p. 33.

47. Lesek Kolakowski, *Toward a Marxist Humanism: Essays on the Left Today* (New York: Grove Press, 1968), p. 66.

48. "Never to accept anything as true that I did not know to be evidently so, that is to say, care for to avoid precipitancy and prejudice, and to include in my judgments nothing more than what presents itself so clearly and so distinctly to my mind that I might have no occasion to place it in doubt"; René Descartes, *Discourse on Method and Other Writings* (Baltimore: Penguin, 1968), p. 41.

49. Carolyn Porter, *Seeing and Being: The Plight of the Participant Observer in Emerson, James, Adams, and Faulkner* (Middletown, Conn.: Wesleyan University Press, 1981), pp. 31–32. See also Werner Heisenberg, *Physics and Philosophy* (New York: Harper & Bros., 1958).

50. Technically, Heisenberg's problem arises only when one attempts microscopic measurement of two properties of one thing. Thus, one cannot know both the position and the momentum of one object at precisely the same time. See

Douglas Hofstadter, *Metamagical Themas: Questing for Mind and Pattern* (New York: Basic Books, 1985), pp. 455–477. The social and philosophical arguments extend this point a bit further.

51. Sartre, *Search for a Method*, pp. 156–157.

52. Andrea Dworkin, *Pornography: Men Possessing Women* (New York: Perigee, 1981), p. 124.

53. Linda Lovelace and Michael McGrady, *Ordeal* (Secaucus, N.J.: Citadel Press, 1980). The same may be true of class. See Richard Sennett and Jonathan Cobb, *The Hidden Injuries of Class* (New York: Alfred A. Knopf, 1972).

54. Anne Koedt, "The Myth of the Vaginal Orgasm," in Koedt, Levine, and Rapone, *Radical Feminism*, pp. 198–207; Ti-Grace Atkinson, "Vaginal Orgasm as a Mass Hysterical Survival Response," in *Amazon Odyssey: The First Collection of Writings by the Political Pioneer of the Women's Movement* (New York: Links Books, 1974), pp. 5–8.

55. Shere Hite, *The Hite Report: A Nationwide Study of Female Sexuality* (New York: Macmillan, 1976), pp. 257–266.

56. Jean-Paul Sartre, *Existential Psychoanalysis,* trans. Hazel E. Barnes (Chicago: Henry Regnery, 1973), p. 20.

57. Peter Berger and Stanley Pullberg, "Reification and the Sociological Critique of Consciousness," *New Left Review* 35 (January–February 1966); Herbert Marcuse, "The Foundation of Historical Materialism," in *Studies in Critical Philosophy,* trans. Joris De Bres (Boston: Beacon Press, 1972); Karl Klare, "Law-Making as Praxis," *Telos* 40 (Summer 1979): 131.

58. Istvan Meszaros, *Marx's Theory of Alienation* (London: Merlin Press, 1972); Bertell Ollman, *Alienation: Marx's Conception of Man in Capitalist Society* (London: Cambridge University Press, 1971); Herbert Marcuse, *Eros and Civilization: A Philosophical Inquiry into Freud* (New York: Random House, 1955), pp. 93–94, 101–102.

59. Sheila Rowbotham, *Women's Liberation and the New Politics,* Spokesman Pamphlet no. 17 (Bristol: Falling Wall Press, 1971), p. 17.

60. See Andrea Dworkin, *Intercourse* (New York: Free Press, 1987).

61. Zora Neale Hurston, *Their Eyes Were Watching God* (Urbana: University of Illinois Press, 1978), pp. 79–80.

### 7. Sexuality

1. See Jane Caputi, *The Age of Sex Crime* (Bowling Green, Ohio: Bowling Green State University Popular Press, 1987); Deborah Cameron and Elizabeth Frazer, *The Lust to Kill: A Feminist Investigation of Sexual Murder* (New York: New York University Press, 1987).

2. A few basic citations from the massive body of work on which this chapter draws are:

    *On rape:* Diana E. H. Russell and Nancy Howell, "The Prevalence of Rape in the United States Revisited," *Signs: Journal of Women in Culture and Society* 8 (Summer 1983): 668–695; D. Russell, *Rape in Marriage* (New York: Macmillan, 1982); Lorenne M. G. Clark and Debra Lewis, *Rape: The Price of Coercive Sexuality* (Toronto: Women's Press, 1977); D. Russell, *The Politics of Rape: The Victim's Perspective* (New York: Stein & Day, 1975); Andrea Medea and Kathleen Thompson, *Against Rape* (New York: Farrar, Straus and Giroux, 1974); Susan Brownmiller, *Against Our Will: Men, Women, and Rape* (New York: Simon and Schuster, 1975); Irene Frieze, "Investigating the Causes and Consequences of Marital Rape," *Signs: Journal of Women in Culture and Society* 8 (Spring 1983): 532–553; Nancy Gager and Cathleen Schurr, *Sexual Assault: Confronting Rape in America* (New York: Grosset & Dunlap, 1976); Gary LaFree, "Male Power and Female Victimization: Towards a Theory of Interracial Rape," *American Journal of Sociology* 88 (1982): 311–328; Martha Burt, "Cultural Myths and Supports for Rape," *Journal of Personality and Social Psychology* 38 (1980): 217–230; Kalamu ya Salaam, "Rape: A Radical Analysis from the African-American Perspective," in *Our Women Keep Our Skies from Falling* (New Orleans: Nkombo, 1980); J. Check and N. Malamuth, "An Empirical Assessment of Some Feminist Hypotheses about Rape," *International Journal of Women's Studies* 8 (1985): 414–423.

*On battery:* D. Martin, *Battered Wives* (San Francisco: Glide Productions, 1976); S. Steinmetz, *The Cycle of Violence: Assertive, Aggressive, and Abusive Family Interaction* (New York: Praeger, 1977); R. Emerson Dobash and Russell Dobash, *Violence against Wives: A Case against the Patriarchy* (New York: Free Press, 1979); R. Langley and R. Levy, *Wife Beating: The Silent Crisis* (New York: E. P. Dutton, 1977); Evan Stark, Anne Flitcraft, and William Frazier, "Medicine and Patriarchal Violence: The Social Construction of a 'Private' Event," *International Journal of Health Services* 9 (1979): 461–493; Lenore Walker, *The Battered Woman* (New York: Harper & Row, 1979).

*On sexual harassment:* Merit Systems Protection Board, *Sexual Harassment in the Federal Workplace: Is It a Problem?* (Washington, D.C.: U.S. Government Printing Office, 1981); C. A. MacKinnon, *Sexual Harassment of Working Women* (New Haven: Yale University Press, 1979); Donna Benson and Gregg Thomson, "Sexual Harassment on a University Campus: The Confluence of Authority Relations, Sexual Interest, and Gender Stratification," *Social Problems* 29 (1982): 236–251; Phyllis Crocker and Anne E. Simon, "Sexual Harassment in Education," 10 *Capital University Law Review* 541 (1981).

*On incest and child sexual abuse:* D. Finkelhor, *Sexually Victimized Children* (New York: Free Press, 1979); J. Herman, *Father-Daughter Incest* (Cambridge, Mass.: Harvard University Press, 1981); D. Finkelhor, *Child Sexual Abuse: Theory and Research* (New York: Free Press, 1984); A. Jaffe, L. Dynneson, and R. tenBensel, "Sexual Abuse of Children: An Epidemiologic Study," *American Journal of Diseases of Children* 129 (1975): 689–692; K. Brady, *Father's Days: A True Story of Incest* (New York: Seaview Books, 1979); L. Armstrong, *Kiss Daddy Goodnight* (New York: Hawthorn Press, 1978); S. Butler, *Conspiracy of Silence: The Trauma of Incest* (San Francisco: New Glide Publications, 1978);

A. Burgess, N. Groth, L. Homstrom, and S. Sgroi, *Sexual Assault of Children and Adolescents* (Lexington, Mass.: Lexington Books, 1978); F. Rush, *The Best-Kept Secret: Sexual Abuse of Children* (Englewood Cliffs, N.J.: Prentice-Hall, 1980); Diana E. H. Russell, "The Prevalence and Seriousness of Incestuous Abuse: Stepfathers v. Biological Fathers," *Child Abuse and Neglect: The International Journal* 8 (1984): 15–22; idem, "The Incidence and Prevalence of Intrafamilial and Extrafamilial Sexual Abuse of Female Children," ibid. 7 (1983): 133–146; idem, *The Secret Trauma: Incestuous Abuse of Women and Girls* (New York: Basic Books, 1986).

*On prostitution:* Kathleen Barry, *Female Sexual Slavery* (Englewood Cliffs, N.J.: Prentice-Hall, 1979); M. Griffin, "Wives, Hookers and the Law," 10 *Student Lawyer* 18–21 (January 1982); J. James and J. Meyerding, "Early Sexual Experience as a Factor in Prostitution," *Archives of Sexual Behavior* 7 (1978): 31–42; United Nations Economic and Social Council, Commission on Human Rights, Sub-Commission on Prevention of Discrimination and Protection of Minorities, Working Group on Slavery, *Suppression of the Traffic in Persons and of the Exploitation of the Prostitution of Others,* E/Cn.4/AC.2/5 (New York, 1976); Jennifer James, *The Politics of Prostitution* (Seattle: Social Research Associates, 1975); Kate Millett, *The Prostitution Papers* (New York: Avon Books, 1973).

*On pornography:* L. Lederer, ed., *Take Back the Night: Women on Pornography* (New York: William Morrow, 1980); Andrea Dworkin, *Pornography: Men Possessing Women* (New York: Perigee, 1981); Linda Lovelace and Michael McGrady, *Ordeal* (Secaucus, N.J.: Citadel Press, 1980); P. Bogdanovich, *The Killing of the Unicorn: Dorothy Stratten, 1960–1980* (New York: William Morrow, 1984); M. Langelan, "The Political Economy of Pornography," *Aegis: Magazine on Ending Violence against Women* 32 (August 1981): 5–7. D. Leidholdt, "Where Pornography Meets Fascism," *WIN News,* March 15, 1983, pp. 18–22; E. Donnerstein, "Erotica and Human Aggression," in *Aggression: Theoretical and Empirical Reviews,* ed. R. Green and E. Donnerstein (New York: Academic Press, 1983); idem, "Pornography: It's Effects on Violence Against Women," in *Pornography and Sexual Aggression,* ed. N. Malamuth and E. Donnerstein (Orlando, Fla.: Academic Press, 1984); Geraldine Finn, "Against Sexual Imagery, Alternative or Otherwise" (Paper presented at Symposium on Images of Sexuality in Art and Media, Ottawa, March 13–16, 1985); Diana E. H. Russell, "Pornography and Rape: A Causal Model," *Political Psychology* 9 (1988): 41–74; M. McManus, ed., *Final Report of the Attorney General's Commission on Pornography* (Nashville: Rutledge Hill Press, 1986).

*See generally:* Diana E. H. Russell, *Sexual Exploitation: Rape, Child Sexual Abuse, and Workplace Sexual Harassment* (Beverly Hills: Russell Sage, 1984); D. Russell and N. Van de Ven, *Crimes Againt Women: Proceedings of the International Tribunal* (Millbrae, Calif.: Les Femmes, 1976); E. Stanko, *Intimate Intrusions: Women's Experience of Male Violence* (London: Routledge & Kegan Paul, 1985); Ellen Morgan, *The Erotization of Male Dominance/Female Submission* (Pittsburgh: Know, 1975); Adrienne Rich, "Compulsory Heterosexuality and Lesbian Existence," *Signs: Journal of Women in Culture and Society* 5 (Summer 1980):

631–660; J. Long Laws and P. Schwartz, *Sexual Scripts: The Social Construction of Female Sexuality* (Hinsdale, Ill.: Dryden Press, 1977); L. Phelps, "Female Sexual Alienation," in *Women: A Feminist Perspective,* ed. J. Freeman (Palo Alto, Calif.: Mayfield, 1979); Shere Hite, *The Hite Report: A Nationwide Survey of Female Sexuality* (New York: Macmillan, 1976); Andrea Dworkin, *Intercourse* (New York: Free Press, 1987). Recent comparative work provides confirmation and contrasts: Pat Caplan, ed., *The Cultural Construction of Sexuality* (New York: Tavistock, 1987); Marjorie Shostak, *Nisa: The Life and Words of a !Kung Woman* (New York: Vintage Books, 1983).

3. Freud's decision to disbelieve women's accounts of being sexually abused as children was apparently central in the construction of the theories of fantasy and possibly also of the unconscious. That is, to some degree, his belief that the sexual abuse in his patients' accounts did not occur created the need for a theory like fantasy, like unconscious, to explain the reports. See Rush, *The Best-Kept Secret;* Jeffrey M. Masson, *The Assault on Truth: Freud's Suppression of the Seduction Theory* (New York: Farrar, Straus and Giroux, 1984). One can only speculate on the course of the modern psyche (not to mention modern history) had the women been believed.

4. E. Schur, *Labeling Women Deviant: Gender, Stigma, and Social Control* (Philadelphia: Temple University Press, 1984) (a superb review of studies which urges a "continuum" rather than a "deviance" approach to issues of sex inequality).

5. This figure was calculated at my request by Diana E. H. Russell on the random-sample data base of 930 San Francisco households discussed in *The Secret Trauma,* pp. 20–37, and *Rape in Marriage,* pp. 27–41. The figure includes all the forms of rape or other sexual abuse or harassment surveyed, noncontact as well as contact, from gang rape by strangers and marital rape to obscene phone calls, unwanted sexual advances on the street, unwelcome requests to pose for pornography, and subjection to peeping toms and sexual exhibitionists (flashers).

6. S. D. Smithyman, "The Undetected Rapist" (Ph.D. diss., Claremont Graduate School, 1978); N. Groth, *Men Who Rape: The Psychology of the Offender* (New York: Plenum Press, 1979); D. Scully and J. Marolla, " 'Riding the Bull at Gilley's': Convicted Rapists Describe the Rewards of Rape," *Social Problems* 32 (1985): 251. (The manuscript subtitle was "Convicted Rapists Describe the Pleasure of Raping.")

7. Kate Millett, *Sexual Politics* (Garden City, N.Y.: Doubleday, 1970).

8. Jacques Lacan, *Feminine Sexuality,* trans. Jacqueline Rose, ed. Juliet Mitchell and Jacqueline Rose (New York: Norton, 1982); Michel Foucault, *The History of Sexuality,* vol. 1: *An Introduction* (New York: Random House, 1980); idem, *Power/Knowledge,* ed. C. Gordon (New York: Pantheon, 1980).

See generally (including materials reviewed in) R. Padgug, "Sexual Matters: On Conceptualizing Sexuality in History," *Radical History Review* 70 (Spring/Summer 1979), e.g., p. 9; M. Vicinus, "Sexuality and Power: A Review of Current Work in the History of Sexuality," *Feminist Studies* 8 (Spring 1982): 133–155; S. Ortner and H. Whitehead, *Sexual Meanings: The Cultural*

*Construction of Gender and Sexuality* (Cambridge: Cambridge University Press, 1981); Red Collective, *The Politics of Sexuality in Capitalism* (London: Black Rose Press, 1978); J. Weeks, *Sex, Politics, and Society: The Regulation of Sexuality since 1800* (New York: Longman, 1981); J. D'Emilio, *Sexual Politics, Sexual Communities: The Making of a Homosexual Minority in the United States, 1940–1970* (Chicago: University of Chicago Press, 1983); A. Snitow, C. Stansell, and S. Thompson, eds., Introduction to *Powers of Desire: The Politics of Sexuality* (New York: Monthly Review Press, 1983); E. Dubois and L. Gordon, "Seeking Ecstasy on the Battlefield: Danger and Pleasure in Nineteenth-Century Feminist Social Thought," *Feminist Studies* 9 (Spring 1983): 7–25.

9. An example is Jeffrey Weeks, *Sexuality and Its Discontents* (London: Routledge & Kegan Paul, 1985).

10. Luce Irigaray's critique of Freud in *Speculum of the Other Woman* (Ithaca: Cornell University Press, 1974) acutely shows how Freud constructs sexuality from the male point of view, with woman as deviation from the norm. But she, too, sees female sexuality not as constructed by male dominance but only repressed under it.

11. For those who think that such notions are atavisms left behind by modern scientists, see one entirely typical conceptualization of "sexual pleasure, a powerful unconditioned stimulus and reinforcer" in N. Malamuth and B. Spinner, "A Longitudinal Content Analysis of Sexual Violence in the Best-Selling Erotic Magazines," *Journal of Sex Research* 16 (August 1980): 226. See also B. Ollman's discussion of Wilhelm Reich in *Social and Sexual Revolution* (Boston: South End Press, 1979), esp. pp. 186–187.

12. Foucault's contributions to such an analysis and his limitations are discussed illuminatingly in Frigga Haug, ed., *Female Sexualization,* trans. Erica Carter (London: Verso, 1987), pp. 190–198.

13. A. Kinsey, W. Pomeroy, C. Martin, and P. Gebhard, *Sexual Behavior in the Human Female* (Philadelphia: W.B. Saunders, 1953); A. Kinsey, W. Pomeroy, and C. Martin, *Sexual Behavior in the Human Male* (Philadelphia: W.B. Saunders, 1948). See the critique of Kinsey in Dworkin, *Pornography,* pp. 179–198.

14. Examples include: D. English, "The Politics of Porn: Can Feminists Walk the Line?" *Mother Jones,* April 1980, pp. 20–23, 43–44, 48–50; D. English, A. Hollibaugh, and G. Rubin, "Talking Sex: A Conversation on Sexuality and Feminism," *Socialist Review* 58 (July–August 1981); J. B. Elshtain, "The Victim Syndrome: A Troubling Turn in Feminism," *The Progressive,* June 1982, pp. 40–47; Ellen Willis, *Village Voice,* November 12, 1979. This approach also tends to characterize the basic ideology of "human sexuality courses" as analyzed by C. Vance in Snitow, Stansell, and Thompson, *Powers of Desire,* pp. 371–384. The view of sex so promulgated is distilled in the following quotation, coming after an alliterative list, probably intended to be humorous, headed "determinants of sexuality" (on which "power" does not appear, although every other word begins with *p*): "Persistent puritanical pressures promoting propriety, purity, and prudery are opposed by a powerful, primeval, procreative passion to

plunge his pecker into her pussy"; "Materials from Course on Human Sexuality," College of Medicine and Dentistry of New Jersey, Rutgers Medical School, January 29–February 2, 1979, p. 39.

15. A third reason is also given: "to the extent that sexism in societal and family structure is responsible for the phenomena of 'compulsive masculinity' and structured antagonism between the sexes, the elimination of sexual inequality would reduce the number of 'power trip' and 'degradation ceremony' motivated rapes"; M. Straus, "Sexual Inequality, Cultural Norms, and Wife-Beating," *Victimology: An International Journal* 1 (1976): 54–70. Note that these structural factors seem to be considered nonsexual, in the sense that "power trip" and "degradation ceremony" motivated rapes are treated as not erotic to the perpetrators *because* of the elements of dominance and degradation, nor is "structured antagonism" seen as an erotic element of rape or sex (or family).

16. P. R. Sanday, "The Socio-Cultural Context of Rape: A Cross-Cultural Study," *Journal of Social Issues* 37, no. 4 (1981): 16. See also M. Lewin, "Unwanted Intercourse: The Difficulty of Saying 'No,' " *Psychology of Women Quarterly* 9 (1985): 184–192.

17. See Chapter 9 for discussion.

18. Susan Brownmiller, *Against Our Will*, originated this approach, which has since become ubiquitous.

19. Annie McCombs helped me express this thought; letter to *off our backs* (Washington, D.C., October 1984), p. 34.

20. Brownmiller, *Against Our Will*, did analyze rape as something men do to women, hence as a problem of gender, even though her concept of gender is biologically based. See, e.g., her pp. 4, 6, and discussion in chap. 3. An exception is Clark and Lewis, *Rape.*

21. Snitow, Stansell, and Thompson, Introduction to *Powers of Desire*, p. 9.

22. C. Vance, "Concept Paper: Toward a Politics of Sexuality," in *Diary of a Conference on Sexuality*, ed. H. Alderfer, B. Jaker, and M. Nelson (Record of the planning committee of the conference "The Scholar and the Feminist IX: Toward a Politics of Sexuality," April 24, 1982), p. 27; to address "women's sexual pleasure, choice, and autonomy, acknowledging that sexuality is simultaneously a domain of restriction, repression and danger as well as a domain of exploration, pleasure and agency." Parts of the *Diary*, with the conference papers, were later published in C. Vance, ed., *Pleasure and Danger: Exploring Female Sexuality* (London: Routledge & Kegan Paul, 1984).

23. Vance, "Concept Paper," p. 38.

24. For examples see A. Hollibaugh and C. Moraga, "What We're Rollin' Around in Bed With: Sexual Silences in Feminism," in Snitow, Stansell, and Thompson, *Powers of Desire*, pp. 394–405, esp. 398; Samois, *Coming to Power* (Berkeley, Calif.: Alyson Publications, 1983).

25. Andrea Dworkin, "Why So-called Radical Men Love and Need Pornography," in Lederer, *Take Back the Night*, p. 148.

26. Susan Sontag, "Fascinating Fascism," in *Under the Sign of Saturn* (New York: Farrar, Straus and Giroux, 1980), p. 103.

27. Robert Stoller, *Sexual Excitement: Dynamics of Erotic Life* (New York: Pantheon Books, 1979), p. 6.

28. Harriet Jacobs, quoted in Rennie Simson, "The Afro-American Female: The Historical Context of the Construction of Sexual Identity," in Snitow, Stansell, and Thompson, *Powers of Desire,* p. 231. Jacobs resisted sex with another white master by hiding in an attic cubbyhole "almost deprived of light and air, and with no space to move my limbs, for nearly seven years."

29. A similar rejection of indeterminacy can be found in Linda Alcoff, "Cultural Feminism versus Post-Structuralism: The Identity Crisis in Feminist Theory," *Signs: Journal of Women in Culture and Society* 13 (Spring 1988): 419–420. The article otherwise misdiagnoses the division in feminism as that between so-called cultural feminists and post-structualism, when the division is between those who take sexual misogyny seriously as a mainspring to gender hiearchy and those who wish, liberal-fashion, to affirm "differences" without seeing that sameness/difference is a dichotomy of exactly the sort that post-structuralism purports to deconstruct.

30. See Sandra Harding, "Introduction: Is There a Feminist Method?" in *Feminism and Methodology* (Bloomington: Indiana University Press, 1987), pp. 1–14.

31. One of the most compelling accounts of active victim behavior is provided in *Give Sorrow Words: Maryse Holder's Letters from Mexico,* intro. Kate Millett (New York: Grove Press, 1980). Ms. Holder wrote a woman friend of her daily, frantic, and always failing pursuit of men, sex, beauty, and feeling good about herself: "Fuck fucking, will *feel* self-respect" (p. 94). She was murdered soon after by an unknown assailant.

32. This phrase comes from Michel Foucault, "The West and the Truth of Sex," *Sub-stance* 5 (1978): 20. Foucault does not criticize pornography in these terms.

33. Dworkin, *Pornography,* p. 24.

34. J. Cook, "The X-Rated Economy," *Forbes,* September 18, 1978, p. 18; Langelan, "The Political Economy of Pornography," p. 5; *Public Hearings on Ordinances to Add Pornography as Discrimination against Women* (Minneapolis, December 12–13, 1983); F. Schauer, "Response: Pornography and the First Amendment," 40 *University of Pittsburgh Law Review,* 605, 616 (1979).

35. John Money, professor of medical psychology and pediatrics, John Hopkins Medical Institutions, letter to Clive M. Davis, April 18, 1984. The same view is expressed by Al Goldstein, editor of *Screw,* a pornographic newspaper, concerning antipornography feminists, termed "nattering nabobs of sexual negativism": "We must repeat to ourselves like a mantra: sex is good; nakedness is a joy; an erection is beautiful . . . Don't let the bastards get you limp"; "Dear Playboy," *Playboy,* June 1985, p. 12.

36. Andrea Dworkin, "The Root Cause," in *Our Blood: Prophesies and Discourses on Sexual Politics* (New York: Harper & Row, 1976), pp. 96–111.

37. See Chapter 12 for further discussion.

38. Dworkin, *Pornography,* pp. 69, 136, and chap. 2, "Men and Boys." "In practice, fucking is an act of possession—simultaneously an act of ownership, taking, force; it is conquering; it expresses in intimacy power over and against, body to body, person to thing. 'The sex act' means penile intromission followed

by penile thrusting, or fucking. The woman is acted on, the man acts and through action expresses sexual power, the power of masculinity. Fucking requires that the male act on one who has less power and this valuation is so deep, so completely implicit in the act, that the one who is fucked is stigmatized as feminine during the act even when not anatomically female. In the male system, sex is the penis, the penis is sexual power, its use in fucking is manhood"; p. 23.

39. Ibid., p. 109.

40. Ibid., pp. 113–128.

41. Ibid., p. 174.

42. Freud believed that the female nature was inherently masochistic; Sigmund Freud, Lecture XXXIII, "The Psychology of Women," in *New Introductory Lectures on Psychoanalysis* (London: Hogarth Press, 1933). Helene Deutsch, Marie Bonaparte, Sandor Rado, Adolf Grunberger, Melanie Klein, Helle Thorning, Georges Bataille, Theodore Reik, Jean-Paul Sartre, and Simone de Beauvoir all described some version of female masochism in their work, each with a different theoretical account for virtually identical observations. See Helene Deutsch, "The Significance of Masochism in the Mental Life of Women," *International Journal of Psychoanalysis* 11 (1930): 48–60; idem in *The Psychology of Women* (New York: Grune & Stratton, 1944). Several are summarized by Janine Chasseguet-Smirgel, ed., in her Introduction to *Female Sexuality: New Psychoanalytic Views* (Ann Arbor: University of Michigan Press, 1970); Theodore Reik, *Masochism in Sex and Society* (New York: Grove Press, 1962), p. 217; Helle Thorning, "The Mother-Daughter Relationship and Sexual Ambivalence," *Heresies* 12 (1979): 3–6; Georges Bataille, *Death and Sensuality* (New York: Walker and Co., 1962); Jean-Paul Sartre, "Concrete Relations with Others," in *Being and Nothingness: An Essay on Phenomenological Ontology*, trans. Hazel E. Barnes (New York: Philosophical Library, (1956), pp. 361–430. Betsey Belote stated: "masochistic and hysterical behavior is so similar to the concept of 'femininity' that the three are not clearly distinguishable"; "Masochistic Syndrome, Hysterical Personality, and the Illusion of the Healthy Woman," in *Female Psychology: The Emerging Self*, ed. Sue Cox (Chicago: Science Research Associates, 1976), p. 347. See also S. Bartky, "Feminine Masochism and the Politics of Personal Transformation," *Women's Studies International Forum* 7 (1984): 327–328. Andrea Dworkin writes: "I believe that freedom for women must begin in the repudiation of our own masochism . . . I believe that ridding ourselves of our own deeply entrenched masochism, which takes so many tortured forms, is the first priority; it is the first deadly blow that we can strike against systematized male dominance"; *Our Blood*, p. 111.

43. Dworkin, *Pornography*, p. 146.

44. Anne Koedt, "The Myth of the Vaginal Orgasm," in *Notes from the Second Year: Women's Liberation* (New York: Radical Feminism, 1970); Ti-Grace Atkinson, *Amazon Odyssey: The First Collection of Writings by the Political Pioneer of the Women's Movement* (New York: Links Books, 1974); Phelps, "Female Sexual Alienation."

45. Dworkin, *Pornography*, p. 22.

46. This is the plot of *Deep Throat*, the pornographic film Linda "Lovelace" was forced to make. It may be the largest-grossing pornography film in the history of the world (McManus, *Final Report*, p. 345). That this plot is apparently enjoyed to such a prevalent extent suggests that it appeals to something extant in the male psyche.

47. Dworkin, "The Root Cause," p. 56.

48. A prominent if dated example is Jill Johnston, *Lesbian Nation: The Feminist Solution* (New York: Simon and Schuster, 1973).

49. This and the following quotations in this paragraph are from P. Califia, "A Secret Side of Lesbian Sexuality," *The Advocate* (San Francisco), December 27, 1979, pp. 19–21, 27–28.

50. The statistics in this paragraph are drawn from the sources referenced in note 2, above, as categorized by topic. Kathleen Barry defines "female sexual slavery" as a condition of prostitution which one cannot get out of.

51. Donnerstein, testimony, *Public Hearings on Ordinances*, pp. 35–36. The relationship between consenting and nonconsenting depictions and sexual arousal among men with varying self-reported propensities to rape are examined in the following studies: N. Malamuth, "Rape Fantasies as a Function of Exposure to Violent Sexual Stimuli," *Archives of Sexual Behavior* 10 (1981): 33–47; N. Malamuth and J. Check, "Penile Tumescence and Perceptual Responses to Rape as a Function of Victim's Perceived Reactions," *Journal of Applied Social Psychology* 10 (1980): 528–547; N. Malamuth, M. Heim, and S. Feshbach, "The Sexual Responsiveness of College Students to Rape Depictions: Inhibitory and Disinhibitory Effects," *Journal of Personality and Social Psychology* 38 (1980): 399–408; N. Malamuth and J. Check, "Sexual Arousal to Rape and Consenting Depictions: The Importance of the Woman's Arousal," *Journal of Abnormal Psychology* 39 (1980): 763–766; N. Malamuth, "Rape Proclivity among Males," *Journal of Social Issues* 37 (1981): 138–157; E. Donnerstein and L. Berkowitz, "Victim Reactions in Aggressive Erotic Films as a Factor in Violence against Women," *Journal of Personality and Social Psychology* 41 (1981): 710–724; J. Check and T. Guloien, "Reported Proclivity for Coercive Sex Following Repeated Exposure to Sexually Violent Pornography, Nonviolent Dehumanizing Pornography, and Erotica," in *Pornography: Recent Research, Interpretations, and Policy Considerations,* ed. D. Zillmann and J. Bryant (Hillsdale, N.J.: Erlbaum, forthcoming).

52. Donnerstein, testimony, *Public Hearings on Ordinances*, p. 36.

53. Ibid. The soporific effects of explicit sex depicted without express violence are apparent in *The Report of the Commission on Obscenity and Pornography* (Washington, D.C.: U.S. Government Printing Office, 1970).

54. Donnerstein and Berkowitz, "Victim Reactions in Aggressive Erotic Films"; Donnerstein, "Pornography: Its Effect on Violence against Women." This conclusion is the cumulative result of years of experimental research showing that "if you can measure sexual arousal to sexual images and measure people's attitudes about rape you can predict aggressive behavior with women";

Donnerstein, testimony, *Public Hearings on Ordinances,* p. 29. Some of the more prominent supporting experimental work, in addition to citations previously referenced here, include: E. Donnerstein and J. Hallam, "Facilitating Effects of Erotica on Aggression toward Females," *Journal of Personality and Social Psychology* 36 (1978): 1270–77; R. G. Geen, D. Stonner, and G. L. Shope, "The Facilitation of Aggression by Aggression: Evidence against the Catharsis Hypothesis," ibid. 31 (1975): 721–726; D. Zillmann, J. Hoyt, and K. Day, "Strength and Duration of the Effects of Aggressive, Violent, and Erotic Communications on Subsequent Aggressive Behavior," *Communication Research* 1 (1974): 286–306; B. Sapolsky and D. Zillman, "The Effect of Soft-Core and Hard-Core Erotica on Provoked and Unprovoked Hostile Behavior," *Journal of Sex Research* 17 (1981): 319–343; D. L. Mosher and H. Katz, "Pornographic Films, Male Verbal Aggression against Women, and Guilt," in *Technical Report of The Commission on Obscenity and Pornography,* vol. 8 (Washington, D.C.: U.S. Government Printing Office, 1971). See also E. Summers and J. Check, "An Empirical Investigation of the Role of Pornography in the Verbal and Physical Abuse of Women," *Violence and Victims* 2 (1987): 189–209; and P. Harmon, "The Role of Pornography in Woman Abuse" (Ph.D. diss., York University, 1987), pp. 65–66. These experiments establish that the relationship between expressly violent sexual material and subsequent aggression against women is causal as well as correlational.

55. Key research is reported and summarized in Check and Guloien, "Reported Proclivity for Coercive Sex"; see also D. Zillmann, "Effects of Repeated Exposure to Nonviolent Pornography" (Report presented to U.S. Attorney General's Commission on Pornography, Houston, June 1986). Donnerstein's experiments, as reported in *Public Hearings on Ordinances* and in Malamuth and Donnerstein, *Pornography and Sexual Aggression,* also clarify, culminate, and extend years of experimental research by many. See, e.g., D. Mosher, "Sex Callousness toward Women," in *Techical Report;* N. Malamuth and J. Check, "The Effects of Mass Media Exposure on Acceptance of Violence against Women. A Field Experiment," *Journal of Research in Personality* 15 (December 1981): 436–446. The studies are tending to confirm women's reports and feminist analyses of the consequences of exposure to pornography on attitudes and behaviors toward women. See Check and Malamuth, "An Empirical Assessment of Some Feminist Hypotheses."

56. G. G. Abel, D. H. Barlow, E. Blanchard, and D. Guild, "The Components of Rapists' Sexual Arousal," *Archives of General Psychiatry* 34 (1977): 895–908; G. G. Abel, J. V. Becker, L. J. Skinner, "Aggressive Behavior and Sex," *Psychiatric Clinics of North America* 3 (1980): 133–155; G. G. Abel, E. B. Blanchard, J. V. Becker, and A. Djenderedjian, "Differentiating Sexual Aggressiveness with Penile Measures," *Criminal Justice and Behavior* 2 (1978): 315–332.

57. Donnerstein, testimony, *Public Hearings on Ordinances,* p. 31.

58. Smithyman, "The Undetected Rapist."

59. Scully and Marolla, " 'Riding the Bull at Gilley's.' "

60. In addition to Malamuth, "Rape Proclivity among Males," Malamuth and Check, "Sexual Arousal to Rape," and Neil Malamuth, Scott Haber, and Seymour Feshbach, "Testing Hypotheses regarding Rape: Exposure to Sexual Violence, Sex Differences, and the 'Normality' of Rapists," *Journal of Research in Personality* 14 (1980): 121–137, see T. Tieger, "Self-Rated Likelihood of Raping and the Social Perception of Rape," ibid. 15 (1981): 147–158.

61. M. Burt and R. Albin, "Rape Myths, Rape Definitions, and Probability of Conviction," *Journal of Applied Social Psychology* 11 (1981): 212–230; G. D. LaFree, "The Effect of Sexual Stratification by Race on Official Reactions to Rape," *American Sociological Review* 45 (1984): 824–854; J. Galvin and K. Polk, "Attrition in Case Processing: Is Rape Unique?" *Journal of Research in Crime and Delinquency* 20 (1983): 126–154. The latter work seems not to understand that rape can be institutionally treated in a way that is sex-specific even if comparable numbers are generated by other crimes against the other sex. Further, this study assumes that 53 percent of rapes are reported, when the real figure is closer to 10 percent; Russell, *Sexual Exploitation.* Idem, "The Prevalence and Incidence of Rape and Attempted Rape in the United States," *Victimology: An International Journal* 7 (1982): 81–93.

62. Scully and Marolla, " 'Riding the Bull at Gilley's,' " p. 2.

63. Sometimes this is a grudging realism: "Once there is a conviction, the matter cannot be trivial enough though the act may have been"; P. Gebhard, J. Gagnon, W. Pomeroy, and C. Christenson, *Sex Offenders: An Analysis of Types* (New York: Harper & Row, 1965), p. 178. It is telling that if an act that has been adjudicated rape is still argued to be sex, that is thought to exonerate the rape rather than indict the sex.

64. R. Rada, *Clinical Aspects of Rape* (New York: Grune & Stratton, 1978); C. Kirkpatrick and E. Kanin, "Male Sex Aggression on a University Campus," *American Sociological Review* 22 (1957): 52–58; see also Malamuth, Haber, and Feshbach, "Testing Hypotheses regarding Rape."

65. Abel, Becker, and Skinner, "Aggressive Behavior and Sex."

66. Robert Stoller, *Perversion: The Erotic Form of Hatred* (New York: Pantheon, 1975), p. 87.

67. Compare, e.g., Hite, *The Hite Report;* with Russell, *The Politics of Rape.*

68. This is truly obvious from looking at the pornography. A fair amount of pornography actually calls the acts it celebrates "rape." Too, "in depictions of sexual behavior [in pornography] there is typically evidence of a difference of power between the participants"; L. Baron and M. A. Straus, "Conceptual and Ethical Problems in Research on Pornography" (Paper presented at the annual meeting of the Society for the Study of Social Problems, 1983), p. 6. Given that this statement characterizes the reality, consider the content attributed to "sex itself" in the following (methodologically liberal) quotations on the subject: "Only if one thinks of *sex itself* as a degrading act can one believe that all pornography degrades and harms women" (emphasis added); P. Califia, "Among Us, against Us—The New Puritans," *The Advocate* (San Francisco), April 17, 1980, p. 14. Given the realization that violence against women *is*

sexual, consider the content of the "sexual" in the following criticism: "the only form in which a politics opposed to violence against women is being expressed is anti-sexual"; D. English, A. Hollibaugh, and G. Rubin, "Talking Sex: A Conversation on Sexuality and Feminism," *Socialist Review* 58 (July–August 1981): 51. And "the feminist anti-pornography movement has become deeply erotophobic and anti-sexual"; A. Hollibaugh, "The Erotophobic Voice of Women," *New York Native,* September–October 1983, p. 34.

69. J. Wolfe and V. Baker, "Characteristics of Imprisoned Rapists and Circumstances of the Rape," in *Rape and Sexual Assault,* ed. C. G. Warner (Germantown, Md.: Aspen Systems, 1980).

70. This statement has been attributed to California state senator Bob Wilson; "Rape: The Sexual Weapon," *Time,* September 5, 1983. He has denied that the comment was seriously intended to express his own views; Letter, *Time,* October 10, 1983. I consider it apocryphal as well as stunningly revelatory of the indistinguishability of rape from intercourse from the male point of view. See also Joanne Schulman, "The Marital Rape Exemption in the Criminal Law," *Clearinghouse Review* 14 (October 1980): 6.

71. Carolyn Craven, "No More Victims: Carolyn Craven Talks about Rape, and What Women and Men Can Do to Stop It," ed. Alison Wells (Mimeograph, Berkeley, Calif., 1978), p. 2.; Russell, *The Politics of Rape,* pp. 84–85, 105, 114, 135, 147, 185, 196, and 205; P. Bart, "Rape Doesn't End with a Kiss," *Viva* 11 (June 1975): 39–41, 100–101; J. Becker, L. Skinner, G. Abel, R. Axelrod, and J. Cichon, "Sexual Problems of Sexual Assault Survivors," *Women and Health* 9 (Winter 1984): 5–20.

72. See the sources on incest and child sexual abuse cited in note 2, above.

73. Olympia, a woman who poses for soft-core pornography, interviewed by Robert Stoller, "Centerfold: An Essay on Excitement," *Archives of General Psychiatry* 36 (1979): 1019–28.

74. It is interesting that, in spite of everything, many women who once thought of their abuse as self-actualizing come to rethink it as a violation, while very few who have ever thought of their abuse as a violation come to rethink it as self-actualizing.

75. See G. Schmidt and V. Sigusch, "Sex Differences in Responses to Psychosexual Stimulation by Film and Slides," *Journal of Sex Research* 6 (November 1970): 268–283; G. Schmidt, "Male-Female Differences in Sexual Arousal and Behavior during and after Exposure to Sexually Explicit Stimuli," *Archives of Sexual Behavior* 4 (1975): 353–365; D. Mosher, "Psychological Reactions to Pornographic Films," in *Technical Report,* pp. 255–312.

76. Using the term *experience* as a verb like this seems to be the way one currently negotiates the subjective/objective split in Western epistemology.

77. S. Rachman and R. Hodsgon, "Experimentally Induced 'Sexual Fetishism': Replication and Development," *Psychological Record* 18 (1968): 25–27; S. Rachman, "Sexual Fetishism: An Experimental Analogue," ibid. 16 (1966): 293–296.

78. Speech at March for Women's Dignity, New York City, May 1984.

79. *Public Hearings on Ordinances;* Margaret Atwood, *Bodily Harm* (Toronto: McClelland & Stewart, 1983), pp. 207–212.

80. This is also true of Foucault, *The History of Sexuality.* Foucault understands that sexuality must be discussed with method, power, class, and the law. Gender, however, eludes him. So he cannot distinguish between the silence about sexuality that Victorianism has made into a noisy discourse and the silence that has *been* women's sexuality under conditions of subordination by and to men. Although he purports to grasp sexuality, including desire itself, as social, he does not see the content of its determination as a sexist social order that eroticizes potency as male and victimization as female. Women are simply beneath significant notice.

81. Masson, *The Assault on Truth.*

82. On sexuality, see, e.g., A. Lorde, *Uses of the Erotic: The Erotic as Power* (Brooklyn, N.Y.: Out and Out Books, 1978); and Haunani-Kay Trask, *Eros and Power: The Promise of Feminist Theory* (Philadelphia: University of Pennsylvania Press, 1986). Both creatively attempt such a reconstitution. Trask's work suffers from an underlying essentialism in which the realities of sexual abuse are not examined or seen as constituting women's sexuality as such. Thus, a return to mother and body can be urged as social bases for reclaiming a feminist eros. Another reason the parallel cannot be at all precise is that Black women and their sexuality make up both Black culture and women's sexuality, inhabiting both sides of the comparison. In other words, parallels which converge and interact are not parallels. The comparison may nonetheless be heuristically useful both for those who understand one experience but not the other and for those who can compare two dimensions of life which overlap and resonate together at some moments and diverge sharply in dissonance at others.

83. Ti-Grace Atkinson, "Why I'm against S/M Liberation," in *Against Sadomasochism: A Radical Feminist Analysis,* ed. E. Linden, D. Pagano, D. Russell, and S. Star (Palo Alto, Calif.: Frog in the Well, 1982), p. 91.

## 8. The Liberal State

1. Illustrative examples can be found in Karl Marx, *The German Ideology* (New York: International Publishers, 1972), pp. 48–52; idem, *Critique of Hegel's Philosophy of Right,* ed. Joseph O'Malley, trans. Annette Jolin (Cambridge: Cambridge University Press, 1970), p. 139 ("substratum"); idem, "Introduction to Critique of Political Economy," in *German Ideology,* ed. C. J. Arthur (New York: International Publishers, 1972), p. 142; idem, *Eighteenth Brumaire of Louis Bonaparte,* in *Selected Works,* ed. V. Adoratsky, vol. 2 (New York: International Publishers, 1936), 344 ("superstructure"); letter from Marx to P. V. Annenkov, December 28, 1846, in *The Poverty of Philosophy* (New York: International Publishers, 1963), p. 181. The concept also occurs pervasively if mostly implicitly throughout *Capital.*

2. In *Selected Works,* 3: 527.

3. Marx, *Poverty of Philosophy,* p. 156.

4. Karl Marx and Friedrich Engels, *The Communist Manifesto,* in *Collected Works* (London: Lawrence & Wishart, 1900), p. 486.

5. See Chapter 2 and *Origin,* pp. 125–146.

6. *Origin,* p. 174.

7. See also Karl Marx, *Early Writings,* ed. and trans. T. B. Bottomore (New York: McGraw-Hill, 1964), p. 20.

8. Marx, *Critique of Hegel's Philosophy of Right,* p. 139. See also Max Adler, *Die Staatsauffassung des Marxismus* (Darmstadt, 1964), p. 49.

9. Lenin urged taking over the state mechanism for the proletariat, but not changing its form. For a discussion of Lenin's *The State and Revolution,* see L. Kolakowski, *Main Currents of Marxism,* vol. 2: *The Golden Age,* trans. P. S. Falla (Oxford: Clarendon Press, 1978), 498–509.

10. This analysis of the political manuscripts is indebted to Eric Hobsbawm, "Marx, Engels and Politics," in *The History of Marxism,* ed. E. Hobsbawm, vol. 1 (Brighton: Harvester Press, 1982), p. 245.

11. Jon Elster, *Making Sense of Marx* (Cambridge: Cambridge University Press, 1985), p. 57. Elster attributes this insight to post-1850 Marx.

12. Representative works include Fred Block, "The Ruling Class Does Not Rule: Notes on the Marxist Theory of the State," *Socialist Revolution* 7 (May–June 1977): 6–28; Ralph Miliband, *The State in Capitalist Society* (New York: Basic Books, 1969); Nicos Poulantzas, *Classes in Contemporary Capitalism* (London: New Left Books, 1975) and *Political Power and Social Classes,* trans. Timothy O'Hagan (London: Verso, 1978); Perry Anderson, *Lineages of the Absolutist State* (London: New Left Books, 1975); Goran Therborn, *What Does the Ruling Class Do When It Rules?* (London: New Left Books, 1978); Claus Offe and Volker Ronge, "Theses on the Theory of the State," *New German Critique* 6 (1975): 137–147; David A. Gold, Clarence Y. H. Lo, and Erik Olin Wright, "Recent Developments in Marxist Theories of the Capitalist State," *Monthly Review* 27 (October 1975): 29–43 and (November 1975): 36–51; Norberto Bobbio, "Is There a Marxist Theory of the State?" *Telos* 35 (Spring 1978): 5–16. Theda Skocpol, *States and Social Revolution: A Comparative Analysis of France, Russia and China* (Cambridge: Cambridge University Press, 1979), pp. 24–33, ably reviews much of this literature. Applications to law include Isaac Balbus, "Commodity Form and Legal Form: An Essay on the 'Relative Autonomy' of the Law," *Law and Society Review* 11 (Winter 1977): 571–588; Mark Tushnet, "A Marxist Analysis of American Law," *Marxist Perspectives* 1, no. 1 (Spring 1978): 96–116; and Karl Klare, "Law-Making as Praxis," *Telos* 40 (Summer 1979): 123–135.

13. Elster, *Making Sense of Marx,* p. 411.

14. Poulantzas' formulation follows Althusser; Louis Althusser and Etienne Balibar, *Reading Capital,* trans. Ben Brewster (London: New Left Books, 1970).

15. Poulantzas, *Political Power and Social Classes,* pp. 14, 16.

16. This discussion usually terms economic realities the "base" and the state and its

laws parts of the "superstructure." Base determines superstructure. An interesting reworking of these relations is Gerald A. Cohen, *Karl Marx's Theory of History: A Defense* (Oxford: Oxford University Press, 1978), p. 216.

17. Ernesto Laclau makes a similar point. Criticizing Ralph Miliband: "It would seem that Miliband is working with a simplistic contraposition, in which the adjective 'relative' constitutes a simple restriction to an autonomy conceived in terms of freedom." Clarifying Poulantzas: "For Poulantzas, on the contrary, the 'relative' character of an autonomy indicates that it belongs to a world of structural determinations, and it is only within this, as a particular moment of it, that the concept of autonomy must be elaborated"; Ernesto Laclau, *Politics and Ideology in Marxist Theory* (London: New Left Books, 1977), p. 65.

18. The Critical Legal Studies movement has worked with these issues without getting much further on this question than this paragraph discloses. See Mark Kelman's able synthesis, *A Guide to Critical Legal Studies* (Cambridge, Mass.: Harvard University Press, 1987), summarizing the criticisms of standard legal discourse by these left scholars. See also David Kairys, ed., *The Politics of Law* (New York: Pantheon, 1982); Duncan Kennedy and Karl Klare, "A Bibliography of Critical Legal Studies," 94 *Yale Law Journal* 461 (1984); Critical Legal Studies Symposium, 36 *Stanford Law Review* 1 (1984). The lack of centrality of a critique of gender to this group's critique of law and society (indeed its lack of encounter with the real world in general) makes this school less useful to theory than it might otherwise be. The olympian conceptual discourse of Roberto Unger, *The Critical Legal Studies Movement* (Cambridge, Mass.: Harvard University Press, 1986), for example, does not advance any substantive theory of power (class or gender) as a basis for his criticisms of the formalism and objectivism of mainstream legal discourse. It is entirely unclear, as a result, just what is at stake in social hierarchy; that is, how and in what way some are concretely benefited, hence enforce and hold onto their position, while others are concretely deprived, hence have an interest in change but may be systematically terrorized and despairing—all in ways that are fundamental to the relation between law and society, the social nature of the state, and legal thinking. Some of the concepts and comments of Critical Legal Studies, such as the "interpenetrated" nature of state and society, are useful. See Kelman, pp. 258–262. Others, such as the "indeterminacy" of law, are less useful for those for whom law is all too determinate. For one attempt within this tradition, see Clare Dalton, "An Essay in the Deconstruction of Contract Law," 94 *Yale Law Journal* 997 (1985).

19. Each of these issues is discussed in detail in later chapters in this section.

20. Recent work attempting to criticize and yet rehabilitate the liberal state, such as Bruce Ackerman, *Social Justice in the Liberal State* (New Haven: Yale University Press, 1980), does not solve these problems. Ackerman, for example, does not question the social sources and sites of power, but only its distribution.

21. Klare, "Law-Making as Praxis"; Judith Shklar, *Legalism* (Cambridge, Mass.: Harvard University Press, 1964).

22. Scholars of power in its political aspect traditionally analyze legitimated physical force. Thus, the organization called "government," the science of which is political science, after Weber became that which successfully upholds its claim to regulate exclusively the legitimate use of physical force in a physical territory; Robert A. Dahl, *Modern Political Analysis* (Englewood Cliffs, N.J.: Prentice-Hall, 1976), p. 3. (See Max Weber, *Theory of Social and Economic Organization* [New York: Free Press of Glencoe, 1957], p. 154.) Dahl and C. E. Lindblom use "control" in a similar way: "In loose language, A controls the responses of B if A's acts cause B to respond in a definite way"; *Politics, Economics, and Welfare* (New York: Harper & Brothers, 1953), p. 94. Pluralist theorists of power have been critical of treating power as a lump in a zero-sum game: you either have it or you don't. Still, for them, it has to do with getting what one wants, with rewards and deprivations, with A getting B to do something A wants independent of what B wants, either from A telling B or from B anticipating what A wants. "A power relation, actual or potential, is an actual or potential causal relation between the preferences of an actor regarding an outcome and the outcome itself"; Jack H. Nagel, *A Descriptive Analysis of Power* (New Haven: Yale University Press, 1975), p. 29. Because he wants it, it happens. On other causal aspects, see Herbert A. Simon, "Notes on the Observation and Measurement of Political Power," *Journal of Politics* 15 (1953): 500–516. Carl J. Friedrich similarly formulates a "rule of anticipated reactions": "if A's desire for X causes B to attempt to bring about X"; *Constitutional Government and Democracy* (New York: Harper & Brothers, 1937), pp. 16–18. According to Dahl, "A has power over B to the extent that he can get B to do something that B would not otherwise do"; Robert A. Dahl, "A Critique of the Ruling Elite Model," in *Political Power,* ed. Roderick Bell, David Edwards, and Harrison Wagner (New York: Free Press, 1969), p. 80. See also Nelson Polsby, *Community Power and Political Theory* (New Haven: Yale University Press, 1962), and R. Dahl, "Power," *International Encyclopedia of the Social Sciences,* vol. 12 (New York: Macmillan, 1968), 405–415. These formulations, while envisioning a somewhat atomistic and individuated social world and a discrete set of decisional interactions, nevertheless do characterize many of the behaviors claimed by feminists as exhibiting power relations between women and men.

   Other concepts of power urged by critics of the traditional approaches capture further dimensions of male power as a political system, emphasizing the more structural, contextual, tacit, and relational dimensions of power. See, e.g., Peter Bachrach and Morton Baratz, "Two Faces of Power," in Bell, Edwards, and Wagner, *Political Power,* p. 94. To these facets, Steven Lukes adds control over agenda, latent as well as observable conflict, and objective as well as subjective interests, emphasizing the "sheer weight of institutions" over explicit decisions; *Power: A Radical Analysis* (London: Macmillan, 1974), p. 18. These concepts also characterize gender relations as power, hence political, relations.

   Given the heated disagreements among these men, it is remarkable the extent to which Robert Dahl is correct in characterizing them all when he observes that political science (which is the study of politics, which is, inter alia, about power) has defined the man/woman division outside its confines, because it is seen to relate to "ancient and persistent biological and physiological drives, needs and wants . . . to satisfy drives for sexual gratification, love, security and respect are insistent and primordial needs. The means of satisfying them quickly and concretely generally lie outside political life"; *Modern Political Analysis*, pp. 103–104. In other words, because the subordination of women is seen as universal and natural, it is not seen as a system of domination, hence a system of power, hence as political at all.

23. Harold D. Lasswell and Abraham Kaplan, *Power and Society* (New Haven: Yale University Press, 1950), pp. xiv, 240.

24. Dahl, *Modern Political Analysis*, p. 3. See also Dahl and Lindblom, *Politics, Economics, and Welfare*. Of course, this is not to say that power is all there is to politics.

25. Kate Millett, *Sexual Politics* (Garden City, N.Y.: Doubleday, 1970), p. 31.

26. See Susan Rae Peterson, "Coercion and Rape: The State as a Male Protection Racket," in *Feminism and Philosophy*, ed. Mary Vetterling-Braggin, Frederick A. Elliston, and Jane English (Totowa, N.J.: Littlefield, Adams, 1977), pp. 360–371; Janet Rifkin, "Toward a Theory of Law and Patriarchy," 3 *Harvard Women's Law Journal* 83–96 (Spring 1980). Additional work of interest on this subject includes Sherry B. Ortner, "The Virgin and the State," *Feminist Studies* 4 (October 1978): 19–36; Viana Muller, "The Formation of the State and the Oppression of Women: Some Theoretical Considerations and a Case Study in England and Wales," *Review of Radical Political Economics* 9 (Fall 1977): 7–21; Irene Silverblatt, "Andean Women in the Inca Empire," *Feminist Studies* 4 (October 1978): 37–61; Karen Sacks, "State Bias and Women's Status," *American Anthropologist* 78 (September 1976): 565–569.

27. Herbert Wechsler, "Toward Neutral Principles of Constitutional Law," 73 *Harvard Law Review* 1 (1959), though a defense of legalized racism, is taken as axiomatic.

28. Peter Gabel, "Reification in Legal Reasoning" (Mimeograph, New College Law School, San Francisco, 1980), p. 3.

29. Shklar, *Legalism*, p. 1.

30. Rawls's "original position," for instance, is a version of my objective standpoint; John Rawls, *A Theory of Justice* (Cambridge, Mass.: The Belknap Press of Harvard University Press, 1971). Not only apologists for the liberal state, but also some of its most trenchant critics see a real distinction between the rule of law and absolute arbitrary force; E. P. Thompson, *Whigs and Hunters: The Origin of the Black Act* (New York: Pantheon Book, 1975), pp. 258–269. Douglas Hay argues that making and enforcing certain acts as illegal reinforces a structure of subordination; D. Hay et. al., eds., *Albion's Fatal Tree: Crime and Society in Eighteenth-Century England* (New York: Pantheon, 1975), pp. 17–31. This seems particularly apparent for criminal law. Michael D. A. Freeman applies this argument to domestic battery of women; "Violence against Women: Does

the Legal System Provide Solutions or Itself Constitute the Problem?" (Mimeograph, Madison, Wis., 1980), p. 12 n. 161.

31. Laurence Tribe, "Constitution as Point of View" (Mimeograph, Harvard Law School, 1982), p. 13.

32. Madeleine Gagnon, "Body I," in *New French Feminisms,* ed. Elaine Marks and Isabelle de Courtivron (Amherst: University of Massachusetts Press, 1980), p. 180. The mirror trope has served as metaphor for the epistemological/political reality of objectification in feminist work. "Into the room of the dressing where the walls are covered with mirrors. Where mirrors are like eyes of men, and the women reflect the judgments of mirrors"; Susan Griffin, *Woman and Nature: The Roaring inside Her* (New York: Harper & Row, 1978), p. 155. "She did suffer, the witch / trying to peer round the looking / glass, she forgot / someone was in the way"; Michelène, "Réflexion," quoted in Sheila Rowbotham, *Woman's Consciousness, Man's World* (Harmondsworth: Penguin, 1973), p. 2; see also ibid., pp. 26–29, and Mary Daly, *Beyond God the Father: Toward a Philosophy of Women's Liberation* (Boston: Beacon Press, 1973), pp. 195, 197. Virginia Woolf wrote the figure around ("So I reflected . . ."), remarking "the necessity that women so often are to men" of serving as a looking glass in which a man can "see himself at breakfast and at dinner at least twice the size he really is." Notice the doubled sexual/gender meaning: "Whatever may be their use in civilized societies, mirrors are essential to all violent and heroic action. That is why Napoleon and Mussolini both insist so emphatically upon the inferiority of women, for if they were not inferior, they would cease to enlarge"; *A Room of One's Own* (New York: Harcourt, Brace & World, 1969), p. 36.

33. Olmstead v. U.S., 277 U.S. 438, 478 (1928) (Brandeis J. dissenting).

34. Alexander M. Bickel, *The Least Dangerous Branch: The Supreme Court at the Bar of Politics* (New Haven: Yale University Press, 1986).

35. Isaiah Berlin, "Two Concepts of Liberty," in *Four Essays on Liberty* (London: Oxford University Press, 1969), pp. 121–122.

36. Lochner v. New York, 198 U.S. 45 (1905). Bickel, *The Least Dangerous Branch,* and others have argued for judicial restraint on many grounds. This is my interpretation of the reality that gave this view the preeminence it has attained.

37. Muller v. Oregon, 208 U.S. 412 (1908).

38. West Coast Hotel v. Parrish, 300 U.S. 379, 399 (1937). Cass Sunstein's insightful analysis of Lochner is extremely helpful. See "Lochner's Legacy," 87 *Columbia Law Review* 873 (1987). A similar set of perceptions underlies Owen Fiss, "Why the State?" 100 *Harvard Law Review* 781 (1987).

39. Judith A. Baer, *The Chains of Protection: The Judicial Response to Women's Labor Legislation* (Westport, Conn.: Greenwood Press, 1978); Clara M. Beyer, *History of Labor Legislation for Women in Three States,* U.S. Department of Labor, Women's Bureau, Bulletin no. 66 (Washington, D.C., 1929). See J. Landes, "The Effect of State Maximum-Hours Laws on the Employment of Women in 1920," *Journal of Political Economy* 88 (1980): 476. In international perspective, see Tove Stang Dahl, *Women's Law* (Oslo: Norwegian University Press, 1987), p. 94.

40. West Coast Hotel v. Parrish, 300 U.S. 379 (1937), overruled the previous rejection of minimum wage laws for women (Adkins v. Children's Hospital, 261 U.S. 525 [1923]), finding a minimum wage for women reasonable because the state has a special interest in protecting women from exploitive work contracts because the health of women "becomes an object of public interest and care in order to preserve the strength and vigor of the race" (p. 394). It is thought that this opened the door for later upholding of the Fair Labor Standards Act under constitutional attack in U.S. v. Darby, 312 U.S. 100 (1940). *West Coast Hotel* was also used to uphold state constitutional amendments that make it unlawful to deny employment on the basis of union membership. American Federation of Labor v. American Sash and Door Co., 335 U.S. 538 (1949). See also Lincoln Federal Labor Union v. Northwestern Iron and Metal Co., 335 U.S. 525, 536 (1948) ("that wages and hours can be fixed by law is no longer doubted since West Coast Hotel").

41. For an excellent discussion of this history, see Mary E. Becker, "From Muller v. Oregon to Fetal Vulnerability Policies," 63 *University of Chicago Law Review* 1219 (1986).

42. See, in a different key, Michael Sandel, *Liberalism and the Limits of Justice* (Cambridge: Cambridge University Press, 1982): "The idealist metaphysic, for all its moral and political advantage, cedes too much to the transcendent, and in positing a noumenal realm wins for justice its primacy at the cost of denying it its human situation" (p. 13).

43. Johnnie Tillmon, "Welfare Is a Women's Issue," *Liberation News Service,* February 26, 1972; reprinted in Rosalyn Baxandall, Linda Gordon, and Susan Reverby, eds., *America's Working Women* (New York: Random House, 1976), pp. 355–358.

44. Sexual harassment, designed in pursuit of the jurisprudential approach argued here, is an exception. So is a recent decision by the Ninth Circuit, Watkins v. Army, 837 F.2d 1429 (9th Cir. 1988), which holds that to deprive gays of military employment on the basis of homosexual status is a violation of the Equal Protection Clause.

45. Chapter 12 provides citations and fuller discussion of this argument.

46. Charles Tilly, ed. "Western State-Making and Theories of Political Transformation," in *The Formation of National States in Western Europe* (Princeton: Princeton University Press, 1975), p. 638.

47. John L. Austin, *The Province of Jurisprudence Determined* (New York: Noonday Press, 1954).

48. H. L. A. Hart, *The Concept of Law* (London: Oxford University Press, 1961).

49. Ronald Dworkin, *Law's Empire* (Cambridge, Mass.: Harvard University Press, 1986). The task of this work is to justify the coercive power of the state through an account of authoritative interpretation which disposes of disagreements on the meaning of laws. The proposed solution is "law as integrity," which is "about principle" (p. 221).

50. This is how Bobbio describes Marx's particular orginality; "Is There a Marxist Theory of the State?" p. 15.

## 9. *Rape: On Coercion and Consent*

1. W. LaFave and A. Scott, *Substantive Criminal Law* (St. Paul: West, 1986), sec. 5.11 (pp. 688–689); R. M. Perkins and R. N. Boyce, *Criminal Law* (Mineola, N.Y.: Foundation Press, 1980), p. 210.

2. One component of Sec. 213.0 of the Model Penal Code (Philadelphia: American Law Institute, 1980) defines rape as sexual intercourse with a female not the wife of the perpetrator, "with some penetration however slight." Most states follow. New York requires penetration (sec. 130.00 [1]). Michigan's gender-neutral sexual assault statute includes penetration by objects (sec. 750.520 a[h]; 720.520[b]). The 1980 Annotation to Model Penal Code (Official Draft and Revised Comments, sec. 213.1[d]) questions and discusses the penetration requirement at 346–348. For illustrative case law, see Liptroth v. State, 335 So.2d 683 (Ala. Crim. App. 1976), *cert. denied* 429 U.S. 963 (1976); State v. Kidwell, 556 P.2d 20, 27 Ariz. App. 466 (Ariz. Ct. App. 1976); People v. O'Neal, 50 Ill. App. 3d 900, 365 N.E. 2d 1333 (Ill. App. Ct. 1977); Commonwealth v. Usher, 371 A.2d 995 (Pa. Super. Ct. 1977); Commonwealth v. Grassmyer, 237 Pa. Super. 394, 352 A.2d 178 (Pa. Super. Ct. 1975) (statutory rape conviction reversed because defendant's claim that five-year-old child's vaginal wound was inflicted with a broomstick could not be disproved and commonwealth could therefore not prove requisite penetration; indecent assault conviction sustained). Impotence is sometimes a defense and can support laws that prevent charging underage boys with rape or attempted rape; Foster v. Commonwealth, 31 S.E. 503, 96 Va. 306 (1896) (boy under fourteen cannot be guilty of attempt to commit offense that he is legally assumed physically impotent to perpetrate).

3. In the manner of many socialist-feminist adaptations of marxian categories to women's situation, to analyze sexuality as property short-circuits analysis of rape as male sexuality and presumes rather than develops links between sex and class. Concepts of property need to be rethought in light of sexuality as a form of objectification. In some ways, for women legally to be considered property would be an improvement, although it is not recommended.

4. For contrast between the perspectives of the victims and the courts, see Rusk v. State, 43 Md. App. 476, 406 A.2d 624 (Md. Ct. Spec. App. 1979) (*en banc*), *rev'd,* 289 Md. 230, 424 A.2d 720 (1981); Gonzales v. State, 516 P.2d 592 (1973).

5. Susan Brownmiller, *Against Our Will: Men, Women, and Rape* (New York: Simon and Schuster, 1975), p. 15.

6. Diana E. H. Russell, *The Politics of Rape: The Victim's Perspective* (New York: Stein & Day, 1977); Andrea Medea and Kathleen Thompson, *Against Rape* (New York: Farrar, Straus and Giroux, 1974); Lorenne M. G. Clark and Debra Lewis, *Rape: The Price of Coercive Sexuality* (Toronto: Women's Press, 1977); Susan Griffin, "Rape: The All-American Crime," *Ramparts,* September 1971, pp. 26–35. Ti-Grace Atkinson connects rape with "the institution of sexual intercourse," *Amazon Odyssey: The First Collection of Writings by the Political*

*Pioneer of the Women's Movement* (New York: Links Books, 1974), pp. 19 ?3 Kalamu ya Salaam, "Rape: A Radical Analysis from the African-American Perspective, "in *Our Women Keep Our Skies from Falling* (New Orleans: Nkombo, 1980), pp. 25–40.

7. Racism is clearly everyday life. Racism in the United States, by singling out Black men for allegations of rape of white women, has helped obscure the fact that it is men who rape women, disproportionately women of color.

8. Pamela Foa, "What's Wrong with Rape?" in *Feminism and Philosophy,* ed. Mary Vetterling-Braggin, Frederick A. Elliston, and Jane English (Totowa, N.J.: Littlefield, Adams, 1977), pp. 347–359; Michael Davis, "What's So Bad about Rape?" (Paper presented at the annual meeting of the Academy of Criminal Justice Sciences, Louisville, Ky., March 1982). "Since we would not want to say that there is anything morally wrong with sexual intercourse per se, we conclude that the wrongness of rape rests with the matter of the woman's consent"; Carolyn M. Shafer and Marilyn Frye, "Rape and Respect," in Vetterling-Braggin, Elliston, and English, *Feminism and Philosophy,* p. 334. "Sexual contact is not inherently harmful, insulting or provoking. Indeed, ordinarily it is something of which we are quite fond. The difference is [that] ordinary sexual intercourse is more or less consented to while rape is not"; Davis, "What's So Bad?" p. 12.

9. Liegh Bienen, "Rape III—National Developments in Rape Reform Legislation," 6 *Women's Rights Law Reporter* 170 (1980). See also Camille LeGrande, "Rape and Rape Laws: Sexism in Society and Law," 61 *California Law Review* 919 (May 1973).

10. People v. Samuels, 58 Cal. Rptr. 439, 447 (1967).

11. Julia R. Schwendinger and Herman Schewendinger, *Rape and Inequality* (Berkeley: Sage Library of Social Research, 1983), p. 44; K. Polk, "Rape Reform and Criminal Justice Processing," *Crime and Delinquency* 31 (April 1985): 191–205. "What can be concluded about the achievement of the underlying goals of the rape reform movement? . . . If a major goal is to increase the probability of convictions, then the results are slight at best . . . or even negligible" (p. 199) (California data). See also P. Bart and P. O'Brien, *Stopping Rape: Successful Survival Strategies* (Elmsford, N.Y.: Pergamon, 1985), pp. 129–131.

12. See State v. Alston, 310 N.C. 399, 312 S.E.2d 470 (1984) and discussion in Susan Estrich, *Real Rape* (Cambridge: Harvard University Press, 1987), pp. 60–62.

13. Note, "Forcible and Statutory Rape: An Exploration of the Operation and Objectives of the Consent Standard," 62 *Yale Law Journal* 55 (1952).

14. A similar analysis of sexual harassment suggests that women have such "power" only so long as they behave according to male definitions of female desirability, that is, only so long as they accede to the definition of their sexuality (hence, themselves, as gender female) on male terms. Women have this power, in other words, only so long as they remain powerless.

15. See Comment, "Rape and Battery between Husband and Wife," 6 *Stanford Law*

*Review* 719 (1954). On rape of prostitutes, see, e.g., People v. McClure, 42 Ill. App. 952, 356 N.E. 2d 899 (1st Dist. 3d Div. 1976) (on indictment for rape and armed robbery of prostitute where sex was admitted to have occurred, defendant acquitted of rape but "guilty of robbing her while armed with a knife"); Magnum v. State, 1 Tenn. Crim. App. 155, 432 S.W.2d 497 (Tenn. Crim. App. 1968) (no conviction for rape; conviction for sexual violation of age of consent overturned on ground that failure to instruct jury to determine if complainant was "a bawd, lewd or kept female" was reversible error; "A bawd female is a female who keeps a house of prostitution, and conducts illicit intercourse. A lewd female is one given to unlawful indulgence of lust, either for sexual indulgence or profit . . . A kept female is one who is supported and kept by a man for his own illicit intercourse"; complainant "frequented the Blue Moon Tavern; she had been there the night before . . . she kept company with . . . a married man separated from his wife . . . There is some proof of her bad reputation for truth and veracity"). Johnson v. State, 598 S.W. 2d 803 (Tenn. Crim. App. 1979) (unsuccessful defense to charge of rape that "even [if] technically a prostitute can be raped . . . the act of the rape itself was no trauma whatever to this type of unchaste woman"); People v. Gonzales, 96 Misc. 2d 639, 409 N.Y.S. 2d 497 (Crm. Crt. N.Y. City 1978) (prostitute can be raped if "it can be proven beyond a reasonable doubt that she revoked her consent prior to sexual intercourse because the defendant . . . used the coercive force of a pistol).

16. People v. Liberta, 64 N.Y. 2d 152, 474 N.E.2d 567, 485 N.Y.S 2d 207 (1984) (marital rape recognized, contrary precedents discussed). For a summary of the current state of the marital exemption, see Joanne Schulman, "State-by-State Information on Marital Rape Exemption Laws," in Diana E. H. Russell, *Rape in Marriage* (New York: Macmillan, 1982), pp. 375–381; Patricia Searles and Ronald Berger, "The Current Status of Rape Reform Legislation: An Examination of State Statutes," 10 *Women's Rights Law Reporter* 25 (1987).

17. On "social interaction as an element of consent" in a voluntary social companion context, see Model Penal Code, sec. 213.1. "The prior social interaction is an indicator of consent in addition to actor's and victim's behavioral interaction during the commission of the offense"; Wallace Loh, "Q: What Has Reform of Rape Legislation Wrought? A: Truth in Criminal Labeling, *Journal of Social Issues* 37, no. 1 (1981). 47.

18. E.g., People v. Burnham, 176 Cal. App. 3d 1134, 222 Cal. Rptr. 630 (Cal. App. 1986).

19. Diana E. H. Russell and Nancy Howell, "The Prevalence of Rape in the United States Revisited," *Signs: Journal of Women in Culture and Society* 8 (Summer 1983): 668–695; and D. Russell, *The Secret Trauma: Incestuous Abuse of Women and Girls* (New York: Basic Books, 1986).

20. Pauline Bart found that women were more likely to be raped—that is, less able to stop a rape in progress—when they knew their assailant, particularly when they had a prior or current sexual relationship; "A Study of Women Who Both

Were Raped and Avoided Rape," *Journal of Social Issues* 37 (1981): 132. See also Linda Belden, "Why Women Do Not Report Sexual Assault" (Portland, Ore.: City of Portland Public Service Employment Program, Portland Women's Crisis Line, March 1979); Menachem Amir, *Patterns in Forcible Rape* (Chicago: University of Chicago Press, 1971), pp. 229–252.

21. Answer Brief for Plaintiff-Appellee, People v. Brown, Sup. Ct. Colo., Case No. 81SA102 (1981): 10.

22. Note, "Forcible and Statutory Rape," p. 55.

23. La. Rev. Stat. 14.42. Delaware law requires that the victim resist, but "only to the extent that it is reasonably necessary to make the victim's refusal to consent known to the defendant"; 11 Del. Code 761(g). See also Sue Bessmer, *The Laws of Rape* (New York: Praeger, 1984).

24. See People v. Thompson, 117 Mich. App. 522, 524, 324 N.W. 2d 22, 24 (Mich. App. 1982); People v. Hearn, 100 Mich. App. 749, 300 N.W. 2d 396 (Mich. App. 1980).

25. See Carol Pateman, "Women and Consent," *Political Theory* 8 (May 1980): 149–168: "Consent as ideology cannot be distinguished from habitual acquiescence, assent, silent dissent, submission, or even enforced submission. Unless refusal of consent or withdrawal of consent are real possibilities, we can no longer speak of 'consent' in any genuine sense . . . Women exemplify the individuals whom consent theorists declared are incapable of consenting. Yet, simultaneously, women have been presented as always consenting, and their explicit non-consent has been treated as irrelevant or has been reinterpreted as 'consent' " (p. 150).

26. Brownmiller, *Against Our Will*, p. 5.

27. Shafer and Frye, "Rape and Respect," p. 334.

28. See R. Emerson Dobash and Russell Dobash, *Violence against Wives: A Case against the Patriarchy* (New York: Free Press, 1979), pp. 14–21.

29. On the cycle of battering, see Lenore Walker, *The Battered Woman* (New York: Harper & Row, 1979).

30. Samois, *Coming to Power* (Palo Alto, Calif.: Alyson Publications, 1983).

31. If accounts of sexual violation are a form of sex, as argued in Chapter 11, victim testimony in rape cases is a form of live oral pornography.

32. This is apparently true of undetected as well as convicted rapists. Samuel David Smithyman's sample, composed largely of the former, contained self-selected respondents to his ad, which read: "Are you a rapist? Reasearchers Interviewing Anonymously by Phone to Protect Your Identity. Call . . ." Presumably those who chose to call defined their acts as rapes, at least at the time of responding; "The Undetected Rapist" (Ph.D. diss., Claremont Graduate School, 1978), pp. 54–60, 63–76, 80–90, 97–107.

33. Nancy Gager and Cathleen Schurr, *Sexual Assault: Confronting Rape in America* (New York: Grosset & Dunlap, 1976), p. 244.

34. Susan Estrich proposes this; *Real Rape*, pp. 102–103. Her lack of inquiry into social determinants of perspective (such as pornography) may explain her faith in reasonableness as a legally workable standard for raped women.

35. See Director of Public Prosecutions v. Morgan, 2 All E.R.H.L. 347 (1975) [England]; Pappajohn v. The Queen, 111 D.L.R. 3d 1 (1980) [Canada]; People v. Mayberry, 542 P.2d 1337 (Cal. 1975).

36. Richard H. S. Tur, "Rape: Reasonableness and Time," 3 *Oxford Journal of Legal Studies* 432, 441 (Winter 1981). Tur, in the context of the *Morgan* and *Pappajohn* cases, says the "law ought not to be astute to equate wickedness and wishful, albeit mistaken, thinking" (p. 437). Rape victims are typically less concerned with wickedness than with injury.

37. See Silke Vogelmann-Sine, Ellen D. Ervin, Reenie Christensen, Carolyn H. Warmsun, and Leonard P. Ullmann, "Sex Differences in Feelings Attributed to a Woman in Situations Involving Coercion and Sexual Advances," *Journal of Personality* 47 (September 1979): 429–430.

38. Estrich has this problem in *Real Rape.*

39. E. Donnerstein, "Pornography: Its Effect on Violence against Women," in *Pornography and Sexual Aggression,* ed. N. Malamuth and E. Donnerstein (Orlando, Fla.: Academic Press, 1984), pp. 65–70. Readers who worry that this could become an argument for defending accused rapists should understand that the reality to which it points already provides a basis for defending accused rapists. The solution is to attack the pornography directly, not to be silent about its exonerating effects, legal or social, potential or actual.


## 10. Abortion: On Public and Private

1. See, e.g., D. H. Regan, "Rewriting Roe v. Wade," 77 *Michigan Law Review* 1569 (1979), in which the Good Samaritan happens upon the fetus.

2. As of 1973, ten states that had made abortion a crime had exceptions for rape and incest; at least three had exceptions for rape only. Many of these exceptions were based on Model Penal Code 230.3 (Proposed Official Draft 1962), quoted in Doe v. Bolton, 410 U.S. 179, 205–207, App. B (1973). References to states with incest and rape exceptions can be found in Roe v. Wade, 410 U.S. 113 n. 37 (1973). Some versions of the Hyde Amendment, which prohibits use of public money to fund abortions, have contained exceptions for cases of rape or incest. All require immediate reporting of the incident.

3. See Kristin Luker, *Taking Chances: Abortion and the Decision Not to Contracept* (Berkeley: University of California Press, 1975).

4. Roe v. Wade, 410 U.S. 113 (1973).

5. Griswold v. Connecticut, 381 U.S. 479 (1965).

6. H. L. v. Matheson, 450 U.S. 398, 435 (1981) (Marshall, J., dissenting).

7. Roe. v. Wade, 410 U.S. 113, 153 (1973) ("a woman's decision whether or not to terminate her pregnancy"); Harris v. McRae, 448 U.S. 297 (1980) (referring to Maher v. Roe, 432 U.S. 464, 474 [1976], on no state responsibility to remove non-state-controlled obstacles).

8. Deshaney v. Winnebago County Dep't of Social Services, 109 S. Ct. 988

(1989) (no due process "liberty" interest created by state child protection statutes and enforcement, in case of permanent injury to abused child of which agency was aware).

9. T. Gerety, "Redefining Privacy," 12 *Harvard Civil Rights–Civil Liberties Law Review* 233, 236 (1977).

10. Kenneth I. Karst, "The Freedom of Intimate Association," 89 *Yale Law Journal* 624 (1980); "Developments—The Family," 93 *Harvard Law Review* 1157 (1980); Doe v. Commonwealth Att'y, 403 F. Supp. 1199 (E.D. Va. 1975) *aff'd without opinion,* 425 U.S. 901 (1976); but cf. People v. Onofre, 51 N.Y. 2d 476 (1980), *cert. denied,* 451 U.S. 987 (1981). The issue was finally decided, for the time, in Bowers v. Hardwick, 478 U.S. 186 (1986) (statute criminalizing consensual sodomy does not violate right to privacy).

11. Tom Grey, "Eros, Civilization, and the Burger Court," 43 *Law and Contemporary Problems* 83 (1980), was helpful to me in developing this analysis.

12. *Abele v. Markle* originally included an allegation that prohibiting abortion discriminated against women in the basis of sex. 452 F. 2d 1121, 1123 (1971). The Second Circuit held instead that prohibiting all abortions was unconstitutional under the Ninth Amendment and the due process clause of the Fourteenth Amendment. Schulman v. N.Y. City Health and Hospitals Corporation, 70 Misc. 2d 1093 (1st Dept. 1973), held that a requirement of identifying women who have abortions publicly discriminates against married and single women by denying them equal protection of the laws as to their right to privacy. This gives women rights but not on the basis of sex. Klein v. Nassau County Medical Center, 347 F. Supp. 496 (1972), won state Medicaid funding for indigent women for medically necessary abortions on grounds that its denial "subjected [indigent women] to coercion to bear children which they do not wish to bear and no other women similarly situated are so coerced" (at 500). This equal protection ruling was thus based on class, not on sex.

13. See Adrienne Rich, *Of Woman Born: Motherhood as Experience and Institution* (New York: Norton, 1976), chap. 3: "The child that I carry for nine months can be defined *neither* as me or as not-me" (p. 64).

14. Kristen Booth Glen, "Abortion in the Courts: A Lay Woman's Historical Guide to the New Disaster Area," *Feminist Studies* 4 (February 1978): 1.

15. Judith Jarvis Thomson, "A Defense of Abortion," *Philosophy and Public Affairs* 1 (1971): 47.

16. Andrea Dworkin, *Right-wing Women* (New York: Perigee, 1983). See also Friedrich Engels on the benefits of removing private housekeeping into social industry, Chapter 2. Note that the Playboy Foundation has supported abortion rights from day one and continues to, even with shrinking disposable funds, on a level of priority comparable to its opposition to censorship.

17. Johnnie Tillmon, "Welfare Is a Women's Issue," *Liberation News Service,* February 26, 1972; reprinted in Rosalyn Baxandall, Linda Gordon, and Susan Reverby, eds., *America's Working Women: A Documentary History, 1600 to the Present* (New York: Random House, 1976), pp. 355–358.

18. See H. L. v. Matheson, 450 U.S. 398 (1981); Bellotti v. Baird, 443 U.S. 622

(1979); but see Planned Parenthood of Central Missouri v. Danforth, 428 U.S. 52 (1976). Most attempts to regulate the right out of existence have been defeated; City of Akron v. Akron Reproductive Health Center, 462 U.S. 416 (1983). More recently, see Reproductive Health Service v. Webster, 851 F.2d 1071 (8th Cir. 1988), *U.S. app. pndg.*

19. A more affirmative vision of the possibilities of *Roe v. Wade* was held by litigators after the decision. See J. Goodman, R. C. Schoenbrod, and N. Stearns, "Doe and Roe: Where Do We Go from Here?" 1 *Women's Rights Law Reporter* 20, 27 (1973). Stearns remarks that "the right to privacy is a passive right. The right to privacy says that the state can't interfere. The right to liberty, particularly founded as it was in the Court's opinion on all of the grave things that happen to a woman's life if she doesn't get an abortion, would seem to imply that the state has some kind of affirmative obligation to ensure that a woman can exercise that right to liberty. That presumably will have very important implications for access questions like Medicaid, for example." Unfortunately, their view that *Roe* guaranteed women a right to abortion as a protected liberty, which is affirmative, rather than as protected privacy, which is passive, did not prevail in later cases.

20. Herbert Marcuse, "Repressive Tolerance," in *A Critique of Pure Tolerance,* ed. Robert Paul Wolff, J. Barrington Moore, and Herbert Marcuse (Boston: Beacon Press, 1965), p. 91.

21. Adrienne Rich, "Conditions for Work: The Common World of Women," in *Working It Out: Twenty-three Women Writers, Artists, Scientists, and Scholars Talk Out Their Lives and Work,* ed. Sara Ruddick and Pamela Daniels (New York: Pantheon Books, 1977), p. xiv.

22. Schlomo Avineri, *The Social and Political Thought of Karl Marx* (London: Cambridge University Press, 1969).

23. Planned Parenthood of Central Missouri v. Danforth, 428 U.S. 52, 69 (1975) ("The state cannot delegate to a spouse a veto power which the state itself is absolutely and totally prohibited from exercising during the first trimester of pregnancy").

24. S. Warren and L. Brandeis, "The Right to Privacy," 4 *Harvard Law Review* 205 (1980). But note that the right of privacy under some state constitutions has been held to include funding for abortions; Committee to Defend Reproductive Rights v. Meyers, 29 Cal. 3d 252 (1981); Moe v. Secretary of Admin. and Finance, 417 N.E.2d 387 (Mass. 1981).

25. Examination of the legal record in *Roe v. Wade* and *Harris v. McRae* reveals that little legal attempt was made to get beyond the gender neutrality of privacy doctrine to frame the abortion issue directly as one of inequality of the sexes—that is, as an issue of sex discrimination. The original complaint in *Roe v. Wade* contained a cause of action for denial of equal protection of the laws, First Amended Complaint CA-3-3690-B (N.D. Tex., Apr. 22, 1970) IV, 5. But the inequality complained of did not, as it developed, refer to inequality on the basis of sex. Oral argument in the district court appears to have been confined largely to the right to privacy. Opinion of the District Court, Civil

Action No. CA-3-3690-B and 3-3691-C (June 17, 1970) 116 n.7. In the U.S. Supreme Court, the Center for Constitutional Rights filed an amicus brief arguing that criminal abortion statutes like those of Texas and Georgia "violate the most basic Constitutional rights of women." "[It] is the woman who bears the disproportionate share of the de jure and de facto burdens and penalties of pregnancy, child birth and child rearing. Thus any statute which denies a woman the right to determine whether she will bear those burdens denies her the equal protection of the laws." Brief *Amicus Curiae* on behalf of New Women Lawyers, Women's Health and Abortion Project, Inc., National Abortion Action Coalition 6 (Aug. 2, 1971). The brief assumes that sex is equal and voluntary, even if pregnancy may not be: "Man and woman have equal responsibility for the act of sexual intercourse. Should the woman accidentally become pregnant, against her will, however, she endures in many instances the entire burden or 'punishment' " (p. 26); "And it is not sufficient to say that the woman 'chose' to have sexual intercourse, for she did not choose to become pregnant" (p. 31).

The complaint in *Harris v. McRae* alleged discrimination "based on poverty, race and minority status, which deprives and punishes the plaintiff class of women in violation of due process and equal protection of the law." Plaintiffs' and Proposed Intervenors' Amended Complaint, McRae v. Califano, 74 Civ. 1804 (JFD) Jan. 5, 1977, para. 74. It does not allege discrimination on the basis of sex. Only one brief argues sex discrimination, and that to argue that since women are *socially* discriminated against on the basis of sex, denying them abortions is an additional hardship, not to make the *legal* argument that not paying for abortions, a state act that hurts only women, is sex discrimination. As framed by NOW, "the plight of indigent women denied medically necessary abortions is exacerbated by the pervasive sex discrimination that impacts especially hard on women in poverty." Brief *Amicus Curiae* for NOW et. al., No. 79–1268 (U.S. Supreme Court, Mar. 18, 1980) 44.

Every social basis for discrimination against women other than the sexual, and every legal basis for discrimination against women other than gender has been used to attempt to support the abortion right. In the United States, with the partial exception of the CCR brief—an effort at once made audacious and impressive and weakened by the fact that sex discrimination by law had just been recognized as unconstitutional—burdens on abortion seem virtually never to have been legally argued as simple sex discrimination.

### 11. *Pornography: On Morality and Politics*

1. Andrea Dworkin, *Pornography: Men Possessing Women* (New York: Perigee, 1981), reviews and demolishes this tradition.
2. To the body of law ably encompassed and annotated by W. B. Lockhart and R. McClure, "Literature, The Law of Obscenity, and the Constitution," 38

*Minnesota Law Review* 295 (1961); and idem, "Censorship of Obscenity," 45 ibid. 5 (1960), I add only the most important cases since then: Stanley v. Georgia, 394 U.S. 557 (1969); U.S. v. Reidel, 402 U.S. 351 (1971); Miller v. California, 413 U.S. 15 (1973); Paris Adult Theatre I v. Slaton, 413 U.S. 49 (1973); Hamling v. U.S., 418 U.S. 87 (1974); Jenkins v. Georgia, 418 U.S. 153 (1974); Splawn v. California, 431 U.S. 595 (1977); Ward v. Illinois, 431 U.S. 767 (1977); Lovisi v. Slayton, 539 F.2d 349 (4th Cir. 1976); U.S. v. 12 200-Ft. Reels of Super 8MM Film, 413 U.S. 123 (1973); Erznoznik v. City of Jacksonville, 422 U.S. 205 (1975); New York v. Ferber, 458 U.S. 747 (1982).

3. "Congress shall make no law . . . abridging the freedom of speech, or of the press . . ." Amendment I, U.S. Constitution (1791). First Amendment absolutism has been the conscience of the First Amendment. Justice Black, at times joined by Justice Douglas, took the position that the Constitution, including the First Amendment, was "absolute." Hugo Black, "The Bill of Rights," 35 *New York University Law Review* 865, 867 (1960); idem, *A Constitutional Faith* (New York: Alfred A. Knopf, 1968); Edmond Cahn, "Justice Black and First Amendment 'Absolutes': A Public Interview," 37 ibid. 549 (1962). For a discussion, see Harry Kalven, "Upon Rereading Mr. Justice Black on the First Amendment," 14 *UCLA Law Review* 428 (1967). For one exchange in the controversy surrounding the "absolute" approach to the First Amendment, as opposed to the "balancing" approach, see, e.g., Wallace Mendelson, "On the Meaning of the First Amendment: Absolutes in the Balance," 50 *California Law Review* 821 (1962); L. Frantz, "The First Amendment in the Balance," 71 *Yale Law Journal* 1424 (1962); idem, "Is the First Amendment Law?—A Reply to Professor Mendelson," 51 *California Law Review* 729 (1963); Wallace Mendelson, "The First Amendment and the Judicial Process: A Reply to Mr. Frantz," 17 *Vanderbilt Law Review* 479 (1964). In the pornography context, see, e.g., Roth v. U.S., 354 U.S. 476, 514 (1957) (Douglas, J., joined by Black, J., dissenting); Smith v. California, 361 U.S. 147, 155 (1959) (Black, J., concurring); Miller v. California, 413 U.S. 15, 37 (1973) (Douglas, J., dissenting). It is not the purpose of this chapter to criticize absolutism as such, but rather to identify and criticize some widely and deeply shared implicit beliefs that underlie both the absolutist view and the more mainstream flexible approaches.

4. Canadian Criminal Code, 1983, Offences Tending to Corrupt Morals, Section 159(1) (c) and (d); People v. Sanger, 222 N.Y. 192 (1918).

5. *The Report of the Commission on Obscenity and Pornography* (Washington, D.C.: U.S. Government Printing Office, 1970) (majority report). Which is not to ignore (a) the widespread criticism from a variety of perspectives of the commission's methodology, e.g., Lane V. Sunderland, *Obscenity: The Court, the Congress and the President's Commission* (Washington, D.C.: American Enterprise Institute for Public Policy Research, 1975); E. Donnerstein, "Pornography Commission Revisited: Aggression—Erotica and Violence against Women," *Journal of Personality and Social Psychology* 39 (1980): 269–277; A. Garry, "Pornography and Respect for Women," *Social Theory and Practice* 4 (Summer

1978); I. Diamond, "Pornography and Repression," *Signs: Journal of Women in Culture and Society* 5 (Summer 1980): 686–701; V. Cline, "Another View: Pornography Effects, the State of the Art," in *Where Do You Draw the Line? An Exploration into Media Violence, Pornography, and Censorship,* ed. V. B. Cline (Provo, Utah: Brigham Young University Press, 1974); P. Bart and M. Jozsa, "Dirty Books, Dirty Films, and Dirty Data," in *Take Back the Night: Women on Pornography,* ed. L. Lederer (New York: William Morrow, 1980), pp. 209–217; (b) the data the commission found and minimized (like the fact that a substantial minority of men were stimulated to aggression by exposure to what the commission studied *(Report of Obscenity Commission,* vol. 8, p. 377) or ignored the significance of (like Mosher's findings on the differential effects of exposure by gender); or (c) the fact that the commission did not focus questions about gender, did its best to eliminate "violence" from its materials (so as not to overlap with the Violence Commission), and propounded unscientific theories like "puritanism" to explain women's negative responses to the materials; or (d) no scientific causality is required to legally validate even an obscenity regulation. The Supreme Court, in an opinion by Chief Justice Burger, stated: "But, it is argued, there is no scientific data which conclusively demonstrate that exposure to obscene materials adversely affects men and women or their society. It is [urged] that, absent such a demonstration, any kind of state regulation is 'impermissible.' We reject this argument. It is not for us to resolve empirical uncertainties underlying state legislation, save in the exceptional case where that legislation plainly impinges upon rights protected by the Constitution itself . . . Although there is no conclusive proof of a connection between antisocial behavior and obscene material, the legislature of Georgia could quite reasonably determine that such a connection does or might exist." Paris Adult Theatre I v. Slaton, 413 U.S. 49, 60–61 (1973).

6. Some of pornography's harm to women is documented in studies. The findings are that exposure to pornography increases normal men's willingness to aggress against women under laboratory conditions; makes both women and men substantially less able to perceive accounts of rape as accounts of rape; makes normal men more closely resemble convicted rapists psychologically; increases all the attitudinal measures that are known to correlate with rape, such as hostility toward women, propensity to rape, condoning rape, and predicting that one would rape or force sex on a woman if one knew one would not get caught; and produces other attitude changes in men like increasing the extent of their trivialization, dehumanization, and objectification of women. Diana E. H. Russell, "Pornography and Rape: A Causal Model," *Political Psychology* 9 (1988): 41–74; idem, "Pornography and Violence: What Does the New Research Say?" in Lederer, *Take Back The Night,* p. 218; N. Malamuth and E. Donnerstein, eds., *Pornography and Sexual Aggression* (Orlando, Fla.: Academic Press, 1984); D. Zillman, *Connection between Sex and Aggression* (Hillsdale, N.J.: Erlbaum, 1984); J. V. P. Check, N. Malamuth, and R. Stille, "Hostility to Women Scale" (Manuscript, York University, Toronto, 1983); E. Donnerstein,

"Pornography: Its Effects on Violence against Women," in Malamuth and Donnerstein, *Pornography and Sexual Aggression,* pp. 53–82; N. Malamuth, "Rape Proclivity among Males," *Journal of Social Issues* 37 (1981): 138–157; N. Malamuth and J. Check, "The Effects of Mass Media Exposure on Acceptance of Violence against Women: A Field Experiment," *Journal of Research in Personality* 15 (1981): 436–446; N. Malamuth and B. Spinner, "A Longitudinal Content Analysis of Sexual Violence in the Best-Selling Erotica Magazines," *Journal of Sex Research* 16 (August 1980): 226–237; D. L. Mosher and H. Katz, "Pornographic Films, Male Verbal Aggression against Women, and Guilt," in *Technical Report of the Commission on Obscenity and Pornography,* vol. 8 (Washington, D.C.: U.S. Government Printing Office, 1971). Also D. Mosher, "Sex Callousness towards Women," in ibid.; D. Zillman and J. Bryant, "Effects of Massive Exposure to Pornography," in Malamuth and Donnerstein, *Pornography and Sexual Aggression,* pp. 115–138; M. McManus, ed., *Final Report of the Attorney General's Commission on Pornography* (Nashville: Rutledge Hill Press, 1986).

7. Jacobellis v. Ohio, 378 U.S. 184, 197 (1964) (Stewart, J., concurring).

8. Justice Stewart is said to have complained that this single line was more quoted and remembered than anything else he ever said.

9. The following are illustrative, not exhaustive: Dworkin, *Pornography;* D. Leidholdt, "Where Pornography Meets Facism," *WIN News,* March 15, 1983, p. 18; G. Steiner, "Night Words: High Pornography and Human Privacy," in *The Case against Pornography,* ed. D. Holbrook (La Salle, Ill: Open Court, 1973); Susan Brownmiller, *Against Our Will: Men, Women, and Rape* (New York: Simon and Schuster, 1975), p. 394; R. Morgan, "Theory and Practice: Pornography and Rape," in *Going Too Far: The Personal Chronicle of a Feminist* (New York: Random House, 1977); Kathleen Barry, *Female Sexual Slavery* (Englewood Cliffs, N.J.: Prentice-Hall, 1979); R. R. Linden, D. R. Pagano, D. E. H. Russell, and S. L. Star, eds., *Against Sadomasochism: A Radical Feminist Analysis* (Palo Alto, Calif.: Frog in the Well, 1982), especially articles by Ti-Grace Atkinson, Judy Butler, Andrea Dworkin, Alice Walker, John Stoltenberg, Audre Lorde, and Susan Leigh Star; Alice Walker, "Coming Apart," in Lederer, *Take Back the Night,* pp. 95–104; and other articles in that volume with the exception of the legal ones; Gore Vidal, "Women's Liberation Meets the Miller-Mailer-Manson Man," in *Homage to Daniel Shays: Collected Essays 1952–1972* (New York: Random House, 1972), pp. 389–402; Linda Lovelace and Michael McGrady, *Ordeal* (New York: Berkley, 1980); Kate Millett, *Sexual Politics* (Garden City, N.Y.: Doubleday, 1977); F. Rush, *The Best-Kept Secret: Sexual Abuse of Children* (Englewood Cliffs, N.J.: Prentice-Hall, 1980). Colloquium, "Violent Pornography: Degradation of Women versus Right of Free Speech," 8 *New York University Review of Law and Social Change* 181 (1978–79), contains both feminist and nonfeminist argument. Also of real interest is Susan Sontag, "The Pornographic Imagination," *Partisan Review* 34 (1967): 181–214.

10. See Chapter 7 for further discussion.

11. Susan Griffin, *Pornography and Silence: Culture's Revenge against Nature* (New York: Harper & Row, 1981).

12. In addition to Dworkin, *Pornography*, see Andrea Dworkin, "The Root Cause," in *Our Blood: Prophesies and Discourses on Sexual Politics* (New York: Harper & Row, 1976), pp. 96–111.

13. The position that pornography is sex—whatever you think of sex, you think of pornography—underlies nearly every treatment of the subject. In particular, nearly every nonfeminist treatment proceeds on the implicit or explicit assumption, argument, criticism, or suspicion that pornography is sexually liberating. See D. H. Lawrence, "Pornography and Censorship," in *Sex, Literature and Censorship*, ed. Harry T. Moore (New York: Viking 1975); Hugh Hefner, "The Playboy Philosophy," pts. 1 and 2, *Playboy*, December 1962, p. 73, and February 1963, p. 10; Henry Miller, "Obscenity and the Law of Reflection," *Tricolor*, 48 (February 1945), reprinted in *The Air Conditioned Nightmare II* (New York: New Directions, 1947), pp. 274, 286; D. English, "The Politics of Porn: Can Feminists Walk the Line?" *Mother Jones*, April 1980, pp. 20–23, 43–44, 48–50; J. B. Elshtain, "The Victim Syndrome: A Troubling Turn in Feminism," *The Progressive*, June 1982, pp. 40–47. For example, "In opposition to the Victorian view that narrowly defines proper sexual function in a rigid way analogous to ideas of excremental regularity and moderation, pornography builds a model of plastic variety and joyful excess in sexuality. In opposition to the sorrowing Catholic dismissal of sexuality as an unfortunate and spirtually superficial concomitant of propagation, pornography affords the alternative idea of the independent status of sexuality as a profound and shattering ecstasy." David A. J. Richards, "Free Speech and Obscenity Law: Toward a Moral Theory of the First Amendment," 123 *University of Pennsylvania Law Review* 45, 81 (1974).

14. The contents of adult bookstores and pornographic movies, the pornographers (who, like all smart pimps, do some form of market research), and the pornography itself confirm that pornography is for men. That women may consume it does not make it any less for men, any more than the observation that men mostly consume pornography means that pornography does not harm women. See also M. Langelan, "The Political Economy of Pornography," *Aegis: Magazine on Ending Violence against Women* 5 (Autumn 1981): 5–7; James Cook, "The X-Rated Economy," *Forbes*, September 18, 1978, p. 18. From personal observation, women tend to avoid pornography as much as possible—which is not all that much, as it turns out.

The "fantasy" and "catharsis" hypotheses, together, assert that poronography cathects sexuality on the level of fantasy fulfillment. The work of Donnerstein, particularly, shows that the opposite is true. The more pornography is viewed, the more pornography—and the more brutal pornography—is both wanted and required for sexual arousal. What occurs is desensitization requiring progressively more potent stimulation, not catharsis. See the works cited in note 9, above, and M. Straus, "Leveling, Civility, and Violence in the Family," *Journal of Marriage and the Family* 36 (1974): 13–29.

15. Lovelace and McGrady, *Ordeal,* provides an account by one coerced pornography victim. See also the brilliant chapter 6, "The Use of Performers in Commercial Pornography," in M. McManus, ed., *Final Report of the Attorney General's Commission on Pornography* (Nashville: Rutledge Hill Press, 1986).

16. Diana E. H. Russell, in a random sample of 930 San Francisco households, found that 10 percent of women had ever "been upset by anyone trying to get you to do what they'd seen in pornographic pictures, movies or books"; *Sexual Exploitation,* pp. 125–127. Obviously, this figure could include only those who knew that the pornography was the source of the sex, which makes it conservative. See also Russell, *Rape in Marriage* (New York: Macmillan, 1982), pp. 83–84 (24 percent of rape victims answered "yes" to the question). The hearings held by the Minneapolis City Council's Committee on Government Operations (with which Andrea Dworkin and I assisted) produced many accounts of the use of pornography to force sex on women and children; *Public Hearings on Ordinances to Add Pornography as Discrimination against Women* (Minneapolis, December 12–13, 1983).

17. A parallel observation is made by Frederic Jameson of tourism in relation to landscape: "the American tourist no longer lets the landscape 'be in its being' as Heidegger would have said, but takes a snapshot of it, thereby graphically transforming space into its own material image. The concrete activity of looking at a landscape . . . is thus comfortably replaced by *the act of taking possession of it* and converting it into a form of personal property"; "Reification and Utopia in Mass Culture," *Social Text* 1 (Winter 1979): 131 (emphasis added).

18. Laura Mulvey has observed that Freud's "scopophilia" means "taking other people as objects, subjecting them to a controlling and curious gaze," the sexuality of which is "pleasure in using another person as an object of sexual stimulation through sight"; "Visual Pleasure and Narrative Cinema," *Screen* 16, no. 3 (1982). As he so often did, Freud interpreted a male norm as an isolated abnormality. Of course, mass media technology has generalized such behaviors.

19. "Explicitness" of accounts is a central issue in both obscenity adjudications and audience access standards adopted voluntarily by self-regulated industries as well as by boards of censor (e.g., Ontario). See, e.g., "complete candor and realism" discussed in Grove Press v. Christenberry, 175 F. Supp. 488, 489 (S.D.N.Y. 1959); "directness," Grove Press v. Christenberry, 276 F.2d 433, 438 (2nd Cir. 1960); "show it all," Mitchum v. State, 251 So.2d 298, 301 (Fla. 1971); Kaplan v. California, 413 U.S. 115, 118 (1973). How much sex the depiction shows is implicitly thereby correlated with how sexual (i.e., how sexually arousing to the male) the material is. See, e.g., Justice White's dissent in Memoirs v. Massachusetts, 383 U.S. 413, 460 (1966); R. D. Hefner, "What G, PG, R and X Really Means," *Congressional Record,* December 8, 1980, pp. 126, 172. Andrea Dworkin brilliantly gives the reader the experience of this aesthetic in her blow-by-blow account in *Pornography.*

20. L. Henkin, "Morals and the Constitution: The Sin of Obscenity," 63 *Columbia Law Review* 391, 394 (1963).

21. It may seem odd to denominate "moral" as female in this discussion of male morality. Under male supremacy, men define things; I describe that. Men define women as "moral." This is the male view of women. Thus this analysis, a feminist critique of the male standpoint, terms "moral" the concept that pornography is about good and evil. The term *female* refers to men's attributions of women, which I am analyzing as "male."

22. A reading of case law supports the reports in Woodward and Armstrong, *The Brethren* (New York: Simon and Schuster, 1979), p. 194, to the effect that this is a bottom-line criterion for at least some justices. The interesting question is why male supremacy would change from keeping the penis hidden so it could be covertly glorified to having it everywhere on display, overtly glorified. This suggests at least that a major shift from private terrorism to public terrorism has occurred. What used to be perceived as a danger to male power, the exposure of the penis, has now become a strategy in maintaining it.

23. One possible reading of Lockhart and McClure, "Literature, the Law of Obscenity, and the Constitution," is that this exemption was their agenda, and that their approach was substantially adopted in the third prong of the *Miller* doctrine. For the law's leading attempt to grapple with this issue, see Memoirs v. Massachusetts, 383 U.S. 413 (1966), and as overturned in Miller v. California, 413 U.S. 15 (1973), with citations therein to Lockhart and McClure. See also U.S. v. One Book Entitled "Ulysses," 5 F. Supp. 182 (S.D.N.Y. 1933) and 72 F.2d 705 (2nd Cir. 1934).

24. Andrea Dworkin and I developed this analysis together. See also her argument about how pornography is an issue of sexual access to women, producing a fight among men, in "Why So-Called Radical Men Love and Need Pornography," in Lederer, *Take Back the Night,* p. 141.

25. Those termed "fathers" and "sons" in ibid. we came to term "the old boys," whose strategy for male dominance involves keeping pornography and the abuse of women private, and "the new boys," whose strategy for male dominance involves making pornography and the abuse of women public. Freud and the accepted generalization of his derepression hypothesis to the culture at large are intellectually central in "the new boys' " approach and success. To conclude, as some have, that women have benefited from the public availability of pornography, so should be grateful and have a stake in its continuing availability, is to say that open condoned oppression is so beneficial compared with covert condoned oppression that it should be allowed to continue. This position ignores the alternative of ending the oppression. The benefit of pornography's open availability is that it becomes easier for women to know whom and what we are dealing with, in order to end it.

26. Miller v. California, 413 U.S. 15 (1973).

27. Paris Adult Theatre I v. Slayton, 413 U.S. 49, 67 (1973). See also "A quotation from Voltaire in the flyleaf of a book will not constitutionally redeem an otherwise obscene publication." Kois v. Wisconsin, 408 U.S. 229, 231 (1972), quoted in Miller v. California, 413 U.S. at 25 n. 7.

28. Penthouse International v. McAuliffe, 610 F.2d 1353 (5th Cir. 1980). For a

study in enforcement, see Coble v. City of Birmingham, 389 So.2d 527 (Ala. Ct. App. 1980).

29. Malamuth and Spinner, "Longitudinal Content Analysis." "The portrayal of sexual aggression within such 'legitimate' magazines as *Playboy* and *Penthouse* may have a greater impact than similar portrayals in hard-core pornography"; N. Malamuth and E. Donnerstein, "The Effects of Aggressive-Pornographic Mass Media Stimuli," *Advances in Experimental Social Psychology* 15 (1982): 103–136 and n. 130. This result is apparently emerging even more clearly in Neil Malamuth's ongoing experiments.

30. Some courts, under the obscenity rubric, seem to have understood that the quality of artistry does not undo the damage. "This court will not adopt a rule of law which states that obscenity is suppressible but well-written [or a technically well produced] obscenity is not." People v. Fritch, 13 N.Y.2d 119, 126, 243 N.Y.S.2d 1, 7, 192 N.E.2d 713 (bracketed words added by the court in People v. Mature Enterprises, 343 N.Y.S.2d 911 [1973]). More to the point of my argument here is Justice O'Connor's observation: "The compelling interests identified in today's opinion . . . suggest that the Constitution might in fact permit New York to ban knowing distribution of works depicting minors engaged in explicit sexual conduct, regardless of the social value of the depictions. For example, a 12-year-old child photographed while masturbating surely suffers the same psychological harm whether the community labels the photography 'edifying' or 'tasteless.' The audience's appreciation of the depiction is simply irrelevant to New York's asserted interest in protecting children from psychological, emotional, and mental harm." New York v. Ferber, 458 U.S. 747 (1982) (concurring). Put another way, how does it make a harmed child not harmed that what was produced by harming him is great art?

31. Women typically get mentioned in obscenity law only in the phrase "women and men," used as a synonym for "people." At the same time, exactly who the victim of pornography is has long been a great mystery. The few references in obscenity litigation to "exploitation" occur in contexts like the reference to "a system of commercial exploitation of people with sadomasochistic sexual aberrations," meaning the customers (all of whom were male) of women dominatrixes. State v. Von Cleef, 102 N.J. Super. 104 (1968). Also, of course, the male children in *Ferber*. Or Justice Frankfurter's reference to the "sordid exploitation of man's nature and impulses" as part of his conception of pornography in Kingsley Pictures Corp. v. Regents, 360 U.S. 684, 692 (1958).

32. Miller v. California, 413 U.S. at 24 (1973).

33. See, e.g., "What shocks me may be sustenance for my neighbor." 413 U.S. at 40–41 (Douglas, J., dissenting); "[What] may be trash to me may be prized by others." U.S. v. 12 200-Ft. Reels of Super 8MM Film, 413 U.S. 123, 137 (1973) (Douglas, J., dissenting). As put by Chuck Traynor, the pimp who forced Linda "Lovelace" into pornography, "I don't tell you how to write your column. Don't tell me how to treat my broads"; quoted in Gloria Steinem,

"The Real Linda Lovelace," in *Outrageous Acts and Everyday Rebellions* (New York: Holt, Rinehart, and Winston, 1983), p. 252.

34. See the *Mishkin* resolution of this for nonstandard sexuality, 383 U.S. 502 (1966).

35. Hopefully, it is obvious that this is not a comment about the personal sexuality or principles of any judicial individual, but rather an analysis that emerges from a feminist attempt to interpret the deep social structure of a vast body of case law on the basis of a critique of gender. Further research should systematically analyze the contents of the pornography involved in the cases. Is it just chance that the first film to be found obscene by a state Supreme Court depicts male masturbation? Landau v. Fording, 245 C.A.2d 820, 54 Cal. Rptr. 177 (1966). Given the ubiquity of the infantilization of women and the sexualization of little girls, would *Ferber* have been decided the same if twelve-year-old girls had been shown masturbating? See Commonwealth of Massachusetts v. Oakes, 410 Mass. 602, 518 N.E. 2d 836 (1988), *cert. granted* 100 L. Ed. 2d 226 (1988). Is the depiction of male sexuality in a way that men think it is dangerous for women and children to see, the reason works like *Lady Chatterley's Lover* and *Tropic of Cancer* got in trouble?

36. Roth v. U.S., 354 U.S. 476 (1957); but cf. Stanley v. Georgia, 394 U.S. 557 (1969), in which the right to private possession of obscene materials is protected as a First Amendment speech right. (One justice noticed this incongruity in the oral argument in *Stanley*; see P. Kurland and G. Casper, eds., *Landmark Briefs and Arguments of the Supreme Court of the United States: Constitutional Law,* vol. 67 [Virginia: University Publications of America, 1975], 850).

37. See, e.g., the charge to the Pornography Commission to study "the effect of obscenity and pornography upon the public and particularly minors and its relation to crime and other antisocial behavior" (McManus, *Final Report,* p. 1).

38. Naomi Scheman, "Making It All Up" (Manuscript, Minneapolis, January 1982), p. 7.

39. For the general body of work to which I refer, which is usually taken to be diverse, see Thomas I. Emerson, *Toward a General Theory of the First Amendment* (New York: Vintage, 1967); idem, *The System of Freedom of Expression* (New York: Vintage, 1970); A. Meiklejohn, *Free Speech and Its Relation to Self-Government* (New York: Harper & Brothers, 1948); Brandeis, J., concurring in Whitney v. California, 274 U.S. 357, 375 (1927) (joined by Holmes, J.); T. Scanlon, "A Theory of Freedom of Expression," *Philosophy & Public Affairs* 1 (1972): 204–226; John Ely, "Flag Desecration: A Case Study in the Roles of Categorization and Balancing in First Amendment Analysis," 88 *Harvard Law Review* 1482 (1975); Z. Chafee, *Free Speech in the United States* (Cambridge, Mass.: Harvard University Press, 1941), p. 245. This literature is ably summarized and anatomized by Ed Baker, who proposes an interpretive theory that goes far toward responding to my objections here, without really altering the basic assumptions I criticize. See C. Edwin Baker, "Scope of the First Amendment Freedom of Speech," 25 *UCLA Law Review* 964 (1978); and idem, "The Process of Change and the Liberty Theory of the First Amendment," 55 *Southern California Law Review* 293 (1982).

40. Stanley v. Georgia, 394 U.S. 557 (1969).

41. Erznoznik v. City of Jacksonville, 422 U.S. 205 (1975); Stanley v. Georgia. See also Breard v. Alexandria, 341 U.S. 622, 641–645 (1951); Kovacs v. Cooper, 336 U.S. 77, 87–89 (1949).

42. See Walker, "Coming Apart," in Lederer, *Take Back the Night;* Diana E. H. Russell, ed. "Testimony against Pornography: Witness from Denmark," ibid.; *Public Hearings on Ordinances.* Cf. Justice Douglas, dissenting in Paris Adult Theatre I v. Slayton: "[In] a life that has not been short, I have yet to be trapped into seeing or reading something that would offend me." 413 U.S. 49, 71 (1973). He probably hadn't.

43. See Chapter 10.

44. Emerson, *Toward a General Theory,* pp. 16–25, and *System of Freedom of Expression,* p. 17.

45. Law contains many examples of pure speech treated as actionable acts. A crime of bribery, for example, is typically defined to occur when a person "confers, or offers or agrees to confer, any benefit upon a public servant upon an agreement or understanding that such public servant's vote, opinion, judgment, action, decision or exercise of discretion as a public servant will thereby be influenced." Section 200.00 N.Y. Penal Law. Offers, agreements, and influence are verbal. A vote is a word. Discretion is exercised, decisions made and executed, through words. In regulating opinions, judgments, and understandings, bribery statutes attempt thought control. Another example is the federal regulation of discrimination in housing, which makes it actionable "to make, print, or publish . . . any notice, statement, or advertisement, with respect to the sale or rental of a dwelling" on a discriminatory basis. 42 U.S.C. Section 3604(c) (1982). Here, the speech is the discriminatory act. Similarly, antiunion speech is an unfair labor practice under the National Labor Relations Act, Section 8, 29 U.S.C. 158. See N.L.R.B. v. Gissel Packing Company, 395 U.S. 575, 617 (1969). Most sexual harassment is done through words. See C. MacKinnon, *Sexual Harassment of Working Women* (New Haven: Yale University Press, 1979), for examples. See also Davis v. Passman, 442 U.S. 228 (1979) (letter treated as actionable sex discrimination); P Santor, "Judicial Indifference to Pornography's Harm: American Booksellers v. Hudnut," 17 *Golden Gate University Law Review* 297, 320, 330 (1987).

46. The absolutist position on the entire Constitution was urged by Justice Black. See, e.g., Hugo Black, "The Bill of Rights," 35 *New York University Law Review* 865, 867 (1968), focusing at times on the First Amendment; and E. Cahn, "Justice Black and First Amendment 'Absolutes': A Public Interview," 37 *New York University Law Review* 549 (1962). Justice Douglas as well as Justice Black emphatically articulated the absolutist position in the obscenity context. See, e.g., Miller v. California, 413 U.S. 15, 37 (1973) (Douglas, J., dissenting); Smith v. California, 361 U.S. 147, 155 (1959) (Black, J., concurring); Roth v. United States, 354 U.S. 476, 514 (1957) (Douglas, J., joined by Black, J., dissenting). Absolutist-influenced discontent with obscenity law is clear in Justice Brennan's dissent in Paris Adult Theatre I v. Slaton, 413 U.S. 49, 73 (1973).

47. See, e.g., U.S. v. Roth, 237 F.2d 796, 812–817 (2nd Cir. 1956) (Frank, J., concurring).

48. 237 F.2d 796, 826 n. 70 (Frank, J., concurring).

49. Werner Heisenberg, *The Physical Principles of Quantum Theory* (Chicago: University of Chicago Press, 1930), p. 63.

50. Pornography and harm are not two separate events anyway if pornography is a harm.

51. Morton Horowitz, "The Doctrine of Objective Causation," in *The Politics of Law,* ed. D. Kairys (New York: Pantheon 1982), p. 201. The pervasiveness of the objectification of women has been considered as a reason why pandering should not be constitutionally restricted: "The advertisements of our best magazines are chock-full of thighs, ankles, calves, bosoms, eyes, and hair, to draw the potential buyer's attention to lotions, tires, food, liquor, clothing, autos, and even insurance policies." Ginzburg v. U.S., 383 U.S. 463, 482 (1966) (Douglas, J., dissenting). Justice Douglas thereby illustrated, apparently without noticing, that somebody in addition to the entire advertising industry knows that associating sex, that is, women's bodies, with things causes people to act on that association.

52. Two boys' masturbating with no showing of explicit force demonstrates the harm of child pornography in New York v. Ferber, 458 U.S. 747 (1982), while shoving money up a woman's vagina, among other acts, raises serious questions of "regulation of 'conduct' having a communicative element" in live sex adjudications. California v. LaRue, 409 U.S. 109 (1972) (live sex can be regulated by a state in connection with serving alcoholic beverages). "Snuff" films, in which a woman is actually murdered to produce a film for sexual entertainment, are known to exist. People v. Douglas and Hernandez, Felony Complaint #NF8300382, Municipal Court, Judicial District, Orange County, California, August 5, 1983, alleges the murder of two young girls to make a pornographic film. Douglas was convicted of murder but the film was never found.

53. Both Susan Griffin (*Pornography and Silence*) and the oldest Anglo-Saxon obscenity cases locate the harm of pornography in the mind of the consumer, where it is thought to start and stop. Regina v. Hicklin, 3 Q.B. 360 (1868) ("tendency to deprave and corrupt those whose minds are open to such immoral influences and into whose hands a publication of this sort may fall"). The data of Court and of Kutchinsky, both correlational, reach contrary conclusions on the issue of the relation of pornography's availability to crime statistics; B. Kutchinsky, "Towards an Explanation of the Decrease in Registered Sex Crimes in Copenhagen," in *Technical Report,* p. 7; idem, "The Effect of Easy Availability of Pornography on the Incidence of Sex Crimes: The Danish Experience," *Journal of Social Issues* 29 (1973): 163–182; cf. J. H. Court, "Pornography and Sex Crimes: A Re-evaluation in the Light of Recent Trends around the World," *International Journal of Criminology and Penology* 5 (1976): 129ff. More recent investigations into correlations focused on rape in the United States have reached still other conclusions. L. Baron and M. Straus have found a strong correlation between state-to-state variations in the rate of reported rape

and the numbers of readers of *Playboy* and *Hustler;* "Sexual Stratification, Pornography, and Rape" (Manuscript, Family Research Laboratory and Department of Sociology, University of New Hampshire, 18 November 1983). The authors conclude: "the findings suggest that the combination of a society which is characterized by a struggle to secure equal rights for women, by a high readership of sex magazines which depict women in ways which may legitimize violence, and by a context in which there is a high level of non-sexual violence, constitutes a mix of societal characteristics which precipitate rape" (p. 16). See also *Report of the Committee on Obscenity and Film Censorship* (London: HMSO, 1979) and the opinions of Justice Harlan on the injury to "society" as a permissible basis for legislative judgments in this area. Alberts v. U.S., 354 U.S. 476, 501–502 (1956) (concurring in companion case to Roth).

54. Lawrence Tribe, *American Constitutional Law* (Mineola, N.Y.: Foundation Press, 1978), p. 662.

55. I am conceiving rape as sexual aggression; see Chapter 9. The work of Neil Malamuth is the leading research in this area. See Malamuth, "Rape Proclivity among Males"; idem, "Rape Fantasies as a Function of Exposure to Violent Sexual Stimuli," *Archives of Sexual Behavior* 10 (1981): 33; Malamuth, Haber, and Seymour Feshbach, "Testing Hypotheses regarding Rape: Exposure to Sexual Violence, Sex Differences, and the 'Normality' of Rapists," *Journal of Research in Personality* 14 (1980): 121–137; Malamuth, M. Heim, and S. Feshbach, "Sexual Responsiveness of College Students to Rape Depictions: Inhibitory and Disinhibitory Effects," *Journal of Personality and Social Psychology* 38 (1980): 399–408. See also the work by Malamuth cited in note 6, above. Of course, there are difficulties in measuring rape as a direct consequence of laboratory experiments, difficulties that have led researchers to substitute other measures for willingness to aggress.

    Apparently, it is impossible to make a film for experimental purposes which portrays violence or aggression by a man against a woman and which a substantial number of normal male experimental subjects do not perceive as sexual; conversation with E. Donnerstein.

56. By this I do not mean erotica, which could be defined as sexually explicit sex premised on equality. See also Zillman and Bryant, "Effects of Massive Exposure to Pornography."

57. See also the "original position" of John Rawls, *A Theory of Justice* (Cambridge, Mass.: The Belknap Press of Harvard University Press, 1971), and idem, "Kantian Constructivism in Moral Theory," *Journal of Philosophy* 9 (1980): 515, 533–535.

58. Immanuel Kant, *Fundamental Principles of the Metaphysics of Morals,* trans. T. Abbott (Indianapolis: Bobbs-Merrill, 1947); Arthur Danto, "Persons," in *Encyclopedia of Philosophy,* vol. 6, ed. P. Edwards (New York: Macmillan, 1967), 10; Margaret Radin, "Property and Personhood," 34 *Stanford Law Review* 957 (1982).

59. Ludwig Wittgenstein, *Philosophical Investigations,* trans. G. Anscombe, 2d ed. (Oxford: Blackwell, 1958), p. 178.

60. E.g., *Capital.*

61. David Hume, "Of Personal Identity," in *A Treatise on Human Nature* (Oxford: Clarendon Press, 1986), bk. 1, pt. 4, sec. 6.

62. Bernard Williams, "The Idea of Equality," pp. 232–234, in *Problems of the Self* 1 (1973).

63. One might ask at this point, not why some women embrace explicit sado-masochism, but why any women do not.

64. Dworkin, *Pornography,* p. 115. "Echoing Macaulay, 'Jimmy' Walker remarked that he had never heard of a woman seduced by a book." U.S. v. Roth, 237 F.2d 796, 812 (2nd Cir. 1956) (appendix to concurrence of Frank, J.). Much of what is usually called seduction, feminists might consider rape or forced sex.

65. American Booksellers Assn., Inc. v. Hudnut, 771 F.2d 323 (7th Cir. 1985).

66. 771 F.2d at 328.

67. In this case, official policy has been expressed through the device of "summary affirmance" of the *Hudnut* result by the U.S. Supreme Court. Hudnut v. American Booksellers Assn., Inc., 475 U.S. 1001 (1986). A summary affirmance resolves a case without briefs or arguments by letting stand a result reached in a court of appeals. Lower courts reviewing the identical issues are bound by the result but not by the reasoning of the decision that is affirmed. Where the issues are not identical, or where the decision departs from established precedent, or where intervening legal developments suggest that the Court would reach a different result, lower courts may not be bound by the result. The Supreme Court may grant full review to the issues without being bound by the previous summary affirmance. Mandel v. Bradley, 432 U.S. 173 (1977); Hicks v. Miranda, 422 U.S. 332 (1975). So while this result is a significant state behavior, it need not be the last word on the subject.

## 12. Sex Equality: On Difference and Dominance

1. Sex inequality was first found unconstitutional by interpretation of the equal protection clause of the Fourteenth Amendment in 1971. Reed v. Reed, 404 U.S. 71 (1971). When Title VII of the Civil Rights Act of 1964 was debated, racist southern congressmen attempted to defeat the provisions on racial discrimination by adding "sex" to the prohibited bases. Their *reductio ad absurdum* failed when it passed; *Congressional Record,* February 8, 1964, p. 2577. See also Willingham v. Macon Telegraph Publishing Co., 507 F.2d 1084, 1090 (5th Cir. 1975).

2. The law of sexual harassment, recognized only recently under sex equality law, is an exception, achieved by putting into practice the analysis argued in this book. See Catharine A. MacKinnon, *Sexual Harassment of Working Women: A Case of Sex Discrimination* (New Haven: Yale University Press, 1979). Sex equality cases that address sexual issues such as rape (Michael M. v. Superior

Court of Sonoma County, 450 U.S. 464 [1981]; Dothard v. Rawlinson, 433 U.S. 321 [1977]) do so in a context of the drawing of gender lines.

3. J. Tussman and J. tenBroek, "The Equal Protection of the Laws," 37 *California Law Review* 341 (1949); were the first to use the term *fit* to characterize the necessary relation between a valid equality rule and the world to which it refers.

4. Royster Guano Co. v. Virginia, 253 U.S. 412, 415 (1920).

5. Craig v. Boren, 429 U.S. 190 (1976).

6. Barbara Brown, Thomas I. Emerson, Gail Falk, and Ann E. Freedman, "The Equal Rights Amendment: A Constitutional Basis for Equal Rights for Women," 80 *Yale Law Journal* 871 (1971).

7. "Regardless of their sex, persons within any one of the enumerated classes . . . are similarly situated . . . By providing dissimilar treatment for men and women who are thus similarly situated, the challenged section violates the Equal Protection Clause." Reed v. Reed, 404 U.S. 71, 77 (1971); Rostker v. Goldberg, 453 U.S. 57 (1981) (because women are differently situated for combat by legislation, male-only registration for draft does not violate equal protection). See also Califano v. Webster, 430 U.S. 313 (1977); Parham v. Hughes, 441 U.S. 347, 355 (1979) (mothers not similarly situated to fathers for purposes of legitimizing children because only fathers have legal power to do so); Schlesinger v. Ballard, 419 U.S. 498 (1975); Michael M. v. Superior Court of Sonoma County, 450 U.S. 464, 471 (1981) (women are dissimilarly situated from men "with respect to the problems and risks of sexual intercourse," meaning pregnancy).

8. There is another approach, gaining ascendancy, discussed in Chapter 13.

9. G. Rutherglen, "Sexual Equality in Fringe-Benefit Plans," 65 *Virginia Law Review* 199, 206 (1979).

10. Brown, Emerson, Falk, and Freedman, "The Equal Rights Amendment."

11. Nadine Taub, "Keeping Women in Their Place: Stereotyping Per Se as a Form of Employment Discrimination," 21 *Boston College Law Review* 345 (1980); See also Barbara Kirk Cavanaugh, " 'A Little Dearer than His Horse': Legal Stereotypes and the Feminine Personality," 6 *Harvard Civil Rights–Civil Liberties Law Review* 260 (1971).

12. Jean Harris, quoted by Shana Alexander in *Very Much a Lady*, in a review by Anne Bernays, *New York Times Book Review*, March 27, 1983, p. 13.

13. See B. Babcock, A. Freedman, F. Norton, and S. Ross, *Sex Discrimination and the Law* (Boston: Little, Brown, 1975), pp. 23–53.

14. The Bona Fide Occupational Qualification exception to Title VII of the Civil Rights Act of 1964, 42 U.S.C. Section 2000e-2(e), permits sex to be a job qualification when it is a valid one. For ERA theory, see Brown, Emerson, Falk, and Freedman, "The Equal Rights Amendment."

15. This observation applies even to enlightened liberals like John Rawls, who rejects the naturalism of social orderings as prescriptive but accepts them as descriptive of unjust societies. Inequality exists in nature; society can accept or reject it. It is not in itself a social construct, nor are differences a function of it;

John Rawls, *A Theory of Justice* (Cambridge, Mass.: The Belknap Press of Harvard University Press, 1971), p. 102.

16. For examples, see Wendy Williams, "The Equality Crisis: Some Reflections on Culture, Courts, and Feminism," 7 *Women's Rights Law Reporter* 175 (1982); Herma Kay, "Models of Equality," 1985 *University of Illinois Law Review* 39; Fran Olsen, "Statutory Rape: A Feminist Critique of Rights Analysis," 63 *Texas Law Review* 387 (1984); Wendy Williams, "Equality's Riddle: Pregnancy and the Equal Treatment/Special Treatment Debate," 13 *New York University Review of Law and Social Change* 325 (1985); Sylvia Law, "Rethinking Sex and the Constitution," 132 *University of Pennsylvania Law Review* 955 (1984); Stephanie Wildman, "The Legitimation of Sex Discrimination: A Critical Response to Supreme Court Jurisprudence," 63 *Oregon Law Review* 265 (1984); Herma Kay, "Equality and Difference: The Case of Pregnancy," 1 *Berkeley Women's Law Journal* 1 (1985); Dowd, "Maternity Leave: Taking Sex Differences into Account," 54 *Fordham Law Review* 699 (1986). Frances Olsen, "From False Paternalism to False Equality: Judicial Assaults on Feminist Community, Illinois 1869–1895," 84 *Michigan Law Review* 1518 (1986), sees the definition of the issues as limiting.

17. Examples in employment: Title VII of the Civil Rights Act of 1964, 42 U.S.C. 2000e; Phillips v. Martin-Marietta, 400 U.S. 542 (1971). Education: Title IX of the Civil Rights Act of 1964, 20 U.S.C. 1681; Cannon v. University of Chicago, 441 U.S. 677 (1979); Delacruz v. Tormey, 582 F.2d 45 (9th Cir. 1978). Academic employment: women appear to lose most of the cases that go to trial, but cf. Sweeney v. Board of Trustees of Keene State College, 604 F.2d 106 (1st Cir. 1979). Professional employment: Hishon v. King & Spalding, 467 U.S. 69 (1984). Blue-collar employment: Vanguard Justice v. Hughes, 471 F. Supp. 670 (D. Md. 1979); Meyer v. Missouri State Highway Commission, 567 F.2d 804 (8th Cir. 1977); Payne v. Travenol Laboratories Inc., 416 F. Supp. 248 (N.D. Miss. 1976). See also Dothard v. Rawlinson, 433 U.S. 321 (1977) (height and weight requirements invalidated for prison guard positions because of disparate impact on the basis of sex). Military: Frontiero v. Richardson, 411 U.S. 677 (1973); Schlesinger v. Ballard, 419 U.S. 498 (1975). Athletics: This situation is relatively complex. See Gomes v. R.I. Interscholastic League, 469 F. Supp. 659 (D.R.I. 1979); Brenden v. Independent School District, 477 F.2d 1292 (8th Cir. 1973); O'Connor v. Board of Education of School District No. 23, 645 F.2d 578 (7th Cir. 1981); Cape v. Tennessee Secondary School Athletic Association, 424 F. Supp. 732 (E.D. Tenn. 1976), *rev'd*, 563 F.2d 793 (6th Cir. 1977); Yellow Springs Exempted Village School District Board of Education v. Ohio High School Athletic Association, 443 F. Supp. 753 (S.D. Ohio 1978); Aiken v. Lieuallen, 593 P.2d 1243 (Or. App. 1979).

18. See Rostker v. Goldberg, 453 U.S. 57 (1981) (upholding male-only draft registration). See also Lori S. Kornblum, "Women Warriors in a Men's World: The Combat Exclusion," 2 *Law & Inequality: A Journal of Theory and Practice* 351 (1984).

19. The undercurrent is: what's the matter, don't you want me to learn to kill . . . just like you? This conflict might be expressed as a dialogue between women in the afterlife. The feminist says to the soldier: we fought for your equality. The soldier says to the feminist: oh, no, *we* fought for *your* equality.

20. On alimony and other economic factors, see L. Wietzman, "The Economics of Divorce: Social and Economic Consequences of Property, Alimony, and Child Support Awards," 28 *UCLA Law Review* 1181, 1251 (1981), which documents a decline in women's standard of living of 73 percent and an increase in men's of 42 percent within a year after no-fault divorce in California. Weitzman attributes to no-fault what, in my view, should be attributed to gender neutrality. On custody, see Phyllis Chesler, *Mothers on Trial* (New York: McGraw-Hill, 1986).

21. For data and analysis see Barbara F. Reskin and Heidi Hartmann, eds., *Women's Work, Men's Work: Sex Segregation on the Job* (Washington, D.C.: National Academy Press, 1986). Comparing the median income of the sexes from ages twenty-five to fifty for 1975–1983, the U.S. Department of Labor Women's Bureau reports that women in 1975 made about $8,000 to men's $14,000, and in 1983 $15,000 to men's $24,000; U.S. Department of Labor, Women's Bureau, *Time of Change: 1983 Handbook of Women Workers,* Bulletin 298 (Washington, D.C., 1983), p. 456. The Equal Pay Act was passed in 1963. On equal pay for equal work, see Christensen v. State of Iowa, 563 F.2d 353 (8th Cir. 1977); Gerlach v. Michigan Bell Tel. Co., 501 F. Supp. 1300 (E.D. Mich. 1980); Odomes v. Nucare, Inc., 653 F.2d 246 (6th Cir. 1981); Power v. Barry County, Michigan, 539 F. Supp. 721 (W.D. Mich. 1982); Lemons v. City and County of Denver, 17 FEP Cases 906 (D. Colo. 1978), *aff'd,* 620 F.2d 228 (10th Cir. 1980), *cert. denied,* 449 U.S. 888 (1980). See also Carol Jean Pint, "Value, Work and Women," 1 *Law & Inequality: A Journal of Theory and Practice* 159 (1983). To see the demise of women's schools on the horizon, combine the result of Bob Jones University v. United States, 461 U.S. 574 (1983) (private university loses tax exemption because internal racial segregation violates public policy) with Mississippi University of Women v. Hogan, 458 U.S. 718 (1982) (all-women public nursing school is sex discrimination).

22. General Electric v. Gilbert, 429 U.S. 125 (1976); Geduldig v. Aiello, 417 U.S. 484 (1974).

23. A recent example of the Supreme Court's understanding this better than the women's movement is California Federal Savings and Loan Assn. v. Guerra, 479 U.S. 272 (1987), concerning statutory maternity leave. No feminist group supported the position the Supreme Court ultimately adopted, that it was not sex discrimination for a state legislature to require maternity leaves and job security for pregnant women. All but one feminist group (which argued that reproduction is a fundamental right) argued that it was.

24. Lemons v. City and County of Denver, 17 FEP Cases 906 (D. Colo. 1978); AFSCME v. Washington, 770 F.2d 1401 (9th Cir. 1985).

25. EEOC v. Sears, Roebuck and Co., Civil Action # 79-C-4373 (N.D. Ill. 1987), "Offer of Proof concerning the Testimony of Dr. Rosalind Rosenberg,"

"Written Testimony of Alice Kessler Harris," "Written Rebuttal Testimony of Dr. Rosalind Rosenberg," Rosalind Rosenberg, "The Sears Case: An Historical Overview" (Mimeograph, November 25, 1985); Rosalind Rosenberg, "Women and Society Seminar: The Sears Case" (Paper, December 16, 1985); Jon Weiner, "The Sears Case: Women's History on Trial," *The Nation*, September 7, 1985, pp. 1, 176–180; Alice Kessler-Harris, "Equal Employment Opportunity Commission v. Sears, Roebuck and Company: A Personal Account," *Radical History Review* 35 (1986): 57–79. EEOC v Sears, 628 F. Supp. 1264 (N,D. Ill., 1986) (Sears did not discriminate), *aff'd*, 839 F.2d 302 (7th Cir. 1988).

26. Phillips v. Martin-Marietta, 400 U.S. 542 (1971).

27. Reed v. Reed, 404 U.S. 71 (1971).

28. Aristotle, *Politics: A Treatise on Government,* trans. A. D. Lindsay (New York: E. P. Dutton, 1912), bk. 3, chap. 16: "Nature requires that the same right and the same rank should necessarily take place amongst all those who are equal by nature" (p. 101); idem, *Ethica Nicomachea,* trans. W. Ross (London: Oxford University Press, 1972), bk V.3, 1131a-b.

29. On women's nature: "Although moral virtue is common to all . . . yet the temperance of a man and a woman are not the same, nor their courage, nor their justice . . . for the courage of the man consists in commanding, the woman's in obeying"; Aristotle, *Politics,* p. 24.

30. J. Landes, "The Effect of State Maximum-Hours Laws on the Employment of Women in 1920," *Journal of Political Economy* 88 (1980): 476.

31. Kahn v. Shevin, 416 U.S. 351, 353 (1974).

32. Schlesinger v. Ballard, 419 U.S. 498 (1975).

33. Dothard v. Rawlinson, 433 U.S. 321 (1977). If courts learned that sexual harassment is as vicious and pervasive and damaging to women in workplaces everywhere as rape is to women guards in men's prisons, one wonders if women could be excluded from the workplace altogether. Meritor Savings Bank, FSB v. Vinson, 477 U.S. 57 (1986), includes a complaint for sexual harassment based on two and a half years of rape by a bank supervisor.

34. Doerr v. B.F. Goodrich, 484 F. Supp. 320 (N.D. Ohio 1979); Hayes v. Shelby Memorial Hospital, 546 F. Supp. 259 (N.D. Ala. 1982); Wright v. Olin Corp., 697 F.2d 1172 (4th Cir. 1982).

35. David Cole, "Strategies of Difference: Litigating for Women's Rights in a Man's World, 2 *Law & Inequality: A Journal of Theory and Practice* 34 n.4 (1984) (collecting cases).

36. It is difficult to document what does not happen. One example is American Booksellers Assn., Inc. v. Hudnut, 771 F.2d 323 (7th Cir. 1985), summarily affirmed by the Supreme Court without argument. 475 U.S. 1001 (1986), reh. denied 475 U.S. 1132 (1986).

37. Michael M. v. Superior Court of Sonoma County, 450 U.S. 464 (1981).

38. Rostker v. Goldberg, 453 U.S. 57 (1981).

39. Nancy Cott, "Passionlessness: An Interpretation of Victorian Sexual Ideology,

1790–1950," *Signs: A Journal of Women in Culture and Society* 4 (1978): 219–236.

40. Personnel Administrator of Massachusetts v. Feeney, 442 U.S. 256 (1979). See also Washington v. Davis, 426 U.S. 229 (1976); U.S. Postal Service v. Aikens, 460 U.S. 711 (1983).

41. Sexual harassment law has mostly avoided requiring women to prove that the man who made sexual advances toward them did so intending to discriminate against women. Katz v. Dole, 709 F. 2d 251, 255–256, esp. 256 n.7 (4th Cir. 1983); but cf. Norton v. Vartanian, 31 FEP Cases 1259, 1260 (D. Mass. 1983). Judges have, for the most part, been brought to comprehend that women who are targets of unwanted heterosexual advances would not be in that position if they were not women. Barnes v. Costle, 561 F.2d 983 (D.C. Cir. 1977).

42. Consider this discussion of the connection between gender issues and motive: "It is clear to me that I was denied tenure because I was a lesbian. It is also clear to me that no one who voted to deny me tenure thought s/he was 'discriminating' against me as a lesbian, but that each thought s/he was making 'a difficult decision about the quality and direction of my work' "; Judith McDaniel, "We Were Fired: Lesbian Experiences in Academe," *Sinister Wisdom* 20 (Spring 1982): 30–43.

43. Furnco Construction Corp v. Walters, 438 U.S. 567 (1978). Cases on Title VII burden of proof that treat race, as this one does, also apply to sex.

44. Ronald Dworkin, *A Matter of Principle* (Cambridge, Mass.: Harvard University Press, 1985), p. 205.

45. The classic articulation of "neutral principles in constitutional adjudication" is by Herbert Wechsler, in his attack on the Supreme Court for de-institutionalizing racial segregation by law in *Brown v. Board of Education*. Herbert Wechsler, "Toward Neutral Principles of Constitutional Law," 73 *Harvard Law Review* 1 (1959).

## 13. Toward Feminist Jurisprudence

1. In the United States, the "state action" requirement restricts review under the Fourteenth Amendment. See Lawrence Tribe, *American Constitutional Law* (Mineola, N.Y.: Foundation Press, 1978), pp. 1688–1720, for summary. In Canada, under the Canadian Charter of Rights and Freedoms, Section 32 restricts charter review to acts of government.

2. Brown v. Board of Education, 347 U.S. 483 (1954); Swann v. Charlotte-Mecklenburg Board of Education, 402 U.S. 2 (1971); Griggs v. Duke Power, 401 U.S. 424 (1971).

3. Herbert Wechsler, "Toward Neutral Principles of Constitutional Law," 73 *Harvard Law Review* 1 (1959).

4. Plessy v. Ferguson, 163 U.S. 537, 551 (1896); Wechsler, "Toward Neutral Principles," p. 33.

5. Karl Marx, *The Poverty of Philosophy* (New York: International Publishers, 1963), p. 174.

6. Karl Marx and Friedrich Engels, *The Holy Family,* trans. R. Dixon (Moscow: Progress Publishers, 1956), p. 157. See generally M. Cain and A. Hunt, *Marx and Engels on Law* (London: Academic Press, 1979).

7. Examples are Loving v. Virginia, 388 U.S. 1 (1967); Brown v. Board of Education, 347 U.S. 483 (1954); some examples of the law against sexual harassment (e.g., Barnes v. Costle, 561 F.2d 983 [D.C. Cir. 1977]; Vinson v. Taylor, 753 F.2d 141 [D.C. Cir. 1985], aff'd. 477 U.S. 57 (1986); Priest v. Rotary, 98 F.R.D. 755 [D.Cal. 1983]), some athletics cases (e.g., Clark v. Arizona Interscholastic Assn., 695 F.2d 1126 [9th Cir. 1986]), some affirmative action cases (e.g., Johnson v. Transportation Agency, Santa Clara County, 480 U.S. 616 [1987]), and California Federal Savings and Loan Association v. Guerra, 492 U.S. 272 (1987).

8. This context was argued as the appropriate approach to equality in an intervention by the Women's Legal Education and Action Fund (LEAF) in Law Society of British Columbia v. Andrews (May 22, 1987) before the Supreme Court of Canada. This approach to equality in general, giving priority to concrete disadvantage and rejecting the "similarly situated" test, was adopted by the Supreme Court of Canada in that case (1989) — DLR (3d) — .

9. See Ill. Rev. Stat. 1985, ch. 38, par. 12–14; People v. Haywood, 515 N.E.2d 45 (Ill. App. 1987) (prosecution not required to prove nonconsent, since sexual penetration by force implicitly shows nonconsent); but cf. People v. Coleman, 520 N.E.2d 55 (Ill. App. 1987) (state must prove victim's lack of consent beyond reasonable doubt).

10. This is argued by LEAF in its intervention application with several groups in Seaboyer v. The Queen (12 July 1988) and Gayme v. The Queen (18 November 1988), both on appeal before the Supreme Court of Canada. The rulings below are The Queen v. Seaboyer and Gayme (1986) 50 C.R. (3d) 395 (Ont. C.A.).

11. LEAF and a coalition of rape crisis centers, groups opposing sexual assault of women and children, and feminist media made this argument in an intervention in The Queen v. Canadian Newspapers Co., Ltd. The Canadian statute was upheld by a unanimous court. (1988)—D.L.R. (3d)—.

12. This is argued by LEAF intervening in The Queen v. Gayme.

13. This argument was advanced by LEAF in an intervention in Borowski v. Attorney General of Canada (October 7, 1987).

14. The Anti–Pornography Civil Rights Ordinance (discussed in Chapter 11 in text accompanying notes 64–67) aims to do this. See Andrea Dworkin and Catharine A. MacKinnon, *Pornography and Civil Rights: A New Day for Women's Equality* (Minneapolis: Organizing Against Pornography, 1988).

# Credits

Earlier versions of parts of this book appeared as "Feminism, Marxism, Method, and the State: An Agenda for Theory," *Signs: Journal of Women in Culture and Society* 7 (1982): 515–544; "Feminism, Marxism, Method, and the State: Toward Feminist Jurisprudence," *Signs: Journal of Women in Culture and Society* 8 (1983): 635–658; "Desire and Power," in *Marxism and the Interpretation of Culture,* ed. Cary Nelson and Lawrence Grossberg (Champaign-Urbana: University of Illinois Press, 1987); "Difference and Dominance: On Sex Discrimination," in *The Moral Foundations of Civil Rights,* ed. Robert K. Fullinwider and Claudia Mills (Totowa, N.J.: Rowman and Littlefield, 1986); "Feminist Discourse, Moral Values, and the Law—A Conversation" (with C. Gilligan, E. Dubois, and C. Menkel-Meadow), 34 *Buffalo Law Review* 11, 20–36, 69–77 (1985); "The Male Ideology of Privacy: A Feminist Perspective on the Right to Abortion," *Radical America* 17 (July–August 1983); "Roe v. Wade: A Study in Male Ideology," in *Abortion: Moral and Legal Perspectives,* ed. J. Garfield and P. Hennessey (Amherst, Mass.: University of Massachusetts Press, 1984); "Not a Moral Issue," 2 *Yale Law and Policy Review* 321 (1984); " 'Pleasure under Patriarchy': The Feminist/Political Approach," in *Theories and Paradigms of Human Sexuality,* ed. J. Geer and W. O'Donohue (New York: Plenum Press, 1987); and *Feminism Unmodified: Discourses on Life and Law* (Cambridge, Mass.: Harvard University Press, 1987); and my doctoral dissertation in the Yale Department of Political Science, "Feminism, Marxism, Method, and the State" (1987).

# Index